Game Change

Game Change

*Obama and the Clintons,
McCain and Palin, and
the Race of a Lifetime*

John Heilemann
and
Mark Halperin

An Imprint of HarperCollins*Publishers*

HarperCollins books may be purchased for educational, business, or sales promotional use. For information please write: Special Markets Department, HarperCollins Publishers, 10 East 53rd Street, New York, NY 10022.

FIRST HARPERLUXE EDITION

HarperLuxe™ is a trademark of HarperCollins Publishers

Library of Congress Cataloging-in-Publication Data is available upon request.

ISBN: 978-0-06-194599-1

10 11 12 13 14 ID/RRD 10 9 8 7 6 5

For Diana and Karen

Contents

Authors' Note

The idea for this book arose in the spring of 2008 out of a pair of firm convictions. The first was that the election we had both been following intensely for more than a year was as riveting and historic a spectacle as modern politics had ever produced. The second was that, despite wall-to-wall media coverage, much of the story behind the headlines had not been told. What was missing and might be of enduring value, we agreed, was an intimate portrait of the candidates and spouses who (in our judgment) stood a reasonable chance of occupying the White House: Barack and Michelle Obama, Hillary and Bill Clinton, John and Elizabeth Edwards, and John and Cindy McCain.

The vast majority of the material in these pages was taken from more than three hundred interviews with more than two hundred people conducted between July 2008 and September 2009. Almost all of the interviews took place in person, in sessions that often stretched over several hours. We set out to speak with every individual named in the book; only a handful declined to participate. Many also provided us with emails, memos, contemporaneous notes, recordings, schedules, and other forms of documentation.

All of our interviews—from those with junior staffers to those with the candidates themselves—were conducted on a "deep background" basis, which means we agreed not to identify the subjects as sources in any way. We believed this was essential to eliciting the level of candor on which a book of this sort depends. To a very large extent, we were interviewing people with whom one or both of us had long-standing professional relationships, and thus a solid basis to judge both the quality of the information being provided and the veracity of the providers.

While we made great efforts to compare and verify differing accounts of the same events, we were struck by how few fundamental disputes we encountered among our sources. In part, this owes to timing. We conducted many of our interviews about the nomination fights in the summer of 2008, when the combatants were out of the heat of battle and ready to talk, but their memories were still fresh. And the same dynamic held true in the months after the general election, when we turned intensely to that topic. In most every scene in the book, we have included only material about which disagreements among the players were either nonexistent or trivial. With regard to the few exceptions, we brought to bear deliberate professional consideration and judgment.

With the help of the participants, we have reconstructed dialogue extensively—and with extreme care. Where dialogue is within quotation marks, it comes from the speaker, someone who was present and heard the remark, contemporaneous notes, or transcripts. Where dialogue is not in quotes, it is paraphrased, reflecting only a lack of certainty on the part of our sources about precise wording, not about the nature of the statements. Where specific thoughts, feelings, or states of mind are rendered in italics, they come from either the person identified or someone to whom she or he expressed those thoughts or feelings directly.

No doubt some of our principal dramatis personae will find images of themselves in these pages that they would rather not see in print. But in every case, we have tried to tell their stories in two ways: as fairly as possible from the outside and as empathetically as we could from behind their eyes. In doing so, we have tried to

address the multitude of vital questions that daily journalism (and hourly blogofying) obsessed over briefly
and then passed by, or never grappled with in the first
place. How did Obama, a freshman senator with few
tangible political accomplishments, convince himself
that he should be, and *could* be, America's first African
American president? What role did Bill Clinton actually play in his wife's campaign? Why did McCain pick
the unknown and untested governor of Alaska as his
running mate? And who is Sarah Palin, really?

Although no work of this kind, lacking the distance
and perspective of time, can hope to be definitive, we
are convinced that some answers are more readily discovered in the ground that lies between history and
journalism—precisely the spot that we were aiming for
and believe this book occupies.

Our first and most obvious debt is to our sources,
who spent countless hours with us in person and on
the phone. We would also like to thank their assistants,
who facilitated many of the interviews.

We are grateful to our bosses, Adam Moss and Rick
Stengel, the editors of *New York* magazine and *Time*,
respectively, who granted us the space we needed to
take on this project; our agents, Andrew Wylie and
Scott Moyers at the Wylie Agency and Jeff Jacobs at
CAA, without whom we would have been lost; Richard

Plepler of HBO, for his encouragement and perspicacity; our editor Tim Duggan, our publisher Jonathan Burnham, and the rest of the team at HarperCollins—Kathy Schneider, Tina Andreadis, Kate Pruss Pinnick, Leslie Cohen, and Allison Lorentzen—for placing a big bet on this book and laboring to make it a success.

A number of friends and colleagues in the journalism racket provided us support, including work from which we drew wisdom or memories that we tapped: Mike Allen, Matt Bai, Dan Balz, David Chalian, John Dickerson, Robert Draper, Joshua Greene, John Harris, Al Hunt, Joe Klein, Ryan Lizza, Jonathan Martin, John McCormick, Chris Matthews, Andrea Mitchell, Liza Mundy, Adam Nagourney, Bill Nichols, John Richardson, Michael Shear, Roger Simon, Ben Smith, Jeffrey Toobin, and Jeff Zeleny. In the closing phase, Aaron Kiersh contributed careful and timely research. And we were assisted throughout by an armada of transcribers, of whom two in particular deserve mention: Frankie Thomas and Steven Yaccino.

A special expression of gratitude is due Elise O'Shaughnessy of *Vanity Fair*, a gifted editor who came up with the book's title and then performed miracles to keep the manuscript from turning into *War and Peace*; we salute her poise under pressure and artful way with the scalpel. Another profound word of thanks is due

Karen Avrich, whose tireless and brilliant work as a writer, editor, and researcher is evident on every page that follows.

FROM JOHN HEILEMANN:

A panoply of pals provided me with less tangible, but no less invaluable, forms of aid and comfort: Kurt Andersen and Anne Kreamer; Chris Anderson; John Battelle; Lisa Clements; David Dreyer; Mike Elliott and Emma Oxford; Mary Ellen Glynn and Dwight Holton; Katrina Heron; Michael Hirschorn; John Homans; Jeff Kwatinetz; Kerry Luft; Kenny Miller, Rachel Leventhal, and my goddaughter, Zoe Miller-Leventhal; Neil Parker and Kay Moffett; Jeff Pollack; Robert Reich; Jordan Tamagni and Michael Schlein; Will Wade-Gery and Emily Botein; Harry Werksman; Fred and Joanne Wilson.

As ever, I am grateful for the example and support of my father, Richard Heilemann, which keep me on the straight and narrow (more or less), and for the memory of my mother, which sustains me in all my endeavors.

Finally, Diana Rhoten, my wife and salvation, deserves a bouquet the size of Botswana. Without her as a perpetual source of patience, reassurance, and inspiration—not to mention the occasional dose of tough love and ample portions of homestretch home cooking—I would never have made it through intact.

FROM MARK HALPERIN:

I send deep gratitude to Josh Tyrangiel and my colleagues at *Time* and Time.com, as well as to Ina Avrich, Bob Barnett, Gary Foster, Kyle Froman, Gil Fuchsberg, Nancy Gabriner, Charlie Gibson, Debbie Halperin, Bianca Harris, Dan Harris, Andrew Kirtzman, Ben Kushner, and David Westin. I am grateful for the guidance and eternal inspiration of Peter Jennings.

Getting the book done required the support and smiles of Megan Halperin, Hannah Halperin, Madelyn Halperin, Laura Hartmann, and Peter Hartmann. Thanks to their parents: RoseAnne McCabe, Gary Halperin, Carolyn Hartmann, and David Halperin. And also many thanks to Morton Halperin, Diane Orentlicher, Ina Young, and Joe Young.

Karen Avrich's awesome professional contributions are noted above. More important than those: almost all of what I have achieved in my work, and in my life, I owe to Karen. By her sense of adventure, her generosity, her strength, her grace, and her example, she makes me a better person.

PROLOGUE

Barack Obama jerked bolt upright in bed at three o'clock in the morning. Darkness enveloped his low-rent room at the Des Moines Hampton Inn; the airport across the street was quiet in the hours before dawn. It was very late December 2007, a few days ahead of the Iowa caucuses. Obama had been sprinting flat out for president for nearly a year. Through all the nights he'd endured in cookie-cutter hotels during the months of uncertainty and angst—months of lagging by a mile in the national polls, his improbable bid for the White House written off by the Washington smart set, his self-confidence shaken by his uneven performance and the formidability of his archrival, Hillary Clinton—Obama always slept soundly, like the dead. But now he found himself wide awake, heart pounding, consumed by a thought at once electric and daunting: *I might win this thing.*

The past months in Iowa had been a blur of high school gyms, union halls, and snow-dusted cornfields. Obama was surging, he could sense it—the crowds swelling, the enthusiasm mounting, his organization clicking, his stump speech catching sparks. His strategy from day one had been crystalline: win Iowa and watch the dominoes fall. If he carried the caucuses, New Hampshire and South Carolina would be his, and so on, and so on. But as Obama sat there in the predawn stillness, the implications of the events he saw unfolding hit him as never before. He didn't feel ecstatic. He didn't feel relieved. He felt like the dog that caught the bus. What was he supposed to do now?

By the morning of the caucuses, Obama was laboring to project his customary aura of calm. "Never too high, never too low" was how he and everyone else described his temperament. His opponents were still out there running around, squeezing in a few last appearances before the voting started. But Obama had decided to chill. He woke up late, played some basketball, went for a haircut with Marty Nesbitt, a pal of his from Chicago. Lazing around the hotel afterward, he and Nesbitt shot the breeze about sports, their kids, and then more sports. Anything, that is, to avoid talking about the election, the one topic that Obama seemed intent on banishing from his head.

The phone rang. Obama picked it up. Chris Edley was on the line.

The two men had known each other for almost twenty years, since Obama was a student at Harvard Law School and Edley one of his professors. Now the dean of Boalt Hall at Berkeley, Edley was one of the few outsiders in whom Obama had confided all year long, with whom he shared his frustrations and anxieties about his campaign, which were greater than almost anyone knew. But today it was the teacher who was stressing while the pupil played Mr. Cool.

"I haven't been able to eat in thirty-six hours, I'm so nervous," Edley said. "How are you doing?"

"I'm serene," Obama said. "I just got back from playing basketball."

"You've got to be kidding."

"Nope," Obama said. "We had a strategy. We stuck to it. We executed it reasonably well. Now it's in the hands of the voters."

Obama's advisers took comfort in his serenity, but share it they did not. The Obama brain trust—David Axelrod, the hangdog chief strategist and self-styled "keeper of the message"; David Plouffe, the tightly wound campaign manager; Robert Gibbs, the sturdy, sharp-elbowed Alabaman communications director; Steve Hildebrand, the renowned field operative behind the campaign's grassroots effort in Iowa—was a worrywartish crew by nature. But their nerves were especially jangly now, and with good reason.

The Obamans had bet everything on Iowa. If their man lost, he was probably toast—and certainly so if he placed behind Clinton. By his campaign's own rigorous projections, an Obama victory would require a turnout at least 50 percent higher than the all-time Iowa record. It would require a stampede of the college kids and other first-time caucus-goers they had been recruiting like mad. Would the kids show up? Obama's advisers had high hopes, but no real sense of confidence. Many of them were convinced that John Edwards would wind up in first place. Others fretted that Clinton would win. The campaign's final internal pre-caucus poll had Obama finishing third.

Anxiety among Obama's brain trust rarely seemed to affect the candidate, but as caucus day morphed into night, his façade of nonchalance began to crack. On a visit to a suburban caucus site with Plouffe and Valerie Jarrett—a tough Chicago businesswoman and politico who was a dear friend to Obama and his wife, Michelle—he saw a swarm of voters in Obama T-shirts and got teary-eyed in the car. Outside the restaurant where he planned to have dinner with a couple dozen friends, Obama was fiending for information in a way his aides had seldom seen before. Overhearing Plouffe and another staffer kibitzing about turnout, he doubled back and peppered them with queries: "What are you guys talking about?" "What did you say?" "What are you hearing?"

Obama sat down with Michelle in the wood-paneled dining room of Fleming's Prime Steakhouse in West Des Moines. Plouffe had warned him to ignore the early returns, which were likely to be skewed against him. But not long into the meal, BlackBerrys around the table buzzed with emails that told a different story. Turnout was massive. Unprecedented. Beyond anyone's wildest dreams. Obama was leading in Polk County. He was leading in Cedar Rapids. Then a phone call came from Plouffe. Obama listened, hung up, and apologized to his friends. "I think I gotta go get ready to give my victory speech," he said.

As Barack and Michelle walked out of Fleming's and headed back to their hotel, the candidate was neither elated nor surprised. He had been too confident the past few days for those emotions now. What Obama felt was something close to certainty: he would be the Democratic nominee. The African American with the middle name Hussein had conquered the nearly all-Caucasian Iowa caucuses. Who could possibly stop him now? Especially given what he'd just learned about the fate that had befallen Hillary.

Terry McAuliffe entered the suite on the tenth floor of the Hotel Fort Des Moines, let in by the Secret Service agent stationed outside the door. Bill Clinton sat alone on the couch, watching the Orange Bowl on TV. McAuliffe had been the chairman of the Democratic National Committee when Clinton was president; now he chaired Hillary's campaign and had just learned the brutal news.

"Hey, Mac, how you doing?" Clinton said casually. "You want a beer?"

"How we doing?" McAuliffe asked, taken aback. "Have you not heard anything?"

"No."

"We're gonna get our ass kicked."

"*What?*" Clinton exclaimed, jumping to his feet, calling out, "Hillary!"

Hillary emerged from the bedroom. McAuliffe filled her in. The data jockeys downstairs in the campaign's boiler room had rendered a grim verdict: she was going to finish third, slightly shy of Edwards and a long way behind Obama.

McAuliffe's words landed like a roundhouse right on the Clintons' collective jaw. They'd known all along that Iowa was Hillary's weakest state. But she and her team kept pouring time and money into the place, pushing more and more chips into the center of the table. On the eve of the caucuses, the people the Clintons trusted most had assured them the gamble would pay off. First place, Hillary and Bill were told. A close second, at worst. Yet here she was, a far-off third—and the Clintons were reeling like a pair of Vegas drunks the morning after, struggling to come to grips with the scale of what they'd lost.

The members of Hillary's high command soon began piling into the suite: Mark Penn, her perpetually rumpled chief strategist and pollster; Mandy Grunwald, her ad maker; Howard Wolfson, her combative communications czar; Neera Tanden, her policy director; and Patti Solis Doyle, the quintessential Hillary loyalist, who served as her campaign manager. Though the suite was the best in the hotel, the living room was small, the lighting dim, the furniture shabby. The atmosphere was clammy and claustrophobic—and became even more so as the Clintons' shock quickly gave way to anger.

How did this happen? the Clintons asked again and again, grilling Penn about his polling and Grunwald about her ads, railing about the unholy amount of cash the campaign had blown on Iowa. (The final tally would be $29 million—for 70,000 votes.) The turnout figures made no sense to them: some 239,000 caucus-goers had shown up, nearly double the figure from four years earlier. Where did all these people come from? Bill asked. Were they really all Iowans? The Obama campaign must have cheated, he said, must have bussed in supporters from Illinois.

Hillary had been worried about that possibility for weeks; now she egged her husband on. Bill's right, she said. We need to investigate the cheating.

"It's a rigged deal," Bill groused.

Hillary was trying to rein in her emotions. The former president was not. Red-faced and simmering, he sat in the living room venting his frustrations. He was furious with New Mexico governor Bill Richardson, the fourth-place finisher, for cutting a backroom deal that had funneled some of his supporters to Obama, after assuring Hillary's campaign that he would make no such pacts. Bill Clinton had appointed Richardson to two high offices during his administration, and now he'd knifed Hillary in the back. I guess energy secretary and U.N. ambassador weren't enough for him, Clinton huffed.

But mostly Bill was enraged with the media, which he believed had brutalized his wife while treating Obama with kid gloves. This is bullshit, he said. The guy's a phony. He has no experience, he has no record; he's not nearly ready to be commander in chief.

"He's a United States senator," Hillary snapped. "That's nothing to laugh at."

He's only been in the Senate three years and he's been running the whole time for president, Bill replied. "What has he really done?"

"We have to be real here—people think of that as experience," Hillary said.

Losing always tests a politician's composure and grace. Hillary had never lost before, and she found little of either trait at her disposal. Presented with the carefully wrought, sound-bite-approved text of the concession speech she was soon supposed to deliver before the cameras, she sullenly leafed through the pages, cast them aside, and decided to ad lib. Her phone call to congratulate Obama was abrupt and impersonal. "Great victory, we're three tickets out of Iowa, see you in New Hampshire," she said, and hung up the phone.

The advisers in the room were all longtime intimates of the Clintons and had experienced their squalls of fury many times. But to a person, they found the display they were witnessing now utterly stunning—and especially unnerving coming from Hillary. Watching her bitter and befuddled reaction, her staggering lack of calm or command, one of her senior-most lieutenants thought for the first time, *This woman shouldn't be president.*

The truth was, the dimensions of Obama's win boggled Hillary's mind. He had beaten her among Democrats and independents, among rich and poor. He'd even carried the women's vote. His victory would destroy her support among African Americans, Hillary was certain of that. Twenty-four hours earlier and all the previous year, she'd been the front-runner, the unstoppable, inevitable nominee. Now Obama stood as the most likely next president of the United States.

Bill Clinton was resolved to do whatever it took to thwart that probability. For months he had held his tongue as his fears escalated—about Iowa, about what he saw as her team's lack of competence, about their unwillingness to take down Obama. It's Hillary's campaign, he'd told himself; he had to let her run it. But now her candidacy was hanging by a thread, and with it the prospect that he held dear of creating a Clinton dynasty. The time had come, he decided, for the Big Dog to be unleashed.

Yet Hillary wondered if it was too late for that. Turning to her husband, she shook her head and sighed. Maybe the problem wasn't Iowa. Maybe the problem wasn't her campaign. "Maybe," she said, "they just don't like me."

John Edwards stood onstage in the ballroom of the Renaissance Savery Hotel in Des Moines, gamely attempting to put the best face possible on his distant second-place finish. "The one thing that's clear from the results tonight is that the status quo lost and change won," he declared. "And now we move on."

Edwards knew better than that, however. When he first learned the outcome from his number crunchers, what he thought was, *Well, we're fucked.*

For Edwards even more than Obama, winning Iowa was the sine qua non of survival. The former North Carolina senator had always kept one foot in the Hawkeye State after the 2004 campaign, in which his surprise second-place finish in the caucuses vaulted him into the vice-presidential slot under John Kerry. Edwards's campaign this time around had been a spirited neo-populist crusade. But compared to Clinton and Obama, he was running a shoestring operation—really, he was running on fumes. To have any chance at all in the states ahead, Edwards needed a clear victory in Iowa to give him the momentum of a contender and to unleash a flood of contributions into his coffers.

But Edwards had no intention of going quietly into any good night. He had a contingency plan. Two months earlier he had asked Leo Hindery, a New York media investor who was one of his closest confidants, to convey a proposal to Tom Daschle, the former Senate majority leader and a mentor to Obama. The scheme was audacious but straightforward: If Edwards won the caucuses, Obama would immediately drop out of the race and become his running mate; if Obama won, Edwards would do the converse. (If Clinton won, it was game over for them both.) Wounding though a loss in Iowa would be to Hillary, she might well prove strong enough to bounce back. The only way to guarantee her elimination would be to take the extraordinary step of uniting against her.

Hindery had presented the proposal to Daschle, with whom he'd long been friends. Daschle brought it to the Obama campaign. The talks were tentative; nothing had been decided.

Now, with the results of Iowa in, Edwards determined it was time to strike the deal. A little while before taking the stage at the Savery, he summoned Hindery to his hotel suite and gave him his marching orders: "Get ahold of Tom."

Hindery considered the timing miserable. *Obama just frickin' won Iowa*, he thought. *Give him a chance to savor it.* But Edwards wanted to set the wheels in motion—tonight.

Hindery left the Edwards suite and tried frantically to locate Daschle, but discovered that he wasn't in Iowa. Calls were placed. Messages were left. No one knew where he was.

As Edwards delivered his speech, Hindery stood a few feet to his right, until an aide suddenly alerted him that Daschle, vacationing with his family in Mexico, was on the phone.

Hindery stepped offstage and took the call, straining to hear Daschle over the noise of the crowd. "Tom? I've got John right here," Hindery said. "You aren't going to believe this, but he's willing to cut a deal right now. He'll agree to be Barack's VP."

Hindery was correct. Daschle was dumbfounded.

"Are you sure you want to do this now?" he asked.

"I'm not, but he is," Hindery replied.

All right, Daschle said. I'll take it to Barack.

The triumph of Barack Obama, the humbling of Hillary Clinton, and the evisceration of John Edwards made January 3, 2008, a night for the history books. It was one of those rare moments in political life in which the world shifts on its axis—and everyone is watching. Obama, Clinton, and Edwards had all come into the caucuses with similar hopes and expectations. And they all left in radically different places: Obama, confident to the point of cockiness; Clinton, desperate but determined to save herself; Edwards, doomed but playing the angles. Looking back on it, they all agreed: Iowa had been a game changer.

Though the world was paying less attention, the Republicans held caucuses in Iowa that night as well, and they were a game changer, too. The GOP nomination race had been in disarray all year, with no clear front-runner. For months, Rudy Giuliani, the former mayor of New York and brusque 9/11 icon, had run first in national polls, but he was fading fast. Mike Huckabee, the former governor of Arkansas, was a charming performer, but his almost exclusively Evangelical base of support was too narrow to make him a plausible nominee. Yet Huckabee won the Iowa caucuses, trouncing former Massachusetts governor Mitt Romney by ten points. The defeat was a vast humiliation for Romney, who'd spent millions on the state and had planned to use a victory there as a springboard to New Hampshire and beyond. By throwing the race into even greater chaos, the caucuses accomplished one thing: they opened the door wide to a candidate who wasn't even in Iowa that evening, John McCain, who instead was in New Hampshire at a town hall meeting, casually telling an antiwar activist that it was "fine with me" if American troops stayed in Iraq for a hundred years.

There was something fitting about the outcomes in Iowa for both parties: the element of surprise, the fundamental way they shifted and shaped the contours of the race ahead. Every presidential contest has its twists and turns, each consequential to some degree. But the 2008 election was a campaign defined by big events, startling revelations, and unexpected episodes that again and again threatened to turn everything on its head. The Reverend Jeremiah Wright. Bill Clinton's outbursts in South Carolina. Allegations about troubles in the McCain marriage. The epic crisis of the global financial system. The mesmerizing, confounding, deeply polarizing emergence of Sarah Palin. Palin's public travails and private nightmares, and the unprecedented steps the McCain team took to cope with their superstar. All developments so extravagant and dramatic that they seemed like elements borrowed from a Hollywood screenplay.

And that was fitting, too. More than any election in memory, 2008 was a battle in which the candidates were celebrities, larger-than-life characters who crashed together to create a story uncommonly emotional for politics; a drama rich and captivating and drenched in modern complexities surrounding race, gender, class, religion, and age; a multimedia spectacle that unspooled 24/7 on the Web, cable television, the late-night talk shows, and *Saturday Night Live*. The drama played out against a backdrop that was itself vividly cinematic: a country at war, an economy on the brink, and an electorate swept up, regardless of party, in a passionate yearning for transformation.

Out in Iowa that January, however, precious little of this was clear. What the candidates knew was that for months, and even years, they'd been working toward that night, positioning, strategizing, calculating. They'd been traversing the country, raising money and cajoling local pooh-bahs, shaking hands and smooching babies. They had no idea what would happen next, where the narrative would take them. Indeed, for Obama and Clinton, the confusion was deeper still: they had no clue that their tale was a love story—or that it had been all along.

PART ONE

1

HER TIME

There were thunderstorms in Chicago, bringing air traffic to a grinding halt in and out of O'Hare. So Hillary Clinton sat on the tarmac at Martin State Airport, outside Baltimore, eating pizza and gabbing with two aides and her Secret Service detail on the private plane, waiting, waiting for the weather to clear so she could get where she was headed: a pair of fundraisers in the Windy City for Barack Obama.

It was May 7, 2004, and two months earlier, the young Illinois state senator had won a resounding, unexpected victory in the state's Democratic United States Senate primary, scoring 53 percent of the vote in a seven-person field. Clinton, as always, was in great demand to help drum up cash for her party's candidates around the country. She didn't relish the task, but she did her duty. At least it wasn't as painful as asking for money for herself—an act of supplication that she found so unpleasant she often simply refused to do it.

As the wait stretched past one hour, and then two, Clinton's pilot informed the traveling party that he had no idea when or if the plane would be allowed to take off. To the surprise of her aides, Clinton displayed no inclination to scrap the trip; she insisted that they keep their place in line on the runway. The political cognoscenti were buzzing about Obama—his charisma and his poise, his Kenyan-Kansan ancestry and his only-in-America biography—and she was keen to do her part to help him.

"I want to go," she said firmly.

By the time Clinton finally arrived in Chicago, she had missed the first fund-raiser. But she made it to the second, a dinner at the Arts Club of Chicago, where Barack and Michelle greeted her warmly, grateful for the effort that she'd expended to get there. For the next hour, Clinton worked the room, charming everyone she met, regaling them with funny yarns about the Senate. Then she and Obama raced off to the W Hotel and spoke at a Democratic National Committee soiree for young professionals. The house was packed, Obama rocked it, and Hillary was impressed.

These people know what they're doing, she said to her aides—then flew back east and gushed about Obama for days. He was young, brainy, African American, a terrific speaker. Just the kind of candidate the party needed more of, the kind that she and Bill had long taken pride in cultivating and promoting. Clinton told Patti Solis Doyle, her closest political aide and the director of her political action committee, HillPAC, to provide Obama with the maximum allowable donation. And that was just the start: in the weeks ahead, Clinton would host a fund-raiser for him at her Washington home, then return to Chicago to raise more money for his campaign.

Clinton's aides had never seen her more enthusiastic about a political novice. When one of them asked her why, she said simply, "There's a superstar in Chicago."

Political superstardom was a phenomenon with which Hillary Rodham Clinton was intimately familiar, of course. She knew the upsides and downsides of it, the pleasure and the pain, as well as anyone in American life. For more than a decade she had been in the spotlight and under the microscope ceaselessly and often miserably, and in the process came to dwell on a rarified plane in the national consciousness: beloved and detested, applauded and denounced, famous and infamous, but never ignored.

Now, at fifty-six and in her fourth year in the U.S. Senate, Clinton was still the bête noire of the Republican right. But she was also one of the most popular Democratic politicians in the country—more so than her party's presidential nominee, John Kerry, and more so than her husband, whose public image was still in rehab after the Monica Lewinsky imbroglio and the Marc Rich pardon scandal.

The trajectory that delivered Hillary to this place was remarkable in every way. In the White House she had been, from the start, a profoundly polarizing presence. (Much to her bafflement, too; what she'd done to provoke such a lunatic corps of haters was a mystery to her.) Her time as First Lady was marred by a horrid cascade of defeats, humiliations, and conspiracy theories: health care and cattle futures, Vince Foster and Whitewater, Lewinsky and impeachment. Yet somehow Hillary emerged from all of it a larger, more resonant figure. The Lewinsky affair, for all its awfulness, marked a turning point, rendering her sympathetic and vulnerable-seeming, a woman who had behaved with dignity and fortitude in the most appalling circumstances imaginable. Her decision to run for the Senate in New York in 2000 went against the advice of many of her friends; some political prognosticators predicted confidently that she would lose. Instead, she won the race in a canter, by a thumping twelve-point margin. Weeks after Election Day, Simon and Schuster agreed to pay $8 million for her memoirs, at the time the second-biggest advance ever for a nonfiction tome (just slightly less than the sum handed to Pope John Paul II). But when the book, *Living History*, was published in June 2003, it earned back every penny, selling out its first printing of 1.5 million copies and then some. And the tour to promote it was a sensation, with her fans camping out overnight to get her autograph and the media comparing her to Madonna and Britney Spears.

The Simon and Schuster paycheck allowed Hillary and Bill to buy her dream house in Washington, a $2.85 million, six-bedroom, neo-Georgian manse that was nicknamed after the leafy, secluded street on which it sat: Whitehaven. But *Living History* did more than that. It sparked the beginning of a flirtation with the idea of running for president in 2004—a flirtation at once serious and so shrouded in secrecy that even the best-informed Democratic insiders knew nothing about it.

It was the book tour that got the ball rolling inside Clinton's head. Everywhere she went, people kept telling her she should run, that she was the only Democrat with a hope of defeating George W. Bush. And not just people, but *important* people—elected officials, big-dollar donors, Fortune 500 chieftains. They were in a panic about the party's extant crop of candidates: Kerry was in single digits in the polls and so broke he would have to lend his campaign money; Dick Gephardt was past his sell-by date, John Edwards was an empty suit, Joe Lieberman a retread. The only one catching on was former Vermont governor Howard Dean, whom the party bigwigs saw as too hot, too left, and too weak to stand a chance in a general election.

Hillary agreed with all of that, especially the part about Dean's unelectability. The Bush machine would chew him up and spit him out, then trample on his remains. She also knew that every public poll with her name in the mix had her within striking distance of the incumbent—and trouncing everyone in the Democratic field by thirty points. Oh, sure, her name recognition accounted for much of that lead. Even so! Thirty points! Without lifting a finger!

Hillary was aware, too, that the notion of her running was gaining traction within Clintonworld. For weeks that summer, Steve Ricchetti, who had served as Bill's deputy White House chief of staff and remained one of his closest political hands, could be heard arguing to anyone in earshot that Hillary faced a Bobby Kennedy moment—in which a terrible war, a torn electorate, and a president who had squandered his chance to unify the nation presented a historic opportunity. Maggie Williams, Hillary's former White House chief of staff and a paragon of caution, was open to the idea;

she saw the nomination and the White House there for the taking. Solis Doyle was more than open: She'd been posting to the HillPAC website a stream of emails from supporters begging Hillary to get in. And now Patti was telling her boss that Mark Penn and Mandy Grunwald said that if Clinton was considering entering the race, some systematic steps were in order, and they were ready to help her take them.

Hillary was surprised. Though both Penn and Grunwald were longtime members in good standing of the Clinton high command, they were currently working on Lieberman's campaign, Penn as its pollster and Grunwald as its media consultant.

"You know how terribly unethical this is?" Solis Doyle said to Clinton.

Of course she did—but Hillary was interested in their pitch, and she couldn't help but love the loyalty and devotion it showed to her cause.

Between the public polls and the shenanigans on the website, speculation in the media was mounting about a Clinton bid. Hillary's public posture was unwavering: not gonna happen. At the New York State Fair in Albany that August she told an Associated Press reporter, "I am absolutely ruling it out."

But in private, Clinton appeared to be inching closer to ruling it in. Over the next three months, she and her

inner circle engaged in a series of closed-door meetings and conference calls to explore the possibility in
detail. Even as Penn remained on Lieberman's payroll,
Clinton dispatched him to do a hush-hush poll of voters
in Iowa, New Hampshire, and nationwide. (The results
did nothing to discourage her.) She enlisted John Hart,
a veteran of Bill's 1992 campaign, to analyze the logistics of a late entry: the filing deadlines, the feasibility of
securing sufficient delegates to claim the nomination.
(Tough, but doable.) She tasked her message team with
devising an answer to explain away the abandonment
of the pledge she'd taken during her Senate campaign
to serve out her full six-year term. (The circumstances
in the country were so extraordinarily dire that she was
compelled to run.)

In the end, nearly all her advisers were in agree-
ment: She should do it. Because there was an opening.
Because she could win. Because, as Solis Doyle told her,
"This could be your time."

But Clinton was not a woman swayed by dreamy
exhortations to seize the moment. She was a rational-
ist, an empiricist, with a bone-deep instinct to calibrate
risk and reward, and a highly developed—maybe over-
developed—sixth sense about the trapdoors that might
lie ahead.

Clinton took her full-term pledge seriously; it was
essential to how she had earned the trust of New York

voters. Yes, her husband as governor had made a similar vow to the people of Arkansas, then cast it aside before his 1992 presidential race on the grounds that the country's need for him outweighed the sanctity of his promise. But Hillary worried about betraying the constituents who had given her a home. She also worried about the political price she would pay for doing so. Wouldn't she get hammered for being dishonest, being cynical, being a rank opportunist? For being . . . well, everything her enemies had said she was lo these many years?

And then there was the possibility that she would lose. The Senate seat gave her a political identity that was distinct and separate from her husband's. If she ran for president now and lost, she'd be done and dusted in the Senate, she thought. The platform that made her more than just a former First Lady would be undermined.

On the other hand, the potential rewards were obvious, both for her and for the country. The prospect was nearly irresistible: another chance for a Clinton to expel a failed Bush from the White House.

Hillary valued what her team had to say about all this, but she didn't completely trust it. They had no idea what it was like to be her. Ambition and caution were the twin totems of her psyche, and she was torn between them. She needed more data, more input, more advice—though she was loath to widen the circle much, for fear of the story leaking.

One day late that fall, Clinton summoned James Carville, the architect of Bill's victory in 1992, to her Senate office. Hillary adored James, had no doubt about his allegiance or discretion—although she hadn't looped him in until now. Having advised against her Senate run, Carville was feeling a little gun-shy, so the counsel he offered was hedged. But Hillary seemed to have the bit between her teeth. I think I can do this, she said. None of these guys who are in the race can beat Bush, and I think he can be had.

Carville sat there thunderstruck. When the meeting was over, he walked out the door and thought, *Shit, she may run!*

Clinton also put in a call to her old friend Tom Vilsack, the governor of Iowa. On November 15, she was scheduled to visit Vilsack's state for the annual Jefferson-Jackson Dinner in Des Moines. The J-J was a big deal every year, but on the eve of the Iowa caucuses in a presidential year, it was the biggest deal in Democratic politics. All the major candidates showed up, kicking off the Iowa homestretch, giving speeches they hoped would provide a rush of adrenaline to carry them across the finish line. Hillary had been invited to deliver the keynote and serve as emcee, an honorary role reserved for a Democratic heavyweight who was not in the hunt for the party's nomination.

Clinton had heard through the grapevine, however, that Vilsack thought she should be running. On the phone, Vilsack said it was true—and then practically begged her to get into the race. The party had to thwart Dean, Vilsack told her, and she was the only one who could do it. "This is going to be a holy war, and we need our A team on the field," Vilsack said, "and you're our A team."

Flattered but conflicted, intrigued but not convinced, Clinton arrived at the J-J Dinner in a haze of ambivalence. And then uncorked a scathing denunciation of Bush— "He has no vision for a future that will make America safer and stronger and smarter and richer and better and fairer"—that whipped the crowd into a lather.

In retrospect, Kerry's performance that night, strong and spirited, would be seen as the start of his comeback. Edwards did fine, too. But Hillary's speech outshone all the rest, and she knew it. As she watched her fellow Democrats work the room—pretenders one and all, free of gravitas or panache, let alone any hope of beating Bush—she thought, *These are our candidates for president?*

With the filing deadlines for key primaries looming in December, decision time was upon her. Hillary called together the innermost members of her inner circle for one final meeting at the Clinton home in Chappaqua, in the Westchester County suburbs of New York. Around the table were her husband; their daughter, Chelsea, and Chelsea's boyfriend; Williams and Solis Doyle; and two Clinton White House stalwarts to whom Hillary was close: Evelyn Lieberman, the sharp-eyed former deputy chief of staff famous for having banished Lewinsky from the West Wing to the Pentagon, and Cheryl Mills, the diamond-hard lawyer who had defended Bill in his impeachment trial.

One by one, Hillary polled the group, listening carefully to what each of them had to say. These were the people whose opinions meant the most to her. Solis Doyle and Williams were in favor, as they had been all along. Lieberman and Mills were down with the program, too. And so was Bill. He had no doubt that Hillary would make a better president than anyone who was running. Just as important, he was sure that she could win.

But Hillary discovered that there was one dissenter in the room. Chelsea believed that her mother had to finish her term, that she'd made a promise and had to keep it, that voters would be unforgiving if she didn't.

Try as she might to convince herself otherwise, Hillary thought her daughter was right. After months of weighing the pros and cons, gaming out the decision from every angle, she simply couldn't get past the pledge. All the artful answers in the world wouldn't satisfy her own conscience or drown out the bleating of the anti-Clinton chorus and their amen corner in the press that would greet her if she launched a last-minute campaign. Hillary could hear it now: ambitious bitch, there she goes again, dissembling, scheming, shimmying up the greasy pole with no regard for principle.

"I'd be crucified," she told Solis Doyle.

Clinton's decision to forego the 2004 race would prove fateful. It is impossible to know whether Hillary would have won either the Democratic nomination or the White House—although the strategists behind Bush's reelection considered her formidable in a way they never did Dean or Kerry. But her entry would have scrambled the Democratic race severely. By closing a door, she opened another, inadvertently setting off a chain reaction that would have enormous consequences for her deferred ambitions. The absence of Clinton in the race left the road clear for Kerry to stage his surprising resurgence. The stunning victory over Dean in Iowa. The landslide in New Hampshire. The knockout blow on Super Tuesday that sealed the nomination and put Kerry in a position to make a decision as unlikely as it was momentous: the tapping of an unknown

Illinois state legislator to give the keynote address that summer at the Democratic National Convention.

The selection of Obama had yet to be announced when Bill Clinton rolled into Chicago on July 2, 2004. The former president was passing through on the book tour for his memoir, *My Life*, which was burning up the bestseller lists even more scorchingly than his wife's had done—a million copies sold its first week on the street. The weather was oppressive that day, criminally muggy, and Clinton was ridiculously overscheduled. So, by the time Bill arrived at his last event, an Obama fund-raiser at the home of billionaire real estate mogul Neil Bluhm, he was exhausted, cranky, and feeling every bit his age. But after heading upstairs at the Bluhm house to freshen up and meet Barack and Michelle, he rallied and gave a juicily Clintonian introduction for Obama, praising his potential to the heavens. When Clinton was done, Obama stepped up and responded with a self-deprecating reference to his meager income relative to the piles of dough that Clinton's book was hauling in: "My life would probably be a lot better if I was just finishing up this book tour," Obama deadpanned.

Clinton laughed and then, being Clinton, reclaimed the floor.

"Sonny," he declared, "I'd trade places with you any day of the week!"

The poignancy of Clinton's comment would be hammered home all too soon. On the Monday night of the Democratic convention in Boston, the former president turned in a triumphal performance—and then saw his speech rendered a footnote to history the next evening by Obama's keynote, which catapulted Barack into the stratosphere. A month later, Clinton, after complaining of heart pains and shortness of breath, underwent an angiogram that revealed arterial blockages of such magnitude (90 percent in several places) that his doctors scheduled him for surgery. On September 6, he was subjected to a quadruple bypass, his breastbone cut open, chest pulled apart, heart stopped for seventy-three minutes. His recovery would be slow, arduous, and beset by complications. In some ways, he would never be the same again.

From his hospital bed, Clinton consulted by phone with Kerry, who for months had seen his prospects minced by the Bush campaign and its conservative-media allies. Kerry had handed the Republicans ample ammunition to paint him as an effete, patrician, liberal flip-flopper—and, more disastrously, had failed to push back against the Swift Boat Veterans for Truth, who challenged both his veracity and his war record.

The advice Clinton gave him was rudimentary: more economy, less Vietnam; "Bush fights for Halliburton, John Kerry fights for kids."

Even in his sick and weary state, Clinton could see the election slipping away. In late October, fresh out of the hospital, looking pallid and gaunt and sounding winded, he made a last-ditch effort to help save his party's standard-bearer, speaking in front of a crowd of one hundred thousand at a Kerry rally in Philadelphia. "If this isn't good for my heart," he declared, "I don't know what is."

Hillary did her part for Kerry, too, crisscrossing the country on his behalf in the campaign's closing days. But she felt little sympathy for him. She had nothing but contempt for Democrats who allowed their public images to be mangled and their characters maligned by the right-wing freak show. This was why she'd thought so little of Dean and why she'd always had doubts about Kerry. She detected a strain of Al Gore in the nominee: a passivity, a weakness, an inability to wield the blade in self-defense, let alone pounce at the right moment to carve up an opponent. She sensed that he lacked the hardness needed to survive the combination meat grinder/flash incinerator that postmodern politics had become—a hardness that had come to her unbidden, but that she now wore like a badge of honor.

The verdict on Election Day was, for Hillary, stark confirmation of these home truths. Another honorable Democrat destroyed, another winnable election lost. But it was also, of course, a kind of blessing: 2008 would now be an open-field run. After two Bush terms, her party would rally behind her—naturally, happily, eagerly. She would have a full term in office as a well-regarded senator under her belt. The pledge would be behind her.

Up in Chappaqua a few days after the election, surrounded by her team, Clinton began the process of positioning for the future. Ever circumspect, she claimed she wasn't yet fully certain that she would be gunning for the White House, but everyone took those assertions as pro forma, as Hillary being Hillary. They harbored no doubts that she believed 2008 would be her time.

But Election Day 2004 had delivered something else as well: a blowout Senate victory for Barack Obama. The superstar in Chicago was on his way to Washington.

2

THE ALTERNATIVE

Obama ambled down the fourth-floor hallway in the Russell Senate Office Building looking for his destination: SR476. It was February 1, 2005, a little less than a month after he'd been sworn in as the third African American senator since Reconstruction, and he was still learning his way around Capitol Hill. His own quarters were a block away, in the larger, more modern, and less prestigious Hart Building. Russell was the tank where the big fish swam—Ted Kennedy, John Kerry, John McCain. It was also where Hillary Clinton occupied the suite that had once belonged to the legendary New York senator Daniel Patrick Moynihan, and it was Clinton whom Obama was coming to see on that cold, clear winter day.

He needed help. The past six months had been sheer mayhem. One day, Obama was a promising but obscure politico with a funny name and an uphill fight to win the Senate race into which he'd leapt. The next, his life was swept up in a whirlwind of nearly unfathomable force. His oration at the Democratic convention—with its stirring calls to unity and common purpose, its rejection of false distinctions between red and blue America, its rejection of "the politics of cynicism" and embrace of "the politics of hope"—had not only struck a chord with countless Democrats but turned him into a worldwide celebrity. Suddenly, Obama was recognized everywhere he went. Crowds waited for him outside his favorite restaurants in Chicago, swarmed around him on the streets. Suddenly, he was on the cover of *Newsweek* and the set of *Meet the Press.*

Precious few people in any walk of life could even faintly comprehend what had happened to him and what it meant. But Hillary would understand completely. Obama's view of her husband was complicated; there was much about Bill Clinton and the creed of Clintonism that he admired, but also much that gave him pause. His feelings about Hillary were, however, more straightforward. He'd liked her from the moment they met. Obama was wonkier, more enthralled by policy, than most people understood, and he saw in Hillary a kindred spirit. He thought she was tough, smart, ballsy, and knew how to win. A number of Obama's campaign aides had worked for John Edwards before he folded his 2004 campaign, and Obama enjoyed razzing them about what would happen if Clinton and Edwards squared off for the Democratic presidential nomination in 2008. "Hillary's gonna kick your guy's ass," he'd say.

Obama also was impressed with how Clinton had handled her transition from the White House to the Senate back in 2001. He knew that his megawatt status could prove problematic in the upper chamber, a hidebound institution where seniority determined power, prestige, and privilege—and where noses easily went out of joint. He wanted Hillary's assistance in navigating the minefield stretched out before him.

They sat together for about an hour that day, amid the tchotchkes and the photos on Clinton's canary-yellow office walls—a picture of Bobby Kennedy, another of her and Bill in the Oval Office, a composite shot of Hillary with her hero Eleanor Roosevelt. Clinton believed that success in the Senate required the sublimation of the ego (or a credible facsimile thereof). And the advice she offered Obama based on that theory was clear and bullet-point concise: Keep your head down. Avoid the limelight. Get on the right committees. Go to hearings. Do your homework. Build up a substantive portfolio. And never forget the care and feeding of the people who sent you here.

Clinton appreciated that Obama had sought her counsel, seemed to see him as a budding protégé, wanted to take him under her wing. During that first year together in the Senate, he would approach her often on the floor (something he did with other colleagues only rarely), and she always took time to chat with him quietly, to try to steer him in the right direction. At one point, Obama gave her a gift: a photograph of him, Michelle, and their two young daughters, Sasha and Malia. From then until the day she left the Senate in 2009—through all the rivalry and rancor that eventually developed between them—Hillary displayed it prominently in her office.

Clinton's staff, however, looked on Obama with a somewhat more jaundiced eye. In the early months of 2005, any number of stories in the press noted approvingly his adherence to the "Clinton model" of cautious advancement. But Hillary's people thought Obama's conduct was nothing like their boss's in her first years in the Senate. Instead of shying away from the national media, he seemed to be courting it, giving innumerable interviews and being trailed constantly by photographers and camera crews.

One day that spring, Hillary's personal aide, Huma Abedin, and another Clinton staffer were loitering just off the Senate floor when they ran into Obama, who greeted them casually: "Hey, what's going on?"

"I saw your picture on a magazine cover," Abedin said, gently chiding him. "It was nice."

To which Obama replied without irony, "Oh, which one?"

The point was made.

He could come across as cocky, that was for sure—and not just to people outside his circle. He was smarter than the average bear, not to mention the average politician, and he not only knew it but wanted to make sure that everyone else knew it, too. In meetings with his aides, he exerted control over the conversation by interrupting whoever was talking. "Look," he would say—it was his favorite interjection, almost a tic—and then be off to the races, reframing the point, extending it, claiming ownership of it. "Whose idea was that?" was another of his favorites, employed with cheery boastfulness whenever something he'd previously proposed had come up roses. His calmness and composure could veer into the freakish, and sometimes concealed his gaudy confidence in himself. But not always. A few hours before his high-stakes convention keynote, a *Chicago Tribune* reporter asked him if he was nervous. "I'm LeBron, baby," Obama replied. "I can play on this level. I got some game."

The self-assurance had been there as long as anyone could remember, alongside the ambition. When Obama started dating a young Chicago lawyer named Michelle Robinson, in the summer of 1989, he mentioned to her brother, Craig, that he might one day want to run for Senate, "possibly even for president." Craig replied, "Okay, but don't say that to my aunt Gracie," attempting to save the poor schlub from embarrassing himself. (Aunt Gracie was the least of Obama's worries; his new girlfriend disdained politics as a cynical game. "[Craig] should have said, 'Don't tell Michelle,'" Mrs. Obama later recalled.)

The 2004 convention keynote and its aftermath moved the possibility of an Obama run for the White House out of the realm of pure theory. The buzz about it had started the moment he climbed down from the stage. David Axelrod and Robert Gibbs, who had piloted him to his Senate win and remained his two main political advisers, both discussed it, but believed it was at least eight years down the road.

Obama agreed. "There's a lot of speculation about what will happen in 2008," he told his new Senate chief of staff, Pete Rouse, right at the start of 2005. "I can assure you there's no way that I'm running—I have two small kids and I'm not that presumptuous."

But for a man who disclaimed any short-range designs on the Oval Office, Obama surrounded himself with a striking number of adjutants whose eyes had long been on that prize. Axelrod, fifty, a former political journalist with a walrus mustache and a world-weary manner, had made the switch to advising candidates in 1984. In 1988, he worked on Illinois senator Paul Simon's presidential run; he consulted secretly with Al Gore on a possible 2004 bid, then joined Edwards's campaign that year. His résumé was studded with other clients with national ambitions: Senator Chris Dodd, Tom Vilsack, and Hillary Clinton. In the trade, Axelrod was known for being interested less in policy than in softer qualities of character and biography. His central gift was a grasp of the power of narrative—his ability to weave his candidate's beliefs and background into an emotionally compelling bundle. In Obama, whom he'd met in 1991 and had guided ever since, Axelrod saw qualities that the nation was hungry for: optimism, dynamism, outsider status, an aversion to hoary ideological dogmas, a biography that radiated the possibility of overcoming divisions and the capacity for change.

Gibbs, too, saw in Obama a figure of national stature. Having worked on Kerry's presidential campaign in its early stages before losing his job in a campaign purge, he had signed on to Obama's Senate race in no small part because he viewed the candidate as a guy who was going places.

And then there was the latest addition to Obama's inner circle. Pete Rouse was a round man in his late fifties with a head of thick salt-and-pepper hair, a gruff manner, and a voice that sounded as if he gargled with gravel. The consummate insider, he had come highly recommended by Tom Daschle, after many years as the former Senate majority leader's chief of staff. Obama had bonded with Daschle the previous fall, when Daschle was on his way to being defeated for reelection in South Dakota, and had been conferring with him ever since. Rouse would be the first of the Daschle Mafia—arguably the only collection of Washington talent to rival the Clinton apparatus—to gravitate toward Obama, most of them hoping to work for a future president.

Obama made it plain to Rouse that his focus was on the Senate, however. He wanted to be effective and strategic, to move ahead as quickly as possible without ruffling feathers, to project an image of diligence and humility. But unlike Clinton, whose national profile was already as capacious as it could get before she arrived in the Senate, Obama wanted to take advantage of his newfound prominence to build a larger brand. His staff was fielding three hundred speaking invitations a week. Grassroots liberal activists, conservative columnists, and his party's leadership all wanted a piece of him.

Together with Axelrod and Gibbs, Rouse developed a strategic plan to capitalize on this outsize interest. The plan—which Rouse and the rest ingeniously dubbed "The Plan"—called for Obama to dive neck-deep into fund-raising for his Senate colleagues. (They'll be coming for you anyway, Rouse told him, so you might as well volunteer.) To give major speeches on national policy: energy, education, economics. To travel abroad as a member of the Senate Foreign Relations Committee to build his credibility on international affairs. To expand his political horizons aggressively and systematically.

Obama put his shoulder to the wheel, but he found many aspects of his new life frustrating, starting with the Senate itself. The glacial pace, the endless procedural wrangling, the witless posturing and pettifoggery, the geriatric cast of characters doddering around the place: all of it drove him nuts. To one friend in Chicago, Obama complained, "It's basically the same as Springfield"—the Illinois capital where he had toiled in the state senate—"except the average age in Springfield is forty-two and in Washington it's sixty-two. Other than that, it's the same bullshit." After enduring an unceasing monologue by Senator Joe Biden during a committee hearing, Obama passed a note to Gibbs that read, "Shoot me now." Time and again after debates on the floor, he would emerge through the chamber's double doors shaking his head, rolling his eyes, using both hands to give the universal symbol for the flapping of gums, sighing wearily, "Yak, yak, yak."

Obama's frustration was magnified by the fact that he was living apart from his wife and daughters. He didn't doubt the decision that he and Michelle had made to keep their home in Chicago; his spouse had her own career in the city; her mother lived nearby; the girls were happy, grounded, in a wonderful school. But Obama missed them all terribly and questioned whether the separation was worth it when all he seemed to be doing in the Senate was nibbling around the edges.

Then, in late August 2005, Hurricane Katrina happened—and brought Obama to a different place. For weeks afterward, he was downcast and angry at the scale of the failure of George W. Bush and his administration. He started speaking about an "empathy deficit" crippling the country, about the severity of the problems that America faced and the epic failure to confront them. Slowly, subtly, tentatively, Obama seemed to be trying on the mantle of a national leader.

Obama's aides were laboring mightily to further that impression, sending him from one end of the country to the other—Virginia, New Jersey, Texas, Arizona, Tennessee—for fund-raising or political events right before and after the off-year elections of 2005. By the end of the year, Obama was exhausted and annoyed: he'd missed three weekends at home in a row, and weekends were sacrosanct to him. Michelle was even more irritated. "It's a tough choice between, do you stay for Malia's basketball game on Sunday or do you go to New Jersey and campaign for [then-senator Jon] Corzine?" she said to a reporter at the time, her voice dripping with sarcasm. "Corzine got it this time around."

Gibbs was in charge of Obama's schedule and well aware that he'd screwed up. So he was bewildered when Obama came to him in November and indicated he might like to speak at the Florida Democratic Party convention on December 10. Florida senator Bill Nelson had asked Obama three times to attend; three times, Obama had said no. The tenth was a Saturday, and not just any Saturday, but one on which Malia had a dance recital in Chicago. But here was Obama, toying with going to the Sunshine State anyway.

"What do you have in mind?" Gibbs asked his boss.

"I've got some stuff I'd like to try out," Obama said. "I want to see what the reaction is."

What Obama wanted to try out was an honest-to-goodness stump speech full of sweeping national themes, crafted by him, Axelrod, and his precocious twenty-four-year-old speechwriter, Jon Favreau. And he was so intent on going to Florida—Florida!—that he was willing to leave his daughter's recital, drive out to the airport, catch a charter plane, fly down to Lake Buena Vista, address the crowd, and jet back to Chicago the same night.

Huh, Gibbs thought. *Interesting.*

On the appointed evening, Obama took the podium in a cavernous ballroom at a Walt Disney World hotel. Edwards and Vilsack—both potential candidates for 2008—had spoken earlier that day and garnered respectful receptions. The crowd was maybe a thousand strong, overwhelmingly white. As Obama unfurled his speech, a narrative about the transition from the twentieth century into the twenty-first and the inability of a generation of leaders to realize that the world had changed, people in the audience began shouting, "You should run!"

"In Washington right now, we don't see the kind of leadership that would give us faith," Obama continued. "It's the timidity, the smallness of our politics that are holding us back."

Another voice from out of the darkness: "You're looking pretty good!"

When Obama finished, a thunderous ovation erupted. He headed to the car, climbed inside, turned to Gibbs, and asked, "So how do you think it went?"

"If you wanted to know whether that would connect," Gibbs replied, "I think you got your answer."

Six weeks later, on January 22, 2006, Obama appeared on *Meet the Press*. It was the second time he'd been on the program and the first in more than a year. At the end of the interview, moderator Tim Russert referred back to Obama's previous turn on the show, when he'd stated that he "absolutely" would serve out his full six-year Senate term, and asked if his thinking had changed. Obama said it hadn't.

"So you will not run for president or vice president in 2008?" Russert pressed.

"I will not," Obama said.

Axelrod was pleased with Obama's answer—any hedging would have unleashed a tsunami of distracting speculation. But some other Obama allies thought he had been too unequivocal, leaving him no wiggle room.

"What if you change your mind?" his old friend Valerie Jarrett asked.

"You can always change your mind," Obama said without concern. "I haven't made a decision at all."

"But you kind of said you wouldn't do it."

"Well, I probably won't."

Obama's attitude could be seen as cavalier—or deeply cynical. But it also reflected an instinctive disdain for the conventional rules of politics. To Obama, the ritual parsing of these kinds of statements was a tedious preoccupation of the media, an obsession that few real Americans shared. If he decided to make a play for the White House, how many voters would give a damn what he'd said to Russert months earlier? Not many.

But what made Obama's answer on *Meet the Press* striking in retrospect was that although the likelihood of his running was seemingly minuscule, the idea had for the first time entered the realm of explicit, tangible possibility in his inner circle. A week before Obama's face-off with Russert, Rouse, on a road trip to see his father in New Haven, Connecticut, had pulled off the highway in the middle of the night, ordered a coffee at a donut shop, and sketched out a memo, an update of his earlier strategic plan, that set forth two alternate paths for Obama in the year ahead: one if he was categorically rejecting a presidential bid, the other if he wanted to keep the door ajar, however slightly.

Rouse knew he was being a bit manipulative by framing the case this way. Even a year earlier, when they first discussed his future, Obama hadn't definitively ruled out running, so why would he want to now? But, more than manipulative, Rouse was being methodical, which was his way. If there was any chance that Obama would end up in the race, there were steps he could and should take beforehand to put himself in the best possible position. He would need to spend more time on the road, showing his face in certain key states. He would need to devote more effort to developing relationships with potential allies, something Obama lacked a feel for and had little interest in.

Obama was planning to travel to Africa later in the year. He was also working on his second book—a follow-up to his successful memoir, *Dreams from My Father*—for which there would be an extensive promotional tour. Those events, together with a full slate of fund-raising and campaigning in the fall for Democratic candidates competing in the midterm elections, could be combined to gin up buzz, and also to measure how much of the energy Obama generated might translate into material support for a presidential run.

Rouse undertook his memo at his own instigation, but he was perfectly in sync with Obama's evolving thinking. In March, Rouse invited another member of the Daschle Mafia, Anita Dunn, to meet Obama in his billet on the seventh floor of Hart. Dunn was one of the party's sharpest political minds, a consultant whose clients had included not only the former Senate majority leader but also Senator Evan Bayh and former senator Bill Bradley, for whose 2000 presidential run she'd served as chief strategist.

Dunn's mission would be to revamp Hopefund, Obama's political action committee. The PAC had raised a fair amount of money in 2005, but its email list of donors was paltry and so was the cash in Obama's own campaign account. Hopefund could become an embryonic infrastructure for Obama's future ambitions. "I haven't made any decision about what I'm going to do yet, but we have to get this thing fixed," Obama said to Dunn. "We need to get organized, we need to grow these lists—at the end of the year, I want to have options."

Within Obama's operation, "the options" became a code phrase, a reference to three live possibilities: launching a presidential run, bolstering his stature in the Senate with an eye toward the VP slot in 2008, or returning to Illinois to run for governor—with a presidential bid so far remaining at the bottom of the option pile. Whatever the eventual outcome, Dunn's plan in the interim would be the same. She had been thinking a lot about the Web, the result of a series of conversations with Axelrod's partner, David Plouffe, who was blazing trails in Internet fund-raising and organizing on Deval Patrick's campaign for the Massachusetts governorship. The scheme Dunn hatched on Obama's behalf revolved around a simple transaction. Every time he did an event for a candidate, Hopefund would require the beneficiary to set up a registration system and then turn over the attendees' email addresses to the PAC.

This was no small thing. As 2006 rolled on, the requests poured in—urgent, desperate pleas from Democratic candidates fervent in the view that a visit from Obama would be their fiscal and political salvation. That added up to a lot of chits, and a lot of email addresses.

The blind faith in, and passion for, Obama was like nothing Dunn had ever seen before. Around Hopefund they joked about it all the time, praying it wouldn't go to Obama's head; his ego was robust enough already. They even conferred on the senator a new nickname: "Black Jesus."

Obama may have been a buckraking messiah, but he was all too aware that he was still just a freshman and therefore at the beck and call of his party's leadership. So when he was summoned one day in July to Senate Majority Leader Harry Reid's office without the slightest explanation why, he promptly hoofed it over there, remarking to Gibbs on his way out the door, "I wonder what we screwed up."

Obama's relationship with the leader was cordial enough, but it was hardly warm or close. Now he found himself sitting in the chair across from Reid in his quarters in the Capitol. From the wall above Reid's desk, the impassive visage of Samuel Clemens, rendered in a giant oil painting, mutely observed the proceedings.

At sixty-six, Reid was a little more than twenty years older than Obama, but in terms of style and demeanor, the generation gap between them seemed much wider. Awkward and halting, vaguely archaic, Reid didn't like wasting words or time. On his mind today was Obama's future in the Senate—and he got right to the point.

"You're not going to go anyplace here," Reid declared soon after Obama took his seat. "I know that you don't like it, doing what you're doing."

In observing Obama for the past year and a half, Reid had sensed his frustration and impatience, had heard rumblings that Obama was already angling to head back home and take a shot at the Illinois governorship. Reid had no idea if it was true, but he knew this much: Obama simply wasn't cut out to be a Senate lifer.

As Obama listened to the senior senator from Nevada, he wasn't sure where the old man was going. But then Reid's disquisition took an unexpected turn, surprising Obama in both its bluntness and adamancy.

Twenty minutes later, the meeting was over, and Obama headed back to his warren in the Hart building. He breezed through the lobby, down the hall, and into Gibbs's office, closing the door behind him.

"So," asked Gibbs from behind his desk, "what did we fuck up?"

"Nothing," Obama replied. "Harry wants me to run for president."

"That whole meeting was about you running for president?"

"Yeah," Obama said, then grinned. "He really wants me to run for president."

Harry Reid wasn't alone among Senate Democrats in the dawning desire to see Obama chuck his hat into the ring. Although Clinton hadn't yet formally declared her intention to enter the race, in political circles it was seen as a foregone conclusion, as was her status as the heir apparent, the prohibitive front-runner-in-waiting. And that was making many Democrats distinctly nervous in the summer of 2006.

The reasons for their unease were many. In her first term in the Senate, Hillary had built a record of bipartisan accomplishment and a wealth of expertise on matters of policy; she had earned a reputation, in the lingo of the Senate, as "a workhorse and not a show horse." But polling revealed that her negative ratings were perilously high across the country, and especially outside the bluest states. She remained, as ever, a polarizing creature, one who would widen the chasmal partisan divide that opened up during her husband's two White House terms and only deepened in those of his successor. Her 2002 vote to authorize the Iraq War made her as toxic to some on the left as she was on the right. Democrats feared she might be unelectable in the best of circumstances—and not merely unelectable, but a catastrophe for the party, her presence atop the ticket hobbling House and Senate Democrats in red and purple states across the board.

And then there was the other thing, which threatened to create something closer to the worst of circumstances. The other thing was Bill—more specifically his personal life, about which rumors were running rampant. Not since the Lewinsky era had they been more pervasive, the topic of tittering in every quadrant of the Democratic Establishment from New York to Boston to Los Angeles. And nowhere was the scuttlebutt flowing more freely than in Washington.

Over lunch one afternoon that summer with a Democratic senator to whom he was close, John McCain exclaimed, "What the hell is Bill Clinton *doing* to Hillary?" McCain was friendly with the Clintons. He meant them no injury. But for his across-the-aisle colleague, the conversation threw into sharp relief the nightmare scenario that was causing so many Democrats such angst: that Hillary would skate to the Democratic nomination—and then be destroyed in the general election when Republicans peddled the details of her husband's reputed dalliances to the press. One party elder described the situation thus: "It's like some Japanese epic film where everyone sees the disaster coming in the third reel, but no one can figure out what to do about it."

Reid was well aware that such thoughts were rippling through the Democratic caucus. In truth, he shared them. After the aching disappointments of 2000 and 2004, and after the depredations Democrats believed Bush had inflicted on the country, the sense of urgency about taking back the White House was bordering on manic. The obvious answer was to find a plausible challenger to Clinton—someone who wouldn't weigh down the rest of the party's candidates, even if he were defeated in the general election.

The problem was that none of the Democrats contemplating a bid fit the bill. Edwards was regarded as a shallow, callow pretender by virtually every one of his former colleagues. Joe Biden, Chris Dodd, and Evan Bayh were fine senators, but all would be crushed by Clinton. Ditto Bill Richardson, Mark Warner, and Tom Vilsack. John Kerry was saddled with more baggage than a curbside porter at Dulles airport. Only Al Gore, rejuvenated by his fiery opposition to Bush on the war and his celebrated climate change crusade, seemed to have what it took to make a credible run at Clinton. But Gore evinced almost zero interest in climbing back into the ring.

The pickings, in other words, were mighty slim—except for Obama.

Years later, Reid would claim that he was steadfastly neutral in the 2008 race; that he never chose sides between Barack and Hillary; that all he did was tell Obama that "he could be president," that "the stars could align for him." But at the time, in truth, his encouragement of Obama was unequivocal. He was wowed by Obama's oratorical gifts and believed that the country was ready to embrace a black presidential candidate, especially one such as Obama—a "light-skinned" African American "with no Negro dialect, unless he wanted to have one," as he later put it privately.

Reid was convinced, in fact, that Obama's race would help him more than hurt him in a bid for the Democratic nomination. He argued that Obama's lack of experience might not be crippling; it might actually be an asset, allowing him to cast himself as a figure uncorrupted and unco-opted by evil Washington, without the burdens of countless Senate votes and floor speeches. And, unlike Clinton, Obama had come out forcefully and early against Bush's Iraq incursion;

in 2002, while he was still a state senator, he'd given a heralded speech in which he said, "I don't oppose all wars. . . . What I am opposed to is a dumb war." Reid wasn't sure Obama could defeat Clinton. Probably he couldn't. But he was the only person in the party who stood a fighting chance—the best available alternative.

Obama had heard these arguments before from other senators. His friend and Illinois counterpart, Dick Durbin, was urging him to run, but that was to be expected. More intriguing were the entreaties he was receiving from New York's Chuck Schumer. Schumer's relationship with Hillary had always been fraught with rivalry and tinged with jealousy; though she was technically the junior member of the New York team in the Senate, she had eclipsed him in terms of celebrity and influence from the moment she arrived on the Hill. By 2006, they had found their way to a mostly peaceful coexistence. Yet because of the circles in which he traveled, Schumer was more familiar than most with the tittle-tattle about her husband's alleged infidelities. He heard people debating what Hillary should do to preserve her political viability when the scandal inevitably broke: Divorce Bill or ride it out (again)?

Schumer was also the chair of the Democratic Senatorial Campaign Committee and, in that role, had seen Obama's efforts up close on behalf of the party's candidates. He was blown away by Obama's fund-raising prowess and the enthusiasm he generated in states traditionally inhospitable to Democrats. The political handicapper in Schumer was fascinated by Obama's potential to redraw the electoral map, a capacity Clinton surely lacked. In conversations with other senators and strategists in 2006, Schumer would make these points over and over. He made them to Obama as well, and repeatedly; in one instance Schumer even double-teamed him with Reid. Although Schumer was careful to signal that home-state decorum would prohibit him from opposing Clinton publicly—"You understand my position," he would say—he left no doubt as to where his head and heart were on the question.

These were not the only senatorial voices impor-tuning Obama. Daschle, too, was on the case, and so was a coterie of senators close to him, including Byron Dorgan and Kent Conrad, both of North Dakota. Ben Nelson of Nebraska, Bill Nelson of Florida, Barbara Boxer of California, and even Ted Kennedy—all were nudging Obama to take the plunge. Their conversa-tions with Barack were surreptitious, a conspiracy of whispers. They told him that 2008 was going to be a change election and that he uniquely could embody transformation. They told him he might never get a better chance. They told him this could be his time.

But they also added the same caveats as Schumer. Keen as they were for Obama to run, they would never be able to bless him with an early endorsement. Coming out against Hillary would pose grave risks. The Clintons had long memories and a vindictive streak ten miles wide. If Hillary prevailed, they feared—no, they were certain—there would be retribution down the line. But they would root for Obama secretly, doing whatever they could to help without affronting the aborning Democratic dynasty.

It would be many months before the Clintons gained any awareness of the incipient betrayal of Hillary by her colleagues in the Senate. And then it would hit them like a ton of bricks in their psychic solar plexus. The Clintons saw themselves as the party's de facto First Family. As the patrons of two generations of Democratic politicians for whom they'd raised stacks of cash, providing aid and comfort on the path to prominence. As the only Democrats in recent memory who had demonstrated a consistent capacity to win na-tional elections. As revered and beloved figures. They were blind to the degree of Clinton fatigue in their world and deaf to the conspiracy of whispers. They had no idea how fast the ground was shifting beneath their feet.

And neither, really, did Obama—until his conversation with Reid.

Like everyone else in Washington, Obama took as a given the fearsome potency of the Clinton machine. Despite all the exhortations to take on Hillary, there were many reasons to believe that such an enterprise would be pure folly. That she was unstoppable, a juggernaut.

But Obama had to wonder. Schumer, Dorgan, Durbin, and now Reid—these four men comprised the upper echelon of the official Democratic leadership in the Senate. Maybe the Establishment wasn't as four-square behind the Clintons as conventional wisdom held. Maybe there was an opening.

A few days after his meeting with Reid, Obama was telling Jarrett about what had happened in the leader's office.

She listened to Obama's description of the Reid meeting and was impressed. But Jarrett wanted to know what it meant in concrete terms. "Is he going to endorse you and support you?" she asked.

No, Obama answered.

"So what good is it for him to tell you that you should run if he's not going to help you?"

"He just thinks that I should do it, but he doesn't want to cross Senator Clinton," Obama replied. "He thinks I can win."

Besides Michelle, Jarrett knew Barack Obama as well as anyone. She had watched him for months as he began to wrestle with the idea of running for president. For the first time, she could see him thinking, *Maybe I can do this.*

3

THE GROUND BENEATH
HER FEET

Bill Clinton knew his wife could do it, and do it damn well, too. From the time they fell in love three decades earlier at Yale Law School, he had been in awe of Hillary. She was the smartest, most committed, most idealistic, most impressive person he had ever met; he thought she hung the moon. Some felt that she had the nomination locked up but would face a daunting challenge in the general election. Bill Clinton believed the opposite—a point he made repeatedly to anyone who would listen. "This primary is gonna be harder than the general," he would say. "I'm just telling all you people this."

Clinton's assessment was based primarily on one thing: the anger of the party's liberal base at Hillary's vote to authorize the Iraq War and her continued refusal to recant it. By the late fall of 2005, the former president was convinced that his wife needed to find her way to a more politically palatable position. With elections in Iraq scheduled for that December, the body count rising, and sectarian violence raging in the region, calls were intensifying for a troop reduction or even a full-scale withdrawal. On November 13, Edwards, whom the Clintons considered Hillary's most serious rival for the nomination, published an op-ed in *The Washington Post* apologizing for his own Senate vote in favor of authorizing the war. (Its first sentence: "I was wrong.") The pressure was mounting on Hillary to do the same.

Mark Penn, Bill knew, argued vehemently that a mea culpa would cause Hillary more harm than good. Penn believed her vote was right on the merits and that defending it was smart politics. He contended that the biggest hurdle Hillary would have to surmount if she ran for president was the doubt that a woman was capable of being commander in chief. At all times she had to project strength, resolution, rough-and-readiness—and do absolutely nothing that signaled squishiness. He told the Clintons that his polling showed that sticking to her guns on Iraq played to her advantage as a character issue. Apologizing now would only invite Republicans to characterize her later as another cut-and-run Democrat in the mold of Kerry, Dukakis, and McGovern.

Bill had enormous faith in Penn and his numbers. The bond between them was forged in 1996, when Clinton's ideologically androgynous Svengali, Dick Morris, brought the pollster into that year's reelection effort and then was caught up in a toe-sucking scandal with a prostitute, leaving Penn with the presidential ear. And it was cemented by Penn's skillful navigation of the survival politics of impeachment and his central role in Hillary's Senate victory.

But even if an apology was off the table, surely there was a middle ground to be claimed, Clinton thought. In 1991, he had faced a comparable situation when he was asked if he would have voted to authorize the elder Bush's Gulf War. His answer was vintage Clinton: "I guess I would have voted for the majority if it was a close vote, but I agree with the arguments the minority made."

The trouble was that Hillary, for all her virtues, lacked the suppleness (or slipperiness) that was one of her husband's fortes. He knew better than anyone that she was less capable of the artful shuck and jive that he could muster on his clumsiest day, so he resolved to assist her in making a pivot to a safer berth. The first step came on November 16, just three days after Edwards's op-ed, when Bill, in Dubai on a swing through the Middle East on behalf of his philanthropic Clinton Global Fund, deviated from his prior support for the war by declaring in a speech that the invasion of Iraq was "a big mistake," adding that "Saddam is gone—it's a good thing, but I don't agree with what was done."

A few days later, Bill landed in Jerusalem and set to work ghostwriting a letter for his wife to email to her constituents reframing her stance on the war. In his suite at the King David Hotel, Clinton labored long into the night, editing and reediting faxed copies of the text in his illegible longhand scrawl.

Well after midnight, he summoned Jay Carson, his twenty-eight-year-old communications director, to his room and showed him the letter. The gist of what Hillary would assert: if Congress in 2002 possessed the information that it had at its disposal today, Bush never would have asked it to authorize the use of force in Iraq—and if he had, he would have been refused.

What do you think? Clinton asked. I think this is good. I think this gets her in the right place. Carson was aware that Hillary and her aides had been furiously debating how to handle her war vote for months—but to see his boss behaving this obsessively reinforced his sense of the gravity of the problem. *Man, this is serious,* he thought.

Carson went back to his room to get some sleep. But a couple of hours later, he was called again to Clinton's suite to repeat the routine. It was nearly three o'clock in the morning now, but Clinton was still twitchy, uncertain. Did the letter go far enough? Did it find the sweet spot? Would it defang the anti-warriors?

I don't know, I just don't know, Clinton said, shaking his head. Hillary can't listen to me or anyone else, because she can't go out there and defend it every day if she doesn't agree with what she's saying. She's got to do what she thinks is right and then just try to weather the storm.

Hillary Clinton had encountered few storms—and certainly none of this magnitude or potential consequence—in her first five years in the Senate. In many ways, her entire time in office had been orchestrated to avoid them. Punctiliously, painstakingly, she had set about remediating her political liabilities, putting herself in the best possible position to lead her party. She had moderated her ideological profile, burnished her credentials, honed her policy chops. Established herself as a diligent legislator. Demonstrated her dedication to her constituents in New York. Sanded down every jagged edge from her formerly serrated public image. She had endeavored mightily, in other words, to place herself firmly in the Democratic mainstream, to make herself a figure of respect and admiration, of party cohesion and not divisiveness—and, not least, to create for herself a separate and distinct political persona and operation from that of her husband.

By 2006, Clinton had achieved all that, with a strategy subtler and savvier than most understood. Her public posture in the Senate, it was widely noted, revolved around bipartisanship and deference, despite her built-in superstardom. Her outreach to Republicans was so ostentatious that it bordered on the masochistic: cosponsoring legislation with forty-nine of them, taking pains to mend fences with those who had voted to impeach her husband, joining a Senate prayer group favored by the GOP's staunchest social conservatives.

In private, however, Clinton's approach was nearly the polar opposite, partisan and assertive to its core. She believed passionately in a more activist government, in a progressive agenda, and she was tired of seeing Democrats flounder in their aims simply because they lacked a coherent message, organizational skills, and a crisp, high-sticking strategy. Convinced that liberals needed an infrastructure to match the network of think tanks and advocacy groups that had bolstered the right for decades, she assisted John Podesta, one of her husband's former chiefs of staff, in launching the Center for American Progress and advised the liberal watchdog group Media Matters for America. Her goal was to better fortify her party against the dense, cold-blooded armament of the Bush White House, to lay a protective groundwork for Democratic interests on the Hill. But she also was thinking ahead—to another Clinton presidential campaign and administration, when those reinforcements could ease her path and abet her power.

Within the Senate she was something of a scold toward her party's leadership, forever prodding Reid to develop a sharper and more consistent approach to battling the Republicans. Her opinion of his predecessor, Daschle, was no better; she had quickly pegged him as ineffectual and weak, a bush-leaguer in a big-league job, and his loss at the polls in 2004 had only confirmed her early verdict.

Clinton's prescription for both her and the party's reformation was rooted in the lessons she drew from recent history, from the failures of 2004, 2000, and especially the nineties. Although her husband had dragged Democrats kicking and screaming into the modern age substantively and ideologically, she considered his administration a tactical and operational disaster: soft, undisciplined, woolly minded, and leaky.

The political machine that Hillary built for herself was its opposite in every regard. The people comprising it—on her Senate staff, at her PAC, and among her outside advisers—were loyal to a fault, smart and ruthless, hardheaded and hard-boiled. With few exceptions, they embraced her conception of politics as total war and shared her reflexive antipathy to the Fourth Estate. They more closely resembled Bush's operation than Bill Clinton's (and were happy, even proud, to admit it). They referred to themselves collectively as Hillaryland, and everyone else in politics did too.

More than any other player, Solis Doyle embodied the culture of Hillaryland. The sixth child of Mexican parents who came to America and settled in Chicago, she started out as Hillary's scheduler in 1991 and steadily amassed duties and influence from there on. She had a ready laugh and a teasing wit, but could be brutal in her role as the chief enforcer of Hillaryland's code of omertà and rarely spoke to reporters. More than her political acumen, it was her almost daughterly connection to Hillary that was her source of power. At forty-one, she was the first and last aide Clinton consulted on any big decision, and was often said to possess the capacity to channel her boss's thinking.

And yet in terms of Hillaryland mojo, Solis Doyle was matched by Penn, who exerted an iron grip on Clinton's message strategy. Appointed CEO of the public-relations behemoth Burson-Marsteller in 2005, he had spent the previous three decades polling on behalf of clients ranging from Ed Koch to Tony Blair—

along with companies such as Microsoft and Avis—
and had made a specialty of carving up the electorate
into itty-bitty demographic and psychographic slices
and propounding micropolicies to satisfy voters' crav-
ings and allay their anxieties. He was fifty-two years
old, doughy, disheveled, and socially maladroit; in the
Clinton White House, his nickname had alternated between Schlumpy and Schlumbo.

Hillary was attached to Solis Doyle and Penn for
different reasons, and they in turn reflected different aspects of her character. What she liked about Solis
Doyle was her crawl-across-broken-glass fealty, her
discretion, and the mind meld the two of them had
achieved; Patti was a comfortable and comforting presence. What she liked about Penn was his data-drivenness,
his tendency to frame even the grubbiest issues and nastiest tactics in lofty policy terms, and, most of all, his certitude; when her own political instincts were muddy, as
they often were, he told her what to do.

The job that the Hillarylanders had done for Hillary
had been masterly by any measure. They helped her
win her Senate seat when people said it was a pipe
dream. They helped her lay waste to the prevailing
caricature of her (an arrogant, corrupt, power-mad,
harsh, hypocritical liberal) and sketched a new picture (a competent, clever, hardworking, determined,

pragmatic centrist) that boosted her popularity ratings to the moon. They were on the way to helping her collect nearly $50 million for her Senate reelection campaign that year, in which she faced only token opposition. And whatever money was left over could be put directly into a presidential bid, assuming she decided to take the plunge into that pool.

But now the controversy over Hillary's war vote threatened to eclipse everything she had accomplished. The King David letter, despite Bill's best efforts, did nothing to subdue her critics. If anything, the attacks only grew more vitriolic in the first half of 2006, as Clinton refused to endorse the demand of some liberal Democrats for a firm timetable for troop withdrawal. To Hillaryland, the assault on her from the left was a test—and the results were not encouraging. The internal deliberations over how to handle the situation consumed dozens upon dozens of meetings and conference calls; her people debated the matter endlessly but never reached a conclusion. What should she do? Introduce legislation? Give a speech? Sit for an interview? And if so, what should she say? Stand her ground? Apologize? What?

Hillary had no intention of saying she was sorry. *I don't have anything to apologize for*, she thought. *You want me to apologize for the fact that the president is an idiot?*

Hillary liked to say that she was blessed (or cursed) with a "responsibility gene." It was no small part of why, as a senator from New York in the wake of 9/11, she had voted to authorize the war in the first place—and why she was resistant to pushing for a date certain for withdrawal now. If she did run for president and wound up in the Oval Office, the decisions regarding Iraq would fall into her lap, and having lived in the White House, she understood the presidential premium on flexibility. Then there were the politics of the matter. "I'm not going to let myself be dragged too far left during the primary season," she explained to one of her most generous donors. If she reversed herself now, she would be buying a one-way ticket to Kerryville: the GOP would tattoo her forehead with the lethal "flip-flopper" label.

And so would the press—of that she was certain. The standards to which she was held by the media, she believed, and not without reason, were so much more strict (and latently hostile) than those applied to any other politician in the country. "Everything I do carries political risk because nobody gets the scrutiny that I get," she told a reporter. "It's not like I have any margin for error whatsoever. I don't. Everybody else does, and I don't. And that's fine. That's just who I am, and that's what I live with."

The Iraq dilemma was vexing, a pure Hobson's choice. She was damned if she did and damned if she didn't—and so she adopted her husband's method and split the difference. In the King David letter, Hillary had claimed that she wasn't voting for war in 2002 but instead for more diplomacy. Now she decided to add her name to legislation that urged the president to begin a "phased redeployment" of the troops by the end of 2006.

How the Democratic base would react to these maneuvers was an open question. In mid-June, brave in a hot-pink pantsuit before a rancorous crowd of several thousand progressive activists at the Take Back America conference at the Washington Hilton, Clinton excoriated the Bush administration's domestic agenda and its handling of Iraq—for having "rushed to war," "refused to let the U.N. inspectors conduct and complete their mission," "committed strategic blunder after blunder," and "undermined America's leadership in the world."

But then Clinton raised her hands defensively and added, with a mild quaver in her voice, "I just have to say it: I do not think it is a smart strategy either for the president to continue with his open-ended commitment, which I think does not put enough pressure on the new Iraqi government, nor do I think it is smart strategy to set a date certain. I do not agree that that is in the best interest of our troops or our country."

The crowd erupted. "Why not?" people yelled amid a cacophony of boos and hisses so raucous that Clinton could barely be heard above the din. Stepping down off the stage, she was serenaded with chants of protest—"Bring the troops home! Bring the troops home!"—as she made her way to the exit.

The antiwar base was sending a fundamental message: Clinton's front-runner status was rooted in shaky ground. As wary as she was of being stereotyped as a conventional liberal à la Kerry or Dean, Hillary didn't fully apprehend that her split-the-difference stance was reviving an equally damaging narrative. With it, and with a handful of other moves that smacked of cynicism—her cosponsorship of a bill to criminalize flag-burning was frequently cited—Clinton was breathing new life into perceptions that she had done so much to slay: that she was a calculating, expedient schemer wedded to no great principle other than her own advancement.

For many Democrats, trimming, triangulating, and poll-tested centrism were among the least appetizing features of the Clinton years. But, of course, there were others—as Hillary herself was reminded all the time, in the most unpleasant ways.

. . .

When she first got the word, she was stunned and angry. *The New York Times* was doing *what?* There was just no way it could be true—but it was, she was told by her press secretary, Philippe Reines, and his counterpart for her husband, Jay Carson.

In the spring of 2006, the Paper of Record was in the midst of reporting a story on the state of the Clinton marriage. And from what the flaks could ascertain from their conversations with the reporter, it wasn't going to be pretty. The thrust of the piece, they believed, was that the marriage was a sham; that Hillary and Bill barely saw each other, rarely slept in the same bed; that their matrimony was a partnership, an understanding, but little more; that Bill's bachelor lifestyle had the potential to derail her presidential aspirations.

How is this a legitimate story? Hillary wanted to know. And not just a story, but a story in the most esteemed newspaper in the country. "It's just fucking unbelievable," she said. "This is my life? I have to deal with this bullshit?"

Carson and Reines suspected that the *Times*'s true intention was more pernicious still: the paper wanted to write about the rumors swirling around Bill Clinton's alleged infidelities and was using a discussion of the

Clinton marriage as camouflage. Within Hillary's and Bill's operations, a series of heated discussions ensued about whether to engage with the reporter, Patrick Healy, or simply say, "No comment." The dominant view inside Hillaryland, with its aversion to the press, was that to participate would do nothing but legitimize the story. Carson and Reines strongly disagreed. Guys, the story is likely to be on page A1 of *The New York Times*, Carson said. It's already legitimized! Carson and Reines considered Healy an ethical reporter, persuadable by the facts. Weighing in, they felt, could influence the piece, soften it, and at least prevent errors or egregious insinuations from appearing in print.

Carson and Reines prevailed in that debate and spent a frantic weekend pushing back on the story. They pulled schedules to demonstrate that the Clintons spent plenty of nights together—more, in fact, than Chuck Schumer spent with his wife, Iris. The Clintons loved each other, the press guys insisted; this was not a marriage in name only.

When the story appeared, on May 23, the Clinton camps were braced for the worst. But although it was indeed on A1, the effects of Carson's and Reines's efforts were evident. The piece was elliptical, full of loaded language and ominous hints, but contained no

damaging facts. Even better from the Clinton perspective, the reaction from readers was harsh—a flood
of letters denouncing the paper for going tabloid, for
slumming in the gutter. (Stung by the criticisms, the
Times's public editor felt compelled to devote a column
to justifying the article.) Months later, Carson would
tell Bill Clinton that the story, for all the agita around
it, turned out to be a blessing in disguise. For as long as
anyone could remember, Carson thought, reporters had
been dying to peek inside the couple's bedroom. The
Clinton people warned them not to do it—there's a big
mean dog in there, they suggested, ready to chew your
face off. Now the *Times* had ventured in and come out
bleeding. From that point on, for two solid years, not a
single reporter approached Clintonworld in pursuit of a
similar story.

Yet the Clinton victory, in the moment, was a pyr-
rhic one. In Washington, the fact that the *Times*—the
prudish, starchy, self-important Gray Lady—had been
willing to go there, however awkwardly, merely turned
up the flame on the burning speculation about Bill's putative priapism. What had been a slow simmer in 2005
became a roiling boil in the summer and fall of 2006, as
the chattering classes theorized about whether and why
the *Times* had pulled its punches. Worse, Clintonworld
was hearing that a gusher of gossip was flowing from

members of the couple's own inner circle—and in particular from Steve Ricchetti, the longtime consigliere to Bill who had been so keen on Hillary running for president in 2004.

Since his departure from the White House, Bill Clinton had not exactly erred on the side of caution when it came to his personal comportment. Within days of settling into the Clintons' new house in Chappaqua in 2001, he could be found at Lange's deli, chatting up the stay-at-home mothers who trundled in after yoga, startling his aides that he already knew all the women by name. He gallivanted around the world with his business partner Ron Burkle, the supermarket magnate and notorious playboy, whose custom-converted Boeing 757 was referred to by Burkle's young aides as "Air Fuck One." Clinton's regular trips to that carnal triptych of Los Angeles, Miami, and Las Vegas struck many of his friends as a recipe, if not for trouble, then at least for undue temptation and embarrassment. But Bill seemed not to care. He was going to do what he wanted to do, appearances be damned.

And yet Bill was ripshit when Carson and Terry McAuliffe informed him of the extent to which tongues were wagging in Washington. Those goddamn people in D.C., Clinton fumed. They don't have anything better to do than talk about my sex life? Goddamn that city! This is why I hated it from the beginning down there. Everybody's got boring lives so they just sit around and talk about someone else's.

All the murmurings about Bill were starting to get back to Hillaryland as well. When Solis Doyle made the rounds of senior party players—members of Congress, major donors, former Cabinet secretaries—to chat about Hillary's prospective presidential run, she was encountering a troubling pattern. Almost uniformly, the Democratic grandees professed their affection and respect for Senator Clinton. She's terrific, they said; she'd be a good candidate and make a great president. But then would come the inevitable addendum: What are you going to do about Bill?

What Solis Doyle invariably would say was "We've got that under control." It was a clever answer she had come up with herself, and it seemed to pacify her listeners.

But Patti was rattled by the specificity of the chatter she was hearing. One rumor was that Bill Clinton was having an affair with a dishy Canadian member of parliament, Belinda Stronach; another involved a wealthy divorcée, Julie Tauber McMahon, who lived in Chappaqua; another revolved around the Hollywood actress Gina Gershon; and the list went on.

Solis Doyle was equally unnerved by the caliber of the people indulging in the speculation. One day she paid a visit to Ricchetti, who mentioned without blinking that he'd recently been on a conference call with a handful of big-name Clinton stalwarts, including former treasury secretary Robert Rubin, which devolved into a prolonged discussion of Bill's supposed indiscretions and the danger they posed to Hillary.

This is a problem, Solis Doyle thought, and not a small one. These were heavy-hitting Clinton supporters who had Hillary's best interests at heart, whose intent was anything but malicious, who were actually trying to help. Solis Doyle decided that she needed to tell Hillary, and quick.

She had brought word to Hillary more than once about the rumors hovering around Bill. "It's not true," Hillary would say, and in any case, she knew how to handle it. She had some experience in this area, after all, and she had always emerged intact. "We'll be ready for it," she said, and then, again, "It's not true."

But Solis Doyle needed Hillary to listen this time, to appreciate the implications of what was happening. You don't understand, she said insistently. They're having conference calls about this—what he's doing, who he's doing it with, how it's going to damage you.

The mention of conference calls snapped Hillary to attention. She demanded to know who was on the calls. Solis Doyle told her. Hillary reeled, first stunned into silence by the betrayal, then loudly livid about their friends trafficking this crap behind her back. How dare they? They don't know anything! Who do they think they are?

Hillary had always been adamant that her and her husband's personal lives were nobody's business but theirs. She immediately froze Ricchetti out of Hillaryland. (The reaction in Bill Clinton's world was even harsher; when other staffers asked Doug Band, the former president's chief counselor, why Ricchetti was no longer included on regular conference calls of old White House hands, Band icily replied, "He's dead to us.")

Hillary wasn't in complete denial about the perils of the situation, however. She had seen the damage that Bill's bimbo eruptions could inflict and knew that his imputed peccadilloes were among the gravest potential impediments to her reaching the White House. Clinton turned to two aides she trusted with the most intimate matters, Solis Doyle and Cheryl Mills, and Solis Doyle included Howard Wolfson in the circle. Together, the trio formed a war room within a war room inside Hillaryland, dedicated to managing the threat posed by Bill's libido. Mills, the lawyer, handled delicate matters where attorney-client privilege might prove useful; Solis Doyle was in charge of the political dimension; and Wolfson worked the media side of the equation.

The war room within a war room dismissed or discredited much of the gossip floating around, but not all of it. The stories about one woman were more concrete, and after some discreet fact-finding, the group concluded that they were true: that Bill was indeed having an affair—and not a frivolous one-night stand but a sustained romantic relationship.

This was exactly the scenario that had incited so many members of the conspiracy of whispers to urge Obama into the race—and what everyone who signed up with Hillary feared each waking day. But whatever storm of emotions Clinton herself might have been experiencing she put aside in the interest of survival. She instructed her team to prepare to deal with the potential blowup of Bill's personal life. For months thereafter, the war room within a war room braced for the explosion, which her aides knew could come at any time.

Yet even without any detonations, the Bill-related rumblings and their reverberations would continue—and be absorbed by Hillary in painful, maddening, and portentous ways. In October, she was scheduled to headline a New York fund-raiser for Claire McCaskill, the Democratic candidate for Senate in Missouri. McCaskill, a plainspoken centrist who held the job of state auditor, had narrowly lost a run for governor in 2004. She'd been expected to take another shot at that office four years later, but had decided against it out of fear that Clinton would be her party's presidential nominee in 2008. According to a story in *The New Yorker* in May 2006, McCaskill had "told people in Missouri and in Washington that a ticket led by Clinton would be fatal for many Democrats on the ballot, and that a Clinton candidacy would rule out her chance to win the governorship."

Hillaryland was not amused by the *New Yorker* piece. But McCaskill smoothed things over with the Clintons, apologizing, claiming she'd been quoted out of context. In September, Bill flew to St. Louis and did a fund-raiser for McCaskill, and now Hillary was set to help fill her coffers, though (not coincidentally) nine hundred miles away from the Missouri media.

The day before the New York fund-raiser, however, McCaskill appeared on *Meet the Press* and was asked by Russert if she thought that Bill Clinton had been a great president. "I do," McCaskill said. "I have a lot of problems with some of his, his, his personal issues." Russert began to speak, but McCaskill cut him off. "I said at the time, I think he's been a great leader, but I don't want my daughter near him."

Reines was in Chicago to attend a wedding and happened to be watching the show. Mortified, he knew that someone had to inform Hillary before the fund-raiser took place. He emailed the quote around Hillary-land. Everyone was aghast—and no one wanted to tell the senator, so Reines was saddled with the unpleasant duty.

"So what's going on?" Hillary asked, when Reines reached her by phone.

Oh, not much, Reines replied, running through the day's news, the guests on the Sunday shows, and then, at the end, sidling up gingerly to McCaskill's comment.

"She said *what*?" Hillary asked incredulously.

Reines read her the quote verbatim: "I think he's been a great leader, but I don't want my daughter near him."

The phone went quiet. Hillary was speechless. A few more seconds passed, and then finally came her voice, hot with fury.

"Fuck her," Hillary said—and then called Solis Doyle and summarily canceled the fund-raiser.

McCaskill would again apologize to Hillary and Bill, writing them letters, begging their forgiveness and forbearance. What she said had been stupid, hurtful, insensitive. But the truth was that McCaskill meant it, just as she'd meant her earlier prediction of the damage to Democrats across the country if Hillary won the nomination. McCaskill was in the market for a different horse—and now, like many other Democrats, she thought she saw one in Obama.

Inside Hillaryland, the notion that Obama might enter the race seemed remote to almost everyone. Harold Ickes, a fabled Democratic operative and long-time adviser to the Clintons, was so dismissive of the idea that he offered to bet Solis Doyle $50,000 that it would never happen. Penn, too, was sure Obama would stay out; that was the skinny he was hearing from inside the Illinois senator's orbit.

Hillary, for her part, had no idea what Obama would do, though she knew that he wouldn't be swayed by the argument that his experience was insufficient. "No one ever thinks they don't have the experience to do this," she told one of her aides. "No one thinks that way. He wouldn't have gotten to this point and then said, 'Oh, I don't have the experience.' You don't think about your weaknesses. You think about your strengths."

But Obama's strengths didn't strike her as especially intimidating, and whether he took his weaknesses seriously or not, they were many and glaring. Sure, he had a great deal of potential, but it was just that—potential. He had no fund-raising network, no tangible accomplishments in the Senate. The speeches he gave—oh, they were pretty, but so what? *You don't change peo-*

ple's lives with words, Hillary thought. *You change them with committed effort, by pushing through the opposition. You change them with a fight.* That was how you won elections, too. With a fight. In his entire career, Obama had yet to be hit with a single negative ad. How would he ever withstand the sheer, unrelenting hell of a presidential race: the constant pummeling by his opponents, the withering scrutiny and X-ray intrusions of the media?

But even as most of Clintonworld dismissed Obama, one dissenter stewed. All that talent. The antiwar credentials. The desire for something different in the country. The combination could be deadly, Bill Clinton kept saying. This guy could be trouble.

4

GETTING TO YES

Obama flew out of Washington on August 18, 2006, and arrived the next morning in Cape Town, South Africa, to start his two-week tour of the continent—and the two-and-a-half-month rocket ride that would carry him to the day of the midterm elections. "Rocket ride" was Gibbs's term, and he wasn't exaggerating. The period would include the publication of Obama's second book, *The Audacity of Hope*, the national book tour to publicize it, and a marathon stretch of campaigning for Democratic candidates from coast to coast. Everyone around Obama understood that the interval would be pivotal to his decision about running for president, which he had consciously put off until November. But most of them assumed that in the end, however tempting he found the idea, practicality would prevail.

The Africa trip turned out to be a revelation for both Barack and Michelle. The last time he had been there was fourteen years earlier, with a pack on his back and not much more than a packet of cigarettes in his pocket. Now, from Chad to Ethiopia to Djibouti, and especially in his father's Kenyan homeland, he was treated like a head of state—or Muhammad Ali in Zaire for the Rumble in the Jungle. In Nairobi, thousands lined the streets and stood on rooftops chanting, "Obama biro, yawne yo!"—"Obama's coming, clear the way!" The crowds were bigger than any he had experienced since the Democratic convention, but unlike that audience, the African throngs were there for him and him alone. Michelle found the spectacle discomfiting. "Part of you just wants to say, 'Can we tame this down a little bit?'" she said at the time. "Does it have to be all this? This is out of hand."

But what Michelle saw as overwhelming, her husband viewed as possibility. He began to entertain the notion that he'd tapped into something remarkable; that by virtue of what he represented, he might be able to effect change on a global scale. It was heady and humbling at the same time, nothing short of an epiphany.

When Obama got home, he had one event on his calendar before the madness of the book tour began: the 29th Annual Harkin Steak Fry. And in its way, it was an even bigger deal than the Africa trip. Taking place every September in Indianola, Iowa, the steak fry was a political fair sponsored by Senator Tom Harkin and attended by hundreds of the state's hardcore Democratic activists—and was thus a coveted speaking venue for any aspiring presidential candidate. Eager to avoid an awkward choice between Clinton, Edwards, Warner, or Vilsack, Harkin offered Obama the keynote slot on the assumption that he wasn't running. Obama's advisers were fully aware that if he accepted, the political world would erupt with speculation about his intentions.

"You have to understand what this is going to indicate to a lot of people," Gibbs told Obama, in a meeting with the senior staff. "They're going to think you're running."

"I understand," Obama said.

The truth was, he was ready to stir the pot. Going to the steak fry didn't commit him to anything. The media might whip itself up, but attending the event would let him take the temperature of Iowa activists—another important data point for decision time after the midterms. Obama was intent on not being sloppy about it, not showing too much or too little leg. "If we're gonna do this, we have to do it right," he said, then glanced around the room. In case he wasn't being sufficiently clear, he added, "Don't fuck this up."

Obama, though, was the one to blunder. After the press reported that he'd agreed to keynote the steak fry, Michelle's phone started ringing off the hook, with people calling about her husband's first foray into Iowa. But Michelle was totally in the dark—and now steamed at him. Obama walked into his Senate office looking sheepish.

"Next time I decide to make a big announcement," he said to Gibbs, "would you remind me to tell Michelle?"

Not screwing up the steak fry itself would require staffing Obama well. And Pete Rouse had an idea—one that made sense on the merits and was sure to draw attention. They would add Steve Hildebrand to Obama's traveling party.

Among Democratic insiders and political reporters, Hildebrand was renowned. A grassroots-organizing savant with close ties to three foundational Democratic factions—women's groups, gay activists, and labor—Hildebrand was yet another former Daschle staffer, which was how he and Rouse were friends. But his claim to fame was having helped deliver the Iowa caucuses for Al Gore in 2000. Goateed, tattooed, and openly gay, Hildebrand was the rare top-shelf national operative who lived outside the Beltway (and way outside, in Sioux Falls, South Dakota). Even rarer, he was passionate about issues and had a romantic streak about politics as wide and verdant as a Paris boulevard.

Hildebrand had not even seen Obama's 2004 convention keynote. A few months before the steak fry, in fact, he had met with Hillary and offered to work for her—but she brushed him off. Hildebrand returned to South Dakota and grew angry at what he saw as Clinton's weaseling over the Iraq War. So when Rouse asked him to accompany Obama to Harkin's event, Hildebrand was game. He knew that his presence in Iowa at Obama's side would set off alarm bells in the political sphere, that he was being used as a tool. *The Obama people are fucking with the Clintons*, he thought. And that was just fine with him.

The scene that greeted Obama in Indianola was pure pandemonium. Nearly four thousand people showed up that day at Balloon Field; for a typical steak fry, the number was fifteen hundred. The crowd had its share of college kids from Drake and Iowa State, and was so thick on the ground and eager to get close to Obama that he could barely move. His speech never quite gelled, but the crowd didn't seem to notice. Afterward, as Obama made his way down an endless rope line, with cameras capturing his every move, fans thrust copies of *Dreams from My Father* at him to autograph. "Thank you for giving us hope," one person told Obama.

Hildebrand was thunderstruck. It reminded him of the images of the Clinton-Gore bus tour after the convention in 1992—the rabid, spontaneous enthusiasm, the palpable sense of connection, the future-is-nowness of it. As they walked to the parking lot afterward, he asked Obama, "How do these people know so much about you?"

"I don't know. The convention speech, and then it just grew from there."

"Is it like this in other places?"

Obama shrugged and said, "It's like this everywhere we go."

The following morning, Hildebrand received an email from Solis Doyle: "Saw your name in *The New York Times*. Hope you don't make any decisions before we have a chance to talk."

Hildebrand laughed. Hillary Clinton? Please. His decision was already made. He would do whatever it took to get Obama in the race, then elect him president.

The Obama book tour was purposefully structured to approximate the rigors of a presidential campaign. Gibbs wanted to give his boss a taste of what nonstop life on the road would be like. Each day of the tour would be in a different city and have three elements: a book signing, a political event, and a thank-you get-together for his donors. Because Obama had missed his deadline repeatedly, the publication date of *The Audacity of Hope* had been pushed back to October 17, shortening the tour to just a week—and also putting the book in direct competition with John Grisham's first nonfiction opus, *The Innocent Man*, which hit the shelves the same day. The Grisham title entered the bestseller lists at number one, with Obama's at number two. When Obama learned of the rankings, he was peevish, a little whiny. "But I want to be number one," he complained.

In Chicago, Jarrett threw Obama a book party at the home of her parents. It was pouring rain, and despite a tent in the backyard and umbrella-toting underlings, many of the attendees got soaked, their shoes ruined by the mud. Jarrett introduced Obama and spoke about *Audacity*'s final chapter, in which he wrote about the stress that the demands of his career put on his marriage, the disruptions to his family life. As Jarrett went on, talking about the sacrifices his wife and girls were making, she saw that Obama was crying—to the point where he couldn't manage to speak when it came his turn. Michelle walked over, put her arm around him, and began to cry as well.

Even Obama's closest friends had never seen him choke up in public before. *He's not emoting about the past*, Jarrett thought. *He's emoting about the future.*

GETTING TO YES · 95

About the fact that the sacrifices he's imposed on his family are only just beginning.

On October 22, Obama returned to Tim Russert's set for another appearance on *Meet the Press.* The day before, he'd ridden down from Philadelphia in a limousine with Axelrod and Gibbs. Axelrod warned Obama that Russert would surely revisit his unequivocal reaffirmation from earlier that year that he would "absolutely" not be on the national ticket in 2008. It took no great genius to see the question coming: Obama's face was on the cover of that week's *Time,* beside a headline that read "Why Barack Obama Could Be the Next President." Axelrod, impersonating Russert, intoned, "And so, Senator, here's the tape. Is that still your position?"

Here was the question that had tied Hillary Clinton in knots in 2003, that twelve years earlier had caused her husband to stage a contrived tour around Arkansas to solicit a release from his pledge not to run for president. But Obama hardly gave the conundrum a moment's thought. He couldn't see any point in shilly-shallying over what was patently true. "I'm gonna tell him no," he said to Axelrod and Gibbs. "I think it's best to say I'm reconsidering."

A few minutes later, Obama was on the phone with Michelle. Following previous orders, Gibbs whispered urgently, "Tell her about tomorrow!" But Obama already had. Michelle wasn't pleased with what her husband planned to say—she had serious doubts about the notion of a presidential bid—but she was under no illusions about what was going on inside her husband's head.

Obama's new answer on *Meet the Press*—Russert: "It's fair to say you're thinking about running?" Obama: "It's fair, yes"—set off a firestorm in the press, all right. A firestorm of febrile excitement over the possibility that he was running, and of analysis about what it might mean and how it might play out. Few in the media seemed to notice or care that Obama had broken his pledge, preferring instead to praise his candor.

With Obama now leaving the door ajar (even if only "a bit," as he said on the air), an even greater frisson suffused his homestretch campaigning in the two weeks before the midterms. He was often doing four events a day, hopscotching from state to state to raise last-minute cash for incumbents and challengers alike. The punishing schedule made Obama grouchy. "Why the fuck am I going to Indiana?" he squawked to Hopefund's political director, Alyssa Mastromonaco.

"There are three candidates, and they're running out of money. If we can go and raise $200,000 at this fund-raiser, we'll keep them on the air through Election Day," she retorted.

"Really?" Obama asked skeptically, but then agreed to go. (All three candidates won.)

On the Sunday before the midterms, Obama attended church in Tennessee with Democratic congressman Harold Ford, Jr., the African American Senate candidate there, whose campaign had been rocked by a negative TV ad that fanned fears of miscegenation, a reminder to Obama that race was still a combustible electoral factor. He did stops in Illinois, Ohio, and Iowa—where Hildebrand could be found handing out hundreds of unauthorized "Obama for President" buttons that he'd had made up—and traveled to St. Louis to campaign for Claire McCaskill.

At that last stop, thousands of people lined up for hours outside the World's Fair Pavilion to hear Obama speak. Among those onstage was former Missouri senator Tom Eagleton, who had briefly been George McGovern's running mate in 1972 and was among the party's most beloved figures. Dressed in yellow pants and a green crew-neck sweater, Eagleton was nearly eighty years old and in poor health; this would be his last major public appearance before his death.

But Eagleton desperately wanted a gander at Obama. When the event was over, he approached McCaskill and marveled, "I haven't seen people want to touch someone that way since Bobby Kennedy."

. . .

On November 8, the day after the Democrats routed
the congressional GOP, retaking control of Congress
and repudiating George W. Bush, Obama drove to the
brick building in the River North neighborhood of
Chicago that housed the offices of Axelrod's consulting firm. He was there to have a private lunch with Bill
Daley. Daley was the seventh and youngest child of the
storied Chicago mayor Richard J. Daley; his brother,
Richie, currently occupied City Hall. A banker now,
Bill Daley had served as the secretary of commerce in
Bill Clinton's second term. Daley knew the Clintons
well—how ruthless they were, how crazy their world
was, and how vulnerable Hillary might be to the right
kind of nomination challenge.

All of which was why Obama was meeting Daley
that day. The midterms were past, it was time to get
serious about "the options," and Obama wasn't wasting
a moment. "Yeah, you gotta run," Daley told him right
off the bat. "Why not? What have you got to lose? Can
you win? I think you can. You know, who knows? You
don't know, but why wouldn't you? What's the negative here? What are you gonna wait for?"

Obama brought up the issue of money: Could he
raise enough to be competitive? "I don't think money's

your problem," Daley said. Judging by his performance the past two years, Obama was a money magnet, and one who might be able to change the game by tapping into small donors to an unprecedented degree. Daley, in fact, suggested that Obama could afford not to rush into the race. Maybe he should take a little more time, prepare himself better for what a challenge to Hillary would entail.

"You don't understand," Daley said. "Running around doing fund-raisers for other people is not running for president. These people, the Clintons, for thirty-five years, this is what they do. You've done this now for a couple of years. This is their life. This is, like, 24/7 for them. Hillary knows where she's going for lunch next March, okay? It's a very different thing here." What Daley was thinking was, *Be ready, because the shit's gonna come at you big-time.*

Daley was struck by how much consideration Obama already seemed to have devoted to his hypothetical candidacy. To the suggestion that he hang back, Obama responded that he didn't have the luxury of time; if he dawdled, Hillary would lock up too many big donors and key operatives. Obama was clear about something else, which also struck Daley—for its chutzpah.

"If I can win Iowa," Obama said, "I can put this thing away."

Yet for all his bravado, Obama was still ambivalent about getting into the race, for reasons personal and political. The personal ambivalence was complex and nebulous, but could be resolved down the road. The political ambivalence was more pressing and revolved around one question: Could he and his advisers chart a plausible pathway to victory?

The cartographic endeavor began in earnest a few hours after his lunch with Bill Daley ended. The setting was the same: the fourth-floor conference room in Axelrod's office. On the table were cookies, bottled water, and soda. Around it were the members of Obama's personal and professional brain trust: Michelle, Jarrett, and his close friend, Marty Nesbitt; Axelrod, Gibbs, Rouse, Mastromonaco, Hildebrand, and Axelrod's business partner, David Plouffe. Over the next few hours, Obama received from the group what amounted to a crash course: Presidential Politics 101—the logistics, the mechanics, the calendar, how the whole thing worked. His knowledge about the topic was limited (alarmingly so, thought some at the table), his initial questions rudimentary. How much of his time would be required? How often would he be on the road? Michelle asked if he could come home every weekend—or at least every Sunday—to be with his family.

"Yes, he can have Sundays off," Hildebrand blurted out.

Bullshit, thought Mastromonaco. *Crazy*, thought Gibbs. Almost to a person, the Obama brain trust was determined that their boss understand how hard running for the White House would be, that none of the bitter realities of the process be sugarcoated. Axelrod and Rouse had long wondered if Obama had the requisite inferno raging in his belly. They wanted him to enter the race eyes wide open, both for his own sake and so there would be no recriminations later.

Hildebrand didn't care one whit about raising Obama's consciousness. He wanted him, needed him, to run. He was so enamored of Obama that he was willing to say just about anything to get him in, no matter how nonsensical. Sundays off? Sure! We'll do things differently, we'll use the Web, we'll make it work, he assured Obama.

No, we won't, Plouffe cut in. And no, you can't come home on Sundays.

Rail-thin, pretense-free, incapable of artifice, Plouffe had run winning campaigns at the senatorial, congressional, and gubernatorial levels, as well as worked on two prior presidentials. He knew the score. You have two choices, he told Obama. You can stay in the Senate, enjoy your weekends at home, take regular vacations, and have a lovely time with your family. Or you can run for president, have your whole life poked at and pried into, almost never see your family, travel incessantly, bang your tin cup for donations like some street-corner beggar, lead a lonely, miserable life.

That's your choice, Plouffe explained. There's no middle ground, no short cuts—especially when you're running against Hillary Clinton.

The estimability of the putative Clinton endeavor hovered over the discussion, weighing on Obama. But the people around the table were no rookies at this game; if you had to start from scratch, they were among the best in the business to start there with. Their attitude toward the Clinton machine was clinical and uncowed. The machine was real, but it could be broken down into two constituent parts: personnel and money. Axelrod assured Obama that there were plenty of top-flight players in the party who wouldn't be working for Hillary, especially in the four states that would kick off the nomination contest: Iowa, New Hampshire, Nevada, and South Carolina.

Iowa loomed large in Axelrod's mind. Twenty years earlier, when he worked for Paul Simon's underdog campaign, the Illinois senator lost the caucuses to another candidate from a neighboring state, Missouri congressman Dick Gephardt, by just one percentage point. The lesson for Axelrod was that proximity mattered; that having Chicago as his home base would allow Obama to penetrate Iowa more readily and thoroughly than his would-be rivals, including Clinton. Focusing on Iowa and the other early contests also addressed the second of Hillary's advantages. Though she would likely raise a ton of dough, nobody doubted that Obama could come up with enough to match her in the first four, modest-sized, states.

Obama himself had been fixated on Iowa since the steak fry. He had a good feeling about the place, but that wasn't enough. If the Hawkeye State was going to be so crucial to his chances, he wanted details. Much of November would be spent gathering them, with Hildebrand quietly dispatched to Iowa to do reconnaissance.

One night later that month, Hildebrand's phone rang in Sioux Falls, waking him from a sound sleep. Obama was on the line. For the next forty-five minutes he quizzed Hildebrand about every conceivable Iowa-related topic: how he would fare against Edwards in rural counties; the impact of media coverage spilling over from Illinois into the Iowa communities along the Mississippi River; which local officials they could expect to bring on board as endorsers. Hildebrand told him that he, Michelle, and the girls would all have to spend a lot of time in Iowa—and also that the catalyst for winning there would be bringing new voters into the process. If we run a traditional campaign, Hildebrand said, we're doomed.

Axelrod had a complementary view, which he laid out for Obama. In every election, Axelrod argued, the incumbent defines the race, even if he isn't on the ballot. Which meant 2008 was going to be defined by Bush. And given the enmity that the president had inspired in the Democratic Party, Axelrod went on, the overwhelmingly liberal primary and caucus electorate would be hungry for a candidate representing the sharpest possible departure from 43: one who promised to be a unifier and not a polarizer; someone nondogmatic and uncontaminated by the special-interest cesspool that Washington had become; and, critically, someone seen as a staunch and principled opponent of the war raging in Iraq. Now, who had a better chance of being that someone—Hillary or Barack? The question answered itself.

Axelrod's contention was bolstered by a conversation that Obama had with Rahm Emanuel. Emanuel, an Illinois congressman and another of Axelrod's clients, was one of the shrewdest and most aggressive pols of his generation. He was also a veteran of the Clinton White House, intimately aware of how the former First Couple operated. They're gonna do what they gotta do to win—and this is not patty-cake, Emanuel told Obama. But could they be had? They could be had. There's a soft underbelly with them.

The contours of Hillary's vulnerabilities were revealed in detail by polling and focus group testing in Iowa that the Obama brain trust secretly commissioned a few weeks later, near the end of 2006. Though the polling put Obama in third place behind Edwards and Clinton, he was within striking distance of both. Not bad, considering that Edwards had been practically living in Iowa for two years already and that Clinton was . . . well, Clinton.

More striking were the focus groups, which were conducted in Des Moines and Cedar Rapids. Almost uniformly, the people in the groups reacted favorably to Obama—to his 2002 speech opposing the war, his rhetoric of change and unity, his freshness and sense of promise. Rarely did they express grave misgivings about his race or his exotic background. The more they knew about his biography and bearing, the more they liked him. In one of the sessions, after watching a video clip of Obama, a white woman said, "There's something about that guy; that's the guy I want. I can't even put it into words."

Observing from behind a two-way mirror, Axelrod was floored. "We can't forget that woman," he said to his colleagues. "We have something special here. I feel like I've been handed a porcelain baby"—something very, very precious, but very fragile.

The results of the focus groups were equally encouraging when it came to Clinton. She was well known, well liked, and well respected, but inspired nagging doubts. She registered with participants as status quo, as the past and not the future; she stirred up memories of the partisan bickering of the nineties, the Clinton-Gingrich contretemps, Monica, and impeachment. Her standing among women was much stronger than it was among men, but there was no sweeping feminist imperative to support her. "I do want a woman to be president of the United States," one female voter said, "but not this one."

By the end of November 2006, Obama could see a route to beating Clinton. Not an easy highway to navigate, by any means, but at least one clearly marked and mapped. And he could also see that the biggest roadblock ahead of him was another woman entirely.

From the get-go, Michelle Obama had made it plain that she didn't want Barack to run for president. She was wary beyond words, for a long time refusing to discuss the concept, even with her closest friends. The citation of spousal hesitation is, of course, a time-worn trope in American presidential politics. Every male candidate loftily affirms that he couldn't possibly go ahead without his wife's full support, but as a matter of course, Y-chromosome ambition trumps X-chromosome reluctance. Really, it's no contest.

But with Barack and Michelle, it was. Obama adored his wife, genuinely believed she was his better half, that he'd be lost without her. He didn't even bother to pretend that he enjoyed anyone else's company remotely as much as he relished being with her and their daughters. As the midterms approached, he told his advisers more than once, I'm not doing this if Michelle's not comfortable, and she's certainly not there yet.

She had always been a gut-level skeptic about the gaga-ness around her husband. In the wake of the drooling adulation poured on him after his convention speech, she suspected that he would be treated like "the flavor of the month," a passing fancy soon discarded by a fickle political culture. As she watched people fawning over him at his swearing-in to the Senate, she said dryly to a reporter, "Maybe one day he'll do something to merit all this attention."

She had no doubt that day would come. Her confidence in Barack was profound and unshakable. But in the meantime, she was perfectly miserable with him being in the Senate. The Robinson family had been close-knit: a homemaker mother, a municipal-employee father, and a basketball-star brother who ate dinner every night together with her in a one-bedroom brick bungalow on the South Side of Chicago. They were immersed in one another's daily lives, the highs and lows, the successes and traumas of childhood and adolescence. She wanted that badly for her daughters, too, and she wasn't getting it. She hadn't signed up for a commuter marriage. She was laboring to make it work, but when she was being honest, she admitted that she hated it; she was lonely too much of the time. There had been strains in their marriage back in 2000, when Barack had run unsuccessfully for Congress. Now she was being asked to talk about his running for president—and it felt like the rug was about to be pulled out from under her even more violently than it had been already.

One night midway through 2006, over a four-hour dinner with Jarrett, Michelle let her frustrations pour out. "This is hard," she said. "Really hard." Jarrett decided not to even mention the presidential chatter. Michelle was in a bad place emotionally. No point in making it worse.

But following the midterms, Michelle had no choice but to grapple with the subject. After that first November meeting in Axelrod's office, the Obamas, Jarrett, and Marty Nesbitt went for dinner at Coco

Pazzo, an Italian joint they loved. Michelle was going on and on about her issues. She had a lot of questions—and also a lot of fears. She'd been worried about Barack's safety since he entered the Senate. Now he would be an even bigger target, and so would she and the girls. Could the campaign keep their family safe?

The atmosphere was tense. Finally, Jarrett interrupted and said, "Let's try this from a different perspective. Michelle, let's say Barack answers all your questions to your full satisfaction and he's got an answer for every one of them. Are you in?"

"I'm in a hundred and ten percent," Michelle said. But she wasn't going to let her husband get away with the "We'll figure it out" bluster that he was prone to employ over contentious matters. Turning to Barack, she said, "You're going to be really specific with me. You're going to tell me exactly how we're going to work it out."

All the stress seemed to drain right out of Obama's posture. His shoulders slackened, his face softened. It was the first time he'd ever heard Michelle say that she could get behind his running. Her list, he knew, would be long and involved, but it would be finite—a mountain that he could scale.

Most of the questions on Michelle's list involved their daughters. How are you going to continue being a father to them? How many days will you be home? How are you going to communicate with the girls when you're away? How often are you going to talk to them? Are you going to come to parent-teacher conferences? What about recitals? But other questions were directed elsewhere. How are you going to take care of your health? Are you going to quit smoking? (That was a deal-breaker, she claimed.) And then there was this: How are we, as a family, going to withstand the personal attacks that will certainly be coming?

Barack knew Michelle was right to be worried about the hammer that would fall on both of them if he ran. But he believed it was possible to rise above the distortions and *j'accuses* that had turned politics into the sort of unedifying blood sport from which so many Americans recoiled. Obama was also resolute about not attempting to turn the onslaught against his opponents. Oh, he'd throw punches when it was necessary—he would never shy away from a vigorous fight. But if he had to become just another hack, gouging out eyes and wallowing in the mud to do this thing, then it wasn't worth doing. If he got in, he told Michelle and his brain trust, he would be in with both feet, for sure. "But I'm also going to emerge intact," he said. "I'm going to be Barack Obama and not some parody."

It was an extraordinary statement, the kind that few standard-issue pols would think to make when planning a long-shot adventure with their advisers. What gave him such an assured posture was his experience of the past two years—an experience that was without precedent in modern American politics. In his brief time on the national scene, Obama had compiled a staggering succession of big-stage triumphs that took the breath away. The convention speech. The Africa trip. The book tour. Appearances on *Oprah* and on the covers of *Time* and *Newsweek*. The reception he'd received from the media had been uniformly glowing, and that fed Obama's sense that he could somehow transcend the horror show. Maybe that was insanely naïve. Maybe it was incandescently mature. But at that moment, he had no reason to believe that it was anything but perfectly sound.

Obama flew to Orange County, California, on December 1 to take part in an event at the Saddleback megachurch run by Rick Warren, the bestselling author of *The Purpose Driven Life*. It was World AIDS Day, and Warren had invited Obama to appear alongside Republican senator Sam Brownback of Kansas. Brownback, speaking first, remarked to Obama, "Welcome to my house," prompting peals from the crowd.

When Obama's turn came, he remarked, "There is one thing I've gotta say, Sam, though: This is my house, too. This is God's house." He quoted Corinthians and advocated the use of condoms to prevent the spread of HIV. At the end, the huge crowd of conservative Evangelicals awarded him a standing ovation.

Saddleback was the start of a feverish two-week sprint before Obama would fly off on his family's annual holiday in Hawaii, where he planned to make his final decision about running. On December 4, he traveled to New York for a meeting in the offices of billionaire financier George Soros with a dozen of New York's heaviest Democratic fund-raisers. From there he proceeded to Washington and sought the counsel of a pair of the capital's proverbial wise men, one a Republican and one a Democrat, one a stranger and one a friend.

The Republican was General Colin Powell, who met with Obama at his office in Alexandria, Virginia. Obama wanted to know about Powell's flirtation with running for the presidency in 1995. Why had he decided against it?

"It was pretty easy," Powell said. "I'm not a politician."

For the next hour, Obama quizzed Powell about foreign policy—and also about race. Did the general think the country was ready for an African American president? I think it might have been ready when I was thinking about running, Powell told Obama. It's definitely more ready now.

Powell had his own set of questions for Obama, but the main one was: Why now? You don't have much of an experience base, Powell pointed out. You're new to the Senate, you have an interesting but limited résumé from before that. So, again, why now?

I think I might have what the country needs today, not four or eight years down the line, Obama responded. I think it might be my time.

The second wise man was Daschle. Like Bill Daley, Daschle knew the Clintons well and wasn't afraid of them. Didn't much like them, either. He considered Hillary an icy prima donna; her husband (who after exiting the White House often called Daschle, imploring him for help in burnishing his legacy), a narcissist on an epic scale; the dynamic between the couple, bizarre; their treatment of their friends, unforgivably manipulative and disloyal. For Daschle, Clinton fatigue wasn't simply a political analysis. It was personal. He was bone-weary of the duo and thought that Obama could and should take them on.

Daschle met Obama at one of his favorite restaurants, an Italian place downtown near his Washington office. The owner set up a table for them in the kitchen so their privacy would be preserved. For three hours they sat drinking red wine and talking, Obama asking question after question: about money, about the microscope he'd be under if he ran, about how great a liability his threadbare CV might be. Daschle reflected on his own contemplation of a White House bid in 2004; he'd decided against it, certain he'd have another chance to run; but now, having lost his Senate seat, that option seemed foreclosed.

Don't assume that you'll get a second window, Daschle told Obama. And don't minimize the salience of being "un-Washington"—or ignore the fact that if you wait, the next time around you won't be un-Washington anymore.

At the end of the meal, the two men embraced, and then Daschle headed home. His wife, Linda, asked if Tom was planning to endorse Obama if he ran. Daschle said, "What the hell—yeah, I am."

That weekend, Obama went on to New Hampshire, his feet making contact with Granite State soil for the first time in his life—an incredible fact for a man on the verge of entering a presidential race. The crowds that met him in Portsmouth and Manchester were, as usual, large and loud and lusty, listening eagerly as he invoked Martin Luther King, Jr., and his longtime pastor in Chicago, the Reverend Jeremiah Wright. But more remarkable was the 150-strong flock of reporters, including many national big feet and thumb-suckers, credentialed for the festivities.

Obama returned to Chicago from New Hampshire, but he wasn't quite finished with his hyperdrive round of buzz-building. He'd begun his sprint at Saddleback with an act of outreach to one religious constituency and now he ended with a play for another: the nation's pro-football fanatics, who were greeted with the sight of Obama at the start of the December 11 ABC broadcast of *Monday Night Football*. Besuited, looking solemn, seated behind a desk, an American flag to his left, Obama began, "Good evening. I'm Senator Barack Obama. I'm here tonight to answer some questions about a very important contest that's been weighing on the minds of the American people. This is a contest about the future. A contest between two very different philosophies. A contest that will ultimately be decided in America's heartland . . . Tonight, I'd like to put all the doubts to rest. I'd like to announce to my hometown of Chicago and all of America that I am ready." With that, Obama placed a Chicago Bears hat on his head and continued, "For the Bears to go all the way, baby!" Then, with a mile-wide grin across his face punctuating a performance of unchecked

charisma, he chanted the descending opening bars—
"Dah, dah, dah, DAH!"—of the *Monday Night Football* theme.

To many, especially those in the Clinton camp, Obama's
early-December itinerary was proof positive that he
was running. But for all the outward signs to the contrary, Obama was still undecided. In Washington, he'd
met with a group of his old friends from Harvard. They
chewed over the prospect for a while, weighing the various points and possibilities. Eventually, someone observed, We've been in this room for two hours talking
about why you should run, and no one has mentioned
that you're black.

While it was true that Obama had rarely considered,
or let himself consider, his skin pigmentation as a possible impediment to his running (or winning), race was
never really absent from his thinking. Now, spontaneously, and quite unexpectedly, he found himself speaking passionately about what it would mean to women
in black churches who had worked so long and so hard
to see their kids grow up safe and have big dreams in
inner-city communities.

He returned to that motif on December 13, when he
and his advisers gathered again in Axelrod's conference
room for a final meeting before the Obamas took off

for Hawaii. "What exactly do you think you can accomplish by getting the presidency?" Michelle asked him pointedly.

"Well," Obama said, "there are a lot of things I think I can accomplish, but two things I know. The first is, when I raise my hand and take that oath of office, there are millions of kids around this country who don't believe that it would ever be possible for them to be president of the United States. And for them, the world would change on that day. And the second thing is, I think the world would look at us differently the day I got elected, because it would be a reaffirmation of what America is, about the constant perfecting of who we are. I think I can help repair the damage that's been done."

Like Obama, his nascent campaign brain trust rarely brought up the subject of race during the deliberations over whether he should run. In part, that was because of a combination of discomfort, confidence, and hope: discomfort in that almost all of them were white and felt presumptuous addressing the issue; confidence in Axelrod, who had a well-earned reputation for steering black candidates across the country to victory with significant white support; and hope that the post-racial appeal that Obama already exhibited would prove to be durable, even transcendent.

Yet the near-silence on the topic also owed something to Obama's combination of optimism and fatalism about it: either the country was ready now for an
African American president, he said, or it wouldn't be
in his lifetime.

Obama's advisers had entered the room still dubious
that he would run. But now it was clear that the proba-
bilities had shifted. For one thing, Michelle's opposition
had eased; that much was obvious. At one point, when
Barack went outside to have a smoke, someone brought
up again the issue of his personal safety. "Well, I've
already gone out and increased our life insurance on
him," Michelle said drolly, with a sly smile. "You just
can't be too careful!"

In Hawaii, Barack and Michelle took long walks on
Waikiki Beach, hammering out the final items on her
questionnaire. (He gave in on everything.) One night
close to New Year's Eve, he called Jarrett and told her
that his decision, in effect, was made. "This is pretty
much done," he said.

But it wasn't. On January 2, just back from Hawaii,
Obama showed up unannounced in Axelrod's office,
wearing blue jeans and a White Sox cap, having come
right from the gym—and expressing renewed ambivalence about undertaking the race. "Being Barack
Obama isn't a bad gig," Obama said. I don't need this to
validate myself; I get plenty of validation as it is; and I

can do some great things from where I am. I like being with my friends, I like being able to watch a ball game, and you guys have made it very clear what the cost of this is going to be.

"I know there are a lot of people who want you to do this," Axelrod replied, "but you don't have to do this." Having been acquainted with his share of presidential candidates, Axelrod knew that the ones who fared well were those who were psychically compelled to be president immediately.

"I think you have ambition, but not that kind of pathological drive," Axelrod went on. "I've worked with Hillary; I know she'll drive herself as hard as is physically possible, because she has to be president, she wants to be, she needs it. I don't sense that in you."

Obama didn't really sense it, either. But he rejected the notion that running for president was a task suited only to the borderline mentally ill. What he knew about himself was that, at his core, he was competitive enough to find the requisite motivation. He trusted the logic that had led him to this point, his perception of where the country was and the work that needed doing. He had come too far to turn back now. The talk with Axelrod constituted his final gut check. And although his insides remained queasy, his head was free of doubt—and in the Obama interior chain of command, the head always outranked the gut.

Obama had one other thing to check. A few days later, he and Michelle secretly flew down to Nashville to have lunch with Al and Tipper Gore. Obama admired Gore immensely. He hoped that down the line he could secure the former vice president's endorsement. But he also knew that the one thing that could kill his candidacy in the crib was an unexpected entry into the race by Gore—which more than a few Democratic insiders in January 2007 still considered a live possibility.

So while the two couples engaged in a general discussion about how to shield a candidate's children from the sharp glare of a presidential race, Obama asked Gore a more pointed question: Is there any chance you'll run?

Not a chance, Gore made clear. And Tipper was equally emphatic: her family, and her husband, would not be making this race.

Obama and Michelle finished up their lunch and flew back to Chicago. The next Monday, Obama said to his team, "All right. Let's do it. What's next?"

He formally launched his campaign six weeks later, on February 10, 2007, on the steps of the Old State Capitol in Springfield, Illinois. Seventeen thousand people packed into the town square on one of those Midwestern winter days so frigid—the high was seven degrees— that every color seems brighter and the horizon line so sharp it could cut glass. Michelle suggested moving the event indoors so that families wouldn't risk frostbite for their kids. But the alternative venue, the Prairie Capital Convention Center, was a sterile, hulking vault, and Axelrod was intent on creating a magical moment and capturing the pretty pictures for use in future ads. Twenty thousand hand warmers were secured and a heater installed in the lectern to keep Obama toasty enough to function.

The speech he delivered laid out all of the themes that would carry him through 2007 and beyond. "I recognize there is a certain presumptuousness in this, a certain audacity to this announcement," Obama proclaimed. "I know that I haven't spent a lot of time learning the ways of Washington. But I've been there long enough to know that the ways of Washington must change." And: "There are those who don't believe in talking about hope: they say, well, we want specifics, we want details, we want white papers, we want plans. We've had a lot of plans, Democrats. What we've had is a shortage of hope." And: "That is why this campaign can't only be about me. It must be about us. It must be about what we can do together." And: "It's time to turn the page."

Obama's performance was nearly flawless, but the launch didn't go quite as planned. Obama's minister,

Reverend Wright, had been scheduled to deliver an invocation at the announcement. But the day before, Obama's team got hold of a story that had just been published in *Rolling Stone*, which included a wildly inflammatory passage concerning the reverend's oratorical style and substance.

"Wright takes the pulpit here one Sunday and solemnly, sonorously declares that he will recite ten essential facts about the United States," the *Rolling Stone* piece said. "'Fact number one: We've got more black men in prison than there are in college,' he intones. 'Fact number two: Racism is how this country was founded and how this country is still run!' There is thumping applause; Wright has a cadence and power that make Obama sound like John Kerry. Now the reverend begins to preach. 'We are deeply involved in the importing of drugs, the exporting of guns and the training of professional KILLERS . . . We believe in white supremacy and black inferiority and believe it more than we believe in God . . . We conducted radiation experiments on our own people . . . We care nothing about human life if the ends justify the means!' The crowd whoops and amens as Wright builds to his climax: 'And. And. And! GAWD! Has GOT! To be SICK! OF THIS SHIT!'"

Axelrod and Gibbs realized immediately that they had a problem on their hands—though its severity wouldn't be apparent for some time. Obama saw the problem, too. He called his pastor and informed him that his role at the announcement was being downgraded: Wright would now lead a private prayer for Obama and his close friends before the event, away from the stage, away from the cameras.

The phone call was painful for Obama. He and Michelle had been married by Wright. Wright had baptized their children. But as soon as Obama read the *Rolling Stone* story, he knew the decision was unavoidable. Staring at Wright's incendiary words on the page, Obama thought, *This doesn't sound real good.*

5

THE INEVITABLES

The December dinner was supposed to be at White-haven, in the dining room with the intense blue walls, where she'd hosted so many fund-raisers over the past six years. But the press got word of the plan; the house had been staked out—a camera crew was right outside—so the supper was moved a few blocks away, to the home of a friend. Clinton would do that sometimes if she wanted to keep a meeting super-secret. Borrow Evelyn Lieberman's place in Cleveland Park or the residence of some other trusty pal. On this particular Sunday night in 2006, the stakeout might have seemed odd, since her guests weren't exactly boldface names: Terry Shumaker, Alice Chamberlin, and Ricia McMahon. But because they were players in New Hampshire Democratic politics, the fact that they had flown down to Washington for a meal with Hillary qualified as news.

She was happy to see the New Hampshirites, all of whom she'd known for years. She had especially warm feelings for Shumaker, who had helped Bill pull off his second-place finish in the Granite State in 1992—the showing that allowed him to dub himself "The Comeback Kid." The group arrived bearing Christmas gifts, and also an eight-page memo by Shumaker on how Hillary should go about setting herself up to win the New Hampshire primary. If she were running, that is.

That was how she kept talking about it throughout the four-hour dinner—"If I run." It seemed strange to Shumaker, who assumed, like everyone, that Clinton was certainly running but just staying publicly mum for strategic purposes. Shumaker's memo was a detailed plan for her New Hampshire rollout in the early months of 2007: the first trip, the small events, the local media plan. "What we are hearing is mainly two things about a possible Clinton candidacy," the memo said. "Either she is 'too polarizing' or 'she can't win.'" But those perceptions could be eradicated by the right kind of campaign. "The challenge," wrote Shumaker, "will be to figure out: How does a 'rock star' do retail?"

Clinton wanted to know about all of it. She was in Hillary the Analyzer mode. But she also kept asking questions about Obama. That very night, he was up in Manchester wowing the party faithful at a sold-out dinner, basking in the spotlight, ginning up the activists who would be crucial to winning the first primary on the nomination calendar. And here was Hillary, huddled quietly in a safe house, speaking of her candidacy in the conditional tense, wanting to know what her potential rival was up to, how he was faring in New Hampshire. *We don't know*, Shumaker thought. *We're here, not there.*

It was, in a way, the perfect metaphor for 2006: Obama out there, always moving, showing leg, gathering momentum—and Clinton hunkered down. She and her team had decided she needed to focus on her Senate race. Her reelection was considered secure, but Hillaryland wanted to win big, to run up the score, and especially to do well outside New York City, to demonstrate her appeal in more conservative suburban and rural precincts. And all of that she had done convincingly, hauling in 67 percent of the vote, carrying fifty-eight of the state's sixty-two counties. The landslide turned out to be costly, though, with her campaign blowing through tens of millions of dollars against nominal opposition. Penn defended the spending by saying that much of it had gone to test-drive sophisticated vote-targeting technologies. But Hillary wasn't sure it was worth it, and her husband was even more doubtful. "Spend forty-five million on a Senate race?" Bill Clinton said, shaking his head. "Whew."

All year long, Hillary hadn't uttered a public word regarding a presidential bid. She wasn't against talking about it, but her advisers insisted she not. They called it the third rail of the reelect—if she touched it, the tabloids would go crazy, New York voters would be turned off, her margin of victory would be impaired. But when it came to preparing for the presidential, the effect was deleterious: 2006 had been a wasted year for her, especially compared with how Obama had spent it.

Now that Election Day was in the rearview mirror, the time had come to gear up for 2008. Since the summer, her high command had been holding meetings—some at Whitehaven, others in Chappaqua, in the converted barn beside the house—to discuss her prospective campaign. Hillary had been nearly as closed-mouthed about the presidential with her advisers as she was in public. Most of them, like Shumaker, simply presumed she was going to run. But the small clutch of Hillarylanders in whom she actually confided were a good deal less certain: Solis Doyle and Williams detected an ambivalence in her that was deep and genuine.

Unlike Obama, Hillary had no political misgivings about running. She was sure she could raise the requisite money, and that was no small thing. She was confident she could put together a crack team—a dream team, in fact. She was certain she could win and that she had something important to offer the country. Bush and his cohorts had driven the nation into a ditch, she thought. She was angry about it, fervently inveighing against this or that Bush policy or executive order, how awful it all was, how much damage that man had caused.

No, Hillary's ambivalence was all personal. Whereas Obama hesitated in the face of the unknown, it was the known that gave Hillary pause. She understood too well what a hellish slog running for president would be. She would be like red meat for the right, and the press would be equally vicious. The *Times* front-pager about her marriage was a preview of how unpleasant it would get—and not only for her, but for Chelsea too, she feared. Just as Obama fretted over how the campaign would affect his girls, Hillary agonized over her daughter. With a job she liked and a steady boyfriend, Chelsea finally had a life that was stable, almost normal, and Hillary wanted to do nothing to disrupt it. She reflected on how smooth the reelection campaign had been, how comfortable and rewarding she found the Senate, how she was on track for a bright future there. (People kept talking about her as a possible majority leader.) Did she really want to plunge back into an old life that was so much more chaotic and traumatic than her new one?

All through November and into December, Clinton kept stalling about getting going, talking about how ridiculous it was that she had to decide so early, constantly citing the fact that her husband hadn't announced until October 1991. At one meeting with her team in the barn in Chappaqua, she asked over and over about how long she could wait to get in. "I don't see why I should have to before late spring," she said.

Hillaryland felt as if it were frozen in place and falling behind. Her people used the specter of Obama as leverage to try to compel her to action. The longer she waited, they warned her, the greater the risk that he would scoop up donors and talented staffers that should have been hers. The practical arguments weighed on Hillary, but she remained unwilling to pull the trigger. As the Clintons took off for the holidays on a trip to Anguilla, Solis Doyle and Williams were convinced there was a decent chance that she would decide against making a run.

On New Year's Day, Hillary and Bill were out on a boat, bobbing along on the blue-green sea, and decided to take a swim. They leapt into the water, swam up to the beach, and then Hillary posed the question directly to the person who knew her best—and who understood as well as anyone alive what running for president entailed.

What should I do, Bill? she asked. Should I do this or not?

You have to ask yourself one question, he replied. Of all the people running, would I be the best president? If you can answer yes, then you need to run. If you're not sure, then you need to think more about it, and if the answer is no, don't do it. That's all I can tell you, Bill said.

Not long after, Solis Doyle's phone rang back in Washington.

"Bill said that if I really feel like I can do this, and do a good job and be the best one, then I should do it," Hillary said. "And I *do* believe that."

Solis Doyle exhaled and smiled.

"Okay! Let's go, then!" Patti said, and they were finally off and running.

The team that Clinton put in charge of her campaign represented a stroll down the path of least resistance. She didn't so much assemble an organization as reconfigure Hillaryland and give its key players new titles. Penn was named the chief strategist, Solis Doyle, the campaign manager. As communications director, Clinton installed her trusted press guru, Howard

Wolfson, whose depth of contacts in the national media was unrivaled and whose reputation for aggression was balanced by a subtle grasp of old media and new. The campaign's ad maker would be Grunwald, whose toughness and capacity to tap into the appealing qualities of her clients had allowed her to succeed in what was basically a boy's business—and inspired enormous confidence in Clinton. Neera Tanden, a brilliant issues wonk with a degree from Yale Law School, would run the policy shop. And Ickes, though working only part time on the campaign, would focus on delegate strategy and help Solis Doyle ride herd on the budget of what would be a multimillion-dollar operation.

Two salient facts about this team stood out above all. The first was its long and deep service to the Clinton cause. All six of the senior players had been involved in both Hillary's election and reelection campaigns to the Senate, and some of them had connections to the couple dating back even further. Both Grunwald and Ickes had labored for Bill Clinton in 1992; Penn had joined the jamboree four years later. Indeed, the only significant outsider whom Hillary brought in was the deputy campaign manager, Mike Henry, a reputed whiz kid who had helped win a succession of tough statewide races, including Tim Kaine's election as governor of Virginia in 2005.

The second fact was that, when it came to Team Clinton, familiarity had failed to breed a spirit of bonhomie. From day one, the operation was a simmering cauldron of long-held animosities—most of them directed at Penn. Solis Doyle, Wolfson, Tanden, and Ickes all were distinctly more liberal than the chief strategist was. (Some considered him a closet Republican.) None of them trusted Penn's poll numbers or the way he wielded them, always in support of whatever strategy he happened to favor. But more than that, the rest of Hillaryland detested Penn personally. They thought him arrogant and amoral, a detrimental force whose perniciousness was amplified by his inexplicably tight bond with the Clintons.

Penn felt no more warmly toward most of his comrades. He regarded Solis Doyle as unqualified for her job. Ickes he routinely called a fabulist and an idiot barely capable of speaking English. When Penn was counseled to be nicer to the team, he found it hard to comprehend. *I'm not nice or un-nice*, he thought. *I'm trying to do my job.*

Solis Doyle, by contrast, was much beloved in Hillaryland. But even among her friends there were concerns that she would be overmatched by the campaign manager's post. Both Ickes and Williams had tried to dissuade her from taking it, arguing that the first manager in many campaigns winds up getting sacked, that she was better off being the power behind the throne. Solis Doyle had heard as well that Bill Clinton doubted her ability, and that McAuliffe, who would be the campaign's chairman, was trashing her behind her back. But Solis Doyle was tired of being a hidden hand. In Hillary's first Senate race, she felt that, in effect, she had run the show—and yet hadn't gotten any credit. *Do I really want to do the job without the title and be little Patti Solis Doyle again?* she thought. The answer was no: she wanted the responsibility and, with it, the recognition.

Hillary was well aware of the knocks against both Solis Doyle and Penn, but she dismissed them. For years she'd seen Patti make the trains run on time with ruthless efficiency, and she saw no reason to think that her protégée wouldn't continue to do it now. About Penn, Clinton's feelings were more mixed. Largely because her husband had such faith in Penn's strategic analysis, she put faith in it too. But she gave him no authority to hire or fire, barred him from decisions regarding budgeting and spending, and told Solis Doyle she preferred that he not have an office at campaign headquarters. (Her distaste for socializing with Penn was evident; once, he'd shown up at Whitehaven uninvited, and Hillary was aghast.)

That Solis Doyle and Penn despised each other didn't bother Clinton at all. Nor did the other discontents that bubbled in Hillaryland. She didn't encourage dissension in her ranks, but she tolerated it and even expected it. Her husband's campaign in 1992 had been fractious, yet that hadn't prevented Bill from winning. And this same team of hers had helped win two Senate races.

Like so many Washingtonians, Hillary had read Doris Kearns Goodwin's totemic book on Lincoln and his Cabinet, *Team of Rivals*. The model made eminent sense to her. And for a while, it even seemed to work.

Clinton announced on her website that she was running. "I'm in," she wrote. "And I'm in to win."

It was January 20, 2007, four days after Obama had formed his exploratory committee and three Saturdays before he declared his candidacy in Springfield. Hillary offered no equivalent grandiloquence. Her Web post contained a link to a one-minute-and-forty-three-second video of her, seated on a beige couch in the sunroom at Whitehaven, wearing a claret-colored jacket over a black blouse, her right arm propped on a chintz pillow. "I'm not just starting a campaign," she said, "I'm beginning a conversation with America. . . . So let's talk. Let's chat. Let's start a dialogue about your ideas and mine."

The launch of Clinton's campaign had been laid out a month earlier in an internal memo by Penn, who argued for positioning Clinton not as a transformational figure, but as a solid, stolid juggernaut. "We are the establishment, experienced candidate," he wrote. "Our goal in this first quarter is to show we have the muscle to win—to live up to the financial expectations. We want to intimidate the possibility of late entrants like Gore. We want to show Obama how it is really done."

In the days leading up to her announcement, Clinton traveled to Iraq and Afghanistan, flashing her national security expertise. Shortly afterward, she began a fund-raising drive that was designed to be a show of overwhelming force. Her campaign proclaimed that it intended to raise $15 million in the first three months of 2007 and $75 million by the end of the year, both aggressive-sounding goals that were in fact low-ball numbers. Behind the scenes, the campaign was pressing its upper-echelon bundlers to raise at least $250,000, and ideally $1 million, apiece. The tacit message to big-dollar Democrats was that it was time to choose between Hillary and Obama. At a book party in Los Angeles attended by scores of potential donors, McAuliffe said, half-jokingly, "You're either with us or against us."

But, lurking just beneath the machismo, there was a defensiveness to the Clinton strategy. Penn's polling found that Hillary was seen by many as unelectable. Her experience as First Lady was discounted and her war vote held against her by the base. The notion of the flagrant, self-serving Clintons returning to the White House still made some voters shudder.

Hillary's rollout was all about addressing these vulnerabilities: "in to win" and the fund-raising push, about electability; the soft-sell video, about her perceived hardness and inauthenticity; the trip to Iraq, about setting the stage for a further leftward shimmy on the war. (On returning, she declared her opposition to the troop surge announced by Bush two weeks earlier.) Penn's strategy was for Hillary to consolidate her strengths and bulldoze her way through her weaknesses.

Not everyone in Hillaryland embraced the course he charted. Wolfson and Grunwald believed that Clinton needed to show her human side, be accessible, empathic. Many of the skeptics of Penn's approach recalled with concern a presentation he'd given in a meeting late in 2006 that summed up what they considered his point of view: Hillary needed to be seen by Democrats as the inevitable nominee. Ickes raised his hand and observed that, back in 1972, he'd worked for another supposedly inevitable Democratic candidate. "How many of you ever shook hands," Ickes asked, "with President Ed Muskie?"

But Clinton was happy prosecuting a front-runner's campaign. She liked being seen as formidable and imposing. She had no taste for softening her image or for pandering to the base. She appreciated that Penn always had an eye on the general election, because she expected to end up there. Really, who was going to stop her? Edwards, true, was white, southern, and male, all qualities possessed by every Democratic president since Kennedy, but Clinton regarded him as a "total phony."

As for Obama, Hillary could still barely fathom that he was in the race at all. She had tried to help him, she'd been on his side. The whole party had rallied around him, lifting him out of obscurity, giving him a chance to grow into something special. But rather than being grateful and waiting his turn, he was now trying to jump the line, with conceivably disastrous results— not for himself but for the party. His constant touting of his early opposition to the war held out the danger of pushing the debate too far left for the Democrats' own good. Hillary assumed that, in time, the party would see him for what he was: infinitely promising, but, right now, naïve, callow, and insubstantial.

There were moments, however, when some doubts crept in. At the DNC's annual winter meeting, in early February at the Washington Hilton, she was standing offstage with an aide when Obama took the podium.

The other candidates had packed the hall with supporters. The Obamans had done nothing—no crowd-building, no buttons, no bumper stickers. (They didn't want to waste the money.) Obama's speech was cool, cerebral, and sober. The audience sat raptly, silently, gazing up at him as if he were some kind of savior. Turning to her staffer, Hillary said quietly, "I don't know if this is going to work out. I don't know how to do this. I really don't know how to deal with these people."

The old Jack Warner house sat on Angelo Drive at the top of Beverly Hills. Built in the thirties, it now belonged to the billionaire entertainment mogul David Geffen, who had spent much of the nineties remodeling the estate from top to bottom. Inside, the walls were covered with world-class art: Rauschenbergs, de Koonings, Pollocks, Gorkys, a Jasper Johns target, a Jasper Johns flag.

On the night of February 20, 2007, Obama was there for a private dinner in his honor. Earlier that evening, Geffen and his partners in DreamWorks SKG, Steven Spielberg and Jeffrey Katzenberg, had hosted a $1.3 million fund-raiser for him at the Beverly Hilton, attended by some three hundred members of the glitterati. From the time the event was announced, it had drawn notice, signifying that at least a portion of

Hollywood, including some longtime backers of the Clintons, was attracted to Obama. Privately, Hillary and her aides were shaken by the symbolism and practical implications of such an encroachment on a world that she'd spent years cultivating. She considered people such as the DreamWorks chiefs more than mere donors; she thought of them as friends. The event for Obama was nothing short of a betrayal.

After the fund-raiser, a more intimate group of thirty-five repaired to Geffen's mansion, spreading themselves out across three tables. Among them were Michelle Obama, Spielberg and Katzenberg, former Disney and Fox studio head Joe Roth, William Morris Agency chairman Jim Wiatt, *Walk the Line* writer and director James Mangold, *Sleepless in Seattle* producer Lynda Obst, and *New York Times* columnist Maureen Dowd.

As the dinner wound down, Geffen approached Obama, holding a printout of a Web page with a column by Dowd that would be appearing in the next day's *Times*. The piece was all about Geffen's disenchantment with the Clintons. It contained harsh words, and lots of them, that would reverberate through the political world for months. Handing it to Obama, Geffen said, "I think I should show you this."

Geffen and Dowd were a colorful pair of friends—a mischievous dyad, each with a long and complicated relationship with the Clintons. Coquettish and flame-haired, Dowd was liberal, but never earnest or doctrinaire, and her scorn for hypocrisy and self-infatuation trumped any ideological predispositions she possessed. She had won the Pulitzer Prize for commentary in 1999, for a series of columns that folded, spindled, and mutilated Bill Clinton over the Monica Lewinsky affair.

Geffen's relationship with Clinton began to change toward the end of Bill's White House years. Before that, the mogul and the president had been tight, the former raising millions for the latter and sleeping in the Lincoln Bedroom more than once. Clinton would phone Geffen all the time—at home, in the car, late at night—and would often stay with Geffen when he was in Hollywood.

Already troubled by Clinton's flaws, Geffen was pushed over the edge in 2001, when the outgoing president pardoned fugitive financier Marc Rich but didn't do the same for Leonard Peltier—a Native American activist who some in Hollywood believed was wrongly convicted and sentenced to life in prison for murdering two federal agents. Geffen lobbied Clinton for the Peltier pardon, and saw Clinton's divergent treatment of Peltier and Rich as a sign of corrupted values. In the years that followed, Geffen heard constant Hollywood chatter about Clinton's exploits with Ron Burkle, who lived around the corner from Geffen in Beverly Hills. When people asked Geffen if he thought Clinton was still fooling around, Geffen would reply, "Do you think the Pope's a Catholic?"

Geffen, meanwhile, had always admired Hillary, regarded her as smart and capable. He contributed to her Senate campaign in 2000, but never felt the personal spark. By contrast, he was dazzled by Obama from the moment he watched the 2004 convention speech. Soon afterward, Geffen called Obama and predicted he would run for president one day. The next year, he invited Obama to his house for dinner with the Katzenbergs and Warren Beatty—and was swept away by Obama's cool demeanor, his lack of entitlement or self-importance, which Geffen found a refreshing departure from the Clintons.

Early in 2005, while making a public appearance in New York at the 92nd Street Y, Geffen was asked a question about Hillary by a member of the audience. "She can't win and she's an incredibly polarizing figure," Geffen replied. "And ambition is just not a good enough reason." The crowd broke into applause, which surprised Geffen, who'd always assumed that the Upper East Side was Clinton country.

Dowd, in the audience, was surprised, too, and started hounding Geffen to let her write a column about what he had said. Over the course of two years, she asked him about it again and again, but Geffen always demurred. "What, are you crazy?" he would tell her. "No!" Dowd understood what a big story Geffen disowning the Clintons would be. So she kept on pushing. Dining at his house the night before the February fund-raiser for Obama, Dowd implored, Let's do an interview. When it's over, if you don't want me to use it, I won't. What do you have to lose? Geffen finally relented.

The interview lasted fifteen minutes. Dowd left and wrote her column, then called Geffen and read it to him. The column quoted him saying that Hillary would be unable to "bring the country together." That her husband was "a reckless guy who gave his enemies a lot of ammunition to hurt him." That the Clintons were "unwilling to stand for the things that they genuinely believe in. Everybody in politics lies, but they do it with such ease, it's troubling."

Dowd warned Geffen that the column would be explosive. She asked if he wanted to take any of his words back. "Absolutely not," Geffen answered, fully dispensing with his past reticence. "That's exactly what I said, that's exactly what I feel."

Now, as Geffen showed the text of the column to Obama, he wondered how the candidate would react.

Obama read it, gave Geffen a wide-eyed what-have-you-done look, and laughed. This is going to cause some conversation, Obama said dryly. They're not going to be happy with this.

"I hope it doesn't cause too much trouble," Geffen said.

"Trouble for whom?" Obama replied and laughed again.

The Dowd column was explosive, all right. It went off like an atom bomb inside Hillaryland. After coming across it on the Web late that night, at 1:15 a.m. Penn shot an email to Wolfson with the subject line "How do we hit back?" Penn suggested releasing any documents from Bill Clinton's still-under-seal presidential library records regarding the Peltier pardon that reflected badly on Geffen. "We should see if we can use this interview to reveal a vicious personal agenda on Geffen's part and undermine the whole 'new politics' agenda of Obama," he wrote. "And consider—will Obama disavow this interview or does Geffen speak for him? (If he disavows, will he give back the money from Geffen? If he does not disavow, then how is this new politics—looks like the old 'slash and burn' he railed against just hours before.)"

Wolfson agreed. For weeks already, Hillaryland had been frustrated by its inability to engage Obama.

Even though the campaign was just under way, Wolfson and Penn already had seen enough evidence to believe that Obama's charmed media ride was going to continue unless an outside force intervened. Here was a chance to do so in a way that would put Obama in a bind. After an early morning conference call among the staff, the high command sought approval from Clinton, who was stumping in Las Vegas. Because of the time difference, she was still asleep, so Solis Doyle, who was traveling with her, woke her up. Still groggy, Clinton heard the outrage in Penn's and Wolfson's voices. "Okay, do it," she said.

By 9:00 a.m., the campaign had put out a press release with the headline "CLINTON CAMP TO OBAMA: CUT TIES & RETURN CASH AFTER TOP BOOSTER'S VICIOUS ATTACKS." Wolfson got on the horn with journalists and went on cable TV to push the Clinton line. But the Obama campaign refused to be boxed in, instead floating placidly above the flap. Obama told a reporter, "It's not clear to me why I should be apologizing for someone else's remarks. My sense is that Mr. Geffen may have differences with the Clintons, but that doesn't really have anything to do with our campaign."

It wasn't long before Hillaryland realized that its response was boomeranging. Suddenly, their stern pushback looked like a defensive overreaction, and a heavy-handed one at that. For Wolfson, it was a seminal moment. In his conversations with reporters, he found they agreed with Geffen. Everyone knows what he said is true, the journalists casually remarked. By the end of the day, Hillaryland was in full retreat.

The reaction to the column stunned Geffen. Besieged by interview requests, he put out a statement saying Dowd had quoted him accurately. Some of Geffen's friends in Hollywood expressed disbelief. Warren Beatty told him, She's going to be president of the United States—you must be nuts to have done this. But many more congratulated Geffen for having the courage to say what everyone else was thinking but was too afraid to put on the record. They said he'd made them feel safer openly supporting or donating to Obama. Soon after, when Geffen visited New York, people in cars on Madison Avenue beeped their horns and gave him the thumbs-up as he walked down the street.

For the Clintons, the episode was more than bad; it was their worst nightmare splashed across the screen in garish Technicolor. Two paragons of the bicoastal liberal Establishment, one from Hollywood and one from the *Times*, conspiring to take down Hillary largely on the basis of her husband. Her campaign putting on the war paint but botching the job, then descending into a round of finger-pointing in the aftermath, with Penn calling the Clintons to blame Wolfson for mishandling the situation, suggesting he was in over his head. And most ominous of all, the press uniformly siding with Obama. The whole thing stank—and the whiff of trouble was only about to get more fragrant.

The semiofficial rules of engagement in Hillaryland—particularly post-Geffen—were not to take on Obama directly for fear that it would only enhance his stature. But Penn and Bill Clinton formed a kind of dissident supercommittee of two. They were talking offline constantly, with Penn stovepiping data and analysis to the former president, each reinforcing the other's urgent certainty that something had to be done.

Penn saw Obama as a "phenomenon," and in his experience phenomena had to be quashed early, before the myths around them grew so potent they were undeflatable. Clinton, too, was increasingly outraged over what he saw as the fawning press coverage of Obama. It reminded him of 1992, the way the media slobbered over his rival Paul Tsongas as the candidate of ideas and principle, when, in Clinton's opinion, Tsongas was neither. But unlike Tsongas and Bill Bradley, two classic progressive reform candidates whom Obama resembled in his outlook and platform, the Illinois senator was certain to capture a large chunk of the black vote—a constituency that had always been a bedrock for the Clintons. In January, an ABC News/*Washington Post* poll put Hillary ahead of Obama by a margin of 60 to 20 percent among black voters nationally; a month later, her lead had shrunk to 44–33.

Penn and Bill agreed they needed a "stopper"— something that would allow the campaign to kill Obama in the cradle. The stopper they seized on was Obama's record on Iraq. Without a majority of the black vote, Hillary would need to perform better among white liberals, and one way to make that happen would be to take Obama down a peg in their eyes. Penn observed that Obama's antiwar image was based almost entirely on his 2002 speech; his voting record in the Senate on Iraq was nearly identical to Hillary's. Now the campaign's research team discovered a pair of potentially damaging quotes from 2004: "I'm not privy to Senate intelligence reports. What would I have done? I don't know," Obama said when asked how he would have voted on authorizing the war had he been in the Senate at the time; and, "there's not much of a difference between my position on Iraq and George Bush's position at this stage."

To Penn and Bill, the quotes seemed like manna from heaven. The Hillaryland press shop went into overdrive trying to peddle them to the media, but reporters evinced scant interest. Bill monitored the situation closely, asking for regular updates about any progress in pushing the story, growing increasingly frustrated when it failed to click. Told that journalists didn't consider it news, he would wail, "Why not? Why not?" That so few reporters were biting reinforced his and Penn's conviction that Obama was getting a free ride.

Invited to speak at a forum at Harvard on March 19 along with the top strategists from the other campaigns, Penn decided it was time to take off the gloves and go public. Suspecting that the rest of Hillary's team would disagree, he chose not to consult them. He did seek permission from Bill Clinton, though. And Bill Clinton was all for it.

That night at Harvard, Penn sat onstage with Axelrod and Jonathan Prince, the deputy manager of the Edwards campaign, and waited for his opening. Helpfully, one of the students in the audience asked about Hillary's war vote—and Penn launched into his spiel about Obama, citing both of the quotes that the research team had unearthed. Axelrod, annoyed, sought to clarify Obama's comments, then lectured Penn, "I really think that it is important, if we are going to run the kind of campaign that will unify our party and move this country forward, that we do it in an honest way, and that was not an honest tactic." Penn didn't care. *That was a well-played segment,* he thought.

And the segment wasn't over. The next day, on a conference call with a group of Hillary's bundlers—to which a reporter was conveniently allowed to listen—Bill Clinton echoed Penn. "I don't have a problem with anything Barack Obama said on this," Clinton stated. But "to characterize Hillary and Obama's positions on the war as polar opposites is ludicrous. This dichotomy that's been set up to allow him to become the raging hero of the antiwar crowd on the Internet is just factually inaccurate."

Hillaryland was livid at the freelancing. On a morning conference call of the high command, Wolfson and the rest pummeled Penn for going off the reservation, for a maladroit attempt to drive a story for which the press had no appetite. They believed that Iraq was a losing issue for Hillary; they wanted not to talk about it. Penn defended himself, saying that Bill Clinton had signed off on the offensive. "Who's running this fucking campaign?" Tanden complained to Solis Doyle.

Where Hillary stood on the supercommittee's frustrations and efforts was unclear to her other advisers. Though she seemed to approve of Penn's ploy and had no doubt that Obama was having it both ways on the war, she was hesitant to raise the matter herself in a speech or at a press conference. And without her front and center, the issue was going nowhere. What it all added up to—the staff conflict, the one-off nature of the hit, the reluctance of Hillary to take the lead—was an early example of how hard the Clintonites would find it to put an effective negative frame on Obama.

The difficulty became all the greater two weeks later, when, on April 4, Obama's campaign released its fund-raising totals for the first quarter of the year. A few days earlier, the Clinton team had unveiled its numbers: $36 million, a staggering-sounding sum that turned out to be somewhat less than it appeared. Roughly $10 million of that was left over from Hillary's Senate reelection campaign and another $6 million was for use only in the general election (if she got there), leaving about $20 million in fresh cash for the nomination contest. The Obama numbers? Total: $25 million. For the primaries: $23.5 million, from a far broader base of donors.

The reaction in Hillaryland was confusion and shock. All along, a core predicate of Clinton's campaign was that she would possess a major financial advantage over everyone in the field. Now that was seriously in question—and Hillary was staring down the barrel of an objective, quantifiable metric of how redoubtable a

combatant Obama would be. A series of frantic conference calls ensued, in which Clinton demanded answers.
"This is a big deal, guys," she said grimly. "How did it
happen?" "Someone explain this to me." "We have to
do better."

Clinton wanted to believe Obama's first-quarter
numbers were a fluke, but when he beat her again in
the second quarter, by even more than in the first—$31
million to $21 million this time—panic set in.

One day that summer, after a fund-raising breakfast at the ritzy Hamptons weekend home of New York
venture capitalist Alan Patricof, Hillary walked into the
kitchen and started talking to Patricof and her finance
director, Jonathan Mantz. Patricof noted that Obama
was raking in money by selling T-shirts, buttons, and
posters with his campaign logo on them. "He's got a
retail merchandise business going," Patricof said.
"Why aren't we doing more of that?"

Hillary turned to Mantz and repeated the question:
Why *aren't* we doing more of that? But before Mantz
could answer, Clinton began to unravel.

We're losing the small-donor race, she said, her voice
starting to rise. Why are we losing? What do we need
to do? I just don't understand!

Hillary was nearly screaming now. Gesturing outside, she exclaimed, "Why don't we have merchandise

being sold out back? We could've set up tables in the back!"

There were a lot of things Mantz could have said: Because you're not leading a movement. Because your donors aren't college kids. Because we're in the Hamptons and you don't hawk souvenirs on the lawn beside the swimming pool. Instead, he thought, *Wow, this is the angriest I've ever seen her.* And then simply said, "I'll fix it."

Fixing the fund-raising was one of many challenges facing Clinton in 2007—but in terms of urgency and long-range significance, none was in even the same galaxy as the problem of Iowa. Right after New Year's, Penn had put their first poll in the field to figure out where Clinton stood in the state ab initio. The results were discouraging: Edwards led with 38 percent, with Clinton and Obama tied at 16. In no other state in the country would Hillary, with her name recognition and national profile and popularity among Democrats, have fared so poorly. But hearing the numbers, she put on a brave face. "It's better than I thought it would be," she said. "We have our work cut out for us."

The members of the Hillaryland high command were less sanguine. Unlike New Hampshire, where the Clinton name was platinum because of her husband,

Iowa was a place where neither he nor she had spent much time. (In 1992, local guy Tom Harkin was in the race and had it sewn up, so the other candidates skipped the caucuses; in 1996, incumbent Clinton ran for the nomination unopposed.) Democrats in Iowa were decidedly liberal, with a peacenik streak; Hillary's war record was more vexatious there than anywhere else. Edwards had been working the state more or less constantly since 2003. Obama lived next door. If Hillary was going to be competitive in Iowa, she would need to go all out. The problem was, she hated it there. Every day felt like she was stuck in a Mobius strip: another barn, another living room, another set of questions about immigration (from people who were anti-) and the war (ditto). She'd get back on the plane, slump into her seat, heave a deep sigh, and grunt, "Ugh."

The Iowans didn't seem to be listening to her, just gawking at her, like she was an animal in a zoo. Hillary would hear from her staff the things voters were saying about her: "She's so much prettier in person," "She's so much nicer than I thought." It made her ill. She found the Iowans diffident and presumptuous; she felt they were making her grovel. Hillary detested pleading for anything, from money to endorsements, and in Iowa it was no different. She resisted calling the local politicos whose support she needed. One time, she spent forty-five minutes on the phone wooing an activist, only to be told at the call's end that the woman was still deciding between her and another candidate. Hillary hung up in a huff.

"I can't believe this!" she said. "How many times am I going to have to meet these same people?"

Over and over, she complained about the system that gave Iowa so much power in selecting the nominee. "This is so stupid," she would say. "So unfair." She bitched about Iowa's scruffy hotels and looked for excuses to avoid staying overnight. But among the sources of her frustration and bewilderment, the absence of connection was paramount. "I don't have a good feeling about this, guys," she told her staff on the plane. "I just don't have a good feeling about this place."

People Hillary respected, experts on Iowa, urged her to spend more time there. She seemed to understand, but her antipathy to the state only grew. Mike Henry grasped the scale of the problem and took a radical stab at remedying it. Dismayed by what he'd seen on a trip to Iowa that spring, Henry concluded that there was a sound case for Hillary bypassing the caucuses. In mid-May, after mulling the idea in private with Solis Doyle, Ickes, and political consultant Michael Whouley, Henry drafted a memo laying out his argument. Iowa, he wrote, was Hillary's consistently weakest state, and was likely to consume $15 million and seventy days of her schedule. "Worst case scenario: this effort may bankrupt the campaign and provide little if any political advantage," he wrote.

Henry sent the memo to Solis Doyle and Ickes, and also, inexplicably, to a friend of his named Sheila Nix, who worked in the office of Illinois governor Rod Blagojevich. Within twelve hours, the memo had been leaked to *The New York Times* and was all over the paper's front page.

Ickes was baffled by Henry's foolishness: "Mike, what goes through your fucking mind?" But he also saw the irony in the situation. Hillary could never recede from Iowa under these circumstances. The leaking of the memo had locked her in, exactly the opposite outcome of what Henry had hoped for.

Henry's screwup, however, was an outward sign of a deeper malady in Hillaryland: the team of rivals the candidate had constructed was longer on rivalry—and backbiting, pettiness, and general-purpose dysfunction—than on teamwork.

Every decision Clinton had made (and not made) in structuring her campaign was coming back to bite her. She had effectively given both Penn and Solis Doyle veto power over hiring—which they regularly exercised to preserve their status, preventing any fresh blood or new ideas from penetrating Hillaryland. She had told Solis Doyle to keep a tight rein on the budget, but astronomical salaries abounded and spending was out of control. (A notorious tightwad, Clinton was forever complaining, "There are too many people on the road. . . . I don't know what all these people do.") She had empowered her senior advisers to govern by consensus, but Penn so frequently went directly to the Clintons to override choices with which he disagreed that his colleagues considered discussion futile. The level of animosity among them all was off the charts. Screaming matches erupted regularly on conference calls and in person. Solis Doyle's preferred name for Penn was "fat fuck."

The result was chaos. Meetings rarely started on time, had any discernible structure, or accomplished their ostensible purpose. Every decision was litigated and relitigated again and again, ad infinitum, ad nauseam. The campaign had neither a political director nor a field director; Henry was de facto both. There was almost no one with experience in Democratic presidential nomination fights. There were no significant budgets or plans in place for any states beyond the first four. The campaign's delegate operation was understaffed and unsophisticated. The most basic operational and political matters were frequently left unaddressed.

From the outside, none of this was apparent. Hillaryland looked like a colossus. Far ahead in the national polls and the hunt for endorsements, she still appeared on track as the inevitable nominee. But Bill Clinton's old hands knew better. Locked out of Hillary's campaign, dismissed as old-school "white boys" by Solis Doyle, they could still see things others couldn't: that Hillaryland was a fractious, soulless mess—and that their old boss, the former president, was on the outside looking in, just like them.

Bill Clinton jumped on the conference call wondering what the point of it was. Carson, his spokesman, told him Hillary's people wanted to have a quick chat before he headed west. For the next three days, over the July 4 holiday, he would be at his wife's side all over Iowa: the state fairgrounds in Des Moines, the Independence Day parade in Clear Lake, private meetings with undecided caucus leaders and potential precinct captains. Hillary had been in the race for coming up on six months—and this was their first joint campaign swing.

The Hillarylanders were nervous about the trip, afraid that Bill would overshadow her, that he'd talk too much—or, more to the point, talk too much about himself and not enough about her. Over the past couple of weeks, they'd worried the trip nearly to death, discussing and diagramming every aspect in minute detail. (Would he sit or stand onstage next to her? How would they work the rope line? Where would they sleep? Would they do any separate events?) Now the high command wished to go over the script again. Just want to make sure you're okay with everything, sir, Carson said. You've got your talking points; you should be fairly brief; turn it over to her and let her rip.

Yup, Clinton said, I got it—but apparently that wasn't sufficient. Grunwald had a few words to say, then Penn, then Wolfson, then Solis Doyle. All of them said the same thing as Carson had, just repackaged in different language.

"Yeah, okay, guys. I *got* it," Clinton said, his voice heavy with sarcasm. "I'll try not to screw it up for her too bad while I'm out there."

Clinton was getting used to this kind of treatment from his wife's campaign—well, not used to it, but by now it was familiar. The press kept saying that he was Hillary's greatest asset, a political genius, the sharpest strategist in the Democratic Party. But his involvement so far in 2007 had been close to nil, and certainly less by most measures than that of a typical candidate's spouse. That was how his wife's people wanted it: they saw him not as a priceless asset, but as a problem to be managed. And Bill hadn't tried to fight his way in. Though he often questioned the campaign's strategy, he knew that he had to stay out of Hillary's way, let her win this thing herself. He just wished that Solis Doyle and all the rest of them would stop treating him like an infant. "You know, I did get myself elected president of the United States . . . twice!" he liked to say.

Bill was rusty. He knew that. Politics had changed a lot since he was in the game for real. After his heart surgeries, he'd lost a step or two, no doubt. And, he allowed, he didn't know beans about Iowa. He found himself parroting the conventional wisdom: Edwards is strong; Obama has a chance; it's Hillary's hardest row to hoe. That was one reason he was thrilled to be getting out there. Finally a chance to sniff around, test his instincts, see what was happening on the ground.

The July 4 trip went off without a hitch. Bill demonstrated discipline, giving the same six-minute speech every time, almost to the word. But the best part, from his point of view, was the time he got to spend in private, recruiting precinct captains and other activists for his wife, getting a handle on how the process worked, drilling down with Teresa Vilmain, the top-drawer organizer whom Hillary had just signed on to run the state for her.

On the flight home, Hillary was uncertain how the trip had gone. She was hoarse and exhausted, worried about the press's parsing of her and Bill's body language, the criticisms that they'd been too programmed. Bill tried to buck her up. You did great, he said. You really touched people—the crowds were hanging on your every word.

But, in truth, Iowa was starting to plague Bill's mind. The campaign's local advisers had told him in no uncertain terms that the one thing Iowans wouldn't abide was negative campaigning, which meant it would be hard to take Obama down in the manner that Bill and Penn thought necessary. After the Henry memo, there was no getting out of Iowa for Hillary. And yet, after all the work she'd done there, she was still struggling as in no other state.

Bill Clinton wondered if Iowa was laying a triple whammy on his wife: she couldn't attack, she couldn't quit, and she couldn't win.

And yet for all that had happened so far in 2007, for all the turbulence and doubts, for all the internal squabbles and external missteps, Hillary publicly didn't appear to be a beleaguered figure as the summer turned to fall. She didn't feel that way, either. While there was cause for disquiet, there were plenty of reasons for confidence. She had entered the year the front-runner and she was still the front-runner—now more than ever. And Obama seemed to be fading, just as she had predicted.

She had whipped him in the interminable series of Democratic debates that had taken place since April. Her mastery of the issues, her knowledge of every jot and tittle about every aspect of public policy, had been on full display—and Obama had been exposed for the naïf she knew he was, coming across as vague and weak and windy. With Penn's help, she had neutralized many of her most glaring vulnerabilities. She had blurred the distinctions between her and Obama on Iraq, adroitly changing the subject from which candidate was most antiwar to who was more qualified to bring the conflict to an end. She had recast her awful history with health care reform, unveiling her long-awaited plan in mid-September and getting rave reviews for her substantive prowess, the detail and clarity of her presentation, and her self-deprecating allusions to her disastrous attempt to overhaul the system as First Lady. She'd watched as Obama's campaign was hammered for producing a proposal that was an obvious rip-off of hers. She'd begun to defuse her rival's message, giving speeches where she said "change is just a word without the strength and experience to make it happen." And, finally, in the third quarter of the year, she had succeeded in raising more money than Obama.

All along, Clinton had held a commanding lead over Obama in the national polls. Now, on October 3, came a new ABC News/*Washington Post* survey that seemed to shift the appropriate description from "clear front-runner" to "prohibitive favorite." The poll put Hillary ahead of Obama by a staggering thirty-three-point margin, 53–20. Despite all the efforts of her opponents to tar her as too polarizing to be electable, the poll found that 57 percent of voters rated her the most likely of the Democratic candidates to win in the fall. More heartening still, not only was Clinton leading decisively among voters who were looking for "strength and experience," but she was beating Obama 45–31 among those seeking "new direction and new ideas." The poll was the talk of the political world. Even in Iowa, the race seemed to be tilting in her favor. Thanks in large part to Vilmain's labors, Hillary was now in a virtual three-way tie in the state.

Two weeks later, Hillary received a piece of news that thrilled her beyond measure. She was getting the endorsement of Georgia congressman John Lewis. Lewis was one of the civil rights era's greatest heroes, an African American student organizer beaten nearly to death by a white mob during the freedom rides of

1961. All year long, despite Hillary's aversion to buttonholing superdelegates—elected officials and other party honchos who would vote automatically at the national convention the next summer in Denver—their endorsements kept falling into her lap, while Obama collected virtually none. But Lewis was a particularly welcome feather in her cap and a harsh blow to Obama.

What all this said to Hillary was that the natural order was reasserting itself. Despite the angst of the past ten months, the elements of Penn's plan were falling into place: the money, the Establishment support, the muscle to win. She was showing Obama, as Penn wrote in his December memo, "how it is really done." And the press corps, for all its disdain for her, was coming around to the opinion that the campaign had sought to instill from the start: Hillary's victory was inevitable.

And she seemed to believe it, too. How confident was Clinton? So extravagantly self-certain that she began to turn her attention to a question no rational candidate would have dared to contemplate this early: Who should be her running mate in the general election? She had already determined without a sliver of doubt that she was not going to choose Obama. She knew she would come under enormous pressure to do so from all corners of the party and the press, and she had already come up with a solution.

Clinton decided she needed to have a prominent African American or two to run her vice-presidential search process. She was inclined to tap Cheryl Mills and Vernon Jordan, a longtime friend of the Clintons and Washington's premier black power broker. When her aides asked who would be at the top of her VP short list, she mentioned Bayh, Biden, Vilsack, and Ohio governor Ted Strickland.

But Clinton was getting even further ahead of herself than that. One day that fall, she summoned her friend Roger Altman to meet with her in Washington. Altman was a major Wall Street player who had served as deputy treasury secretary in the Clinton administration. As they sat in her basement hideaway office in the Capitol, Hillary asked Altman to undertake a secret project on her behalf. She wanted him to start planning right away for her eventual transition to the White House, on the assumption that she would win the general election. I don't want to get to the point, she said, where we're scrambling to do a transition. I want to be in the opposite position.

Altman already knew what Clinton was going to ask him to do. A few days earlier, he'd had a call from John Podesta, who told him that Hillary wanted them together to undertake the transition effort. For about half an hour, Altman and Clinton discussed how the plan would work, setting up a schedule for the next few months and focusing on the selection of chairs and co-chairs to run the preparation on a variety of issues. Hillary made clear how important it was that word of the endeavor not leak. She had devised a cover story: that the Altman-Podesta-led meetings were merely part of a project on presidential transitions already under way at Podesta's Center for American Progress.

At the Clinton campaign headquarters in Ballston, Virginia, just a few minutes outside Washington, the few aides who were aware of the transition preparations were alarmed by the whole scheme—by the presumptuousness of it, and even more by the risks involved. If news broke that Hillary had already started working on her presidential transition, the ensuing media maelstrom would be crippling, undermining the campaign's efforts to tamp down the perception of Clinton's arrogance and sense of privilege. Altman and Podesta, for their part, believed the undertaking was just another sign of Clinton's methodical commitment to preparation. *She's such a planner*, Altman thought. But they were spooked by the notion that Hillary might be jinxing herself. Let's hope this isn't the bell that tolls the finale for the campaign, they joked.

One night in October, as Clinton flew back east from a campaign stop in Arizona, she cracked open a bottle of white wine and kicked around the latest media offer on the table—a cover shoot and an accompanying inside photo spread in *Vogue*. Anna Wintour, the magazine's glamorous editrix, and her people were wheedling the campaign. It will be good for Hillary, they said. Great photos. The first woman president-in-waiting. She should do it.

Clinton's aides thought it was a fabulous idea, another opportunity to humanize their boss, but Clinton was skeptical.

I don't think a *Vogue* photo shoot is going to be helpful, Hillary said. I'm still trying to convince white men that I can be the commander in chief, and me looking pretty in a dress isn't gonna do that.

Hillary took a sip of wine and let her mind drift toward the future.

"You realize," she said to her aides, "we're only Iowa away from winning this."

6

BARACK IN A BOX

Obama walked into the eighth-floor conference room in the downtown Washington offices of Perkins Coie, the law firm where his attorney, Bob Bauer, was a partner. It was February 2007 and the room was filled with expectant faces, some familiar and some new to Barack: the team of pollsters, image makers, and consultants assembled at lightning speed by Axelrod and Plouffe to help Obama reach the White House. They were seated around a big rectangular table—a dozen of them.

"Whoa," joshed Obama, looking around the room. "Am I paying all you people?"

The group was replete with top-flight national political talent, although few of them resided in the capital. They came from Chicago, New York, Los

Angeles, San Francisco, Sioux Falls. Almost all were men. Almost all were white. They would play a large role in shaping Obama's destiny over the next twenty months, but it was the first time they'd all been together in the same space. It would also be the last.

Obama sat down and listened as David Binder, the focus group impresario from San Francisco, ran through the results of the sessions he'd recently conducted in the first four states: Iowa, New Hampshire, Nevada, South Carolina. To the voters he sampled, Obama was an unknown quantity, Binder said, but their first impressions were positive. When Binder showed them video of Obama, they were struck by his sincerity, his genuineness, his not-the-same-old-same-old-politician-ness. They loved his convention keynote, of course, and were also impressed by the prescience of his 2002 speech in opposition to the Iraq War.

Obama's lead pollster, Joel Benenson, presented the findings of surveys he had done in New Hampshire. And these, too, were encouraging. Obama was only four points behind Hillary in a state in which the Clintons had a reservoir of goodwill, and among voters following the race closely, he actually had a ten-point lead. The numbers showed that, although Hillary was popular with Democrats, there seemed to be a ceiling on her support. The party's antiwar wing was suspicious of her; others questioned whether her duties as First Lady should count as a qualification for the presidency. Most important, voters were looking for change over experience by a two-to-one margin, and even rock-ribbed partisans craved a candidate who could move the country past the bitter polarization of the previous fifteen years—with which Hillary (and Bill) was strongly identified.

Obama took it all in with a mixture of interest and amusement, asking questions occasionally but not obsessively. The thing that jumped out at him, however, involved Benenson's analysis of the change-versus-experience dynamic. "I gotta believe Hillary has people just as smart as our team all around her," Obama said. "Aren't they going to realize this and try to take our message?"

"You know, Barack," David Axelrod cut in, "Joel used to work for Mark Penn, so he knows him pretty well."

"I do know him pretty well," Benenson said. "I know his blind spots. He believes that you play to your strengths and not your weaknesses."

Benenson and Axelrod detested Penn; they thought he represented the dark side of the business. To them, he was a money-crazed mercenary, an arrogant prick, a thug whose chief claim to fame was Bill Clinton's

1996 reelection in which there was no nomination contest. Benenson told Obama that Penn would resist shifting strategy with every fiber of his being. He'll just keep plowing down the same path, the pollster said, because he wants so desperately to be right from the beginning.

Obama nodded, but he was wary of any explanation so rooted in psychobabble. He wondered if they could really count on the obstinacy of Hillary's chief strategist to keep pushing her down the road to ruin. He found the depth of Axelrod's antipathy for Penn slightly inexplicable—but kind of funny. A few weeks later, when Obama's message maestro called to recount in copious and animated detail the Harvard event at which Penn had tried to undermine Obama's antiwar cred, Barack laughed and said, "You really don't like that guy, do you?"

But Obama had enormous faith in Axelrod's judgment and intuitions—a faith that had served him well since they'd become politically entwined nearly fifteen years earlier. He also had faith in the early-state strategy that Axelrod and Plouffe had laid out before he decided to enter the race. At another meeting that February in Washington, this time with a handful of his African American advisers, Obama was confronted with their concerns: some in the press had questioned whether he was "black enough" to appeal to voters of color. In terms of personal identity, he said, "this is very painful for me." But the questions would fade as a campaign issue as black voters became better acquainted with him—and besides, the issue was more or less irrelevant to the larger construct of the race.

"Hillary is running on inevitability, and if we win Iowa, that's gone and this is ours," Obama said firmly. "We'll be able to wrap it up in a month."

For a novice presidential candidate who launched his bid with virtually no concrete preparation, Obama's brio and self-assurance at the start were otherworldly. Everything that happened in the campaign's first few weeks fed his sense of confidence. From the announcement speech in Springfield, he flew to Iowa on a chartered Boeing 757 with his wife, daughters, and fifty-seven reporters in tow. Two thousand people showed up for his first town hall meeting, in Cedar Rapids. The next day, seven thousand at the Iowa State University basketball arena in Ames. Two weeks later, twenty thousand at an outdoor rally in Austin, Texas, standing and cheering in the rain.

The crowds confirmed Obama's basic instinct: *The country really is hungry for something fresh and new,* he thought. And he was it.

But it wasn't just the crowds that amped him up. There was also the money. The campaign had set an ambitious goal: $12 million for the first quarter. Penny Pritzker, his national finance chair, had him running flat-out, his schedule crammed with back-to-back fund-raising events, sometimes six or seven in a day, and his call sheet was even denser. Obama didn't relish pleading for cash any more than Clinton did, but he wasn't going to do it half-assed. He did what he had to—and he was good at it. He knew how to work an elite room, how to come off as, well, the un-Clinton, in front of big donors who were seeking an alternative to the front-runner.

Take Orin Kramer, one of the New York financial titans Obama had met with in December. Kramer was a Clinton stalwart who'd raised millions of dollars for Gore and Kerry as well. Hillaryland was working him hard, dispatching Penn to call him and make the sale. But when Kramer told Penn that he thought 2008 was going to be a change election, which would pose problems for Hillary, Penn was airily dismissive.

Obama, by contrast, didn't outsource his pitch. He neither dissed the hedge fund kingpin nor sucked up to him. Rather, he talked to him in person, over a meal, and calmly and cogently laid out his theory of the case. And he waxed lyrical about how his operation planned to use the Web in transformational ways for both fund-raising and organizing. The riff on connectivity baffled Kramer, but it enhanced his perception of Obama as an avatar of the future—and by the end of the dinner, he was on board.

Still, Obama was as shocked as anyone when his fund-raising team more than doubled its goal and beat Clinton in the first quarter. The Web had almost nothing to do with it; that electronic goldmine would be tapped only much later. Instead it had everything to do with big-time bundlers such as Kramer and other Wall Street players such as Soros and Robert Wolf, Hollywood types such as Geffen and Edgar Bronfman, African American music barons such as Andre Harrell and L.A. Reid, as well as a new generation of "baby bundlers," who were looking for a seat at the table but believed that in the House of Clinton all the chairs were already taken.

Obama watched as his fund-raising success fueled a virtuous circle: money plus big crowds equaled glowing press, which in turn equaled bigger crowds and even more money. Out in Iowa, Hildebrand and his partner, Paul Tewes, were opening field offices, recruiting precinct captains, training volunteers. In the Chicago headquarters, the campaign hired a pair of Internet whiz kids—one a veteran of Howard Dean's pathbreaking online operation in 2004, the other a technologist who had worked at the travel site Orbitz—to build a state-of-the-art Web presence with links to Facebook and YouTube. Every day, Obama talked to Plouffe, getting updates on the progress they were making on all fronts, and every day, what he heard said one thing to him: *This is real.*

Inside Obama's campaign, the reigning metaphor for what they were doing was taking off in a jet airplane while they were still bolting on the wings. And in a few short weeks, Air Obama was soaring in the sky. But attaining such altitude so fast brought with it great expectations and close scrutiny, which was about to reveal that Obama's weaknesses as a candidate were every bit as great as his strengths.

The first signs of trouble came in quick succession in the last week of March. Out in Las Vegas, Obama took part in the campaign's first issue-specific forum—the topic was health care—and watched from the wings as Clinton knocked the cover off the ball. She was sharp, passionate, and detailed; the crowd ate it up. Obama, for his part, was only casually prepared, assuming he could wing it. *It'll be like when I'm on Charlie Rose,* he thought. It wasn't. Vague and platitudinous, mouthing generalities and making excuses for not having his health care plan in order, Obama came across as amateurish. The union audience was both surprised and mildly offended.

Back on the plane afterward, Obama was glum, and seemed slightly intimidated by Clinton. "She was terrific," he said to Gibbs. "I was not."

Four days later, in Washington, Obama spoke at the annual legislative conference of the Building and Construction Trades Department, appearing last after all the other Democratic presidential candidates. He was flat, listless, uninspiring; he thought he bombed. Back in his Senate office, he spotted Gibbs and asked him to take a walk. "I don't know what's going on," Obama said as they made their way to the Capitol, where he had to cast a vote. Nothing was clicking, he said. He wasn't finding his rhythm. He couldn't understand why. He felt like he was alone in the middle of the ocean without a raft. Gibbs listened intently, attempted to offer consolation, but nothing he said helped. He thought it was the saddest he'd ever seen Obama.

Thus began a spring and summer of misery for the candidate. He'd been warned how hard this was going to be, but he had silently scoffed. And for the first few weeks, it hadn't been hard at all—it had been a rush. But now the initial adrenaline surge was wearing off and Obama was facing the wretchedness of the reality he'd signed up for. It wasn't long before Axelrod and Plouffe wondered if he was nurturing second thoughts about his decision to run.

The schedule was killing him. The fatigue was all-consuming. The events piled up on top of one another, making his temples ache. He tried not to bitch and moan too much, except when it got out of hand— meaning almost every day. Once, at five in the afternoon on the bus in Iowa, he turned to his body guy, Reggie Love, and asked, "How many more things do I have today?" Reggie: "Three." Barack: *"Are you kidding me?"* What made it all the worse was the books— always with the books, these people desperate for his signature. So many nights on the trail, after his final event of the day, with Obama wanting nothing more than to get back to his hotel and hit the sheets, he'd find them stacked up in the holding room: fifty, a hundred, a hundred and fifty copies of *Audacity* or *Dreams*, awaiting his John Hancock. He'd look at the pile, shake his head, then wearily pick up his pen. Obamamania had its costs. This was one of them.

The loss of privacy, of control over his life, was another. On that Austin trip back in February, he was mobbed at the airport when he tried to catch a Southwest flight to Chicago; he could no longer fly commercial. He often joked ruefully that his life was now controlled by the twenty-two-year-olds who planned his days. Then there was the Secret Service, which began watching over him in May. Man, how he chafed at that. Not long after his protection started, he returned to Chicago from New Orleans looking forward to a haircut. The Service guys said, Sure, but we've got to case the place first. "Why can't I just go to my barber?" Obama groaned. "I've been going to him for years!" (The staff, on the other hand, adored the Service. They helped keep the perennially late Obama on schedule; he didn't like to make the agents wait around for him.)

Most of all, he missed his girls, all three of them. Every time they came out on the trail with him, he was a different man. He laughed, for one thing. Smiled, for another. Didn't gripe so much. But they were hardly ever there; Michelle saw to that. She told the staff she would be on the road only one day a week, and that was that. She assented to abbreviated day trips to Iowa sometimes—but she always insisted on being back by nightfall, and she was rarely with Barack. The debates made her queasy, so she stayed away from all but one of them. (And at that one, she turned to Jarrett and said, "Do you think anyone would notice if we leave in the middle?")

In the late spring, Axelrod, Plouffe, and Rouse took Obama out to dinner in D.C. He had been complaining in front of the staff more than usual, so they decided to give him a chance to vent. A few minutes into the meal, Obama caught the drift and said, "Okay, is this an intervention?"

None of it would've been so bad if he had been performing up to snuff. But he wasn't, and he knew it, and it pained him. Of all the things he'd questioned when he was mulling the race, the one he never doubted was that he would be terrific on the hustings. His whole life he had been a star, able to switch on the juice at a moment's notice, impressive, charming, and memorable. Feelings of inadequacy had therefore never been a big part of the Obama psychic profile. But when it came to playing the role of a presidential candidate, he was experiencing them all the time.

At town hall meetings, he tried to treat voters with respect by giving them adult, sound-bite-free answers, but he was coming across as professorial and pedantic, taking ten minutes to respond to the simplest queries. The memory of his convention keynote had his audiences anticipating a kind of orgiastic uplift—"People are expecting to come crying out of every speech I give," he told Gibbs—that was impossible for him to provide day after day. After he'd riffed for months on his announcement address, his stump speech was flabby and overlong. He could feel that he wasn't connecting.

The debates were even worse—in no small part because he was suffering mightily by comparison to Clinton, who was just so much better than he or anyone around him had ever imagined she would be: always on message, always in control, her mastery of bullet points and talking points solid, her style an admixture of unexpected breeziness and earnest sapience. And he had a bad habit of handing Hillary a stick with which to thump him. At the first Democratic debate that April, in Orangeburg, South Carolina, NBC's Brian Williams asked Obama how he would change the nation's military stance if America were hit again with two simultaneous attacks by Al Qaeda. "Well, the first thing we'd have to do is make sure that we've got an effective emergency response," Obama replied, slowly winding his way to "potentially" taking "some action to dismantle that network." Clinton's answer mentioned retaliation within ten seconds; in the debate spin room later, her team pounded on Obama for his limp-wristedness.

Obama had a lot to say and wasn't good at spitting it out quickly or concisely, tending to back into his responses. Rather than sell one idea well, he tried to squeeze in as many points as possible. "I have sixty seconds," he said in prep. "How much do you guys think I can get into sixty seconds?"

When Axelrod showed him video of the debates, he grimaced. *It's worse than I thought* ran through his mind. He pledged to do better. "I need to figure out how to get this right," he said. But as the debates went along and he continued to founder, Obama's frustration mounted. He started showing up late for prep sessions or cutting them short. Or spending the whole time on his BlackBerry. Or finding excuses to avoid them altogether. "You guys don't have this together," he said at one mildly disorganized run-through. "I'm going to take a nap."

The superficial way the debates were scored by the press corps annoyed him no end. At the CNN/YouTube debate in Charleston, South Carolina, that summer, a questioner asked if Obama would "be willing to meet separately, without precondition . . . with the leaders of Iran, Syria, Venezuela, Cuba, and North Korea, in order to bridge the gap that divides our countries?" Obama didn't flinch: "I would. And the reason is this, that the notion that somehow not talking to countries is punishment to them—which has been the guiding diplomatic principle of [the Bush] administration—is ridiculous."

Hillary's post-debate spinners called his answer irresponsible and jejune. Even some of Obama's own team thought he should walk it back.

The next morning, Obama made a surprise appearance on a staff conference call and declared: I want to be clear. I said what I meant and I believe it. We should go on offense here, because what Hillary is saying is she wants to do what Bush and Cheney do. It's the sort of typical Washington groupthink that I hate.

Obama believed that he was right on the substance and on the politics. But the conventional-wisdom mongers in the media bludgeoned him for weeks, swallowing the Clinton line, slamming him for dropping the ball again on a national security question.

The debates fed a narrative that was becoming pervasive in the press: Edwards was running on bold ideas (universal health care, a new war on poverty); Hillary was the mistress of the nitty-gritty; and Obama was a lightweight, all sizzle and no steak. This is what the media did—it put every candidate in a neat little box and slapped a pithy label on it. Obama understood. But for the past three years, as the press fawned over him, the box he was stuffed into bore a succession of tags that were flattering and advantageous. New. Fresh. Inspiring. Post-racial. He'd never had a negative run of press on the national level, and therefore never developed the kind of thick protective hide that repelled the media's slings and arrows.

What made it worse was that Obama knew he'd helped build this box himself; that he'd left himself open to, and even invited, the charges of insubstantiality that were bedeviling him. He had signed on to the strategy of stressing thematics over specifics, on the grounds that waging a battle with Clinton on the policy margins would pay paltry dividends. But now he was having his doubts.

He wanted to be seen as substantive. He *was* substantive. And not being viewed that way was hurting his chances, he thought. I've spent my whole life caring about policy, he told his staff. I want to have new ideas, I want them to be specific. I want to make sure that no one can say they're not specific enough. Obama had imagined at the outset of the campaign that he would set aside hours to consult with world-class experts, delving into the issues, devising innovative solutions. He kept asking for more time to do that, but his schedule was too jam-packed with fund-raisers and campaign events. All he was doing was reading memos from his policy shop—and getting pummeled by the press for being a cipher.

The media was in his head on this topic, for sure, but there were other voices in there, too, and other causes for concern. Michelle was worried about the national polls: Why aren't we moving? she kept asking. She feared that the campaign, with its monomania about Iowa, was failing to build a broad base of support across the map. It struck her that the campaign's post-racial demeanor, while politically expedient, was neglecting one of the central motivations that had driven Barack to enter the race. More than anything, it bothered her that her husband was losing—and that he seemed disconsolate in the bargain.

Michelle's disgruntlement was echoed in Obama's ears by another source—one from outside the bubble that enveloped him. For months, he had been swapping emails with his former law school professor Chris Edley, sharing his myriad dissatisfactions with how things were going. Edley had worked in the Carter and Clinton White Houses and been issues director on the Dukakis presidential campaign. Even from the remove of the deanship of Berkeley's law school, Edley had strong views about what caused presidential campaigns to fail. And he was stoking Obama's fear that his bid was headed in that direction.

The candidate decided it was time to stage an intervention of his own.

In mid-July, Obama let Plouffe know he wanted to set aside a few hours for a meeting of the senior staff. Everyone was aware that Obama wasn't happy, so they braced for an unpleasant evening. At 7:30 on the appointed night, the extended Obama brain trust— Axelrod, Plouffe, Gibbs, Hildebrand, Mastromonaco, Pritzker, Jarrett, Nesbitt, communications aide Dan

Pfeiffer, a few others, and Michelle—convened at Jarrett's Chicago apartment, where they were joined by Edley. To everyone in the room besides the candidate's wife, the dean was a stranger.

Obama had invited Edley to the meeting without giving him any instructions as to what his input should be. It was a halfway-to-Iowa review, Obama said, and that was all. Now Edley was sitting there between Michelle and Jarrett, directly opposite Obama, with everyone crowded around the giant oval table in Jarrett's dining room. After listening to the candidate's opening remarks—We've come a long way, we have a long way to go, there are things we need to do better— the dean unloaded.

You people, Edley said, referring to Mastromonaco, the scheduler, and Julianna Smoot, the chief fundraiser, are being too relentless, too greedy for Barack's time. He's being overprogrammed, overscheduled, treated like a standard-issue candidate—when nothing could be further from the truth.

"This is a guy who likes to think, he likes to write, he likes to talk with experts," Edley said. "You folks have got to recognize what he's in this for. He's in this because he wants to make contributions in terms of public policy ideas, and you've got to make time for him to do that."

Edley wasn't speaking calmly. He was all riled up. He believed that the campaign was putting at risk the whole point of Obama's candidacy. And he was certain that Obama felt the same, because Obama had told him so. "With all due respect to all you here," he said, nodding toward Axelrod and Plouffe, "you should just get over yourselves and do what the candidate wants."

Around the table, the members of Team Obama either stared straight down or shot daggers at Edley. Quietly, the room seethed. *With all due respect?* thought Gibbs. *Who the hell are you to come in here and tell us "with all due respect"?*

But Edley was far from done. The policy work at the campaign was perfunctory, he said. Just laundry lists of mediocre stuff. They needed to develop some conceptually ambitious, "frame-breaking" proposals, rooted in Obama's personality and values, and then integrate those ideas thoroughly into his message, Edley said.

Axelrod, bristling with resentment, spoke up in defense of the campaign. "We do spend time with him on policy," he protested, citing a focus group they had recently conducted in Michigan. Edley's jaw nearly hit the table. "A focus group isn't policy making," he said derisively.

Edley raised the question of constituency politics, suggesting that the Obama team's obsessive focus on Iowa was causing them to pay too little attention to minorities and that the campaign was blowing off women because of Clinton's strength among female voters—both dangerous games politically that could create problems long term.

Obama wasn't wavering on the early-state strategy and its focus on Iowa, though. "I think it's the right strategy," he said. "I think it's the *only* strategy, and I don't think we should change it." But he was bothered by Clinton's lead with black voters. "They don't want to be taken for granted," Obama said, noting that he didn't appreciate the carping of the African American leadership, with its claims that he was trying to downplay his blackness. "And I don't think we can concede women to Clinton, even though she's going to win the majority of them," he added.

The meeting lasted for more than three hours, covering many topics. But it was the impression left by Edley that lingered. In the eyes of the Obama staff— and especially Axelrod, Plouffe, and Gibbs—his words were counterproductive. They fueled Obama's fixation on policy, which the political professionals considered a distraction from the real tasks at hand. And Edley's demeanor was worse than that. The Obamans viewed him as an obnoxious ass and prayed they'd never see his face again.

But not everyone in the room shared that assessment (even though, looking back on it later, Edley himself would acknowledge his insufferableness). All throughout his comments, Michelle and Jarrett were conspicuously nodding their heads. Obama's campaign, from the start, had been controlled with an iron grip by the troika of Axelrod, Plouffe, and Gibbs—"the suits," as they were nicknamed internally by those wary of their degree of power. Over the previous few months, as Obama's distress grew, Michelle and Valerie had come to see the suits as forming a circle around Barack that was too tight and too resistant to dissenting opinions for his own good. They were thrilled to have an outsider at the table and avidly absorbed what Edley was saying. *He's channeling Barack*, thought Jarrett.

Obama's own feelings about the Edley intercession were opaque, however—in the moment, at least. He neither supported his friend's fiercest contentions nor defended Axelrod and Plouffe when Edley laid into them. He refused to show his hand even privately to the dean, who never heard a word from Obama about the meeting. But after Edley returned to Berkeley, he did hear from Jarrett.

You were terrific, she told him—fiery and provocative, the perfect foil.

What did Barack think? Edley asked.

You played exactly the role he wanted you to play, she said.

A month later, at the end of August, the Obamas made their usual summer sojourn to Martha's Vineyard. Nothing about Barack's political fortunes had brightened in the time since the Edley meeting. If anything, they had darkened. A few weeks earlier, he had given a speech advocating military strikes under certain circumstances against terrorist targets in Pakistan—and been whacked again for an alleged gaffe by the Clinton campaign and the foreign-policy panjandrums. The national polls were stuck stubbornly in place: Obama trailed Clinton by some twenty points. And the situation in be-all and end-all Iowa was hardly cheerier. For all the time and money the campaign had poured into the state, Obama had put no distance between himself and Hillary or Edwards.

Among Obama's donors, sturm und drang was the order of the day. Having sunk more than $50 million into Obama, they were jittery about the possibility that they had thrown good money after a bad candidate. Frantic calls and emails were flooding in to Pritzker, complaining about Obama, his advisers, and their strategy, offering theories on how to fix all three—the loudest of which was that Obama needed to go negative on Clinton.

Much of Washington agreed. Chuck Schumer was up in arms, telling fellow senators that Obama needed to take a two-by-four to Hillary, prophesying that Barack's reluctance to do so indicated that he wasn't tough enough to win. Claire McCaskill was serving as a backchannel to Obama for the whispering conspirators, those Democratic senators privately rooting for him but afraid to cross the Clintons. Tell Barack this, they would say to her, and then advise that he take out his truncheon. He has to go after her, they urged. There's so much there. He has to do to her now what the Republicans will do to her in the fall, or at least remind Democrats what's in store for us if she wins the nomination.

McCaskill dutifully took the messages to Obama. "It won't work," he said. "It's not what this campaign is." And besides, Obama added, "We're gonna win Iowa."

"You know, Barack," McCaskill replied, "every candidate running for president says they're going to win Iowa."

I know, said Obama. A long pause. "We're gonna win Iowa."

Up on the Vineyard, though, as he and his family luxuriated in eight days of bike rides and beachcombing at a house in Oak Bluffs with Jarrett, the Nesbitts, and the family of another close friend from Chicago, Eric

Whitaker, Obama brooded and pondered. He still had faith in his strategy, his team, and himself. But he knew the time was fast approaching in which his campaign would have to step up its game—and more to the point, *he* would have to step up his game. His staff might have thought the Edley meeting was just a passive-aggressive tactic on Obama's part, a way for him to let off steam by proxy. But for Obama, it was the moment when he began to take control of his campaign.

Obama had long talks on the Vineyard with Jarrett and Rouse (who happened to be vacationing there, too) about how the operation had to change. He trusted Axelrod, Plouffe, and Gibbs, and preferred to deal with as few people as possible—the campaign may have been pushing bottom-up democracy, but he was a top-down guy. Yet Obama had come to agree with Michelle and Jarrett that the innermost circle needed to be broadened beyond the suits. He asked Rouse, who was still living in Washington, to start commuting to Chicago so he could have a more active hand at headquarters. And he asked Jarrett, whose role had been informal until then, to join the campaign full time.

Bringing Valerie on board was no small thing. Her relationship with both Barack and Michelle transcended politics. They had all known one another since 1991, when Jarrett was working as Richie Daley's deputy chief of staff and Michelle Robinson presented herself for a job. The bond the women struck was nearly instantaneous and soon extended to Michelle's fiancé. Barack now thought of Jarrett almost as a sibling. He had faith in her judgment, her intuitions, and her motives. Her desire to see him win was overwhelming, but she cared just as much about his remaining true to himself.

Obama returned to the mainland to discover an unwelcome development. Just as he'd feared in February, Clinton was trying to encroach on his message. Over Labor Day weekend, Hillary and Bill had traveled together to New Hampshire and Iowa, rolling out a brand-new slogan for her campaign—"The Change We Need." Up in Concord, on a stage set bearing a placard that read "Change + Experience," Hillary intoned, "Some people think you should have to choose between change and experience. Well, with me, you don't have to choose." Softening her stance as a partisan warrior, she touted her record in the Senate as a bipartisan pragmatist. Out in Des Moines she told audiences that her candidacy, too, was a history-making proposition, a chance to nominate a woman and thus break "the last and biggest glass ceiling."

The arrival of October brought more bad news: the ABC News/*Washington Post* poll that put Obama thirty-three points behind Clinton nationally, followed by a *Des Moines Register* poll that had him third in Iowa, seven points behind Hillary and one behind Edwards.

The day the *Register* poll appeared, in early October, Obama's national finance committee, comprising a couple hundred of the campaign's richest fund-raisers, was gathered in Des Moines—and now in something close to open panic. Obama arrived that unseasonably cold Sunday afternoon and spoke to the bundlers, calming their nerves. But many were left still wondering if it was too late to stop Hillary, especially if Obama was unwilling to kneecap her.

Obama wondered, too. The Iowa homestretch was drawing near, and he believed that on his present trajectory, he was headed for a respectable second place. *And I ain't running*, he thought, *to be a respectable second.* He needed a plan to change the dynamic. He needed a plan to change the game.

Four days after the finance committee meeting, Obama and his brain trust convened in the conference room of a law firm in downtown Chicago. The candidate opened the proceedings with a blunt and bracing statement: "I think everybody around the table would admit that we're losing right now."

I'm not gonna yell, Obama went on. Look, everybody here has worked extremely hard and done a very good job. No question about that. And we're in a position to win this thing, but the fact is, right now we are losing. We've got ninety days to turn this around, and we're going to figure out in this room what we have to do to make sure we win. We're all on the same team here. Everybody's got to check their egos at the door. But we've got to be honest about where we're falling short and what we need to do to succeed.

Obama raised an issue that had been bothering him for months: the change-versus-experience dichotomy. He'd always grasped the rationale behind homing in on transformation. He'd accepted, though not eagerly, the campaign's decision to make its slogan "Change We Can Believe In." (It struck him as too pat, but he preferred it to the other option on the table, "United We Stand," which he rejected as sounding "like an airline slogan.") But Obama was reluctant simply to cede experience to Hillary. Being a state senator wasn't nothing, he said. He had a real record, had passed legislation—some of it important, such as ethics and death penalty reform—in Springfield. He had more elected experience than Clinton, as a matter of fact.

Like Obama, the pollsters in the room had been grappling with the issue all year long. Time and again they would hear in their focus groups expressions of unease about Obama's greenness and his barren résumé. "He's too new," people would say. "Why doesn't he wait four years?" "Why doesn't he just take the vice presidency?" "He doesn't know about foreign policy."

But what was true when Obama's advisers met back in February was still true in October. Voters wanted change over experience by about a two-to-one margin. "Change is still the way to go," Benenson said. "Believe in the message. It's still right on."

The problem now, Benenson observed, was that the campaign's polling showed Clinton making inroads with her new change-centric pitch. And though the national numbers may have been meaningless, she seemed to be gaining ground in Iowa. Everyone in the room understood from day one that they had to beat her there. The imperative was clear: The campaign had to prevent Hillary from swiping the mantle of change from Obama.

Obama called on Axelrod to present a memo he'd prepared for the meeting. There are three pillars to the kind of change voters want, Axelrod reminded them. They're looking for a president who can bring the country together, who can reach beyond partisanship, and who'll be tough on special interests. Obama could embody that sort of change, but Hillary could not, Axelrod said. In fact, she could be painted as the embodiment of everything Americans despised about the Washington status quo. As Larry Grisolano, another Obama strategist, often put it, If Clinton wanted to tout her experience, they had to make her *pay* for her experience.

Axelrod was a master of the dark arts of negative campaigning. (The first major profile of him, twenty years earlier in *Chicago Magazine*, was titled "Hatchet Man: The Rise of David Axelrod.") Having worked on Clinton's Senate race in 2000, Axelrod had seen the background research that exposed her vulnerabilities: the apprehension among voters who thought of her as calculating, triangulating, slippery with the truth. Obama and Axelrod had agreed all along about Clinton fatigue, that it was bubbling out there, just below the surface of her popularity—and her husband's. The trick would be to incite it subtly, by implication and inference. To revive the voters' worst memories of the Clinton years without so much as mentioning her name. To eviscerate her without damaging Obama's reputation as an exponent of clean politics. To go negative, in other words, without seeming nasty.

We will do this, Obama said, but he was adamant that certain ethical boundaries not be breached. A few months earlier, his campaign's opposition research department had prepared a memo linking Clinton's campaign contributions from Indian Americans to her husband's India-related investments and speaking fees. The headline on the document referred to her as "Hillary Clinton (D-Punjab)." When the memo came out, Obama was angrier at his team than he'd been at any time during the campaign.

Now he reemphasized that such behavior was verboten. I told everybody at the start of this, he said, that I would not change who I am in this campaign. That I will come out the other side the same person I was on the way in. Don't any of you do anything that's going to embarrass me or make people think that I've changed who I am in order to win. If I ever catch anyone digging into the Clintons' personal lives, you will be fired. But I'm perfectly happy having a debate with her; I need to have a debate with her about who can actually change Washington, and that's the debate we should have.

The plan was now set. The following month, Obama would be appearing with all the other candidates at the annual Jefferson-Jackson Dinner in Des Moines. That would be the perfect place to unfurl the new strategy in earnest. There was precedent for the event providing a stage for a campaign relaunch. Gore and Kerry had come into the J-J on the ropes in Iowa and turned in revivifying performances. The campaign would pull out all the stops to turn the event into a display of its organizing muscle. And Obama would devote the time required to crafting a knockout address—an idea that instantly appealed to him. He thought of himself as a big-game player, the kind of guy who rose to the occasion. He liked the pressure, he loved the spotlight, he reveled in the intensity of the moment. If the solution to a political problem was a speech, hoo boy, he was good to go.

But the J-J was in November, more than a month away, too long to let the new approach to the Clintons sit dormant. Obama had been agitating to spend some more time with national reporters—and this seemed the moment to strike. He would accept a long-standing interview request from *The New York Times* as a way of setting up the next debate in Philadelphia at the end of October. Obama's communications wizards had determined that the media narrative that emerged from each debate was dictated by the first two questions and answers. And the easiest way to influence those questions in Philly was to have Obama take a few pokes at Hillary in the *Times* a day or two beforehand; such catnip would be impossible for the moderators to resist.

As Obama rose to leave the meeting, he brimmed with confidence again. "We're going to win this," he said brightly. All year long, he had been dancing around Clinton. Now he was ready to engage. He would bring many hidden advantages to this fight, not least the receptivity of the press to an anti-Clinton message. But he would also have one thing on his side that was plain for everyone to see: an ally of convenience whose determination to sink Hillary was every bit as great as, and even more rabid than, his own.

7

"THEY LOOOOOVE ME!"

John Edwards never expected to be the third wheel in the 2008 campaign. The race was going to be Hillary versus him. That was how he saw it from the start. She would be the front-runner, of course; he knew that. He wasn't naïve. But as sure as night follows day, there would be an alternative, an anti-Hillary, and he would be it. And once he had her one-on-one, he was certain that he could take her. He thought she (and her husband) represented the arrogance wrought by power. He believed she lacked the common touch, had no feel for regular people, working people—which, needless to say, he possessed in abundance. He mocked Hillary in meetings with his advisers: "There's Main Street's candidate!" Obama he didn't give all that much thought to. At least, not at the start.

Edwards came off the blocks much earlier than the other two, and his decision to run was free of the ambivalence they felt—the weighing of pros and cons, the doubts, the dark nights of the soul. Before the dust had settled on 2004, he was planning for 2008. On the day that Edwards and John Kerry conceded defeat to Bush and Dick Cheney, he discovered that his wife, Elizabeth, had breast cancer; a few days after that, he was on the phone with his pollster and close friend Harrison Hickman, gaming out the race four years hence, talking about tailoring his message to take on Clinton from the left. In early December, Edwards called his political team over to his place in Georgetown—the six-bedroom row house on P Street that he and Elizabeth had bought two years earlier for $3.8 million—to discuss how to spend the next couple of years in the optimal fashion.

Having given up his Senate seat to run for president, Edwards was unemployed. He needed to beef up his foreign-policy credentials, so he would make some trips abroad. He would court labor, schmooze donors, and nurture his connection to Iowa, where he had finished a surprising second in the 2004 caucuses. He also said he wanted to set up some kind of antipoverty nonprofit. The plight of the poor wasn't a slam-dunk political winner, but Edwards declared that it was something he cared about, and his advisers knew it was no bad thing for a candidate to embrace what moved him. They also knew it would rhyme with the neo-populist stance he would strike in his challenge to Clinton.

The pathway was clear to Edwards: beat Clinton in Iowa, survive New Hampshire, then kill her off in the South Carolina primary, which he carried in 2004. Over and over, he proclaimed to his aides, "I am *going* to be the next president of the United States." Some of them dismissed his outsize confidence as pro forma, but others took it as a sign of something deeper—a burgeoning megalomania.

He was not the same guy who'd come out of no-where and beaten the incumbent Republican, Lauch Faircloth, to become the junior senator from North Carolina in 1998. Back then, everyone who encountered him was struck by how down-to-earth he seemed. He had fewer airs about him than most other wealthy trial lawyers, let alone most senators. He was the son of a textile mill worker, the first in his family to attend college, optimistic, cheerful, eager, and idealistic. The first time he met Hickman, the pollster asked Edwards, as he did every candidate whom he was considering working for, what one word his intimates would use to describe him. Most politicians said impatient, aggressive, or ambitious. Stretching the word with his southern drawl, Edwards said, "Niiiiice." And it was true—disarmingly so.

Some of his friends started noticing a change after he was nearly chosen by Al Gore to be his running mate in 2000: the sudden interest in superficial stuff to which he'd been oblivious before, from the labels on his clothes to the size of his entourage. But the real transformation occurred during the 2004 race. When Edwards caught fire in late 2003, he started getting a rush from the larger crowds, and lost interest in smaller rooms or individual meetings. "Why am I doing this trip? There's no big event," he griped to his schedulers. After emerging as Kerry's main challenger, he waged the most open, relentless campaign to get on the ticket of any potential VP in the modern era. That success swelled his head, and his experience during the general election seemed to inflate it to the point of bursting. He reveled in being inside the bubble: the Secret Service, the chartered jet, the press pack following him around, the swarm of factotums catering to his every whim. And the crowds! The ovations! The adoration! He ate it up. In the old days, when his aides asked how a rally had gone, he would roll his eyes and self-mockingly say, "Oh, they *love* me." Now he would bound down from the stage beaming and exclaim, without the slightest shred of irony, "They looooove me!"

The loss on Election Day and Elizabeth's diagnosis set him back on his heels. For a few months, he was closer to his old self again, but soon enough, what one of his aides called "the ego monster" returned. Once, Edwards had been warm and considerate with his staffers; now he was disdainful, ignoring them, dismissing their ideas, demanding that they perform the most menial of tasks on his behalf. He made his schedulers find out what movies were available on different flights so he could decide which ones to take. He would fly only first class or on private planes he cadged from donors. At the same time, he started blowing off his most generous contributors, failing to return their phone calls and refusing to see them.

As Edwards's mistreatment of his staff and supporters got worse through 2005, some of the people closest to him interceded, trying to set him straight. "You can't talk to people that way," Hickman scolded him after one off-putting display. You didn't get any smarter just because you were on the national ticket, he went on. People are attracted to the nice John Edwards, and for a lot of them, you're not that John Edwards anymore.

Edwards bridled at the criticism, disputing the idea that solicitousness was required to win. "Kerry didn't do any of that and he got nominated," Edwards observed. Other times, he reacted with anger. "I don't know where that's coming from," he said to Hickman at one point. "You have to consider the source," Edwards rationalized. "A lot of these people are hangers-on."

One of the lessons that John and Elizabeth took away from 2004 was that they had relied too much on aides, advisers, and consultants. The political people hadn't helped Edwards; they'd hurt him, gotten in his way. If they'd just let John be John, he might have been president. Edwards had a phrase he used all the time to describe the problem: "the valley of staff." In his next bid for the White House, he and Elizabeth agreed, they would circumvent the handlers, while John forged his own path. It wouldn't be a campaign at all in any conventional sense, they said. Instead, it would be—*he* would be—a "cause."

The denizens of the valley of staff were astonished by the narcissism that seemed to have infused their candidate. Distraught and dispirited, too. But for a long time, they continued slaving in the service of the illusion at the core of Edwards's political appeal: that he remained the same humble, sunny, aw-shucks, son of a mill worker he'd always been. The cognitive dissonance was enormous, sure, but they were used to that. Because for years they'd been living with an even bigger lie—the lie of Saint Elizabeth.

. . .

Even before the cancer, she was among her husband's greatest political assets. In one of the focus groups conducted by Hickman in Edwards's Senate race, voters trashed him as a pretty-boy shyster—until they saw pictures of Elizabeth, four years his senior. "I like that he's got a fat wife," one woman said. "I thought he'd be married to a Barbie or a cheerleader." The Edwardses' eldest son, Wade, had been killed in a car crash in 1996; for a long time, Elizabeth went to his grave site every day and read softly to the tombstone. She gave birth to their youngest daughter, Emma Claire, at age forty-nine, and their son Jack at fifty. The combination of her suffering, resilience, and imperfections made her a poignant figure. But it was the illness that elevated Elizabeth to a higher plane, rendering her iconic.

She learned she might be sick on the Friday before Election Day in 2004. Her chemotherapy treatment started almost immediately. John was at her side throughout it, and everyone remarked on his warmth and attentiveness, and on the closeness of their bond. She confronted her illness with bracing courage and wry humor, emerging quickly as one of the most outspoken and widely admired cancer survivors in history. By July, she was shopping a book proposal on her ordeal, and by October, she'd struck a deal.

No one in the Edwards political circle felt anything less than complete sympathy for Elizabeth's plight. And yet the romance between her and the electorate struck them as ironic nonetheless—because their own relationships with her were so unpleasant, they felt like battered spouses. The nearly universal assessment among them was that there was no one on the national stage for whom the disparity between public image and private reality was vaster or more disturbing. What the world saw in Elizabeth: a valiant, determined, heroic everywoman. What the Edwards insiders saw: an abusive, intrusive, paranoid, condescending crazywoman.

With her husband, she could be intensely affectionate or brutally dismissive. At times subtly, at times blatantly, she was forever letting John know she regarded him as her intellectual inferior. The daughter of a navy pilot, Elizabeth had lived in Japan when she was a girl and considered herself worldly. She called her spouse a "hick" in front of other people and derided his parents as rednecks. One time, when a friend asked if John had read a particular book, Elizabeth burst out laughing. "Oh, he doesn't read books," she said. "I'm the one who reads books."

As far back as the 1998 senatorial campaign, she had been prone to irrational outbursts that perplexed and worried John's advisers. The first time Hickman witnessed an explosion during that race, he attributed it to the strain of her being pregnant with Emma Claire and her lingering grief over Wade. But a close friend of the Edwardses from law school informed him otherwise. "She's always been this way," the friend said—the sharp manner, the cutting comments, the sudden and inexplicable fulminations.

During the 2004 race, Elizabeth badgered and berated John's advisers round the clock. She called Nick Baldick, his campaign manager, an idiot. She accused David Axelrod of lying to her and insisted he be stripped of the responsibility for making the campaign's TV ads. She would stay up late scouring the Web, pulling down negative stories and blog items about her husband, forwarding them with vicious messages to the communications team. She routinely unleashed profanity-laced tirades on conference calls. "Why the fuck do you think I'd want to go sit outside a Wal-Mart and hand out leaflets? I want to talk to persuadable voters!" she snarled at the schedulers.

Elizabeth's illness seemed at first to mellow her in the early months of 2005—but not for long. One day, she was on a conference call with the staffers of One America, the political action committee that was being turned into a vehicle for John's upcoming 2008 campaign. There were forty or fifty people on the call, mostly kids in their twenties being paid next to nothing (and in some cases literally nothing). Elizabeth had been cranky throughout the call, but at the end she asked if her and her husband's personal health care coverage had been arranged. Not yet, she was told. There are complications; let's discuss it after the call. Elizabeth was having none of that. She flew into a rage.

If this isn't dealt with by tomorrow, everyone's health care at the PAC will be cut off until it's fixed, she barked. I don't care if nobody has health care until John and I do!

The health care call immediately attained wide infamy in the Edwardses' political orbit. The people around them marveled at Elizabeth's callousness—this from a woman whose family had multiple houses and a net worth in the tens of millions. (They marveled as well at the tight-lippedness of their operation, the loyalty to John that kept any of the stories about the other side of Elizabeth from seeing the light of day.) Yet no one called her out on her behavior, least of all her husband. When she demeaned him, he pretended not to notice; when people complained about her behavior, he brushed them off. His default reflex was to mollify her or avoid her. No one doubted that, as her condition improved, the increase in John's travel had a lot to do with steering clear of his wife.

The Regency Hotel on Park Avenue in Manhattan was the preeminent clubhouse outside Washington for Democratic politicians and those who loved—and funded—them. Its restaurant, 540 Park, served the city's most storied power breakfast, and its bar, The Library, was a prime site of lubrication and transaction between supplicants and benefactors. The Regency was Edwards's hotel of choice when he was staying in New York.

One early evening in February 2006, Edwards was hanging out in the bar, having a glass of wine with one of his donors and his young traveling aide, Josh Brumberger, when a woman sitting at a nearby table with some friends recognized him, walked over, and introduced herself. "My friends insist you're John Edwards," Rielle Hunter said. "I tell them no way— you're way too handsome."

"No, ma'am. I'm John Edwards," the candidate replied.

"No way! I don't believe you!"

Brumberger saw this kind of thing all the time. Women were always hitting on his boss. He and Edwards had a well-oiled system in place for dealing with these situations tactfully and politely.

"He is John Edwards," Brumberger interjected, "and I'm sorry, but we're in the middle of something. Thank you."

"Oh, I'm sorry," Hunter said, and retreated to her table.

From the get-go, Brumberger thought that she was trouble. Everything about her screamed groupie. She looked like a hybrid of Stevie Nicks and Lucinda Williams, in an outfit more suitable for a Grateful Dead concert than an evening at the Regency. A few minutes later, after Edwards departed for a dinner around the corner, Hunter came back over to Brumberger and started quizzing him on his job. "I think I can help you guys," she said, and handed him her business card. The inscription read, "Being Is Free: Rielle Hunter—Truth Seeker."

After Hunter left, Brumberger sat there chuckling, having another glass of wine with one of his colleagues from Team Edwards, who had joined him. A little while later, he looked up through the window and clocked Hunter and one of her friends cornering his boss on his way back from dinner. "Holy shit, that crazy lady just cut him of!" Brumberger yelped and sprinted outside, where he broke up the scene, leading Edwards back into the hotel.

"Thank you," Edwards said, apparently relieved. "I'm lucky you saw that, because those women, I don't think they would have quit."

Brumberger would always wonder about that evening: Was Hunter's presence really an accident? Had she and Edwards met before? Did she slink into the hotel and spend the night with him after Brumberger went home to his New York apartment? Because a few months later, without warning, Hunter was back—in a big way.

"Get ready to get mic'd up," Edwards told Brumberger in June, before a speech the candidate was set to deliver at the National Press Club. We're gonna have a camera operator and a documentarian traveling with us, Edwards said. We're gonna show the world what it's really like to be John Edwards.

The idea was that Hunter would produce a series of Web videos documenting life on the road with Edwards. Edwards told Baldick, now running his PAC, that he liked the concept, that they should do it. Baldick objected for any number of reasons—but not because he had the slightest worry that Edwards was fooling around with Hunter. That was one thing the people in the Edwardsphere never stressed over when it came to John, who they believed had long ago made the decision not to fall into that trap. And, anyway, he had always seemed . . . well, sorta asexual, at least to his staff.

No, Baldick's concerns revolved around the way the project would feed the ego monster. *Oh, great, a camera with you,* he thought when Edwards raised the subject. *This is gonna be a really good idea.* Baldick also quailed at the cost—the proposed budgets Hunter submitted ran into hundreds of thousands of dollars. For months, Baldick used the price tag as a reason to resist signing her contract. But Edwards kept poking at him, calling him weekly, saying, It'll be really cool! It'll be on the Web! We've got to push the envelope! Eventually, a big check came in from one of Edwards's donors, and that gave John his trump card. "Now Nick can't tell me no," he said to Brumberger triumphantly.

By then, Hunter was already a constant presence on the road with Edwards. Who needed a contract? There was history to be made! All summer long and into the fall, she traveled with him everywhere—Pennsylvania, Texas, Iowa, Ohio, and New York, even on a trip to Africa, where they visited Uganda. Nothing about it was secretive: her name was always on the flight manifests, and even Elizabeth's allies thought Hunter was legit, that Elizabeth had probably approved the project, given her fascination with the Web.

There was nothing legit, however, about Hunter's behavior. It was freaky, wildly inappropriate, and all too visible. She flirted outlandishly with every man she met. She spouted New Age babble, rambled on about astrology and reincarnation, and announced to people she had just met, "I'm a witch." But mostly, she fixated on Edwards. She told him that he had "the power to change the world," that "the people will follow you." She told him that he could be as great a leader as Gandhi or Martin Luther King, Jr. She told him, "You're so real. You just need to get your staff out of your way." She reinforced everything he already believed, told him everything he wanted to hear.

Edwards swooned, of course. Gobbled up her every word like so much pop-psych popcorn. He spent hours talking to her, listening patiently to her ideas about the state of American democracy and her advice on media strategy. (She had intuitions about Chris Matthews.) He ate every meal with her, sat next to her on the plane and in the car, offered to wheel her bags through air-ports. He told the staff to treat her like a principal. He behaved as if she were a combination of an adviser and a spouse. When Baldick suggested that she not take this or that trip—It's all meetings, he would say; we don't need footage of those; let's save some money— Edwards would resist. When Hunter wanted access to some event that Brumberger thought she shouldn't attend, Edwards would order, "Let her do it." Or plead, "C'mon, just let her do it." Or lean over and whisper conspiratorially, "Just let her do it *this one time.*"

It didn't take a genius to suss the warning signs, and Brumberger was no fool. He had been worried about Hunter since she first came on the road, when he Googled her and discovered that, in her party girl past, she had been the model for the "ostensibly jaded, cocaine-addled, sexually voracious" character Alison Poole in Jay McInerney's novel *Story of My Life.* It took Josh a while to screw up his courage, but he finally did, knocking on Edwards's hotel room door one day that summer in Ohio.

I'm not accusing you of anything, Brumberger nervously said. But I need you to know there's a perception out there that you have a different relationship with Rielle than you do with everybody else, and we're in the perception game, and we know that perception becomes reality. I just need you to be cognizant of it, because your staff is starting to talk.

Edwards nodded and smiled reassuringly. I get it, he said. Thank you. Say no more. I hear you loud and clear.

Brumberger exhaled and walked out of the room thinking, *Yes! Home run!*

But nothing changed.

If anything, Edwards's behavior became even more brazen. At the end of August, he brought Hunter over to the family's new mansion outside Chapel Hill. She spent the whole afternoon and evening exploring the place, shooting footage of his family with her video camera. His parents were there, happily answering questions about their son. His two younger children were there, too, and Rielle lingered with them, interviewing both one-on-one on camera, delighting them by showing an interest in their opinions.

Elizabeth was up in Cambridge that day, dropping off their oldest daughter, Cate, at Harvard Law School. Hunter made herself at home, prowling comfortably around the big house, taking off her shoes, curling up on the sofa. She stayed for dinner with Edwards, the children's nanny, and some family intimates.

Brumberger's dealings with Hunter, meanwhile, were getting testy. Increasingly, she treated him and the rest of the staff as if they worked for her—and Edwards was doing nothing to stop it. On a trip to Missouri over Labor Day weekend, it had been decided that Edwards would fly back east on the private plane alone, with the staff traveling commercial. Hunter objected, demanding a seat on the jet with Edwards. An argument ensued. Edwards sided with Hunter. Brumberger was fed up. Arriving back home in New York, he picked up the phone and called his boss.

This is hard, Brumberger began. I don't know how to say this, but I'm really worried about where your head is. I came to you in Ohio, I thought I got through, but the problem has just escalated and gotten a lot worse, and I'm really, really worried.

"Okay," Edwards said frostily. "Anything else?"

Brumberger was beside himself now. He flew down to Washington and met with Baldick, Peter Scher, who'd been Edwards's chief of staff for the 2004 general election, and Kim Rubey, Edwards's press secretary. For Baldick, the alarm bells had already started ringing, when he got a look at the first webisode produced by Hunter. It was filled with so much flirty banter and overfamiliarity between her and Edwards that it made Baldick cringe. When he and his wife watched it at home in bed on Baldick's laptop, she turned to him at once and said, Oh, my God! He's fucking her!

Somebody senior had to confront Edwards, they all agreed. The first to try was Hickman, who'd known him the longest and was often tapped for difficult conversations with John. Hickman phoned and gingerly said that people were talking about him and Hunter. One of the things people most admire about you is your commitment to Elizabeth, he said. You don't want to mess that up. "I know what you're saying," Edwards replied. "I'll deal with that."

Scher was next to raise the issue, traveling up to New York from Washington and meeting Edwards in his room at the Regency.

"So you think I'm fucking her?" Edwards asked.

Well, are you? Scher pressed.

Edwards said he wasn't.

Well, if you're not, everyone thinks you are, Scher replied. So unless she's going to play some vital role in your future that I don't understand, he continued, it seems to me that she shouldn't be traveling with you anymore.

Edwards calmly agreed—so calmly, in fact, that Scher took it as a clear indication that he and Hunter were having an affair. *If someone accused me of cheating on my wife, I'd say, "Go fuck yourself!"* he thought.

A few days later, Brumberger flew from New York to Chicago to join Edwards, who'd come in from North Carolina, for the start of a trip to China. "Hey, I need to talk to you," Edwards said abruptly when they met in the terminal at O'Hare. They walked together to the airline's premium lounge, where Edwards had reserved a private meeting room for their conversation. "Sit," Edwards said—and then tore into Brumberger.

Stuff from the road is getting back to people, and it's obviously you who's doing it, Edwards said angrily, his southern drawl rapidly rising. You didn't recognize who you work for. You don't work for Nick and Peter. You work for me. I trusted you like a son, but you broke my trust. I can't have you around me anymore. You're not coming to China and you're never working for me again.

Brumberger's heart sank. "I'm sorry you feel that way," he said. "I always thought my goal in all of this was to do everything I could to help you become the next president of the United States."

"Why didn't you come to me?" Edwards asked.

"I did come to you! I came to you in Ohio. I called you after Labor Day! I tried!"

"No," Edwards said. "Why didn't you come to me like a fucking man and tell me to stop fucking her?"

They were both yelling now at the top of their lungs, red-faced and teary-eyed. ("You're a twenty-seven-year-old kid and I'm a grown man!" Edwards railed. "Don't you think I've thought about this?") But when Edwards finally regained his composure, he seemed to recognize the implications of sacking Brumberger. Let's talk about all this when I get back, he said.

But Brumberger had had enough. Crushed and mortified, he was finished with Edwards. It would be a very long time before they spoke again.

Brumberger's firing sent shock waves through the Edwardsphere. Baldick, Rubey, and longtime communications adviser David Ginsberg followed him out the door. All three gave Edwards other pretexts for quitting, but there was no escaping the conclusion that the candidate was diddling Hunter, and that he was hellbent on resisting the efforts of the people closest to him to save him from himself.

The departure of much of Edwards's inner circle only weeks before he planned to declare his candidacy didn't seem to trouble him. Most of his team had clashed with Elizabeth, so he could chalk it up to that. The valley of staff was getting smaller; so much the better. Hunter was still traveling with him everywhere, while Elizabeth had been a distant figure from the campaign for much of the fall. Her new book, *Saving Graces*, was a huge success, charting high on the bestseller lists. She was even more famous now, more iconic, more beloved than her husband by a mile. She appeared on *Oprah* and countless other TV shows, establishing a broad constituency of fans.

Elizabeth had never crossed Hunter's path—until the afternoon of December 30, 2006, in Chapel Hill, at the last stop on the announcement tour for John's presidential bid, which Rielle was on hand to shoot.

Elizabeth and her family were waiting at the campaign headquarters in a small room with big windows overlooking an expansive lawn below. Hundreds of people were there for the rally, milling around outside, listening to a bluegrass band. Edwards and his aides arrived straight from the airport and breezed into the room. Hunter was toting her camera, sticking like glue to Edwards, acting the way she always did—too familiar, too intimate. Always jealous of anyone, male or female, who seemed close to John, Elizabeth watched

Hunter working the room. The expression on Mrs. Edwards's face said: Who *is* this woman? And what is she doing here? Icily, Elizabeth asked Hunter to back off. "Excuse me, we're trying to have some privacy," she said.

As Edwards took the stage, Hunter rushed to get into position to film his speech. Elizabeth, her brother, and her sister-in-law observed Hunter's movements. Onlookers watched them engage in an animated conversation in which Elizabeth was visibly upset.

When the whole wretched business eventually became public, Elizabeth would claim that her husband revealed to her the next morning that he had slept with Hunter—but that it had happened only once and afterward he was consumed with remorse. Her first reaction, she would say, was that John should leave the race, but he convinced her that dropping out immediately after the announcement would raise suspicions that would be hard to put to rest.

Whatever was actually said between them, by the next afternoon, Elizabeth was on the phone with members of Team Edwards, issuing marching orders: Hunter's contract was to end, the webisodes pulled from the Internet, the raw video retrieved as soon as possible.

That woman is crazy—get rid of her, Elizabeth said.

And John professed agreement.

"We have to get the tapes back," he told one of his aides. "She's dangerous."

And with that, Rielle Hunter disappeared. But not really. And not for long.

They all sat in silence around the square table in the middle of the Edwardses' living room in the new estate on Old Greensboro Road. It was late in the afternoon on March 21, 2007, and John and Elizabeth had called their closest aides together to talk about her health. It had been a roller coaster of a day, with Elizabeth at the hospital for hours of tests and difficult talks with her doctors. The news had been dark, pitch-black dark, for a while, but now it was merely bad, which made it seem almost good. John explained that Elizabeth's cancer had returned and moved from breast to bone. Calmly, clinically, he explained the diagnosis and prognosis: it was treatable, but incurable.

Among the handful of aides gathered in the room and listening in by phone, more than a few wished that Edwards would use the development as an excuse to leave the race. And if Elizabeth really wanted him to quit after learning about the affair with Hunter, this presented the perfect opportunity for him to do so, no questions asked. For the past three months, as the campaign got under way, Elizabeth and John had been fighting savagely on the road, sometimes causing events to be delayed. She was telling friends that John had changed, that he no longer cared about anybody but himself. To a longtime aide, she put the question "Don't you think he's kind of messianic?"

But Elizabeth didn't ask her husband to get out. She insisted that he stay in. We can't let my cancer impact the future of the country, she told the group that day. He has to run. He has to be president. I believe it's the most important thing that we can do.

Their decision set off a national debate: Should a candidate continue with a grueling campaign when there was serious illness at home? Was it fair to Elizabeth? Was it fair to their children? Would it be fair to the country if he won to have a president with such a trauma consuming his attention?

But John and Elizabeth insisted they were doing what they knew was best—for themselves, their family, and the voters. And despite whatever doubts existed in some quarters, it generally was accepted that Elizabeth had a right to determine how she spent her time, even if she preferred to continue the exhausting fight to get her husband elected president rather than rest quietly at home.

Edwards's position in the race was strong at the start. He'd come flying out of the gate, offering up a flurry of bold and concrete policy plans, notably on health care and global warming. He was in the driver's seat in Iowa. His relationship with labor was tight. His early fund-raising was surprisingly robust: $14 million in the first quarter of the year, not nearly as much as Clinton or Obama, but double his take in the same period four years earlier. Obama's entry, John and Elizabeth believed, didn't alter their original assessment of the contest. Barack was a phenomenon, no doubt about that, but one that would pass.

In the wake of the Hunter flare-up and the recurrence of Elizabeth's cancer, the dynamic between husband and wife shifted in the context of the campaign. He was more deferential to her; she was even more assertive. Former congressman David Bonior, the campaign's new manager, had no experience running a presidential operation and struck much of the staff as an extremely nice but very clueless guy. Elizabeth seemed to love having Bonior nominally in charge, because it meant that, in effect, *she* was in charge. On everything from hiring to advertising, her influence was singular.

She pushed John hard on policy—always to the left. On health care, in particular, she lobbied vociferously, in meeting after meeting, for him to embrace a single-payer plan as the route to universal coverage. In television interviews, on blogs, and on the trail, Elizabeth was outspoken in support of her causes, at times advocating policies—in favor of gay marriage, for instance—more progressive than her husband's. In 2004, Edwards's campaign had been sunny, centrist, and thematic. Elizabeth prodded him toward being hotter, more populist, and more sharply ideological and anti-establishment. And in that cause she enlisted a new ally, bringing into the campaign that spring the consultant Joe Trippi—for whom tilting at the Establishment was akin to breathing.

Trippi was a piece of work. At fifty, he had toiled for seven previous presidential hopefuls, from Ted Kennedy to Gary Hart to Dick Gephardt to Howard Dean. Brilliant, eccentric, and mildly unbalanced, he'd long been a pioneer in applying new technology to politics. Though John Edwards was interested in Trippi mainly because he thought the shaman had some magic formula for turning the Web into a fund-raising spigot, Elizabeth was enamored of his heady talk of transforming the campaign into a movement.

Trippi thought John was high on his own vapors in considering himself equal to Clinton and superior to Obama. But he also believed that if Edwards could beat them both in Iowa, it might be enough of a game changer to propel him to the nomination.

The day after Trippi joined the campaign in mid-April, he got a call from a reporter inquiring about whether Edwards had received a $400 haircut. (Another question he heard early on from a member of the Edwardsphere struck him as even more unsettling: "What are you gonna do about the girlfriend?" *Dude, what are you talking about?* Trippi wondered.) Trippi soon learned that the haircut was, in fact, just one of three interrelated imbroglios that would plague Edwards for months. Inside the campaign, they called them "the three *H*s": the haircuts, the hedge fund, and the house.

Edwards's advisers had warned John about the perils of the new house from the first time they saw the blueprints. It was a two-building complex totaling 28,200 square feet, with an indoor basketball court, swimming pool, and squash court, two theatrical stages, and a room designated "John's Lounge." Staring at the designs, Baldick said, "Is there any foliage to cover the house?" At which Hickman cracked, "Are you kidding? They clear-cut a whole forest to build it!"

But the house was a cancer thing, a gift to Elizabeth at the time when the disease first appeared. When John's advisers pointed out that such a gaudy manse might be a political liability for an aspiring neo-populist, he said, "It's Elizabeth's project" and "I can't deny her this." When the place was ridiculed in the media—by Jay Leno, among many others—Elizabeth responded that her new home was "not grand" but "functional."

The hedge fund was John's deal to be a "senior adviser" to Fortress Investment Group, in New York, from which he reaped a minor fortune. Edwards signed on in October 2005 without even telling his team he was doing it. He justified it by saying he needed the money. (The Edwardses burned through cash at an astounding rate, on everything from real estate to Internet shopping, to which Elizabeth was apparently addicted, filling their house with unopened boxes containing items she'd bought online.)

By December 2006, John had left Fortress. But the damage was done—especially since he kept some of his money in the fund, which was implicated in a welter of foreclosures in New Orleans after Hurricane Katrina and a ton of subprime lending, two damning facts that became subjects of considerable media interest in 2007.

Edwards already had an image problem when it came to his hair, due to a bootleg YouTube video, set to a sound track of "I Feel Pretty," that caught him fussing with his glossy coif before a TV interview. But now there was a story that he'd received two $400 cuts from a posh Beverly Hills stylist who later revealed that he'd once charged Edwards $1,250 for a session back in 2004.

The instinct of Team Edwards was to make a joke of John's follicular follies, but Elizabeth had other ideas. The story drove her to distraction—to the point where, over the summer, she shot a homemade response video in the backyard of their beach house, with her and John boasting about how little they paid for her engagement ring. She sent the staff the video and told them to post it on the campaign's website. Cooler heads eventually prevailed.

The Edwards campaign was certain that the Clintonites were driving the three *H*s, planting the stories in the press at the national level and in the four early states. And it was true: frustrated by the media's indifference to its attempts to stoke negative coverage of Obama, the Clinton operation was pushing the hedge fund and the haircuts. (In fact, the Obamans were also hawking the stylist story.)

The Edwardses saw the effort as a sign of respect, an indication that Hillary was feeling threatened by John. Their advisers tried to spin journalists that the three *H*s were nothing more than a preoccupation of the media, that voters didn't give a damn. But, in fact, the campaign's research suggested otherwise, especially regarding the house. Fair or not, the impact on Edwards's image was undeniable. The three *H*s reinforced doubts about his substantiveness, and, more damaging, his authenticity.

Problematic as all that was, however, it paled beside another threat that returned as the summer turned to fall. Suddenly, it appeared that a fourth *H* might be added to the list—an *H* that could have stood for "honey" or for "hussy," but either way stood for "Hunter."

Roger Altman picked up the phone in his thirty-eighth-floor office on the East Side of New York and found John Edwards on the line. Altman, the former deputy treasury secretary who was then secretly planning Hillary Clinton's White House transition, was chairman of the investment group Evercore Partners. Since 1999, Evercore had owned a stake in American Media, the publisher of the *National Enquirer*—and it was that connection that prompted an agitated Edwards to call Altman one day in the first week of October.

There's a story about to come out in the *Enquirer*, Edwards said, which is going to allege that I had an affair with a woman who used to travel with my campaign. The story is untrue and outrageous, he insisted. It's going to be extremely hurtful to my family. Could you please do something to stop it?

Altman barely knew Edwards, but could tell he was upset. "I haven't heard a word about this," Altman said. "I'll look into it, but there's really nothing I can do."

He had some sympathy for Edwards. The *Enquirer* had been a thorn in Altman's side for years, especially when it published embarrassing pieces on his powerful friends. So he called David Pecker, the *Enquirer*'s publisher, and asked him about the story. We have evidence, Pecker told him. "This thing could have a big impact on this guy, so let's be triply sure," Altman said. Pecker replied that he already was.

A little later, Altman's phone buzzed again. This time it was Elizabeth, in tears.

You must do something about this, she begged. It's cruel, it's unfair, and it's untrue. This is way too much for me. I can't take it. It's killing our family. It's killing me.

Altman was torn up by Elizabeth's distress. He knew, of course, that she was ill. He considered her the victim in this sordid episode. But Altman's hands were tied. "I'm really sorry, Mrs. Edwards," he said. "I'm really, really sorry."

The *Enquirer* story didn't come completely out of left field for the Edwardsphere. Back in April and May, there had been whispers that Hunter had reappeared, with rumored sightings of her at hotels where Edwards was staying. (Once, an advance staffer sent up to his boss's room to retrieve something had come upon a woman matching Hunter's description.) Then, over the summer, a reporter from the Huffington Post began digging into the sudden disappearance of the webisodes from the One America site. The HuffPo story, published in September, was mild—full of insinuations but no direct allegations.

There was little that was elliptical about the *Enquirer* story that hit the streets on October 10, however. "Presidential candidate John Edwards is caught in a shocking mistress scandal that could wreck his campaign" was the lead, and the article went on to cite a "bombshell e-mail message" in which the other woman "confesses to a friend she's 'in love with John,' but it's 'difficult because he is married and has kids.'"

The next morning, John and Elizabeth were scheduled to fly out of Raleigh to separate destinations—he to South Carolina, she to Iowa. But when the traveling staff arrived at their home, they found Elizabeth out of sorts, disconsolate, still in her bathrobe. She had drafted a blog post that she wanted to have published, defending her husband from the accusations against him. This kind of tawdriness was something the Clintons would be involved in, she wrote, but not the Edwardses.

The staff persuaded Elizabeth that posting such an item would do more harm than good. But she was livid about what she saw as the campaign's feeble response to the story. After pulling herself together, she and John set off for the private aviation terminal at the airport— but partway there, their car pulled over, and John got out and jumped into the staff car, saying in an exasperated tone, "I can't ride with her."

At the terminal, the couple fought in the passenger waiting area. They fought outside in the private parking lot. Elizabeth was sobbing, out of control, incoherent. As their aides tried to look away, she tore off her blouse, exposing herself. "Look at me!" she wailed at John and then staggered, nearly falling to the ground.

John tried to bring down the temperature, remaining calm and impassive, but his apparent standoffishness only seemed to infuriate and disorient Elizabeth more. Finally, after talking to her doctor on the phone, Edwards sent his wife home and flew off to South Carolina. There, outside a barbecue joint in Summerton, Edwards was asked by a reporter about the *Enquirer* story; he offered a paean to Elizabeth—"I've been in love with the same woman for thirty-plus years, and as anybody who's been around us knows, she's an extraordinary human being, warm, loving, beautiful, sexy and as good a person as I have ever known"—coupled with the blanket claim that "the story's just false" but no denial of the specific allegations it contained.

Out of view, the Edwards campaign was in damage-control mode, going into overdrive to dissuade the mainstream media from picking up the story, denouncing it as tabloid trash. Their efforts at containing the fallout were remarkably successful. The *Enquirer*'s exposé gained zero traction in the traditional press and almost none in the blogosphere. Edwards's relief was palpable, as was his gratitude to the small coterie of aides who had corralled the story. "It's John," he began in a voice mail to one of them. "I just wanted to call and thank you for everything you've done in the past few days. It hasn't been easy, I know that, and I want you to know how grateful I am for everything you've done. We'll get through this together. Don't worry, man."

The next voice mail in the staffer's queue was from Elizabeth, who vented her fury that the story had appeared in any form, suspicious that the very aides who had kept the matter from mushrooming had somehow enabled the affair.

"You're to have nothing more to do with this!" Elizabeth hissed. "Nothing more! You stay away from our family! You are poison! You're dead to us!"

For John Edwards, the narrow escape should have been hair-raising, his wife's humiliation chastening. But instead of being tossed into turmoil or depression, Edwards seemed as resolved and optimistic as ever about his prospects. To his way of thinking, he was as plausible a nominee in October 2007 as he had been ten months earlier—and the outside world agreed.

He had much less money than Clinton or Obama, that was true. But he had enough to hold his own in Iowa, and that was all he needed. He was consistently rated in the top tier alongside Clinton and Obama, the rest of the field dismissed as a jumble of interchangeable long shots. The press corps credited his Iowa-only strategy and saw him as having a decent chance there. Obama's poor standing in the national polls seemed to confirm Edwards's long-held view that the upstart was a passing fad.

How to get past Hillary was the question. At the urging of Trippi, Edwards had recently adopted a harsher tone with the front-runner, attacking her for being too close to corporate power and tainted by the special-interest corruption in Washington. At a debate in Chicago sponsored by the AFL-CIO, Edwards fired a populist broadside at a recent appearance of Clinton on the cover of a national publication—with her smiling face above the headline "Business Loves Hillary!"

"I want everyone here to hear my voice on this," Edwards declared. "The one thing you can count on is you will never see a picture of me on the front of *Fortune* magazine saying, 'I am the candidate that big corporate America is betting on.' That will never happen. That's one thing you can take to the bank."

To Edwards's eye, his punches seemed to be landing on the mark. When he ran into Clinton backstage at the event, her hostility was evident—which delighted him. "She won't look at me," Edwards told his aides triumphantly. "I'm getting under her skin."

But Edwards knew that even if he beat Clinton in Iowa, she would be a resilient foe. He began to ponder the possibility of a novel, and radical, anti-Hillary strategy: teaming up with Obama to run on a joint ticket against Clinton after the caucuses. He raised the idea with Hickman early that fall.

"Who's going to be number one and number two?" the pollster asked. Edwards replied, "He would be my running mate."

The idea was far out, certainly, but no less odd than pretty much everything about Edwards's situation as he hurtled into the Iowa homestretch. Rielle Hunter was hanging over his head. His wife was apparently on the verge of a breakdown. But Edwards was undaunted. All he needed was a little help. If he could just get Obama to lend him a hand, everything in the end might, just might, turn out golden.

8

THE TURNING POINT

They took the stage in the auditorium at Drexel University just before 9:00 p.m. on Wednesday, October 30: Biden, Clinton, Dodd, Edwards, Obama, Richardson, and Ohio congressman Dennis Kucinich. The candidates in various combinations had appeared at more than a dozen previous debates or forums. Their interchanges had been informative (on occasion), entertaining (less often), and almost entirely free of impact on the basic contours of the race. Clinton was the comfortable front-runner, Edwards and Obama her obtrusive challengers, and the rest irrelevant also-rans.

But the debate at Drexel would be different. Looking back on it later, the candidates and their advisers would all agree: what happened that night in Philadelphia changed everything.

Dominating debate after debate had bred a certain complacency in Clinton—and a distinct disdain for Obama. After many of them, Hillary would privately lambaste Obama for comparing his meager record to hers and Dodd's and Biden's. (Every now and then onstage, the three of them would share furtive eye-rolls over Obama's self-regard.) "What an asshole," Clinton, employing her favorite profanity, grumbled to her aides. "Am I the only one who sees the arrogance? Does that not bother people?"

Hillary knew that Obama intended to play offense at Drexel. The Sunday before the debate, *The New York Times* had run a front-page story based on the table-setting interview that Obama and his team had planned weeks earlier. In it, Obama claimed Clinton was being less than truthful about her positions. That she was acting like a Republican on foreign policy. That she was too divisive to win a general election or unify the country. "We have to make these distinctions clearer," he said. "And I will not shy away from doing that."

The Obama plan worked. The initial question of the debate was directed at him by moderator Brian Williams; the topic was the *Times* story. But Obama bobbled the ball, backing away from his charges. "I think some of this stuff gets overhyped," he said.

In the opening segment of the debate, Edwards's attacks on Clinton were repeated and razor-sharp, while Obama reverted fully into his passive, prolix, professorial mode. Edwards wondered what the hell was wrong with him. Puncturing Clinton was their mutual objective, with time running out, but only Edwards was wielding the blade. During the first intermission, he pulled Obama aside and stared him in the eyes. "Barack, you need to focus!" Edwards implored. "Focus! Focus! Focus!"

The next segment opened with Hillary answering a question about her electability and appropriating a phrase of Obama's about the need to "turn the page" (she applied it to Bush and Cheney). Obama thought, *She stole my line!* And was mocking him in the process! That did it. He finally pounced.

"I'm glad that Hillary took the phrase 'turn the page,'" he said sarcastically. "It's a good one." After smacking her for refusing to release records of her time as First Lady held by the National Archives, he went on: "Part of the reason that Republicans, I think, are obsessed with you, Hillary, is that's a fight they're very comfortable having. It is the fight that we've been through since the nineties. And part of the job of the next president is to break the gridlock and get Democrats and independents and Republicans to start working together to solve these big problems, like health care or climate change or energy. And what we don't need is another eight years of bickering."

What ensued then was one of the more extraordinary group assaults in the history of presidential debates. It was seven on one—five candidates (Kucinich refrained) and two moderators pounding on Clinton mercilessly.

With just eight minutes left on the clock, Clinton had withstood the fusillade—at least she was still standing. Then, the other moderator, Tim Russert, asked her if she supported the idea of giving driver's licenses to illegal immigrants, as New York's Democratic governor Eliot Spitzer had proposed.

Clinton ducked Russert's query, saying she sympathized with Spitzer, then pivoted to stress the need for comprehensive immigration reform. But when Dodd declared his opposition to the plan, Clinton jumped back in: "I did not say that it should be done, but I certainly recognize why Governor Spitzer is trying to do it."

"Wait a minute!" interjected Dodd. The senator from Connecticut considered Hillary a friend; all year long he had held back from going after her, against the advice of many of his advisers, who were virulently anti-Clinton. But this rigmarole that she was spouting struck him as absurd. "You said yes, you thought it made sense to do it."

"No, I didn't, Chris," Clinton replied, and started squabbling with Dodd. Voices escalated. Eyebrows arched. The back-and-forth got heated. Finally, Russert stepped in and asked Clinton to clarify her position: Did she support Spitzer's plan or not?

"You know, Tim, this is where everybody plays gotcha," Clinton said, gesticulating with both hands. "What is the governor supposed to do? He is dealing with a serious problem. We have failed and George Bush has failed. Do I think this is the right thing for any governor to do? No. But do I understand the sense of real desperation, trying to get a handle on this? . . . He's making an honest effort to do it."

Watching the exchange on TV in the staff room, Clinton's aides felt as if they were witnessing a car crash in slow motion. Grunwald pleaded with Hillary's pixelated image on the screen as if she were trying to advise her candidate telepathically. Okay, that's enough, she cried. No! No! No! Stop!

But it was too late. Williams tried to segue to a new topic, but Edwards wouldn't let go. "Unless I missed something, Senator Clinton said two different things in the course of about two minutes," he noted, "and I think this is a real issue for the country." Obama nodded vigorously and Williams asked him why. "I was confused on Senator Clinton's answer," Obama said with a smirk. "I can't tell whether she was for it or against it."

Clinton exited the stage both bloodied and bowed. Of the sixty-two questions at Drexel that weren't part of a "lightning round" in which all the candidates were asked the same thing, more than half were either directed to her or elicited answers that ended up being attacks on her. Only five times did any candidate go after someone besides her. Among the questions put to Obama: Did he believe in life on other planets? What would he do to fix air travel? And what would he dress as for Halloween?

On the flight home to Washington, Clinton asked her aides, How bad was that? Grunwald tried to be gentle but candid about the driver's license cockup: It wasn't great. We're gonna catch some crap. We're gonna need to clean it up.

The next day, however, Clinton's people didn't clean it up at all—they made an even bigger mess. A statement was issued that simply reformulated her muddled position from the night before. Then her press shop clarified the clarification, saying Clinton backed "the basic concept" of giving driver's licenses to illegals absent immigration reform. At the same time, the campaign posted on the Web a thirty-second video titled

"The Politics of Pile-On," with intercut images of the other candidates assailing Hillary at the debate, set to music from Mozart's *Marriage of Figaro*. The day after that, in a speech at her alma mater, Wellesley College, Clinton noted that the school had "prepared me to compete in the all-boys' club of presidential politics."

The combination of Clinton's debate performance and the suggestion that sexism was at work unleashed a torrent of scorn from the media. And her opponents were no less scathing. The Edwards campaign produced a Web video of its own, highlighting Clinton's obfuscations at the debate, called "The Politics of Parsing." The Obama campaign made a video, too, featuring unflattering shots of Clinton against a soundtrack of "Did You Ever Have to Make Up Your Mind?" Obama personally vetoed the video as too mean. But he did go on the *Today* show and characterize Clinton as a whiner: "One of the things that she has suggested why she should be elected is because she's been playing in this rough-and-tumble stage. So it doesn't make sense for her after having run that way for eight months, the first time that people start challenging her point of view, that suddenly, she backs off and says: Don't pick on me."

The scale and intensity of the backlash stunned Hillary. "We need to stop talking about gender," she instructed her staff. All year long she had shied away from putting her femaleness front and center, out of fear that it would undercut the tough-as-nails image she required to clear the commander-in-chief threshold. She had approved the piling-on video, but thought it had nothing to do with sexism—and was furious at her campaign for letting it be cast that way. But her deeper anger was directed at the media. Obama had been bad in so many debates and been given a free pass, she thought. And yet here she was, batting a thousand until then, getting pilloried for whiffing once by a press corps lying in wait for the first excuse to nail her. She found the unfairness of it galling.

The dynamics that drove the coverage were both more complex and simpler than that, of course. The press always wants a race. The press always loves conflict. Driver's licenses for illegals was a hot topic. Clinton stumbling was a man-bites-dog story—and the way she stumbled reinforced an existing stereotype of her, to which the media was certainly receptive. Nor was Clinton's campaign blameless in fomenting some of the ill will toward her. Its approach to the Fourth Estate, reflecting the candidate's disposition, had fluctuated throughout the contest between heavy handed and outright hostile.

But whatever the confluence of causes and effects, the damage to the front-runner from the Drexel debate and its aftermath was more severe than anyone in Hillaryland knew. The inevitable candidate was suddenly revealed as vulnerable. The flawless campaign looked fallible. The Clinton juggernaut had a hole in its hull—and the water was rushing in.

Hillary looked down at the text of her speech and felt ill. She'd picked up a rotten cold on the road and was struggling to shake it, but that wasn't the only reason for the dull throbbing in her skull. It was Friday, November 9, ten days after what had turned out to be the most important debate of 2007 and one day before what was expected to be her most important address of the year. In a little more than twenty-four hours, she would be standing on a stage in Des Moines at the Jefferson-Jackson Dinner, holding forth without notes or the aid of a TelePrompTer, in the round, before nine thousand Democrats. And yet here she was, sitting with her aides at Whitehaven, laying eyes on her speech text for the very first time—and saying, No, let's change this.

The internal debates over what Clinton should say at the J-J had dragged on for weeks and arrived at no place good. In the past months, Obama had developed a fiery call-and-response that had become a trademark flourish: "Fired up! Ready to go!" For the J-J, Clinton would have an incantation of her own: "Turn up the heat!" (On the Republicans.) Nobody in Hillaryland liked it except Penn, who claimed it tested well in his polling and would reinforce Clinton's image as a fighter against the GOP—in contrast to the weak and platitudinous Obama.

The Clinton campaign's organizational efforts were equally haphazard. The J-J was a fund-raiser for the Iowa Democratic Party. The more tickets you bought, the more supporters you could bring. Teresa Vilmain kept badgering the people at the Ballston headquarters: Gang, either we come up with more money now or we lose out, she said. But the Iowa team had trouble getting the budget for the J-J approved. Its request for cash to hire a band to play outside the hall to rouse the troops was rejected. When the funds for crowd-building finally arrived, it was too late—the Obama campaign had already snatched up the prime seats in the place.

On the night of the event, Clinton and her team arrived late to Veterans Memorial Auditorium and Hillary retreated to a trailer to squeeze in a rushed final read-through or two. She would be the penultimate speaker, followed by Obama. The dinner had been plodding along for more than three hours already by the time she took the stage. Because it was so late, and because her supporters tended to be older, her crowd, which was smaller than Obama's to begin with, had thinned out appreciably. Astonishingly, Clinton's rendition of her text was letter perfect. Dressed in a black pantsuit with a yellow top, she gamely built toward her signature theme. "I'll tell you what I want to do," Hillary said. "I'm not interested in attacking my opponents. I'm interested in attacking the problems of America and I believe that we should be turning up the heat on the Republicans! They deserve all the heat we can give them!"

Out in the darkness of the hall, Obama's brain trust was incredulous at Clinton's message. She was talking about fighting, rather than uniting, playing right into their hands.

Obama's speech—indeed, the entire Obama operation at the J-J—could not have been more different than the Clinton effort. Steve Hildebrand, Paul Tewes, and the Iowa field team treated the event as if it were a dry run for caucus night, scheduling a concert by John Legend for the foot soldiers beforehand. The Obama ranks were young, energetic, and eardrum-splitting. They went wild when their hero took the stage, as the PA system blasted an introduction by the Chicago Bulls announcer Ray Clay: "And now, from our neighboring state of Illinois, a six-foot-two force for change, Senator Barack Obama!"

Unlike Hillary, Obama had prepared meticulously for his speech. He had road-tested it a week before, in Spartanburg, South Carolina. He'd spent hours in his hotel room over several days memorizing and rehearsing it. As for his message, there was never even the slightest doubt or dithering. His indictment of Hillary—and her husband—was subtle but unmistakable, his takedown of them a deft blend of coded language and clear implication.

"We have a chance to bring the country together in a new majority," Obama declaimed. "That is why the same old Washington textbook campaigns just won't do in this election. That's why not answering questions because we are afraid our answers won't be popular just won't do. That's why telling the American people what we think they want to hear instead of telling the American people what they need to hear just won't do. Triangulating and poll-driven positions because we're worried about what Mitt or Rudy might say about us just won't do." And also, "I am not in this race to fulfill some long-held ambitions or because I believe it's somehow owed to me."

The decimation was interwoven with flashes of inspiration: "A nation healed. A world repaired. An America that believes again." The crowd adored it all. When Obama walked offstage to Stevie Wonder's "Signed, Sealed, Delivered," the ovation was thunderous. His supporters raised the rafters with their cries of "Fired up! Ready to Go!" Backstage, Obama spotted Axelrod, smiled, and said, "That was solid, right?"

That Obama won the night dramatically was apparent even to Clinton's staunch allies. Ohio governor Ted Strickland, who'd accompanied Hillary to the dinner, thought the shift of momentum to Obama was palpable, almost visible. Penn and Grunwald attempted to spin reporters on the notion that the youth of Obama's supporters was a negative. "Our people look like caucus-goers and his people look like they are eighteen," Grunwald remarked, adding dismissively, "Penn said they look like Facebook." Clinton's chief strategist chimed in, "Only a few of their people look like they could vote in any state."

Hillary's loyalists took pains to praise her at a party afterward, not insincerely. But McAuliffe expressed dismay at Obama's greater show of force in the auditorium, and Vilmain acknowledged that the opposition had more people in the hall.

"Why?" asked Hillary.

They got their money in sooner and they had more of it, Vilmain explained.

"Oh," Clinton said and walked away.

But Hillary wasn't satisfied with Vilmain's answer. She had a lot of questions and a lot of worries—a cascade of concerns that had been growing for a while, but that the J-J unleashed full force. She was worried that Obama seemed to be building some kind of movement in the cornfields. "Movement" was the word she kept hearing from Maggie Williams, who told her it was easy to run against a man, but devilishly hard to run against a cause. "I think there's something going on under the surface here," Clinton said to Penn.

She was worried that Obama's team seemed to be reaching out to a new universe of potential caucus-goers. Vilsack relayed to her that her rival's canvassers were knocking on doors of Republicans and independents—an unheard-of practice in Iowa's Democratic caucuses. Clinton wondered if her side should do the same or if she should be making a play for students, especially young women. But Hillary feared that her war vote would get her hooted off any campus where she spoke. And Vilsack and Vilmain assured her that come caucus night, if history was any guide, the non-Democrats would remain at home and the college kids, lazy or unserious, would stay in their rooms and on their Wiis.

Hillary was worried, too, that the caucus system was unfair. The process required that voters show up in person and hang around for several hours on a frigid January evening; absentee ballots weren't allowed. For people who worked the night shift, single mothers, the elderly, and active-duty military—all key elements of her constituency—the rules made it difficult or even impossible to participate.

She was worried about some indications that Iowa simply didn't cotton to female candidates. Recently, she'd been informed by the *Des Moines Register*'s David Yepsen, the dean of the Iowa press corps, that no woman had ever been elected to Congress or the governorship there. The factoid stunned Hillary—and she started repeating it constantly.

Yet in spite of all her worries, Clinton decided to double down on Iowa. Millions of additional dollars started pouring into the state. Her local advertising budget soared, her staff there was increased twofold, her calendar was packed with Iowa travel. Hillary hated spending the money but was convinced she had no choice. And the J-J had only reinforced that conviction. Within days, Penn's polling found that Obama was starting to open up a lead.

The political gamble here was evident, but the upside was huge: If Clinton carried the caucuses, the nomination would be in the bag. If she didn't, her strength in New Hampshire and the big states on Super Tuesday might dissipate. There was another gamble, however, involved in doubling down on Iowa—a financial wager that Solis Doyle and Harold Ickes laid out for her one day in her Senate office.

Hillaryland was burning cash at a prodigious rate, her advisers said. If she won Iowa, her fiscal health would be jake—money would come gushing in to her campaign's coffers. But if Clinton fell short in the Hawkeye State, a yawning deficit loomed.

Hillary was taken aback by the forecast. *Where in God's name did all the money go?* she thought. She looked at Solis Doyle and Ickes, set her jaw, and said, Well, then, I guess we'd better win Iowa.

Bill Clinton's involvement in his wife's campaign was still minimal at that point. He took part in few conference calls, had no briefing books, and was only rarely sent on the road to campaign for or with her. (The fear of him overshadowing Hillary persisted. Let's make sure that he's not going to get a bigger crowd than she's going to get, Solis Doyle told the Iowa staff whenever Bill visited for separate events.) But now his status was about to change.

Much of Clinton's political acumen lay in his ability to synthesize three streams of data: the polling, what was happening on the ground, and what was happening with the candidate. With Hillary's campaign, his intake had been limited mainly to the numbers being fed to him by Penn, and for much of the year, those numbers had been good—deceptively good. But now

Bill was hearing ominous chatter from the members of his old political circle, most of whom had either absented themselves from Hillaryland or been locked out. His friend Carville opined that Hillary's team was stocked with joyless misanthropes who loved neither politics nor people. Well, you have to call Hillary and tell her, Clinton said beseechingly.

Bill was keenly aware of Hillary's political (and human) liabilities, but he found it difficult to discuss them with her without raising her hackles. One day that fall, they were on a plane together and he tried to give his wife a pep talk, while at the same time gently broaching the topic of her perceived haughtiness. "I know you're working hard," he said, "but you need to let people know how hard you're working for *them*, and you have to really dig in there. There's a belief that you're above them, and you need to really let them know who you are."

"Bill, I'm working *eighteen hours a day*," Hillary snapped, ending the discussion.

The former president thought he could rely on Penn as his instrument inside of Hillary's campaign. But Penn was stymied in his efforts to go negative against Obama. His colleagues at headquarters and in Iowa were firmly opposed to running attack ads; the press showed little interest in the dirt the Clinton press shop was peddling under the table; and Hillary refused to rule in favor of strafing Obama.

The whole thing baffled Bill. Over the past months, his assessment of Obama had hardened. Yes, he was exciting. Yes, he was talented. Yes, he was the future. But he was also, Bill thought, an "off-the-rack Chicago politician" who had figured out how to have it both ways— appearing to be above bare-knuckle tactics while his team practiced them with a vengeance. In early November, for example, *The Atlantic* had published a story in which an unnamed Obama official plopped down next to the author and inquired as to "when reporters would begin to look into Bill Clinton's postpresidential sex life." The incident enraged Bill for reasons that went beyond the obvious. Obama was constantly bragging on the cleanness of his campaign. Yet no one in the media saw fit to call him out when his hired guns egged on the press to start rummaging around in Bill's boudoir. What more evidence did anyone need that the media was in the tank for Obama? It was as if the referees were on the field wearing the opposing team's jerseys, Clinton said.

Clinton grasped the rhythm of a presidential campaign as well as anyone alive. He knew there always came a moment, late in the game, when a candidate either found his voice or didn't, when the soufflé either rose or fell. For him, the moment had come in the autumn of 1991, with a series of third-way policy speeches that propelled him into the lead. Clinton could see that the J-J had done the same for Obama—and that his wife was headed in the opposite direction. Ever since Philly, the press had been all over Hillary, and not just about the debate. There were stories about her staff planting questions at town hall meetings in Iowa. About her failing to leave a tip at a Maid-Rite diner. She was being buffeted by external flaps, distracted by overblown hassles, coping with internal disagreements, and all the while not only failing to find her home-stretch groove, but looking ever more lost out there.

Hillary sensed it, too. Her Iowa stump speech was a themeless pudding, laundry-listy and flat, but she was too busy lurching from crisis to crisis to find time to fix it. The story about her not leaving a tip was bullshit, plain and simple, and the one about the planted questions . . . well, that was true, and, man, did she give her staff an earful about it. She asked them, What are we doing? We're supposed to have this organization that's the best in the world. Why do we keep making these mistakes? The press is gonna turn molehills into mountains, but can we please stop giving them so many molehills to work with?

One night around Thanksgiving, the Clintons held a private meeting with Penn to discuss what they should do to stanch the bleeding and turn Iowa around. Once again, Bill and Penn pressed the argument for going negative against Obama on TV. Hillary had been hitting Obama harder of late. ("Voters will judge whether living in a foreign country at the age of ten prepares one to face the big, complex international challenges the next president will face," she'd said in Iowa. "I think we need a president with more experience than that.") But her team was ineffective in backing her up when she took on Obama. She told Penn that she felt like a general running up a hill with a sword in her hand but no troops behind her. For months, she'd tried to stay on the high road—but now she'd had enough. She was ready, she announced to Penn and her husband, to commence the carpet-bombing.

Bill had definite ideas about how to nuke Obama. He was still obsessed, and so was Penn, with Obama's Iraq record. He was also fixated on Obama's habit of voting "present" in the Illinois state senate, his less-than-pristine history of taking campaign cash from lobbyists, and his ties to the shady Chicago developer Tony Rezko.

At Penn's instruction, Grunwald produced an array of ads revolving around those issues. She made harsh ads, mild ads, mean ads, funny ads—but when they were tested with Iowa voters, every one of them fell flat. Grunwald showed the spots to the Clintons at a meeting at Whitehaven. She explained her difficulty in finding anything that stuck. Bill told her to keep trying, offering ideas in granular detail about the scripts and visuals.

But nothing worked. It began to dawn on Grunwald that the problem was that Iowans simply didn't want to hear trash talk about Obama from Hillary. They liked him and they didn't like her, and there would be no changing that—her negatives were just too deeply cooked into the casserole.

The Clintons flew out to Iowa just after Thanksgiving in a state of irritation and anxiety. On the first night of December, they had drinks at Azalea, a swish restaurant in Des Moines, with the editorial board of the *Register* and some of its political reporters. Hillary was working hard for the paper's endorsement; Bill was gathering intelligence, chatting up the beat reporter who was covering Hillary's campaign. The reporter told him that the Obamans were regularly feeding her negative information about Hillary—but that no one from the Clinton team was doing the same regarding Obama.

When the drinks were over, Bill related the story to Hillary. The next morning, she woke up simmering— and then received yet more bad news. One of her most trusted aides confided that he'd spoken the night before with Karen Hicks, a veteran field organizer who had been dispatched to Des Moines to fortify the Iowa operation. Karen's unhappy, the aide told Hillary. The Iowa team isn't getting what it needs from headquarters. Phone calls aren't being returned. Decisions aren't getting made. Hillary's aide didn't cast blame explicitly on Solis Doyle or Henry, but Hillary had no difficulty in drawing the inference.

Clinton picked up the phone and got on the morning briefing call with her senior advisers—and promptly blew a gasket. Our communications shop isn't getting the job done, she growled, mentioning what she and Bill had learned during drinks the previous night. No one is engaging with reporters, she said. Nothing we throw at Obama is sticking. Everything he throws at us is. All the decision makers are back in Washington, doing God knows what. Clinton seethed uninterrupted for five minutes; when she finished, there was silence.

Finally, Solis Doyle offered meekly, "I'll have a plan for you this afternoon."

"I've been asking you this for weeks, Patti!" Hillary angrily replied.

After the call, Clinton phoned Solis Doyle directly and ordered her and all the rest of the Ballston high command to head to Iowa. You need to get out here,

Hillary said. This is too important. Pretend that nothing else exists in the country.

Clinton could hardly believe where she'd found herself five weeks out from caucus day. Frustrated, panicky, still steaming over what she'd learned that morning, she went before reporters at an afternoon news conference in Cedar Rapids. After criticizing Obama for insisting that his health care plan was universal when it wasn't, Clinton was asked if her opponent's lack of candor on the topic meant he had a character problem.

"It's beginning to look a lot like that," Hillary said. "I have said for months that I would much rather be attacking Republicans and attacking [the] problems of our country, because ultimately that's what I want to do as president. But I have been for months on the receiving end of rather consistent attacks—well, now the *fun* part starts."

9

THE FUN PART

For Obama, the fun part had already been under way for weeks. The J-J had been a slingshot for him; he was flying now. His media team put the speech front and center in TV advertising and direct mail. And its message became the core of what Obama was saying four or five or six times each day on the stump. At the end of November, the latest *Register* poll confirmed the Obama uptick: he was three points ahead of Clinton and four ahead of Edwards (a swing of ten and five points, respectively, since October). In early December, his friend Oprah Winfrey traveled to Des Moines and anointed him in front of eighteen thousand fans. "There are those who say it's not his time, that he should wait his turn," Oprah proclaimed. "I'm sick of politics as usual. We need Barack Obama."

Since the start of Obama's bid for the nomination, Plouffe had been chanting a mantra in his ear: "You need to own Iowa." Owning Iowa meant establishing a deep and intimate connection to the state. It meant visiting any county and remembering what had happened the last time he was there—whom he'd met, why they mattered. It meant doing more than appreciating the grassroots machine that Hildebrand and Tewes were building. It meant being invested in it, living it and breathing it, becoming one with it.

It took Obama a long time to get there, but now something had clicked. All of a sudden, he was asking, How many people am I getting? How many supporter cards? How many precinct captains? Instead of begging off making calls, he was reaching for the phone. At rallies, he started bringing organizers up onstage and giving props to them by name, a nice idea that impressed Plouffe all the more because it was Obama's. After town hall meetings, he would take a group picture with his volunteers—and then another with the high school students in attendance, because those who'd be eighteen by the general election were eligible to participate in the caucuses. To Penn, they might have looked like Facebook. To Obama, they looked like victory.

Obama was enjoying himself, too, at Hillary's expense. He and his advisers took no small pleasure in the planted-question story. (The Obama press shop pushed it sub rosa with reporters and found plenty of takers.) The episode was a perfect illustration of what Obama meant when he dissed "textbook" campaigns, and it reinforced the negative frame that Axelrod wanted to place around Hillary's portrait: that she'd do anything to win. At town halls, Obama would slyly mock Clinton by saying to the crowd, "You know what? Ask me any question. I haven't asked anybody here to ask me a certain question." The line always got a laugh.

As Clinton began to take more shots at Obama, his advisers—especially Axelrod and Gibbs, both summa cum laude graduates of the school of rapid-response politics—were dying to return fire. But many of her shots were so maladroit that Obama found them easy to slough off. On the day she announced that the fun part was starting, her campaign put out a press release that cited an "essay" written by a four- or five-year-old Obama with the title "I want to be president." (The point was that Obama was more ambitious than he pretended to be.)

"It's the silly season," Obama said with a shrug at an event that night in Des Moines. "I understand she's been quoting my kindergarten teacher in Indonesia."

Obama's team wanted to make even more hay with the kindergarten kerfuffle. One of his ad makers hacked together a goofy Web video featuring still photos of Obama as a child dressed up to look like a buccaneer. "Barack Obama wanted to be president when he was in kindergarten but there were other things he wanted—he wanted to be a pirate," the voice-over intoned melodramatically. "Do we really want a pirate president?" (Michelle put the kibosh on that idea; she thought it diminished her husband.)

Ambition wasn't the only youthful excess of Obama's that the Clinton campaign injected into the conversation, however. On December 12, Billy Shaheen, one of Hillary's national co-chairs and a veteran of New Hampshire politics, gave an interview to *The Washington Post* in which he cast doubt on Obama's electability.

"Republicans are not going to give up without a fight," Shaheen said, "and one of the things they're certainly going to jump on is his drug use"—a reference to Obama's acknowledgment in *Dreams* that he'd dabbled with cocaine and marijuana as a young man. "It'll be, 'When was the last time? Did you ever give drugs to anyone? Did you sell them to anyone?'"

Obama tried to brush off Shaheen's insinuations as garden-variety cheap politics. But it hadn't gone unnoticed by him that two Clinton volunteers had recently been caught forwarding emails suggesting that Obama was a Muslim with vague connections to jihadists trying to destroy America. Things seemed to be taking a turn for the ugly, and he and Michelle were certain it was no accident. Obama's brain trust agreed: Shaheen was acting as a puppet for one or both Clintons.

Their suspicions weren't unreasonable. The Clintons talked about Obama's drug use with some regularity in private, citing it as another example of the willful failure of the press to vet Obama. Why are they giving him a free ride on this? the couple would complain. Why isn't it out there?

Hillary's reaction to Shaheen's remarks was "Good for him!" Followed by "Let's push it out!" Her aides violently disagreed, seeing what Shaheen had said as a PR disaster. Grudgingly, Clinton acquiesced to disowning Shaheen's comments. But she wasn't going to cut him loose. Why should Billy have to fall on his sword, she asked, for invoking something that had been fair game in every recent election?

Hillary was in Washington for votes in the Senate. So was Obama. The next day, as both of them prepared to fly to Des Moines for another debate, they found themselves boarding their campaign planes at the same time at Reagan National Airport. One of the strangest things about presidential campaigns is how rarely the candidates are ever in close proximity to one another. They might greet voters one county apart or brush past each other in a debate hall, but private conversations almost never happen.

Yet now came an exception.

"Senator Clinton would like to speak with you," one of her advance people told Obama. Obama ambled over to Clinton as she stood there on the tarmac.

I'm sorry about what Billy said, Hillary began. I didn't know he was going to do that. I'm not running that kind of campaign.

That's fine, Hillary, Obama replied, but this wasn't an isolated incident. There were those emails in Iowa . . .

Now, hold on a second! Clinton said, cutting Obama off, uncorking the long list of grievances she'd been stewing on for months. What about Geffen? What about attacking her about her White House papers? The list went on and on.

For the next several minutes, the two went at it in animated fashion. Bug-eyed, red-faced, waving her arms, Hillary pointed at Obama's chest. Obama tried to calm her down by putting his hand on her shoulder— but that only made her angrier. Finally, they broke from the clinch, stalking back to their respective planes.

"Wow, that was surreal," Obama told Axelrod. He was struck by her fury, and more than that, he thought that she seemed shaken. "You could see something in her eyes," he said, something he hadn't seen before. Maybe it was fear. Maybe desperation. "You know what?" Obama said. "We're doing something right."

On her plane, Clinton related her interpretation of what had happened. I tried to apologize, she told her people, but then he started yelling. The way Obama came back at her told her that *he* was rattled. She couldn't believe he'd put his hand on her, violated her personal space. "He's got a lot of nerve," she said.

Later that day, Clinton, under pressure from her New Hampshire staff, agreed to excommunicate Shaheen. But she still had plenty of surrogates ready to sink their canines into Obama's keister. That night on MSNBC's *Hardball*, Penn appeared in a segment from the debate hall spin room with Trippi and with Axelrod via remote. Chris Matthews asked about the Clinton team's turn toward negativity, and Penn replied, "The issue related to cocaine use is not something that the campaign was in any way raising."

"He just did it again! He just did it again! Unbelievable!" Trippi interrupted indignantly, pointing at Penn. "He just said 'cocaine' again!"

"I think *you're* saying 'cocaine,'" Penn chuckled. "I think *you're* saying it."

Axelrod shook his head mournfully at the sleaziness on display. Trippi fulminated further. And Penn returned to Clinton's Des Moines headquarters giddy as a schoolgirl, giggling to his colleagues, "Did you notice how many times I said 'cocaine'?"

And then there was Hillary's husband. As part of a book tour to promote his latest tome, *Giving*, Bill Clinton appeared on *Charlie Rose* the night after the verbal fisti-cuffs on the tarmac. He spent most of the show talking earnestly about philanthropy, but when Rose nudged him into the realm of politics, he couldn't restrain him-self. A year's worth of agitation flooded out. Voters had to decide, Clinton said, if they wanted a nominee with the experience to be a change agent or were willing to "roll the dice" on "somebody who started running for president a year after he became a senator because he's fresh, he's new, he's never made a mistake, and he has massive political skills." Bill dinged Obama for repeating a "total canard" about his wife pursuing a decades-long scheme to run for president. He reamed out the press for being "stenographers" for Obama and attributed Barack's strength in Iowa to the fact that he lived in a neighbor-ing state. He predicted that people would "watch this interview and parse everything I said" in order to "get a political story and a fight going."

He was right about that. His denigration of Obama on the eve of the caucuses had everyone talking. But Clinton didn't care. His attitude toward politics was in some ways simple: always be on offense, never on defense; if someone is standing in your way, the only sensible course is to crush him. Fuck it, he thought. *Somebody has to say this stuff about Obama, and Hillary's campaign isn't going to. I know I shouldn't have done it, but I'm glad I did.*

Hillary didn't blame her husband for the controversy his comments engendered, in no small part because she believed that every word he said was true. But she could see that her side's negative barrage was backfiring, that it looked like indiscriminate flailing, that all the energy in Iowa remained with Obama.

Clinton began to despair. "If he's who they want, they can have him," she said dejectedly.

Then came a bolt from the blue. In years past in Iowa, the next most influential occurrence after the J-J had been the *Register* endorsement. Both sides had courted the paper assiduously, slavishly, and the Clintons especially so. (Vilsack plotted out their strategy; surrogates such as Madeleine Albright were enlisted to call ed-board members; and Bill laid the charm on thick with the editorial chief.) Because of the paper's leftish leanings, though, most believed Obama had it cinched.

Clinton happily learned otherwise on a frigid mid-December day while she was flying on a tiny chartered jet from New York to Washington. A loud, mysterious buzzing sound kept going off on the plane. Her Secret Service detail began to panic, thinking that it must be an emergency alarm. But then someone noticed an ancient air phone tucked under Hillary's seat. Headquarters was on the line with the good news about the *Register*. Clinton did a little dance for joy—it was the best news she'd heard in weeks.

Penn and others inside Hillaryland thought the *Register* endorsement could be a game changer. A rapid shift of strategy was called for. Out with the negative. In with the positive. Showcase Hillary's softer side. The internal advocates of humanizing her were thrilled, although they worried that it was too late. The price tag on the Iowa campaign was already stratospheric— more than $25 million had now been spent—but no expense would be spared in the last two weeks before the caucuses. To put Clinton in front of as many voters as possible, a private helicopter was secured. (The sleek, navy blue Bell 222 chopper was promptly christened the Hil-o-copter.) And, maybe most remarkable of all, Chelsea Clinton would hit the trail in Iowa.

She had done so only once before, a couple of weeks earlier, on the same day that Oprah arrived to campaign for Obama. Hillary detested the idea, fought it tooth and nail. Her protectiveness of Chelsea had been unwavering and fierce since the Clintons went national. Her daughter was an adult now, sure, old enough to make her own decisions. But Hillary was nervous anyway about throwing her into the middle of the mayhem—and if Chelsea made a mistake or was harassed, Hillary would feel the sting of responsibility.

The prohibition against deploying Chelsea—intelligent, poised, and charming as she was—struck many of Clinton's advisers as nuts. ("Is the daughter dead?" Vilmain asked incredulously on learning that Chelsea wouldn't be accompanying her parents on their July 4 Iowa swing.) And Chelsea desperately wanted to help, lobbying her mother insistently, enlisting aides to make her case. She knows you don't want her to do it, Clinton's traveling chief of staff, Huma Abedin, told Hillary. But *she* wants to do it—she keeps calling and telling me she wants to do it. Finally, Hillary relented.

For five days leading up to Christmas, Hillary embarked on what *The New York Times* described as a "likability tour" of Iowa. She brought her husband along to vouch for her warm and fuzzy side. She brought her best friend from sixth grade. She brought farmers from New York to tell Iowans how she'd helped them. She even brought Magic Johnson to a few events. Gone from her speeches were any strident tones. Speaking as if she were on Quaaludes, her voice was bedtime-story soft, her cadences syrupy slow. In a Des Moines grocery store, she told reporters, "I know that people have been saying, 'Well, you know, we've got to know more about her, we want to know more about her personally.' And I totally get that. It's a little hard for me. It's not easy for me to talk about myself."

The hokiness of Hillary's likability tour was over-powering—and the inconsistency of it with her message all year long even more so. But there were signs that whatever Clinton was doing, it was working.

A few days before Christmas, Hillary awoke to a new CNN poll that had her in first place in Iowa, two points ahead of Obama and four ahead of Edwards. On her staff call that morning, she was loose and frisky. Wolfson informed her that journalists thought her campaign had stabilized since the *Register* endorsement. Clinton agreed. Obama's support outside Des Moines is thin, she said. "We need to start thinking about Edwards." She mentioned that she'd seen him quoted saying he was the most consistent candidate among the Democrats.

Hillary scoffed. Edwards and Obama were very different cats, but they shared something in common. Both were "gripped in delusion," she said.

If Edwards had any doubts about his sanity, he didn't have to look far for signs that would assuage them.

The collective media assessment was that Iowa was still a down-to-the-wire three-way race, with an Edwards victory no less plausible than a Clinton or Obama win. In one twenty-four-hour stretch in mid-December, Edwards graced the cover of *Newsweek*—looking serious and determined, sleeves rolled up, tie loosened—flanked by the headline "The Sleeper"; appeared the same morning on *This Week with George Stephanopoulos* and *Face the Nation*; and received the endorsement of Iowa governor Chet Culver's wife, Mari, whose preference was seen by some as a proxy for her husband, who had pledged to stay neutral.

Edwards was bolstered on the trail by the presence of his children and Elizabeth, who had returned to the road after a month-long absence. During the four long weeks of her hiatus, John's advisers had fielded countless press calls asking about her health: Had it taken a turn for the worse? But now here she was, back on the hustings, as feisty and outspoken as ever, monitoring the debates, turning up on cable television, receiving wild cheers at rallies. Everything seemed to be back to normal.

Then the *Enquirer* struck again.

On December 18, the tabloid published a follow-up to its October exposé on Edwards's affair—and this one was a doozy. Whereas the first *Enquirer* story had failed to name Rielle Hunter, the new piece did that and much more. It included a photograph of her six months pregnant, and bore a headline that read "UPDATE: JOHN EDWARDS LOVE CHILD SCANDAL." And it claimed that Hunter had told "a close confidante that Edwards is the father of her baby!"

Team Edwards had known that the *Enquirer* story was coming for some time. Fred Baron, John's friend and finance chair, had scrambled to coordinate statements from lawyers for the candidate and Hunter denying John's paternity, which the piece included. It also introduced a new character to the drama: Edwards's longtime personal aide, Andrew Young, who was asserting that *he* was the father.

The details in the article around Young's involvement were as squirrely as could be. The *Enquirer* reported that Hunter was living in a rented house near the home of Young, his wife, and children in Governors Club, an exclusive gated community in Chapel Hill. When an *Enquirer* reporter confronted Young face-to-face, he first denied his identity and knowing Hunter—this despite the fact that the car she was driving was registered in his name—before announcing the next day through his attorney that he was the sire of the unborn baby. Drawing out the obvious implication from this curious chain of events, the story noted, "Some insiders wonder whether Young's paternity claim is simply a cover-up to protect his longtime pal Edwards."

The new *Enquirer* story rocked the Edwardsphere to its core. Crazy as it sounded, the idea that Young was taking the fall for John had the deafening ring of truth. An attorney in his early forties, Young had a history of run-ins with the law and a rumored alcohol problem. Though he'd done some fund-raising over the years, his main role with Edwards was menial: household chores, personal errands, airport runs for the family. His devotion to his boss was comically servile. One Edwards staffer liked to joke, "If John asked Andrew to wipe his ass, he would say, 'What kind of toilet paper?'"

Edwards denounced the *Enquirer* piece vehemently to his staff. On the campaign bus, he railed at the tabloid: "How could they fucking say this? How could they do this to me? How could they do this to Elizabeth?"

Some Edwards aides believed John's denials, thought the story was too far-out to be true. The campaign's press shop, as it had in October, moved rapidly to contain the damage. Between Edwards's and Hunter's categorical denials and Young's paternity claim, reporters would have a hard time advancing the narrative—the story might just be survivable.

But other Edwards staffers decided to stop spinning the candidate's disavowals to the media, so certain were they that their boss was lying. Too many of them knew that Young had talked openly about having a vasectomy a few years earlier, after the birth of his third child, sharing details with anyone who would listen. A bit of math and a glance at a calendar made clear that Hunter had gotten pregnant around June, within months of the recurrence of Elizabeth's cancer, right around the time Hunter popped up again. Despite the terrors Elizabeth inflicted on the staffers, their sympathy for her now was huge.

Elizabeth's presence back on the trail, however, created a situation of massive instability. Even before the second *Enquirer* piece, she had turned against Trippi and Jonathan Prince, her husband's deputy campaign manager. (Prince, she was sure, had helped facilitate the Hunter affair; Trippi had lost her confidence by becoming friends with Prince.) She was alternately paranoid about and jealous of their closeness to John, attempting to banish both advisers first from Iowa and then from the campaign bus. Before the final pre-Iowa debate in December, she insisted that they be excluded from John's prep sessions. John begged Trippi and Prince to understand. Elizabeth is a little upset right now, he said; she's going through a lot of stress. Edwards arranged to meet with the two aides secretly to get ready for the debate.

After the story broke, things went from bad to worse. John and Elizabeth were fighting all the time, sometimes all night long. More than once, she announced to the staff that she could no longer speak in public on her husband's behalf or stay in the same hotel with him. Once, in the middle of the night, she woke up a trip director and commanded, Get me out of here! I'm not campaigning for this asshole another day!

At other times, Elizabeth seemed intent on convincing herself that Young was indeed the father. She ordered the campaign staff to assemble an elaborate chronology of the previous months, establishing the nights when Young and Hunter might have been in the same city. "When were they together?" she demanded. "We need to figure this out, how many times they were together."

It's been a humiliating few weeks, Elizabeth told a friend. I wish I could wring Andrew Young's neck.

One night in the last week before the caucuses, she and John had dinner at Azalea with Kim Rubey and David Ginsberg, two of the former aides from 2004 who had left the Edwardsphere in large part because of the looming threat of Hunter. They had come to Des Moines with mixed emotions and motives: to help their old colleagues handle the mammoth workload and to witness the final days of Edwards as a presidential candidate. They had been there at the start. They wanted to be there at the end. And they believed this *was* the end.

Edwards had invited Ginsberg and Rubey to supper after seeing them at one of his events. He seemed touched that they were in Iowa, in light of the circumstances, about which he knew they were better versed than most.

"Can you believe this is Andrew?" Elizabeth said over dinner. "How has Andrew done this to our family?" She solicited everyone's opinion about Young and Hunter. Had Ginsberg and Rubey ever seen them together?

The two former aides squirmed in their seats and held their tongues—while John sat staring silently at them from across the table. They left the dinner astonished by Elizabeth's herculean efforts at willingly suspending disbelief. But as disquieting for them as the scene at Azalea was, even more disturbing was the possibility that they were wrong about how Edwards would fare in Iowa. What if he won? What would they do? What *should* they do?

The thought was occurring in the minds of many old Edwards hands that week, in Iowa and farther afield. The mainstream media, yet again, was determinedly ignoring the *Enquirer.* If that trend continued, there was a chance, however remote, that John could win the nomination—and thus deliver the White House to the GOP on a platter when the story eventually, inevitably, was proved true.

Tentatively, unhappily, but soberly and seriously, the Edwards old guard began discussing their obligation to the party to come forward with what they knew. When should they leak the truth to *The Washington Post* or *The New York Times*? Which of them would make the call?

Two days after Christmas, Obama delivered what his aides billed as his "closing argument" in Iowa, in the basement of the Scottish Rite Temple in Des Moines. With a law professor's attention to detail and a litigator's argumentativeness—plus a hint of the defensiveness of a politician under fire—he included rebuttals to almost every criticism that Clinton had hurled at him down the homestretch. For a month he'd been telling Axelrod he still wasn't happy with his response to the charge of insufficient experience. But his research team helped him solve that puzzle with the discovery of a quote from a source both gilt-edged and delicious to invoke.

"The truth is, you can have the right kind of experience and the wrong kind of experience," Obama said in the Masonic temple's basement. "Mine is rooted in the real lives of real people and it will bring real results if we have the courage to change. I believe deeply in those words. But they are not mine. They were Bill Clinton's in 1992, when Washington insiders questioned his readiness to lead."

For all Obama's confidence, however, his advisers were worried about Hillary's apparently strong last-minute push and Edwards's entrenched and loyal following. The Obama campaign's internal tracking poll on December 27 made the race a three-way tie, with Clinton and Edwards at 26 percent and Obama at 25. The trouble was, the trend lines were moving in the wrong direction. By December 30, the final Obama tracking numbers were Clinton, 27; Edwards, 26; Obama, 24. But the Obama campaign was still phone-banking like mad, calling thousands of voters a day. The calls, his team was pleased to discover, suggested more support for Obama than their tracking poll did, and they all had faith in their turnout operation.

As he headed for his final event in an eventful year, at Iowa State University, in Ames, Obama was exhausted. A quiet dinner with his wife was on the schedule for late that night. For all her reluctance at the outset, Michelle had poured her heart into Iowa in the closing days. Every voter who met her loved her. Her skill at inducing supporters to sign up had become legend. Michelle was competitive. She was constantly teasing Barack about how she was better at the game than he was. "I got fifteen supporter cards today," she said to him. "What'd you do?"

What greeted Obama at Iowa State on New Year's Eve was a healthy crowd and an extraordinary piece of news: the results of the last *Register* poll before the caucuses on January 3, ricocheting from BlackBerry to cell phone. Everyone had been on tenterhooks for the *Register*'s results. The paper's polling team was highly esteemed, with a long-held reputation for producing numbers of startling accuracy. And these were certainly startling: Obama, 32; Clinton, 25; Edwards, 24. The assumptions beneath the numbers were even more eye-popping. The paper forecast "a dramatic influx of first-time caucusgoers, including a sizable bloc of political independents," with both groups heavily favoring Obama.

Onstage, a hoarse Obama reveled in the numbers: "Up six points, maybe it's seven. Six or seven. It's beyond the margin of error. So we might just pull this thing off. We might just pull this thing off, Iowa. Who woulda thunk it?"

For the rest of the night, the wails of Clinton and Edwards operatives could be heard above the clink of champagne flutes all over Des Moines. At the 801 Grand steak house, Trippi piled into the booth of every journalist in sight and explained in numbing detail the glaring flaws in the poll's methodology: too many first-time voters, too many independents, a turnout model that defied the laws of caucus physics. (In 2004, 124,000 showed up; the *Register* seemed to be predicting at least 220,000 this year.) And Vilsack, who knew the caucuses like the back of his hand, took one look at the numbers and said, "That can't be right."

The Clintons didn't know what to think. After all the confidence that stirred before Christmas, their postholiday return to Iowa brought back a familiar disquiet. Outside a church in Indianola one frosty morning, Hillary made a surprise visit to her press bus, bringing the reporters hot coffee and bagels, making a joke at the expense of her spokesman, expressing her sympathies with those who were away from their "significant others"—and was greeted with stony silence. "Why do they hate me so much?" she asked one of her aides plaintively afterward.

Hillary had labored hard to comprehend the rules of the caucus system, and now she finally understood enough—enough to worry, that is. There were successive rounds of voting, with candidates who didn't get 15 percent of the attendees at a caucus site forced out after each round. Her campaign had hoped to strike deals with Biden and Richardson to send their voters to

Clinton if they failed to reach the threshold. But the negotiations had fallen apart. Hillary considered Biden and Richardson friends (though the former more so than the latter). Why weren't they being more cooperative?

On caucus eve, January 2, Clinton's spirits brightened momentarily. Her final rally at the Iowa Historical Society was jam-packed, the music thumping, the reception for her rapturous. Backstage afterward, she and Bill talked with Vilsack and McAuliffe—both of whom were flying high, telling her she was either going to win or come in a close second.

The next morning, however, an email arrived in Hillary's in-box from Penn. The pollster was hedging his bets. If turnout was similar to 2004, then Clinton would do just fine, Penn said. But if turnout was "radically different," it would be because of "another organization," and "the outcome will be radically different."

Hillary went apeshit and called Solis Doyle, demanding an explanation.

"I'm as stunned as you are," her campaign manager replied.

Hillary was still agitated when she got on her final pre-caucus conference call with her team that afternoon. Everyone else was tense and anxious, too. Curtly, she thanked the group and hung up. Then she hunkered down with her husband to await the returns.

Around seven o'clock, McAuliffe wandered over to the campaign's second-floor boiler room in the Hotel Fort Des Moines. Thirty-odd kids hunched over computers, monitoring the turnout numbers as they came in from caucus sites around the state. Every so often someone would yell out an overall turnout estimate: 125! 140! 150! As the numbers kept climbing—165! 185! 195! 205!—McAuliffe started to wonder if something was wrong. He glanced over at Vilmain. She looked like she'd been hit with a poleaxe. Wolfson, walking by on his way to grab some pizza, said, "We're gonna get our asses kicked."

McAuliffe asked Vilmain if it was true. She said it was.

"Someone needs to prepare Hillary," McAuliffe said. "Are we going to get second?"

"Probably not."

Just then, McAuliffe's BlackBerry buzzed. Bill Clinton's counselor, Doug Band, had emailed: the former president wanted to see him upstairs, and pronto.

The next four hours were a blur for Hillary Clinton. Reeling from the loss, she appeared onstage for a televised speech surrounded by old and pale faces— Madeleine Albright, Wesley Clark, her husband—that created an unflattering contrast with the young and multiracial tableau presented by Obama. Back upstairs at the hotel, she had to be coaxed into thanking her Iowa staff and major fund-raisers, who were gathered in a nearby suite. "Yeah, okay," she said. Standing on a chair, steadied by McAuliffe, she told the crowd that everything would be all right. It was just one loss, the race ahead would be long; she was on to New Hampshire. But the expression on her face belied her words: with her frozen smile, her dazed eyes, she looked as if she were having an out-of-body experience.

Returning to her suite, Clinton found it even more crowded than before. Chelsea was there, along with Hillary's mother, Dorothy Rodham, who sat on the bed looking inconsolable. Vilsack walked over to Hillary and apologized for having been too optimistic. "I'm sorry," he said. "I thought we could win."

"It's okay," she said—but didn't mean it.

Hillary began to pack her things. She was eager to put Iowa behind her and move on to the Granite State. But its primary was just five days away. The Clintonites had to decide, and decide right then, how they were going to halt the momentum that Obama now possessed—in particular, if they were finally going to go full-on negative, blasting him with both barrels, including TV ads.

Most of Clinton's advisers remained uneasy at the prospect—and now there was the risk, too, of making Hillary seem a sore and desperate loser.

"Can we win with a positive message?" Wolfson asked.

"I don't think so," Hillary said. "I don't know what it would be. I'm open to suggestions."

"This may be a movement," Wolfson said. "It's tough to beat a movement."

Penn could barely believe his ears. "We didn't go negative here, and it cost us!" he snapped at his colleagues. "This is what we have to do! This is how we're going to survive and win!"

Bill Clinton took control of the meeting. His instincts had all along aligned with Penn's, and now he'd been proved right. Hillary's team had told him that she couldn't win Iowa if she went negative . . . and she'd finished third. *The hell with this,* Clinton thought.

He demanded to see the best negative television ads the campaign already had in the can. Grunwald sat down next to him on the couch and opened her laptop. Over the past few months, she'd made literally hundreds of negative Obama spots—not one of which, she believed, would have done them a bit of good.

Bill studied the available options, then polled the room: Should they go negative or not? Penn, McAuliffe, and Vilsack said yes. Everyone else said no.

It was nearly midnight now. An overnight flight to New Hampshire awaited them. As the suite emptied out, they all assumed that the negative air war would begin the next day—if only because the former president was adamantly in favor.

Yet no one really knew where Hillary Clinton stood. She went back and forth. Throughout the campaign, her uncertainty at crucial junctures had been profound, but never more so than it was at that moment. All the past year, during which she'd been the undisputed leader in the race, Grunwald had reminded her that front-runners never waltzed to the nomination. Somewhere along the line, they inevitably received a shock, an event that threatened to topple them from their pedestal, but which they almost always survived.

Clinton was versed enough in history to know that it was true. But this felt more like a coronary event than a typical front-runner's scare. Sitting on her small private jet before it took off for New Hampshire, she leaned back and called Penn, who was flying in a separate plane with McAuliffe and the press corps.

The confusion that gripped her went beyond questions of strategy and tactics, beyond going negative or not. It went to the existential core of her candidacy. In a voice infinitely weary, Clinton asked her Svengali, "What are we going to do now?"

As Penn started to answer, his plane took off. Hillary heard only static.

10

TWO FOR THE PRICE OF ONE

She touched down in Manchester before dawn that Friday morning, January 4, traveled north to the Centennial Hotel in Concord, cleaned up, changed clothes, then headed back south to Nashua to begin her five-day sprint for salvation. Parlous as her circumstances were, bedraggled as she was from lack of sleep, Hillary took comfort in the steadier footing she had on this fresh soil. If Iowa was terra incognita for her, New Hampshire was terra firma: familiar, friendly, safe. There were no byzantine rules to deal with here, just one that made perfect sense: whoever gets the most votes wins. And hustling and rustling votes in New Hampshire was a Clinton specialty.

Hillary knew she had to make changes, big changes, and had to make them fast. The near-universal assumption was that Obama's momentum from Iowa would propel him to a win in New Hampshire, where he'd already been gaining ground. A fight the previous year between states jockeying for electoral influence had pushed New Hampshire to hold its primary much sooner than normal after Iowa. No one could be sure how that would shape the dynamics of the race, but Clinton's supporters feared—and her rival's fans hoped—that it would favor Obama. And that a second quick victory would all but ensure him the nomination.

As Hillary's big red-white-and-blue bus rumbled down Interstate 293, she thought about the advice that Bill had given her that morning: she should do more town hall meetings, take questions from her crowds, engage more directly with voters. That was how he turned things around in New Hampshire back in 1992, when he was on the ropes because of Gennifer Flowers, the draft, and all of that. Hillary could see the logic, though she didn't embrace the whole connecting thing with the relish that her husband did. "It would be a mistake not to appear more open"—not *be* more open, but *appear* that way—was how she put it to her senior staff on her early morning briefing call.

But when her bus rolled into the airplane hangar at Boire Field, where her first rally was being held, she discovered that her New Hampshire team apparently hadn't gotten the memo. Her state director, Nick Clemons, ran through the program: give your speech, pump up the crowd, don't take questions from the audience, hightail it out of there. Hillary shook her head and said, "I'm taking questions." Clemons tried to dissuade her, said they didn't want to drain the energy from the room. Thank you for the advice, Hillary said firmly, but I'm gonna take *every* question.

Backstage, Bill paced back and forth, talking to their old friend Terry Shumaker about the uphill climb they were facing. We could turn this around if we had the traditional eight days between Iowa and New Hampshire, he said. "I'm just not sure we have enough time."

The first-person plural was no slip of the tongue. For a year, Hillary had been content to keep her husband at arm's length, but now she pulled him close. Nobody knew New Hampshire the way Bill Clinton did. He had been to every town and hamlet, remembered the locals and the layout, the demographics, where every cache of votes was stored. For the next hundred hours, until the polls closed on Tuesday, Hillary and Bill would run her campaign together. She needed his expertise, his feel for the state, its quirks and biorhythms. She needed him for his doggedness, his buoyancy, and his trademark Houdini juju. She needed him because, even on his worst day, he was a font of ideas about how to win—as opposed to everyone else on her campaign, whom she increasingly saw as completely and maddeningly useless.

Take the conference call that morning, for instance. For the first time anybody could remember, Bill was on the line—and what he heard confirmed all his doubts about his wife's operation. Here she was, hanging by her fingertips, trying to hatch a comeback plan. And there was her team, beaten down, barely capable of speech. Penn's voice was so thick and sluggish that it sounded like he was drugged. Solis Doyle was inexplicably absent. When Hillary rattled off her analysis of what had gone wrong in Iowa—they'd "ceded people under thirty," appealed to older women at the expense of younger ones, made "a big mistake in not recognizing that Edwards was an equal threat"—her advisers added nothing. When she offered remedies, they offered silence. "We need to do things differently," Hillary said. "We need to mix it up."

More silence.

"This has been a very instructive call, talking to myself," she said. "Goodbye."

Exasperated though she was, only Hillary could resolve the open question from the night before: Were they going to run negative TV ads against Obama? She turned to Grunwald, a veteran of New Hampshire campaigns, including Bill's in 1992. Grunwald contended that there wasn't enough time to accomplish much by blitzing Obama from the air. Better for Hillary to throw herself into the New Hampshire mosh pit and body-slam him there.

Bill and Penn were all for the slamming, naturally. Penn's analysis was that, unlike Iowa, New Hampshire had been for Hillary all year long—and though Obama's big mo would cause some voters to shift to him, she could get them back (especially the women) if she laid out sharp and specific contrasts. A debate was set for the following night, January 5, at Saint Anselm College, just outside Manchester, among the four candidates still standing after Iowa: Clinton, Obama, Edwards, and Richardson. It was there, Clinton's advisers all agreed, that she would begin her anti-Obama counteroffensive.

Bill showed up at her debate prep session—another first—full of piss and vinegar. Still steaming over how Obama must have cheated in Iowa, he argued for Hillary to pop him hard with that accusation in the debate. Around the room at the Centennial, her advisers squirmed; it was tough to tell a former president that his advice was loopy. Hillary had a different idea: she wanted to whack Obama for his inconsistency on health care. And when debate time came, that was what she did.

Obama defended himself—but not as stridently as Edwards defended him. "Senator Obama and I have differences," Edwards said, "but both of us are powerful voices for change. . . . What will occur every time he speaks out for change, every time I fight for change, the forces of [the] status quo are going to attack. Every single time!"

Double-teamed, Hillary hit back. "Making change is not about what you believe, it's not about a speech you make," she said. "I think it is clear that what we need is somebody who can deliver change. And we don't need to be raising the false hopes of our country about what can be delivered." A few minutes later one of the moderators asked what Hillary would say to voters who regarded Obama as more likable than her. "Well, that hurts my feelings, but I'll try to go on," she said, with a wistful smile. "He's very likable. I agree with that. I don't think I'm *that* bad."

Obama glanced up from his notes and said icily, "You're likable enough, Hillary."

After the debate, Hillary marveled, yet again, at the insufferability of Obama's arrogance. And also at another instance of the double standard applied to the two of them. Can you imagine if I'd made a crack like that? she complained to her aides. The press would've guillotined her on the spot and played soccer with her severed head.

That night Penn publicly released a memo that questioned why, even after Iowa, Obama and Hillary were still tied in New Hampshire polls; its headline was "Where Is the Bounce?" By the next day, he had his answer. A new round of surveys showed Obama pulling ahead to a double-digit lead. Hillary's donors were in a panic. Advice was gushing in from every quarter—over the heads and around the backs of her top advisers. Chelsea and Carson cornered Hillary on her bus, arguing that she had to be more accessible to the reporters, chatting them up, schmoozing them off the record, traveling with them, having a press availability every day.

Out on the trail, Hillary was doing all of that and more, almost pleading with people not to be stampeded into voting for Obama. "Everybody needs to be tested and vetted," she said. "The last thing Democrats need is to just move quickly through this process."

Meanwhile, Bill was on the phone with Clemons, probing him about how they might make up ground, strategizing with Hillary at the hotel—taking advantage of a rare five nights under the same roof. The Clintons thought they were feeling tremors, seeing encouraging signs. Her staffers thought they were tripping. One likened the couple to a pair of dying patients delirious from too much morphine.

Early Monday morning, with just a day to go, Hillary summoned Solis Doyle to her suite in the Centennial.

What's going on? Clinton asked her campaign manager. Where do things stand?

Solis Doyle had anticipated this talk and had been dreading it. The polling, the money, the press—all were deeper in the shithouse than Hillary knew, and the implications even grimmer. *Someone has to be straight with her,* Solis Doyle thought. *Who else is gonna tell her?*

But Patti didn't want to tell her then, not just as Hillary was about to head out for her last full day of campaigning before the primary. You're gonna be late for your first event, Solis Doyle said. You don't want to have this conversation now.

I want to do it now, said Hillary.

Solis Doyle sat down across the table from her boss and sketched out the dismal picture. Penn's data matched the public polls: Hillary was going to lose New Hampshire, probably by a lot, and it was even possible that she would finish third, behind Edwards. The most influential union in Nevada, the culinary workers, had decided to endorse Obama, which would likely tip the caucuses there two weeks later to him. After Obama's win in Iowa, African Americans were swinging hard his way, and given the size of the black vote in South Carolina, Hillary would definitely lose there, too. She had $18 million in the kitty to get her through Super

Tuesday, when twenty-two states would hold contests awarding more than half the total pledged delegates at stake. But once she lost New Hampshire, her fundraising was bound to dry up, while Obama's would go through the ceiling.

Hillary was taken aback. What do you think I should do? she asked.

Look, I love you, Solis Doyle said. My primary concern is you and your future. We need to think about how four straight losses are going to look. You're an icon now, but if you stay in the race and embarrass yourself, that could be destroyed. Maybe the right thing to do is just drop out after New Hampshire.

Hillary reeled. From the start, people had warned her not to put Solis Doyle in the campaign manager's chair. And Hillary knew well that Patti had her weaknesses. But she had decided to ignore all that, to disregard the risks, because of Solis Doyle's signal virtue: a loyalty so fierce that she would run through a wall for Hillary. But after one setback, one lousy loss, Patti was ready to surrender. The person she thought would be the last to abandon her had turned out to be the first. She struggled for air. She struggled for words. She muttered a few things.

I don't want women out there to see me as a quitter, Hillary said limply.

Solis Doyle, on the brink of tears, forced herself to continue. If you're gonna stay in, she said, you're gonna have to make a show of shaking up the campaign. You're gonna have to fire people, and bring in some new ones.

As they talked, Bill walked in and asked what was going on. Hillary told him that Solis Doyle was raising the idea that she drop out. It rang familiar. Sixteen years earlier, in his darkest hour in New Hampshire, some of Bill's aides had recommended that he withdraw. But his credo then was the same as it was now: Fighting hard and losing was honorable. Throwing in the towel was not. Strange stuff happens in campaigns. He had well earned his reputation as a survivor, and in her own way, Hillary had, too. So much bound them together, but one ingredient at that moment was predominant: Clintons aren't quitters.

"As long as you have enough money for an airline ticket," Bill told Hillary, "you should go out there and make your case about why you would make the best president."

The Clintons were both running late for their first events of the day. Solis Dolis told her boss, We're definitely going to talk about this later; this isn't a closed conversation.

Hillary went downstairs, got on her bus, and set off for her morning stop: a roundtable with undecided voters at a coffeehouse in Portsmouth. Huma Abedin noticed that Hillary seemed out of sorts, emotional, and raw. Inside the café, in her sapphire-blue pantsuit with the black piping, she sat down and took questions. Someone asked innocuously how she kept herself looking so good despite the rigors of campaigning. "It's not easy," she started to answer, "and I couldn't do it if I didn't passionately believe it was the right thing to do. You know, I have so many opportunities from this country. I just don't want to see us fall backward."

The next thing she knew, her eyes were welling up, her voice was quaking, and words were escaping from her lips that sounded like they'd come from someone else . . . someone vulnerable. "You know," she said, "this is very personal for me—it's not just political, it's not just public. I *see* what's happening."

On TV, the talking heads said (wrongly) that tears were streaming down her cheeks. Solis Doyle was in a meeting when she heard that Hillary had broken down. A wave of guilt rushed over her.

Fuck. I did this, she thought.

Obama was on his campaign bus that Monday morning, rolling between events in Lebanon and Rochester, when one of his aides pulled up video on his laptop of Clinton's display. The members of his brain trust issued a collective snort of derision. Some called it a "Muskie moment"—a reference to Ed Muskie in 1972 weeping in the back of a flatbed truck in Manchester, thereby dooming himself in New Hampshire. Others thought Hillary was faking it. But Obama expressed some sympathy for his shaken rival. "You know what, guys?" he said to his team. "This isn't easy."

Then again, Obama could afford to be gracious. He was staring at a certain loser.

The past three days had been an exultant blur for Obama, a march to assured victory. He had sailed into New Hampshire with the winds of history and destiny apparently gusting at his back. Everywhere he went, the crowds were massive, overflowing, with lines of people stretching for blocks, waiting for hours in the frigid air to catch a glimpse of him, soak up his soaring cadences. Even the most hard-bitten members of the press were agog at what was unfolding before their eyes. Obama's donors were flying in from around the country to witness the coronation.

Obama took it all in stride. This was how it was supposed to happen—the dominoes were falling in just the way that Axelrod and Plouffe had predicted. His brain trust told him about the offer that Daschle had conveyed from Edwards the night before: that the North Carolinian was prepared to drop out of the race and become Barack's running mate, driving a stake through Clinton's heart. Obama rejected the entreaty out of hand. By winning the Granite State, he could plunge that dagger in all by himself. What did he need Edwards for?

Obama's confidence in New Hampshire was over-whelming—and overweening. On his first day in the state, he declared to *Newsweek*, "At some point people have to stop asserting that because I haven't been in the league long enough, I can't play. It's sort of like Magic Johnson or LeBron James who keep on scoring and their team wins. But people say they can't lead their team because they're too young."

Obama had won just one caucus, but that didn't faze him. He was cruising now. In Iowa, his campaign had been relentless in responding to attacks. But in New Hampshire, when Hillaryland sent out direct mail assailing him for voting "present" on abortion legislation in the Illinois state senate, the Obamans more or less let it slide. The candidate was too busy talking about hope to stoop to refutation. He didn't add a jot of substance to his economic message (this in a state where kitchen table issues were always paramount). He went from mega-rally to mega-rally, eschewing town hall meetings. All of a sudden, the narrative line of 2007 was flipped on its head. The insurgent candidate was running on inevitability. He was going to win because he was going to win.

But if Obama was unperturbed by Clinton's near-tears moment, his brain trust was slightly rattled. The last thing Obama needed was people feeling sorry for Hillary Clinton. The suits cringed at Edwards's ungallant reaction: "I think what we need in a commander in chief is strength and resolve, and presidential campaigns are tough business, but being president of the United States is also tough business."

Back at Obama's New Hampshire headquarters, Plouffe monitored the wall-to-wall media coverage of Clinton in the café. Now dominating the final news cycle before the voting began, it threatened to scramble the dynamic in unpredictable ways.

Plouffe, his stomach churning, phoned Axelrod and said, "I don't like this."

Hillary didn't like it, either. She thought it was a Muskie moment, too. Having labored so long to highlight her strength, to prove to the world she was tough enough to be commander in chief, she worried that she had blown it with one ill-timed display of the turmoil bubbling just below the surface. One of her aides tried to ease her mind by pointing out that crying had become fashionable in politics: "Bush can tear up! Mitt Romney can

tear up! All the guys are tearing up!" Hillary couldn't
see how the analogies applied. "I didn't cry," she kept
insisting. It made you seem real, seem human, some of
her advisers argued. But the realm of emotional resonance was, for her, a foreign country. "I'm an *information* person," she said.

The rest of Hillary's day was no less eventful. At
her next stop on the trail, a gym in Dover, she gave
an interview to Fox News in which she responded to
Obama's claim that she was denigrating the value of
leaders, such as Martin Luther King, Jr., whose stock
in trade was the raising of hopes. "Dr. King's dream
began to be realized when President Johnson passed
the Civil Rights Act," Clinton said. "It took a president
to get it done."

Hillary's point was that words alone weren't enough
to effect change. But the interview caused a flap on
cable TV and the blogs, where it was cast by some as a
slight against King. The Clinton campaign realized immediately that what Hillary had said was problematic,
and she moved quickly to walk it back, inserting remarks into an early evening speech in Salem effusively
praising King.

While Hillary was trying to dance delicately through
a minefield of racial sensitivities, Bill was working the
remote western and northern parts of the state. At a

town hall meeting at Dartmouth College, in Hanover, he uncorked the argument that he and Penn had been longing to make for a year. Hoarse-voiced and finger-wagging, he ripped into Obama's claims of antiwar purity and the media's complicity in letting those claims go unchallenged:

"It is wrong that Senator Obama got to go through fifteen debates trumpeting his superior judgment and how he had been against the war in every year, enumerating the years, and never got asked one time—not once!—'Well, how could you say that when you said in 2004 you didn't know how you would have voted on the resolution? You said in 2004 there was no difference between you and George Bush on the war and you took that speech you're now running on off your website in 2004 and there's no difference in your voting record and Hillary's ever since.'

"*Give . . . me . . . a . . . break*," the former president moaned. "This whole thing is the biggest fairy tale I've ever seen!"

And Clinton was just getting warmed up. "What did you think about the Obama thing, calling Hillary the 'Senator from Punjab?' Did you like that?" he continued. "Or what about the Obama handout that was covered up, the press never reported on, implying that I was a crook, *scouring* me, *scathing* criticism over my financial reports. . . . The idea that one of these campaigns is positive and the other is negative, when I know the reverse is true and I have seen it and I have been blistered by it for months, is a little tough to take. Just because of the sanitizing coverage that's in the media doesn't mean the facts aren't out there."

Bill was infinitely pleased with his performance. "I thought that was good, didn't you?" he said to an aide as he pulled out of Hanover. Back at the Centennial afterward, he told Penn and others, "I finally was able to get the whole case out there."

The morning of the primary, the Clintons woke up girding themselves for defeat. But Hillary kept working with manic intensity all day, scrounging for every last vote. She visited four polling places and a Dunkin' Donuts (shades of 1992 again) before noon, then interrupted an afternoon nap to cram in one last campaign event in Manchester.

The rest of her day was a swirl of intrigue and whispered conversations. If Hillary was to be defeated in New Hampshire, the Clintons had decided they would hang a silver lining around the loss. For days before Solis Doyle suggested a shake-up, the couple had been discussing a retooling of Hillary's plainly dysfunctional campaign. After Iowa, their friends, associates, and informal advisers had started filling their ears with long-suppressed complaints about Solis Doyle and Penn. The chief strategist's bond with the Clintons was too durable for Penn to get the axe. ("You're indispensable," Hillary emailed him.) But Solis Doyle, her relationship with Hillary irreparably ruptured by their conversation the previous day, would be demoted. And a clutch of old Clinton hands would be imported to right the ship: Texan adman Roy Spence; Bill's former White House political director, Doug Sosnik; and Hillary's former chief of staff, Maggie Williams, whom she wanted to run the show.

Solis Doyle was getting ready for breakfast with a reporter when an email arrived from Hillary. Its subject line: "Moving forward." A number of our friends who have our best interests at heart have suggested that we need a new team, Hillary wrote with odd formality. Solis Doyle would retain her title but would relinquish much of her responsibility to Williams.

Patti read the message and cried. She'd suggested that Hillary needed to make changes, but never really thought she'd be the one to take the hit. Hillary loved her like a daughter. (*Supposedly*, Patti thought.) Being dumped via email—the indignity was almost as bad as the betrayal. (*Pick up the phone, at least!*) Solis Doyle believed that she'd done a good job, that many of the campaign's flaws could be laid at Hillary's feet. She was prepared to take her share of the blame. But keep her job in name only and let Williams run everything? No way.

I understand, she emailed Clinton, but I really don't want to stay on. I'll do everything I can to help with the transition, but I don't want my title. I'll just go home to my kids.

Hillary emailed her back: I don't accept your resignation.

For the next several hours, Solis Doyle's closest friends in Hillaryland streamed in and out of her room. Wolfson, Tanden, Ickes, Henry—all sat shiva with Solis Doyle, who alternated between disbelief and hysteria. Everyone agreed that if Hillary lost, they would quit en masse. Everyone agreed that it should have been Penn who was given the boot.

By late afternoon, as word seeped out into the campaign, Hillary started hearing from those who thought getting rid of Solis Doyle would be a mistake. Too many people in Ballston are loyal to Patti, Ickes told Clinton. The move would cause too much chaos at a time when order—and the perception of order—was vital.

Hillary hated personal conflict, avoided it like the plague—hence the demotion via email. But around five o'clock, she went up to Patti's room and knocked on the door.

"Let's talk turkey," Hillary said with forced cheer as she walked in, trying to lighten the mood. And then, even more awkwardly, "Let's talk ham. Let's talk tortillas."

The attempt at levity did nothing to lessen Solis Doyle's discomfort. Sitting down on the bed, Hillary asked her to stay: People are gonna leave if you leave, they need you around, you're the glue, I can't do this without you, she said. Solis Doyle told Hillary she'd think about it. What she told herself was, *I'm outta here.*

After Hillary left, Wolfson trundled in, bearing data from the first wave of exit polls.

"Can you believe this?" he said. "We may only lose by single digits."

Solis Doyle tried to be happy. But it felt to her like someone had died.

Barack and Michelle had a bad feeling the whole day. Michelle was especially edgy. At lunch at their hotel in Nashua, though the polls had been open only a few hours, she dispatched Jarrett to Axelrod and Plouffe's table to ask if they'd heard anything about how things were going.

The first wave of exit polls from the networks late that afternoon began to provide an answer, and not the one the Obamans were expecting. The early returns from blue-collar Manchester were terrible, the first indication that Obama might have trouble with white working-class voters. The suits kept Obama apprised as the numbers went from worrying to scary to depressing. Standing in the hallway in front of his boss's suite, Axelrod said dejectedly, "It looks like she may inch us out."

Jarrett came up from her room and found the Obamas swallowing hard to choke down the bitter pill. *What on earth am I going to say to make this okay?* she thought.

But before Jarrett had a chance to open her mouth, Barack put one hand on her shoulder and said, "This is going to be a good thing. You'll see."

Michelle was steelier, less reassuring. "This is going to be a test," she said. "It's going to be a test to see if they're really with us or not."

In the Clinton suite up in Concord, however, there was less certainty that the primary was truly over. Hillary, who made a practice of never watching election returns on TV, was nowhere to be seen. Her husband, in a pair of jeans and a sweater, his reading glasses perched on his nose, presided over the room with his game face on, serious and concerned.

Bill was closely monitoring the late returns from the Hanover area, eager to see if his broadside at

Dartmouth had worked. But now, as he sifted through pages of precinct-level results, Clinton reached a dispiriting conclusion. If Obama wins Hanover by three to one, we're gonna lose this thing, he said. One minute, the networks were about to call the race for his wife; the next, they were saying, hold on, we're not so sure.

Clinton's knowledge of New Hampshire allowed him to be his own decision desk, more finely tuned than the networks' data models and teams of analysts. Clinton phoned Clemons, from whom he'd been hoovering fresh numbers every fifteen minutes all evening. A new batch from Hanover had just come in. "We're gonna win it!" Bill exclaimed.

It was after ten o'clock when excitement finally washed over the room. The networks had certified Hillary's win. The candidate came in and hugged everyone. "I felt it all day," she said. Bill boasted about how his "fairy tale" attack had been pivotal to the outcome—it had held down Obama's margins in Hanover.

Racing out of the hotel, they sped to Manchester for Hillary's victory speech. "I come tonight with a very, very full heart," she began. "Over the last week, I listened to you, and in the process, I found my own voice."

When it was over, Hillary marched down a hallway backstage, with her husband and Chelsea at her side.

She looked like a quarterback who'd just completed a last-second Hail Mary pass in overtime—pointing at her aides, high-fiving them, smiling from ear to ear. "This is amazing," one of them said. "I'm so proud of you! You did this! You did this!"

Hillary nodded and puffed out her chest.

"I get really tough when people fuck with me," she said.

It would take a while for Obama and his brain trust to figure out what happened in New Hampshire. The sight of Hillary being bludgeoned in the debate, her tearing up, and her gritty performance at the end— all of it while Obama was coasting—had done exactly what Penn said Clinton needed to do: bring home the women voters who had been with her before but who had drifted briefly, in the wake of Iowa, into the unde- cided column or into a flirtation with Obama.

Obama's initial analysis was more rudimentary. Back at his hotel late that night with friends, he com- pared himself to a comet—and the next morning, at a fund-raising breakfast in Boston, to Icarus. But his calm philosophizing masked a deeper disquiet about his situation after New Hampshire. The candidate won- dered again if he might benefit from a broader circle of advisers, something he'd been pushing for, albeit sporadically, since the summer of 2007. His brain trust was gobsmacked. The campaign's internal polls had been just as far off base as the public ones—Clinton ended up winning by three points—and its strategy was in tatters. The momentum out of Iowa that was supposed to carry Obama to the nomination had been stopped in its tracks just five days later. With one win of her own, Hillary had changed the game again.

Obama looked at the calendar and took no comfort in what he saw. Super Tuesday, February 5, was Hillary's firewall; she'd been saying for months that the race would be decided that day, when a gaggle of the big states where her support was robust would render their verdict. Obama realized that, for him to prevail, the contest would have to continue well into the spring—and he was already exhausted. In Boston, one of his donors asked him what the New Hampshire loss might mean.

"It means I'm not gonna get any sleep," he said. "And I'm dying to get some sleep."

11

FEAR AND LOATHING IN THE LIZARD'S THICKET

The Ballston headquarters of Hillaryland occupied three floors in a building that once belonged to the U.S. Immigration and Naturalization Service—and looked the part. The place was charmless, soulless, drab, and gray, suburban-office-park neo-brutalist in every detail. The single homey touch was Solis Doyle's conference table, which in an earlier era had been the Clintons' kitchen table in the Arkansas governor's mansion.

The day after New Hampshire, Hillary convened a rolling meeting around that nostalgic piece of furniture, beneath seven framed covers of *Time* magazine that bore her image. The meeting ran from the late afternoon until nearly midnight and included a sprawling cast of characters: Bill, Chelsea, the original high command, and many of the old-guard Clintonites now being hauled into service. The only person missing from Solis Doyle's office was . . . Solis Doyle. (The staff had tried to find her all day long; her whereabouts were unknown.)

Hillary rarely ran a campaign meeting, but this was an exception. She wanted to get her arms around the situation facing her in the weeks ahead. Having just staged a once-in-a-lifetime comeback, she should have been flying high. Instead, she was acting like she'd just been annihilated—she was angrier even than she was after Iowa, angry in a way that the old hands in the room hadn't seen since Bill's impeachment. She began with a seething soliloquy that lasted fifteen minutes but seemed a whole lot longer.

"I'm not putting up with this anymore," she fumed.

Everyone stared down at their shoes.

The sources of Hillary's ire were manifold, each more maddening than the last. A year into her campaign, her advisers were still squabbling over what her message should be. Don Baer, who had served as Bill's communications director during his second term and was now an associate of Penn's at Burson-Marsteller, suggested she adopt a new motif: "the politics of common purpose." Grunwald advocated an update of her husband's old theme of "putting people first." Doug

Sosnik said that she should focus on "the future"; Roy Spence argued for "solutions." At this late date, it was as if they were starting from scratch.

Wasn't there any lesson to be drawn from what had worked in New Hampshire? The Clintons thought so: Hillary had won because they'd attacked Obama, she at the debate and Bill at Dartmouth. The faction of Hillaryland that for months had been pressing for her to show a softer side had a different view. Wolfson offered an analogy to the movie *The Queen*. You know how, at the end, Queen Elizabeth becomes sympathetic when she displays her humanity? he said. That's what happened in New Hampshire.

Hillary looked uncomprehendingly at Wolfson, as if he were speaking Portuguese.

Having no message was one thing. Having no money was another. Historically, nothing agitated the Clintons more than the prospect of being outspent in a campaign; the fear of it drove them to such extremes as the renting out of the Lincoln Bedroom. Hillary had raised more than $100 million in 2007. She'd known that if she lost Iowa, her wherewithal would be strained—but she never imagined it would be this bad, that she would basically be broke.

"The cupboard is bare," Ickes said. And replenishing it would not be easy: Clinton's donors were tapped out. "We have to win in order to raise," said her finance director, Jonathan Mantz. "If we don't win, we're not gonna raise."

But Hillary didn't even want to compete in the next two contests. So certain was she of losing both, she thought it was pointless. Next on the calendar was Nevada, another caucus state. It would be like Iowa, only worse, she said, with caucus sites in the casinos on the Las Vegas Strip rife with fraud and abuse, and the culinary union rigging the outcome for Obama. As for South Carolina, turnout was likely to be at least 50 percent African American. Meaning, she was screwed.

"You can't skip Nevada *and* South Carolina," Sosnik said emphatically, and the rest of the room agreed. With the campaign running on empty, losing two in a row before Super Tuesday would be debilitating—and, who knows, maybe even fatal.

Worn down, Hillary relented and agreed to play in Nevada, where both her team and her support among Hispanics were solid. (A decision about South Carolina was deferred.) But she could scarcely comprehend the situation in which she now found herself—gasping for air after just two contests, her campaign on the edge of bankruptcy, with no clear plan for how to win.

The person Clinton blamed most for her predicament was the one who wasn't there: Solis Doyle. Yet in the last twenty-four hours, Hillary had reaffirmed that she couldn't afford to dispense with Patti after all. She didn't need any more instability, and dumping Solis Doyle would invite mayhem. She didn't want to deal with awkward questions from the press. And she couldn't risk a backlash among Hispanics over the firing of the highest-ranking Latino political operative in the country; in an awful lot of the states ahead, Hillary was relying on the votes of that community to pull her through.

Solis Doyle had gone off the grid to think things over. She had little desire to stay, but Hillary implored her, and Patti caved. The next day, she resurfaced and began talks with Williams about finding a workable modus vivendi for their jointly running the campaign. Williams was busy with a consulting business and had clients demanding her time. Her appetite for being in Ballston was as minimal as Patti's—but her loyalty to Clinton was deep. The conversations between Williams and Solis Doyle were uneasy and tense. Once, they had been close friends, the two most powerful women in Hillaryland; now they were the usurper and the usurped. It was a recipe for, if not disaster, then paralytic discord.

Hillary, meanwhile, was gone—off to Nevada, South Carolina, Super Tuesday, and beyond. Winning in New Hampshire had given her new life, but had also allowed her to defer the hard choices required to right her operation. Solis Doyle and Penn were still in place, augmented now by a corps of reluctant conscripts. Nobody in Ballston knew who was in charge. Nobody *wanted* to be in charge.

In politics, though, as much as in the realm of physics, nature abhors a vacuum. And in this case, nature—or, at least, a force of nature—promptly stepped in to fill it.

Bill Clinton picked up the phone a few days later and called an old friend, a member of Congress to whom he and Hillary had long been close. I knew we could do it and I was right, he crowed about the victory in New Hampshire. The congressman congratulated Clinton, expressed his admiration for the upset that Hillary had pulled off. But he was discomfited by the way that Bill was claiming credit for the win. He urged Clinton to step back, to give his wife some running room. "It's her campaign, Mr. President," the congressman said. "You have to let her win this thing herself. You have to let go."

But Clinton couldn't let go—especially now that the situation was so perilous that everyone was (finally) reaching out to grasp his hand. In the days since the Ballston meeting, Williams and Sosnik had swiftly moved to incorporate him into the campaign in a way Solis Doyle and the other Hillarylanders had resisted. For the first time, he was provided with a briefing book on the campaign's policies and plans. A morning conference call was set up to give him talking points and a read on the day's press coverage. And he was assigned the task of calling countless superdelegates, whom Hillary continued to fail to court.

One day that week, over takeout Chinese food in the dining room at Whitehaven, Clinton received from the campaign's high command his maiden formal presentation on the road ahead. Hillary's newish political director, Guy Cecil, explained that they faced a lengthy war of attrition over delegates. For all the talk about Super Tuesday being Hillary's firewall, the reality was that, having poured so much cash into Iowa, the Clintonites hadn't conducted a poll in almost any of the February 5 states; in many of them, their operations were skeletal or nonexistent. Cecil put a chart in front of Bill that laid out Hillary's best-case scenario on Super Tuesday: a net gain of no more than sixty delegates out of nearly seventeen hundred up for grabs that day.

"Goddamn it," Clinton said, the familiar flush coloring his cheeks. "What are we doing?" Studying the chart, he shook his head. "All this money, all this work, and this is all we're going to get out of it?"

The deeper Clinton delved into the workings of his wife's campaign, the more upset he got. But in truth he was even more agitated about what was going on beyond Ballston. Seemingly out of nowhere, the race had suddenly turned racial, with both Bill and Hillary being accused of insensitivity at best and perniciousness at worst.

The dynamic had been unleashed the night of New Hampshire, when the talking heads on TV began to speculate about whether Obama's collapse in the nearly all-white state was due partly to racial factors—and the Clintons' comments of the previous day came in for closer inspection. The next morning, January 9, *The New York Times* published a scalding editorial that accused the Clintons of running an "angry campaign" that "came perilously close to injecting racial tension" into the contest, citing Hillary's remark about MLK and LBJ and Bill's "bizarre and rambling attack" on Obama at Dartmouth. Two days later, the *Times* published a front-page story in which South Carolina representative James Clyburn, the highest-ranking African American in Congress, echoed those charges, focusing on the former president and what Clyburn saw as a broad assault on Obama's candidacy. "To call that dream a fairy tale, which Bill Clinton seemed to be doing, could very well be insulting to some of us," Clyburn said.

Clinton's first reaction was astonishment, followed shortly by rage. Bill had been talking about Obama's record on the war—nothing more. Hillary had been making a historical observation—nothing more. Their words were being twisted, bent out of shape in a way that suggested that something more malign than mere misinterpretation was behind it.

The *Times* made Bill especially mental. I can't believe these assholes are sitting there writing this, he wailed to one of many friends he called that week to complain about the editorial. After everything I did for civil rights in Arkansas! After everything I did in the White House! They know damn well I don't have a racist bone in my body!

What cranked up the thermostat on Clinton's umbrage were signs he saw that the Obama campaign was stirring the pot with liberal media outlets and black radio and websites. A few days after New Hampshire, a memo surfaced, produced by Obama's South Carolina operation, that grouped together MLK/LBJ and "fairy tale" along with other race-freighted incidents—including Billy Shaheen's and Penn's invocations of Obama's youthful cocaine use—to suggest that the Clintons were playing the race card. Then there was Illinois congressman and Obama campaign co-chair Jesse Jackson, Jr., who went on MSNBC and noted that while Clinton had teared up in New Hampshire, she never cried over Hurricane Katrina. "Those tears also have to be analyzed," Jackson said, "particularly as we head to South Carolina, where forty-five percent of African Americans will participate in the Democratic contest."

To Bill, the picture was all too clear. By accusing him and Hillary of slapping the race card on the table, the Obama campaign was doing exactly that itself. And though it infuriated him, he couldn't help but respect the artfulness of the play. The Obamans were tough; they weren't just sitting back and letting the nomination slip away. I wish our people were more like that, Bill said.

Clinton could see the danger of the racial back-and-forth to Hillary's campaign, and also to his own reputation. Seeking to contain the fallout, he made the rounds on black talk radio, clarifying his statements, defending himself—even talking up Obama. "There's nothing fairy tale about his campaign," Clinton told Al Sharpton on his syndicated show a few days after New Hampshire. "It's real, strong, and he might win."

What Clinton might have added, if he were being candid, was: But not if I can do anything to stop it.

Obama and his brain trust arrived in Nevada determined to apply the lessons of New Hampshire. They would home in laser-like on kitchen table issues, from health care to the subprime mortgage mess. They would scale down their mega-rallies, and instead hold town halls and roundtables with average voters. But now they found a race bomb had been dropped in their laps—and it blew that plan to pieces.

On Obama's first full day in the Silver State, the Sunday before the Saturday caucuses coming up on January 19, the campaign learned that across the country in South Carolina, Bob Johnson, the founder of Black Entertainment Television, had become the latest Clinton surrogate to bring up (albeit obliquely) Obama's drug use. Defending the Clintons' record on race with Hillary at his side, Johnson declared that they had been "deeply and emotionally involved in black issues when Barack Obama was doing something in the neighborhood—and I won't say what he was doing, but he said it in his book." He then went on to compare Obama to the Sidney Poitier character in *Guess Who's Coming to Dinner*.

The suits had no doubt that the Clintons were playing the race card, that they were trying to blacken up Obama in a way that would hurt him with both white and Hispanic voters on Super Tuesday and beyond. For the Obamans, the Johnson incident was part of an increasingly troubling pattern. *One thing is a coincidence*, thought Gibbs. *Five are a strategy.*

Obama himself had not viewed "fairy tale" as racially loaded, though he was annoyed by what he saw as Clinton belittling him and distorting his record on Iraq—and MLK/LBJ hadn't bothered him at all. But the Johnson remark he found outrageous. Beyond his pique, however, he was worried that the simmering racial stew was on the verge of boiling over. And he was angry at his own campaign's role in turning up the burners underneath it. When he was told about the memo put out by his South Carolina team, Obama erupted. How could this have happened? he demanded of Gibbs. All through the campaign, the Obamans had sought, for reasons of not just principle but strategy, to downplay race. It was hard to see how a wildly polarized electorate would rebound to Obama's benefit.

"This thing is getting way too hot," Obama warned his team the morning after the Johnson comments. "Regardless of who's done what to get us to this point, I'm going to try and defuse it." At a hastily arranged press conference in Reno, Obama told reporters, "We've got too much at stake at this time in our history to be engaging in this kind of silliness. I expect that other campaigns feel the same way."

Obama's effort to turn down the temperature lasted only a few hours. Having tried to put out one fire, he quickly turned around and ignited another. Sitting down with the editorial board of the *Reno Gazette-Journal*, Obama started riffing on history. "I think Ronald Reagan changed the trajectory of America in a way that, you know, Richard Nixon did not, and in a way that Bill Clinton did not," he said. Obama added that, although the GOP was now in intellectual ruins, it was "fair to say the Republicans were the party of ideas for a pretty long chunk of time there over the last ten to fifteen years, in the sense that they were challenging the conventional wisdom."

Gibbs tried to downplay the strange spectacle of his boss celebrating the Reagan Revolution in the midst of a Democratic nomination fight, pointing out that Obama had paid tribute to the Gipper before. But Marty Nesbitt saw something more forward looking and calculated at work. The day before, Obama had told his friend that he once again feared he was headed for "a respectable second place if we don't figure out how to move the needle." Nesbitt agreed: "You gotta do something, but I don't know what it is." Now, catching a glimpse of the Reagan story on TV, Nesbitt thought, *Wow, brilliant*: Obama had set a trap for the Clintons by striking at their pride.

Whatever Obama's motives, he certainly succeeded in getting a rise out of the couple. To her team, Hillary railed at Obama for his imprecation against her husband.

"Who does he think he is?" she exclaimed on a conference call. "Drives me nuts. Drives me nuts! He has no sense of history at all!"

Penn and Grunwald theorized that Obama, the darling of the left, was pandering to conservative Democrats in northern Nevada. He's become a chameleon, one of them said.

"He has! We should call him that!" Hillary said, proposing a TV ad that somehow pictured Obama as a color-shifting lizard. "We need a visual," she said.

"We can't," Grunwald replied.

"Why?" Hillary asked.

The color thing, Grunwald said. We'd get hit for dabbling with race.

"*Oh Gawwwd*," Hillary groaned. "Give me a break."

Bill Clinton was even more livid than his wife about the Reagan swipe. He didn't see it as a tactic. He thought that Obama might actually believe that Reagan's tenure had been superior to his own. In private, he recited statistics from the eighties and nineties that showed how much better the economy fared under him than Reagan—while in public, he vented his indignation with an attack that contorted what Obama had said almost as wantonly as Clinton's critics were doing with "fairy tale."

"Her principal opponent said that since 1992, the Republicans have had all the good ideas," Clinton said while stumping in Pahrump, Nevada. "So now it turns out you can choose between somebody who thinks our ideas are better or the Republicans had all the good ideas."

In the closing days before the Nevada vote, Bill was everywhere—traipsing from the casino floors to half-empty community centers outside Vegas, sometimes with Chelsea in tow. Along with his assaults on Obama, he inveighed against the rules that governed the caucuses and lobbed accusations of voter intimidation and vote suppression hither and yon. "Today, when my daughter and I were wandering through the [Bellagio]," he said in a tiny gym in North Las Vegas the afternoon before the caucuses, "and all these culinary workers were mobbing us telling us they didn't care what the union told them to do, they were gonna caucus for Hillary. There was a representative of the organization following along behind us, going up to everybody who said that, saying, 'If you're not gonna vote for our guy, we're gonna give you a schedule tomorrow so you can't be there.'"

The chances that a union representative engaging in such strong-arming would have done it within earshot of a former president were close to nil. But Clinton didn't care. He'd done his job: muddying up the water with an unverifiable story that implied Obama's supporters had dirty hands, attempting to discredit the caucuses in the event that Hillary lost—which the Clintonites believed was the likeliest outcome.

When the smoke cleared on caucus day, however, Hillary had beaten Obama 51 to 45 percent in the popular vote. Team Obama gamely (and accurately) pointed out that, due to caucus mathematics, their man would actually emerge with more delegates than his rival. But technicalities could do nothing to diminish the thrill of victory for the Clintons—especially for Bill. Once again, Hillary had won a race that almost everyone, including her, believed was beyond reach. And once again, Bill had been the spark, the wild card, shaking things up and making things happen. On the flight home to New York, he reveled in the triumph they'd achieved.

"I knew we were golden," Bill proclaimed, "when I saw we'd carried the Mirage!"

Obama flew back to Chicago from Vegas, spent a night at home, and then set off on Sunday morning for South Carolina by way of Atlanta. Having lost two contests in a row, he understood that winning the next one was essential. His lead in Palmetto State polls was anywhere from just six to thirteen points—and with the Big Dog now unmuzzled and on the loose, that was too close for comfort. On the plane to Atlanta with Axelrod, Gibbs, and Jarrett, Obama focused on a single quandary: how to handle Bill.

"Look, I know he's a former president," Obama said. "There's a certain amount that goes with that." Clinton would always have a blaring megaphone and be accorded a large degree of deference. But Obama was alarmed at his campaign's passivity in dealing with the Bill problem. From New Hampshire through Nevada, they had let Clinton run free—and Obama had paid a heavy price.

No more, Obama said. In South Carolina, Clinton could never go unchallenged. If he stepped out of line, they had to play aggressive defense, hitting back fast and hard. But Obama also wanted to go on offense, and knew he had to do it himself. Later that day, he took the first chance that presented itself.

"The former president," he told ABC News, "has taken his advocacy on behalf of his wife to a level that I think is pretty troubling."

Up in Washington, meanwhile, Penn and Solis Doyle were in agreement for once: South Carolina was unwinnable, and neither Hillary nor Bill should spend much time there, in order to reduce the attention on the state and lessen the oomph of Obama's inevitable victory. A schedule was drafted that had each Clinton spending no more than a day or two there—just enough to avoid the perception that they were dissing South Carolina or the black vote writ large. Hillary would decamp to the Super Tuesday states in the West and East, while Bill would concentrate on other southern states and raising money for the campaign's depleted coffers.

But Bill was apoplectic when he saw the schedule. An email from Doug Band soon arrived in the in-boxes of Solis Doyle and others. In essence, it said: The president thinks you're a bunch of fools.

Clinton's counterproposal was radical. He wanted to spend every day of the coming week in South Carolina. He had confidence in his roots in the state, in his relationships with both the Bubbas and the black voters—in his ability, at least, to keep the primary close, to beat the spread, and, hey, who knows, maybe even pull off another shock-the-world upset for Hillary.

"I gotta go to churches, I gotta campaign hard. I think I can do it," he told one of his new-old allies on the campaign. "You can't win if you don't compete."

Hillaryland resisted, begging Bill to embrace the proposed schedule. But Clinton was implacable. "I'm going," he said, and that was that.

. . .

As the campaign rolled into South Carolina, another fraught psyche was churning and whirling. Since his distant third-place finish in New Hampshire, John Edwards had seemed inclined to heed the counsel of Trippi to stay in the race as long as possible, even if victory was unobtainable, for the sake of amassing delegates. Like the Obamans and the Hillarylanders, Trippi foresaw a protracted delegate fight ahead. But he went further, forecasting the possibility of a brokered convention, with Obama and Clinton obtaining fewer than the 2,025 delegates required for the nomination—a historically unlikely outcome, to be sure, but one that might give Edwards just enough leverage to force his way onto the ticket.

Both the Obama and Clinton camps were in fervent covert communication with Edwards and his advisers. The Clinton people hoped he would get out promptly, ideally before South Carolina, and provide his endorsement to Hillary, allowing her, in theory, to consolidate the white working-class vote. The Obamans hoped for an endorsement, too, but absent that, they were eager for Edwards to follow Trippi's advice and stay in at least through Super Tuesday, to siphon off white votes from Clinton. Plouffe, in the dark about Clinton's destitution, remained terrified of her strength on February 5. More than once he shared internal polling with Team Edwards, showing all the states in which the North Carolinian could play a decisive role—to Obama's benefit.

Edwards was still doing his best Monty Hall imitation: Let's make a deal. Although he maintained publicly that he never desired to be a running mate again, Edwards was, in fact, quite open to the idea. But he was also willing to consider more modest rewards. Having been rebuffed on the notion of teaming up with Obama after Iowa, he once again dispatched Leo Hindery to make a revised offer.

"John will settle for attorney general," Hindery emailed Tom Daschle.

Daschle shook his head. *How desperate is this guy?*

"Leo, this isn't good for John," Daschle replied. "This is ridiculous. It's going to be ambassador to Zimbabwe next."

Daschle warned Hindery that this new offer, like the last one, was sure to be rejected. And it was. When Obama heard about the suggested quid pro quo, he was incredulous.

That's crazy, he told Axelrod. If I were willing to make a deal like that, I shouldn't be president!

Edwards wondered if Clinton might be more open to cutting a deal. For all his previous distaste for her, he was beginning to find her more agreeable than Obama—less aloof, more brass-tacks. But Edwards knew his options were rapidly running out. He had no money, the press was ignoring him, and his vote totals were spiraling toward zero; he'd won just 3.8 percent in Nevada.

Then again, Rielle Hunter was only eight months pregnant.

So Edwards still had another month to strike a bargain.

The South Carolina contest began in earnest on January 21, Martin Luther King Day, with a debate in Myrtle Beach. Even before the three candidates took the stage, the rowdy vibe of the crowd announced one thing: Toto, we're not in Kansas—or Iowa or New Hampshire or even Nevada—anymore. The political culture of South Carolina was wide open and down and dirty. Anything went, and everything always somehow boiled down to race. Given the events of the past two weeks, circumstances were ripe for a blowup.

The Clintonites were eager to avoid that eventuality. In debate prep, Hillary's team advised her that African Americans didn't want to see her trashing Obama. Their advice was unambiguous: Be big, be gracious, be positive, keep any criticisms muted. Obama's aides were less kissy-kissy. If she slugs you, you have to counter-punch, they said. Still, there was one caveat, delivered to the candidate by Axelrod: Don't make this about you and Bill Clinton; you're running against her, not him.

But Obama didn't wait for so much as a jab to start throwing haymakers—aimed squarely at Bill. "President Clinton says that I wasn't opposed to the war from the start or says it's a fairy tale that I opposed the war. That is simply not true," he said. "President Clinton asserts that I said that the Republicans had had better economic policies since 1980. That is not the case."

Hillary interjected that Obama had indeed said "he really likes the ideas of the Republicans over the last ten to fifteen years."

"That is not true," Obama said. "What I said is that Ronald Reagan was a transformative political figure because he was able to get Democrats to vote against their economic interests to form a majority to push through their agenda, an agenda that I objected to. Because while I was working on those streets watching those folks see their jobs shift overseas, you were a corporate lawyer sitting on the board at Wal-Mart."

The Myrtle Beach crowd had been hoping for fireworks. They were getting the Fourth of July. Ooohs and aaahs filled the auditorium at the most personal attack that Obama had launched in the entire campaign.

Clinton fired back that she wasn't talking about Reagan.

"I didn't mention his name," she said.

"Your husband did," Obama retorted.

"Well, I'm here. He's not."

"Okay, well, I can't tell who I'm running against sometimes."

The crowd cheered again, but Clinton wouldn't let go of her point about Obama's apparent embrace of Republican brainstorms.

"Yes, they did have ideas, and they were bad ideas," she said. "Bad for America, and I was fighting against those ideas when you were practicing law and representing your contributor, Rezko, in his slum landlord business in inner-city Chicago."

Obama's association with Rezko was one of the missteps from his past that the press had barely touched—much to the chagrin of Bill Clinton and Penn. Although Penn had told Hillary before the debate that this wasn't the time or place to raise Rezko, the chief strategist couldn't contain his visceral excitement in the moment. Watching the debate on TV with his colleagues, Penn yelled out, "Yes!"

No one was belting out affirmations in the Obama staff room; everyone was too busy grimacing at Barack's performance. The candidate had presented an image—caustic, sarcastic, and thin-skinned—at striking variance with public perceptions of him. It was a side of Obama, however, that his aides sometimes saw in private, and one they feared might cause voters to view him as an angry black man if it were displayed in public. After catching the clips on TV afterward, Obama didn't disagree. "I probably went a little too far," he told Jarrett over dinner, "but she did, too."

Hillary shared that assessment, but believed she had justification. "I'm sorry," she told her aides as she exited the stage, "but he was such an asshole."

The "brawl on the beach," as it was instantly known, made all the previous fifteen Democratic debates look like sewing circles. In every respect, it perfectly foreshadowed what lay ahead. The hot tempers. The lack of control. The jolts of pure adrenaline. And, of course, the focus on the man who wasn't center stage—but soon would be, for good or ill, and for the duration.

Bill showed up the next morning for breakfast at the Lizard's Thicket restaurant in Columbia, wearing gray pants, a taupe blazer, and an electric-orange tie. The menu board listed black-eyed peas and chicken livers, but Clinton went easy on his fragile arteries and had a veggie omelet. A bank of cameras captured his every move; a throng of reporters craned their necks to catch the pearls that fell from his lips.

Clinton looked like the cat who'd swallowed an entire flock of canaries: calm, carefree, and sated. When one of the journalists asked about a comment made the day before by Jim Clyburn—that the former president "needs to chill a bit"—Clinton answered mildly, "I'm pretty chilled out, don't you think?"

In truth, Clyburn was only saying publicly what Clinton was being told privately by members of his party. All through Nevada, he'd been fielding calls from prominent Democrats, Ted Kennedy and Rahm Emanuel among them, urging him to tone down his attacks on Obama, saying they were unwarranted and unseemly, and that they threatened to rend the Democratic family. When a voter at the Lizard's Thicket offered the same point—"I think there's a party perception that coming back on the attack doesn't help"—Bill made it clear that he had no intention of laying off, that he had skin in the game now.

"Well, for three to four months in Iowa, [Obama] attacked [Hillary] every day and she never said a word," he answered, "so you think we should go back to that?"

As Clinton got up to leave the restaurant, a reporter asked a member of his cadre if the boss was as good a politician as he was in 1992. Clinton turned and answered the question himself: "He's rusty and old and creaky."

Maybe he was and maybe he wasn't, but the press corps regarded him as a more than worthy adversary for Obama. With Hillary in Washington, D.C., about to head to California, *The New York Times* captured succinctly the media's framing of the contest: "Mrs. Clinton's campaign this week in South Carolina is essentially running Mr. Clinton against Mr. Obama."

Worried as the Hillarylanders were about Bill's long-term stay in the state, they comforted themselves with the thought that he seemed to be rattling their foe. In Greenville that afternoon, Obama got into a testy confrontation with a reporter he knew well, Jeff Zeleny, late of *The Chicago Tribune* and now at *The New York Times.*

"Are you letting Bill Clinton inside your head?" Zeleny shouted out as Obama worked a rope line.

"I am trying to make sure misstatements by him are answered," Obama said with a peevish tone through a forced grin. "Don't you think that's important?"

Zeleny tried to shout another question from the other side of the barricade.

"Come on, Jeff, don't try cheap stunts like that. You're better than that," Obama said, walking away.

Then he turned around and walked back. "My suspicion is, I think, that the other side must be rattled if they're continuing to say false things about us."

The unflappable Obama was plainly flapped—but he had another arrow in his quiver. Since the plane flight on Sunday night, his campaign had devised another means of piercing Bill Clinton: a "truth squad" comprised of Daschle and a number of Obama's leading South Carolina supporters. Daschle took the lead on the press conference call announcing the effort and made it clear they were going after Bill, not Hillary. "It's not in keeping with the image of a former president," Daschle said of Clinton's behavior.

The most famous (and infamous) local member of the truth squad was former Democratic state party chairman Dick Harpootlian. Once a supporter of both Hillary and Bill, Harpootlian was a media magnet, glib and hard-edged, a perfect combination of down-home grit and steely sophistication. He possessed an unerring gift for feigning indignation with reporters in a way that was provocative and witty—and therefore sure to drive a story to an interesting destination.

Team Obama knew that Harpootlian was itching to take on Bill. They also knew there were risks involved. Harpootlian was volatile, unpredictable, messy—a human IED. He could detonate at will but not necessarily on command, and it was impossible to know where the shrapnel would land after one of his explosions.

That Tuesday afternoon, January 22, Harpootlian showed up in person at a midday event of Bill Clinton's in Aiken. He told reporters that the Clinton campaign was "reprehensible," that it was using the playbook of the late GOP strategist Lee Atwater, the progenitor of a shameful litany of racially exploitive Republican campaign tactics. (Willie Horton, anyone?) The Clintons, he added, were practicing the politics of "personal destruction."

"Bill Clinton loves his wife more than he loves his country," Harpootlian said, "and this is all about continuing some kind of Clinton dynasty as opposed to doing what I believe is best for the country." He went on, "It's distressing to me that we have to follow the former president of the United States to make him tell the truth."

"All great contests," Bill Clinton once said, "are head games."

Clinton had always regarded political contests as the greatest contests of all. He loved them, lived for them, mastered them—in no small part because he understood the psychological rules so well. Successful combatants, Clinton said, had to put "distance between them and these withering attacks" they would face. "You just have to know they're coming in different ways and you just can't let yourself be defined by them." You couldn't let them undermine your judgment. Couldn't let yourself be paralyzed. "Only a small percentage of what voters are looking for is whether any of this stuff is true," he said. "What they're really looking for is to see, how is this person going to react?"

For two weeks now, Clinton had been playing a head game with Obama and had arguably been winning. But suddenly, the terms of the contest had shifted, and Dick Harpootlian was playing a head game with *him*.

The next day, Clinton was leaving a town hall in Charleston when a reporter asked him about Harpootlian's comparison of his tactics in Nevada to those of Atwater.

Removing his reading glasses, Clinton leaned in and responded.

"Dick Harpootlian wasn't in Nevada," he said, adding that Hillary's campaign had received hundreds of complaints of voter suppression during the caucuses. "Now, it's okay. We're not hung up about it; we just pointed it out, and we won anyway—we fought hard and we won. But to say that's Lee Atwater, stating a fact, is a little stretch."

On the surface, Clinton seemed calm as he started speaking, his tone even, his volume low. But inside he was steaming, the bile rising in his throat. The drumbeat of criticism against him since "fairy tale" hadn't let up. He was still being pilloried for playing the race card, crucified by people he'd been friends with forever, people who knew better. His frustration, his hurt, his anger—all were off the charts. But even greater was his epic sense of incredulity. Here he was—Bill Clinton!—smack in the middle of a Democratic primary, trying to win black votes for his spouse while fending off the most absurd charges imaginable. Charges that cut to the core of his self-conception and sense of his own virtue. Charges being taken at face value and amplified by a media that was desperate, as he liked to put it, not to be "on the wrong side of history." And now here was some reporter who barely knew who Atwater was—oh, Clinton was sure of that—asking him (Bill Clinton!) if he and Atwater, that diabolic demon, bore any traits in common.

Lee Atwater? Me? Clinton thought.

He should have ended the exchange. Should have shut his mouth. But Clinton forgot his own rules of political combat, let his judgment take leave of him, along with his equilibrium. He couldn't stay mum. He couldn't walk away. Because this was . . . just too much.

So Clinton kept talking. For five minutes he kept talking. His finger wagging, his face turning magenta, his tone growing sterner and preachier.

As the cameras rolled, he attacked Obama for negative campaigning and praised his own restraint: "When he put out a hit job on me at the same time he called her the senator from Punjab, I never said a word. And I don't care about it today. I'm not upset about it."

He accused the Obama campaign of playing the race card and lashed out at the charges against him: "This is almost like once you accuse somebody of racism or bigotry or something, the facts become irrelevant. There are facts here."

He castigated the media for falling for the Obamans' baleful spin: "They are feeding you this because they know this is what you want to cover. This is what you live for . . . And the Obama people know that."

He lashed out at his nemesis: "Harpootlian calls me Lee Atwater . . . He doesn't care what happened. He just knows he can call you a name and you guys will cover it."

Finally, Clinton seemed to finish and headed toward the door, when another reporter called out to him, "But do you think the Obama people . . ."

Clinton turned around and glanced back at the press pack with a look of scorn.

"Shame on you!" he said—and then, at last, Elvis left the building.

Clinton's outburst reverberated through the remaining days before the primary, playing in an infinite loop on cable and on YouTube. The performance was, in many ways, unprecedented. Never before had anyone seen a former president behave this way. Never had anyone seen a candidate's spouse behave this way. On garish display was Clinton violating the cardinal rule that was supposed to govern his conduct from the start of Hillary's campaign: don't overshadow your wife. Airing his private (and deep, and bitter) grievances in public. Assailing the media on a rope line. For elites, the picture was damning. What it said to them was that Clinton had lost more than a head game with Harpootlian. He'd lost the mental battle with Obama.

For all those reasons and many others, the reaction in Hillaryland was horror. Solis Doyle had been hearing the same analysis from advisers inside and outside the campaign since New Hampshire: they had to stop Bill's spasms. Beyond everything else, they were fueling a damaging argument that the Obama campaign was now making openly. As Greg Craig—a Washington attorney who had known the Clintons since Yale Law

School, coordinated Bill's impeachment defense, and now was advising Obama—observed in an interview in that week's *Newsweek*, "Recent events raise the question, if Hillary's campaign can't control Bill, whether Hillary's White House could."

There was a frantic scramble in Ballston to lasso Bill. "What's he doing in South Carolina?" Tanden, in a panic, said to Solis Doyle. "Get him out!"

"We've been trying to get him out for days, and he won't leave," Patti said.

Solis Doyle raised the subject with Hillary. He's causing huge agita for us, she said. It's not good.

Hillary tried to change the subject and then defended Bill. He's getting a raw deal, she insisted. But Hillary knew that the problem was real; she simply couldn't bear to confront her husband directly about it. Instead, she delegated others—Penn, Williams—to implore him either to leave the state or to pipe down. To no avail, at least at first.

"Goddamn it, I'm doing this," Bill said when Williams reached him by phone.

But by the following morning, Thursday, Clinton seemed to have grasped the need to rein himself in. Deflated, crumpled, and clearly exhausted, he attended a town hall meeting in Lexington and began by saying, "I feel like a little scrambled egg."

A sympathetic voter in the audience suggested that Clinton "stop taking the bait from Obama."

"When I was running, I didn't give a rip what anybody said about me," Clinton explained piteously. "It's weird, you know, but if you love somebody and you think that they'd be good, it's harder." Clinton spent the rest of Thursday and Friday doing wonky events and steering clear of criticizing Obama.

With primary day finally upon them, Hillary's advisers surveyed the wreckage of the week. For all the fears many of them had always nursed about the risks entailed by Bill, no one could have imagined an implosion quite this bad or this baffling. All during the campaign, media and cocktail party psychobabble had abounded as to whether the former president actually wanted his wife to win. Now, for the first time, Hillary's closest aides began to contemplate the question seriously—asking themselves whether, on some unconscious level, he'd been trying to sabotage her.

Months later one of them shook his head and said in wonder, "It would take ten Freudians to explain what Bill Clinton did to Hillary in South Carolina."

Obama watched the meltdown of the Clinton campaign with a mixture of shock and amusement. When he was told about Clinton's on-camera implosion, he could only laugh. But his advisers continued to worry that Bill Clinton was pursuing some masterfully nefarious racial strategy: sacrificing South Carolina's black vote in order to transform Obama from a candidate who was black into the black candidate, thereby helping Hillary with white voters in states such as Ohio and Pennsylvania down the road. Michelle Obama was on board with that theory. In the closing days of South Carolina, a scathing fund-raising email went out under her name that accused Bill of "misleading accusations," "disingenuous attacks," and "smear tactics."

What effect the racially tinged theatrics of the past two weeks would have on the results was the looming question on primary day. There was little doubt that Obama would win, but how polarized would the outcome be? One late poll suggested the answer might be: very. It showed Obama ahead by just eight points and claiming a meager 10 percent of the white vote.

Harpootlian thought such polls were hogwash. That Friday night, just hours before the voting got under way, he showed up at an Obama rally in Columbia, gazed out at the sea of white faces in the crowd, then went backstage and assured the candidate that he'd win at least 50 percent of the vote. Obama wrapped a bear hug around Bill Clinton's tormentor, then laughed approvingly and marveled, "You're a *crazy* son of a bitch."

Harpootlian was right: the result the next day was what Axelrod described as "a good, old-fashioned butt-kicking." Obama prevailed by a whopping margin of 55 to 27 percent, while claiming a quarter of the white vote. More stunning, he essentially tied Clinton among Caucasian men and captured more than half of white voters under thirty.

Obama's victory speech was at once uplifting and defiant. Like his riff at the Iowa J-J, it had the Clintons in its crosshairs but never mentioned the couple. "We're up against the conventional thinking that says your ability to lead as president comes from longevity in Washington or proximity to the White House," Obama said. "Against decades of bitter partisanship that cause politicians to demonize their opponents . . . the kind of partisanship where you're not even allowed to say that a Republican had an idea, even if it's one you never agreed with. . . . Against the idea that it's acceptable to say anything and do anything to win an election."

The anti-Clinton thrust of Obama's remarks gained even greater resonance as word trickled in about a parting shot taken by Bill earlier in the day. Standing with two African American members of Congress who were supporters of Hillary's, he was asked by a reporter why two Clintons had been required to take on Obama in the primary.

"Jesse Jackson won South Carolina in '84 and '88," Clinton said. "Jackson ran a good campaign. And Obama ran a good campaign here."

When Obama heard Bill's utterance, he said to Gibbs, "Now, why would he say that?"

For many in the Democratic Party, the answer was all too clear. Clinton was comparing Obama to Jackson to diminish the former's victory, and to accomplish the blackening that Obama's advisers suspected was his objective all along. (The Jackson comparison circulated in Clintonworld the night before, in an email from Bill's former White House aide Sidney Blumenthal, which prophesied, "After Feb 5, Obama may prove to be a lesser version of Jackson.")

In the days that followed, Bill Clinton would indulge in an orgy of rationalization over what he'd said. He would defend it as a mere historical observation. He would cite African Americans, including Jackson himself, who claimed they took no offense. He would blame the Obama campaign and the press for seizing on his comments to hobble him and Hillary.

Whatever one made of the Jackson comment, there was no rationalizing away the effects of South Carolina. The black vote was permanently lost to Hillary; Obama now owned it, just as he'd predicted a year earlier he would. The Clinton brand had been badly tarnished.

The Obama campaign's goal of reviving memories of the Clinton soap opera had been achieved. In addition to her money troubles, her organizational dysfunction, and her strategic confusion, Hillary now had a Bill problem on her hands.

For Obama, all of that would have been sufficient to summon his million-dollar smile. But there was more. For much of the Democratic Establishment, white and black, South Carolina was the moment when it became conceivable—safe, acceptable, even de rigueur—to come out against the Clintons publicly and throw in with the challenger.

How true that was would become apparent just forty-eight hours later, when the most potent symbol of Establishment support would put his full weight behind Obama. Barack didn't generally give a fig about endorsements. But the backing of Edward Moore Kennedy was an entirely different matter.

12

PULLING AWAY AND
FALLING APART

In the big-game hunt for big-name endorsements, Ted Kennedy was the elephant that every Democrat yearned to bag. There was no potentate in the party, besides perhaps Al Gore, whose backing carried more emotional and electoral wallop. In the yearlong run-up to 2008, Kennedy had been courted avidly by Edwards, Obama, and Clinton. But there was no way he was endorsing anyone as long as Chris Dodd, one of his best friends, was still in the race. The question was what would happen after Dodd was out—and Teddy was in play.

Kennedy had long-standing ties to both Clinton and Edwards, but from early on he was smitten with Obama. The youth, the vigor, the idealism, the appeal across generational and racial lines—it wasn't just the fawning press corps that saw Obama as Kennedyesque. Teddy was also moved by the sentiments of the ladies in his life, who were unswayed by any gender-based allegiance to Hillary. His brother Bobby's widow, Ethel, had publicly anointed Obama two years earlier, calling him "our next president." Ted's wife, Vicki, adored Obama, and so did his niece Caroline's daughters, who raved about the passion that Obama's candidacy was stirring among their teenage peers.

Caroline Kennedy Schlossberg herself weighed an Obama endorsement through much of 2007. Famously reserved, Kennedy Schlossberg had never taken part in politics with great relish or involved herself (except in 1980, when Ted challenged Jimmy Carter) in an intra-party scrum. Caroline liked and admired Hillary; they moved in similar social circles in New York. But after furtively sizing up Obama—slipping into two of his events in Manhattan without attracting notice—and being encouraged by her kids, Kennedy Schlossberg was leaning in his direction.

As Iowa drew near, many of Caroline's New York pals were being enlisted to fly out and canvas there for Clinton. Hillaryland was under the impression that Caroline was willing to make the trip. But Caroline, in fact, was dreading a call from Hillary asking her to go. She would have found it impossible to refuse, and once she had campaigned for Clinton, siding with Obama would be off the table.

Hillary, however, as was her wont, had one of her staffers phone Caroline rather than doing it herself. Caroline ducked the call ("I'm sorry, she's not in right now," said a voice that sounded awfully like hers to the ears of Clinton's aide), and later told friends she was chagrined at being fobbed off on Hillary's staff. But she was also relieved to be free to follow her heart. Once Iowa conferred credibility on Obama, Caroline informed him that she was in, and his campaign started scheming about when to unveil her endorsement for maximum impact.

The Iowa results also induced Dodd's departure from the race, and the Clintons reckoned they now had a shot at landing Teddy. Surely he knew that no one would fight harder than Hillary for his dream of universal health care. Kennedy had twice taken the Clintons sailing on his fifty-foot schooner across Nantucket Sound; surely those voyages on the *Mya* had cemented the dynastic bond.

But as badly as Hillary bungled Caroline, Bill's handling of Ted was even worse. The day after Iowa, he phoned Kennedy and pressed for an endorsement, making the case for his wife. But Bill then went on, belittling Obama in a manner that deeply offended

Kennedy. Recounting the conversation later to a friend, Teddy fumed that Clinton had said, A few years ago, this guy would have been getting us coffee.

Kennedy's displeasure with the Clintons only grew through New Hampshire and Nevada; he believed they were playing a dangerous and divisive game with race. With each passing day, he was more inclined to follow Caroline into Obama's arms. Beyond his status as a liberal legend, Teddy was a cagey operator. Working the phones, consulting his far-flung network of counselors, he discerned a path that could carry Obama to the nomination—and the role he could play in helping to propel him down it. Kennedy also appreciated Obama's approach to seeking his endorsement. Obama asked for his support, then gave him space, having Daschle, to whom Kennedy was close, check in regularly but apply no pressure.

Bill Clinton took the opposite tack: he got up in Ted's grille. In a series of follow-up calls, Clinton went from arguing heatedly to pleading desperately with Kennedy. (At one point, Kennedy told a friend, Clinton went so far as to say, "I love you"—a declaration that Kennedy rendered mockingly in a Boston-Irish imitation of Clinton's Arkansan twang.) When Ted indicated he was going with Obama, Clinton adopted a lawyer's mien, quizzing Kennedy on his motives. "The only reason you're endorsing him is because he's black," Clinton said accusingly. "Let's just be clear."

The day after South Carolina, January 27, Caroline publicly cast her lot with Obama in a Sunday *New York Times* op-ed. The next morning, she stood onstage with her uncle and Obama at American University, in Washington, the site of one of JFK's most famous speeches, as Teddy offered his own endorsement. But Kennedy did more than that. In his distinctive, ringing voice, he vivisected the Clintons and sanctified Obama as his brother's rightful heir.

"There was another time, when another young candidate was running for president and challenging America to cross a New Frontier," Kennedy thundered. "He faced public criticism from the preceding Democratic president, who was widely respected in the party. Harry Truman said we needed 'someone with greater experience' and added: 'May I urge you to be patient.' And John Kennedy replied: 'The world is changing. The old ways will not do. It's time for a new generation of leadership.' So it is with Barack Obama. He has lit a spark of hope amid the fierce urgency of now."

The overt passing of the Kennedy torch touched something in Obama. Gazing out at the crowd of euphoric college kids filling AU's Bender Arena, overcome by what the media would describe as a "Camelot moment," he found himself choked up. But gusts of sentiment rarely stayed with Obama long, and that day, his reaction shifted quickly from emotional to political. Riding high, Obama saw the perfect chance to lunge in for the kill.

Let's get Gore on the phone, he told his aides right after leaving the arena.

It had been a year since Barack and Michelle trekked to Nashville for lunch with Al and Tipper. Obama had kept in regular touch with the former veep, soliciting his advice on policy, but also cajoling him for his support. When Gore came on the line, Obama once again made the request, attempting to use the leverage from the Kennedy coup to engineer a devastating elder-statesman double header.

There was much Gore found attractive about Obama—from his stance on the war to the grassrootsy, Web-enabled nature of his campaign—and he could scarcely say the same for the Clintons. His relationship with Hillary had been strained and hostile since their White House years, when she and Gore were, in effect, co–vice presidents, competing for power and influence. (Gore felt he had less of both than Hillary; the Clintons neither disagreed with his analysis nor cared.) And while time might have quelled Al's and Tipper's resentments toward Bill over l'affaire Lewinsky, impeachment, and their fallout in the 2000 election, the Gores still looked askance at the Clinton marriage, seeing it as an inscrutable codependency that coughed up chaos and melodrama in equal proportion. The idea of a Hill-Bill restoration caused them both to blanch.

Gore had reasons to hold his tongue, however, in the context of the campaign. His stature and status now were rooted in a realm beyond (and, to his mind, above) partisan politics. His backing of Howard Dean in 2004 had misfired embarrassingly. Most of all, Gore knew that if he came out for Obama, his endorsement wouldn't be the story. The story would be his repudiation of the Clintons. If 2000 had taught Gore anything, it was that the press had an insatiable appetite for Clinton-Gore psychoanalysis—and Gore detested being put on the couch. His gut told him his endorsement might wind up boomeranging on Obama, diverting the spotlight away from the candidate and his vision for the future and training it on a sideshow from the past.

Obama tried to persuade Gore, extolling his gravitas, telling him that the importance of his endorsement would transcend the media chatter, assuring him they would plow through it together. But Gore wouldn't budge. He was prepared to enter the fray only if Obama was in real trouble—or if the Clintons went nuclear negative and he thought that his endorsement could end the war before serious damage was done.

Yet in the wake of South Carolina and the Kennedy consecration, Gore didn't see Obama as a man in need of help. He saw a candidate who'd managed to bundle together into one extended news cycle two of the biggest game changers of the race.

A few blocks down Massachusetts Avenue from AU, Hillary was holding a meeting at Whitehaven with her advisers. Her bitterness over the bestowal of the Kennedy imprimatur on Obama was chilling and close to the surface. "There was nothing I could do about this," she told her aides. "[The Kennedys] have always hated us, always resented me and Bill as new people who aren't like them."

Hillary had another reason to be in a foul mood that Monday. The Clintons had just lent $5 million of their own money to her cash-starved operation to see it through Super Tuesday. It was her husband's idea, and Hillary didn't like it one bit. Her midwestern frugality made her a highly nervous Nellie about debt. But Bill kept insisting: Don't worry. I'll do more speeches; it'll be fine. *This campaign is a money pit*, Hillary thought. Having started the shoveling, she wondered when— and if—it would ever end.

That night, Clinton trooped up to Capitol Hill to attend Bush's final State of the Union address. Hillary had a checkered history with SOTUs. One year, she'd been criticized for talking too much during the president's speech; another, for rolling her eyes; still another, for chewing gum. Invariably, she found herself embroiled in some pseudo-scandal—and this year was no exception.

As the chamber of the House of Representatives filled up, Obama and his new best friend from Massachusetts strutted in like a pair of cocks of the walk, slapping backs, shaking hands, reveling in the kudos of their colleagues. When Hillary headed their way, they watched her warily, eyebrows arched, whispering to one another. Then Clinton, resplendent in fire engine red and wearing a rictus grin, reached out to shake Kennedy's hand—and Obama turned his back on her and began chatting with Claire McCaskill.

"The snub" was what the tabloids dubbed it, though Obama denied it was any such thing; he was just answering a question from McCaskill, he said. But the truth was that the Obamans had snubbed Hillary well before the speech—by rejecting an invitation from the Clintonites for the candidates to sit together during the address. After the carnage in South Carolina, Hillary's staff saw value in creating "a picture of unity," as one of her aides put it on a conference call. The Obamans preferred the picture of Barack and Teddy joined at the hip.

The Kennedy effect on Obama's fortunes was hard to overstate. For superdelegates, Ted's stamp of approval was at once a potent symbol and a permission slip. It dominated the news in the run-up to Super Tuesday—receiving a boost that weekend when Maria Shriver, another of Teddy's nieces and the First Lady of California, climbed aboard the Obama bandwagon. On TV, on the Web, and in the papers, the story line was one that both elites and the rank and file understood in the same way: Obama was ascendant, the Clintons were in free fall, and a new Democratic order was aborning.

Both campaigns revised their Super Tuesday delegate projections as the poll numbers shifted across the country, the Obamans ramping theirs up, the Clintonites tamping theirs down. Further adjustments were required when Edwards at last quit the race on January 30, done in by his third-place finish in South Carolina. Whom Edwards would endorse, and what he might extract, remained open questions. But what had been a de facto two-horse race since Iowa was now officially mano a womano. And with Obama's momentum surging, it seemed possible that he might not only breach Hillary's supposed firewall but reduce her candidacy to ashes.

As the results rolled in the night of Super Tuesday, however, those expectations seemed to have been dashed. Hillary captured four of the five largest states in play: California, New Jersey, New York, and Massachusetts (a victory made sweeter by Kennedy's perfidy). And she was on track to carry the popular vote for the day. It appeared that the House of Clinton was still standing—indeed, that Hillary had won the night.

Out in Chicago, David Plouffe pored over the returns into the wee hours. Plouffe was a man who found the kind of beauty and meaning in a spreadsheet that others saw in a Van Gogh—and what he divined from the numbers now was pulchritudinous in the extreme.

Hillary might win the night's popular vote, but Plouffe could tell that her advantage was infinitesimal (50.2 to 49.8 percent was the final score) and based on millions of early votes the Clintonites had banked before South Carolina and Kennedy changed the game. Obama was on course to claim more states than his rival—thirteen to her nine. And even more important, he was going to emerge with a handful more delegates than Hillary.

Delegates had been Plouffe's obsession from day one. His eyes were set firmly on the only number that mattered: 2,025. Starting in the fall of 2007, he and his national field director, John Carson, began deploying people and money to the seven Super Tuesday caucus states, believing they would be fertile ground for Obama—low-turnout affairs dominated by progressive activists and susceptible to grassroots force. Team Clinton, by contrast, with its depleted resources and Hillary-and-Bill-fueled aversion to caucuses after Iowa, devoted next to no assets to those states. Running essentially unopposed, Obama carried six of them by vast margins, which allowed him to rack up enough delegates to more than compensate for the ground he lost to Hillary in the large-state primaries.

His team was clearly out-organizing, out-strategizing, and out-hustling the other side. And now it looked like the Obamans would be able to out-muscle the Clintonites, too.

In the previous few weeks, an extraordinary thing had happened: money had begun gushing into O-Town through the Web. From the outset, the campaign had labored to build the tech infrastructure to enable that flow, but it wasn't until after New Hampshire that the phenomenon took off. In January, Obama's campaign had raised an astonishing $32 million, much of it online, compared to $13 million for Clinton. And since South Carolina, the pace had only accelerated, fueled by the debut of the singer will.i.am's "Yes, We Can" YouTube video, in which a multiracial array of celebs performed a soulful musical rendition of Obama's speech from the night of the New Hampshire primary.

Plouffe didn't yet know that Hillary had been forced to lend her campaign money; he would find out the next day, with the rest of the world, even as his operation was putting out word that $6 million had poured into its coffers in the span of the previous twenty-four hours.

The significance of Obama's new financial edge was magnified by the calendar. In the weeks between Super Tuesday and March 4—when Texas, Ohio, Rhode Island, and Vermont would vote—there would be eleven contests, four of them caucuses and four primaries with a big share of black voters. With Obama able to outspend Hillary by two or three to one, Plouffe was convinced that his candidate would win nine or ten of the remaining February races, and amass a redoubtable lead in pledged delegates.

Ever since the failure to put Clinton away in New Hampshire, Plouffe had feared that Super Tuesday might be Obama's Waterloo. Now, at three in the morning, he realized it had been Clinton's. Looking up from his tabulations, Plouffe was gripped by the sort of certitude that a math teacher has about multiplication tables.

My God, he thought. *We're going to win the nomination.*

Plouffe would be proved wrong about one thing. Obama didn't win nine or ten of the rest of the contests in February—he won all eleven, in many states trouncing Clinton by margins far wider than Plouffe dared dream of.

Even when things had been going reasonably well, Clinton had never exactly been a buoyant Hubert Humphrey on the stump. But now her unhappy warriorhood was painfully evident. For two solid weeks during Obama's winning streak, she hauled herself to state after state in which she knew she was destined to be routed. She didn't have any choice but to go and scrap for every stray delegate. But the forced-march nature of the stretch only made her agony more acute.

That she was losing—losing eleven in a row, losing the nomination—would've been bad enough by itself, but more wrenching was the way she was losing. Every day seemed to bring some fresh indignity clanging down on her head.

Three days after Super Tuesday, Clinton woke up in Seattle for a day of campaigning ahead of the caucuses in Washington State. On her morning briefing call, Wolfson recapped the past day's coverage, noting that

MSNBC's David Shuster was getting blowback for an on-air comment he'd made about Chelsea—something about her role on the campaign trail, about calls she'd been placing to uncommitted superdelegates.

Clinton had been traveling, had heard nothing about it. What did Shuster say?

He said that Chelsea was, ahem, being "pimped out," Wolfson explained.

After a long silence, Clinton exclaimed, "Are you *kidding*? He said *what*?"

Wolfson read the full Shuster quote to her verbatim: "Doesn't it seem as if Chelsea is sort of being pimped out in some weird sort of way?"

Clinton had long before accepted that it was open season on her and her husband on cable and the Web. But this was something else again. Some cable bloviator had referred to her daughter, in effect, as a prostitute.

Another extended silence filled the air, until Hillary spoke again. Her throat catching, her voice quaking, she wasn't angry, she was distraught—and clearly in tears.

How could he say that? How can they get away with that? It's one thing for them to go after me; it's another thing for them to go after my daughter. Where were the women's groups? "If they let them get away with this," Clinton said, "they deserve what they get."

Still crying, she kept rambling—until, out of nowhere, patched in from the road by one of her aides, an unexpected voice piped up.

"Hi, Mom, it's me," Chelsea said. "I'm okay."

The voice of her daughter brought Hillary instantly back to composure. And, almost as quickly, her feelings shifted from upset to outrage. When the call was over, she told Solis Doyle she wanted to pull out of an upcoming debate in Cleveland being sponsored by NBC and MSNBC. More than that, she wanted her supporters to boycott those networks—she wanted retribution. Solis Doyle talked her off the ledge. The NBC brass was apologizing profusely. Shuster had been suspended indefinitely and was writing her a letter of contrition. When Hillary read it, her reaction was tart. "What a bunch of bullshit," she said.

Two days later, Clinton returned to the capital to try once again to clean up the mess that her campaign had become. She still had no strategy, no message, no path to victory. Decisions still weren't being made. Phone calls still weren't being returned. Solis Doyle seemed checked out. Williams, frustrated with trying to share power with Patti, was threatening to leave.

Clinton arranged to meet Solis Doyle that Sunday morning to figure things out, air their respective grievances. Patti tried to reschedule at the last minute, citing a child care issue, but Hillary was ready to move on. She organized a conference call and announced that Solis Doyle would henceforth be doing Hispanic outreach and Williams would be running the campaign solo.

Maggie, you stay on the call and get everything moving, said Hillary, signing off.

Um, I'm just finding out about this, Williams told the group. I'll have to call everyone back.

Clinton wanted Solis Doyle to stick around, maybe travel with her, help out in Texas. But Patti was done. Two days later, she sent Hillary a lengthy exit memo in which she warmly praised most of her colleagues—but savagely stripped the bark off Penn. "He is mean and untrustworthy," Solis Doyle wrote. "He is demeaning. People hate him. The staff hates him. The media hates him . . . [He] has sucked the soul and humanity out of this campaign."

While Patti's departure left Hillary without one of her most fervent loyalists, another had become a deeply troubled asset. Two months earlier, Bill Clinton had been the best-loved Democrat in the country and maybe the most popular person on the planet besides the Pope. Now, in something like a heartbeat, he'd been transformed into a figure of derision and scorn.

The day after South Carolina, one of Hillary's senior advisers had told her, We have a problem. If you can't control your husband in the campaign, how are you going to control him as president?

"Well, someone will have to talk to him," Hillary said.

"*You* need to talk to him," the adviser replied.

"I can't talk to him," Hillary said.

But Hillary knew Bill's role had to change, and so did the rest of Clintonworld. Alongside his anger, there was now a self-pity that was nearly all-consuming. The day of the Kennedy endorsement, Bill sent a wave of discomfort through the crowd at a high-dollar fund-raising lunch for Hillary in Manhattan. After giving some good-humored opening remarks, he was asked in the Q&A about Kennedy and suddenly went all Mr. Hyde. Rattling off a laundry list of favors he'd done as president for Teddy—from making his sister Jean the ambassador to Ireland to keeping the Coast Guard out searching for John F. Kennedy, Jr.'s plane when it went down in 1999—Clinton seemed to be suggesting that Kennedy's failure to back Hillary was the equivalent of reneging on a debt.

Some days later, Bill received a phone call from George W. Bush. The current and former presidents spoke more often than almost anyone knew; from time to time, when 43 was bored, he would call 42 to chew the fat. In this case, Bush, tucked away at Camp David, had a more distinct objective. He wanted to reassure his predecessor that *he* didn't think Clinton was a racist.

The irony of the situation tickled Bush, but he also felt sympathy for Bill. Hey, buddy, Bush said, I know you're coming under attack; you just gotta keep your chin up. Clinton thanked Bush—then treated him to a fifteen-minute tirade about the injustices that had befallen him and the sources of his suffering.

Bush was the highest-ranking personage serenaded with this rant. But few people who spoke to Clinton that February (or for months thereafter) didn't hear a version of it. His daily conference calls with the campaign took on a *Groundhog Day* quality: morning after morning, the same litany of woe, same howls of protest, same wails about his persecution. On more than one call, Clinton became so overwrought that he broke down in tears. How extreme was the infatuation of the press corps with Obama? "I'll tell you," Bill said. "They just want to cream in their jeans over this guy."

Given Clinton's state of mind, the consensus in Hillaryland was that it might be wise to keep him away from cameras and microphones as much as possible. With Williams in charge and Mills running the campaign's daily operations, Bill's internal influence grew, as they brought him into the decision-making loop on advertising and other matters. But his public visibility was greatly reduced. From then on, he would spend much of his time in rural areas, places that, as the campaign put it, had "never seen a president."

Hillary agreed with the plan, though her attitude toward Bill remained the same as it had been through all their years together. Even at his most scandalous, most inconvenient, she still found her husband a marvel. "When he dies, they should study his brain," she'd say.

On February 19, Obama won his tenth straight contest, administering a 58–41 drubbing to Clinton in the Wisconsin primary, carrying virtually every demographic group, and opening up a pledged-delegate lead of 159.

The next day, Plouffe, on a conference call with reporters, basically declared the race over. Given the rules governing the allocation of delegates in the Democratic Party, Plouffe argued, Clinton would have to win Ohio and Texas by thirty points each, and then win the Pennsylvania primary in April by forty, to close the gap. "This is a wide, wide lead right now," he said. "The Clinton campaign keeps saying the race is essentially tied. That's just lunacy."

Plouffe was aware his comments would be interpreted as an attempt to drive Hillary from the race. He knew he risked rallying her supporters. But Plouffe also knew Obama might wind up just short of the magic 2,025 delegates—leaving the possibility of Clinton prevailing by dint of the superdelegates. Plouffe therefore thought it imperative to start driving the argument, with supers and the press, that the leader in pledged delegates should be, and would be, the party's eventual nominee.

Cold-eyed calculation wasn't the only thing fueling Plouffe's taunts. Frustration also played a part. The longer Clinton stayed in, the more money the Obamans would have to waste in pursuit of a foregone conclusion—millions of bucks that would be better spent on the general election.

Obama was frustrated, too. By the end of his winning streak, the thrill of victory had lost a modicum of its luster for him. He complained to his aides about the sameness of the succession of mega-rallies, about a certain staleness creeping in. Axelrod likened Hillary to Freddy Krueger, and that made Obama laugh. "My God, these people never die," Barack said. Yet he chafed at the party's acquiescence in her continuing her quest. If I had lost eleven in a row, he told Gibbs, I can assure you there wouldn't be a lot of debate about me sticking in the race. Everyone would be pushing me out.

Obama's irritation was leavened by a grudging respect for Hillary's tenacity. *Damn, she's tough,* he thought. But mostly he was confused. Obama had never considered Clinton irrational, yet her refusal to surrender just seemed crazy.

During the course of the campaign, Obama had asked the suits—as well as Emanuel, who had become his on-call expert regarding all things Clinton—countless questions about the tactics and tendencies of the couple. Now he had only one: What on earth was Hillary thinking?

Clinton took the stage in an open-air plaza in downtown San Antonio wearing a dark pantsuit and a pasted-on smile to disguise the depth of her desperation. Under the pantsuit, she had on an orange top that matched the color of the sign fastened to the lectern in front of her: TEXAS—CLINTON COUNTRY. Hillary thought it was true, but she wasn't sure. She wasn't sure of much anymore.

It was nearly ten o'clock at night on February 29, less than four days before primary day in Texas and Ohio. Clinton was exhausted. But San Antonio always gave her a boost; it was a special place for her and Bill. Thirty-six years earlier, they'd come down here from Yale to work for George McGovern, getting their first taste of national politics. And although everyone was duly dazzled by Bill back then, there were those who saw greatness in Hillary, too. A local organizer named Betsey Wright, who later became an indispensable figure in Bill's rise, told her that she might have what it took to become the nation's first female president.

But now, as Hillary looked out on a crowd of three thousand a stone's throw from the Alamo, that dream seemed to be crumbling in her hands. She knew that she had to beat Obama in Texas and Ohio to justify carrying on—even Bill had said so publicly a few days earlier. She was doing fine in Ohio, but in Texas, where Obama was outspending her by a mile, she was slipping. This might be one of the last big rallies of her political life.

So, despite her fatigue, her bone-weariness, and the aching throat that had turned her voice into a raspy growl, Clinton launched into her spiel with gusto—and then, suddenly, the power failed, killing the lights and the sound system, too. Clinton didn't pause. Standing there in the dark, she just plowed right on through.

What was sustaining her? What *was* she thinking? It was simple. She thought Obama wasn't qualified to be commander in chief. And she thought the Republicans would destroy him in the fall, preying on his inexperience and insubstantiality, prying him open and disemboweling him.

That morning her campaign had released a new ad in Texas that went directly to those points. Titled "3AM," it was a concoction of Penn's drawn from a script he'd drafted a few days earlier on his laptop in a file called "gamechangers." The ad was aimed at men in Texas and was basically an update of the famous red-phone spot that Walter Mondale used against Gary Hart in 1984. There were sleeping children, the sound of a phone ringing, and a question: When an international crisis hits, who do you want picking up the receiver in the Oval Office? A shot of Hillary, assured and calm, phone to ear, provided the answer; Obama's name was never mentioned.

Even so, "3AM" was the first ad the Clintonites had run that challenged Obama's fitness for office. But Hillary didn't have a moment's hesitation about airing it. For days, the Obama campaign had been hitting her with negative direct mail on health care and NAFTA—even as Obama continued to play the part of holier-than-thou lord of uplift. *What a phony*, she thought. *What a hypocrite.* Her dander was up.

After more than a year of battling Obama, she'd concluded he was a cipher. In prepping for their debate a week earlier in Cleveland, she had argued with her staff over whether she should call him a "blank slate." She compared him to a preacher, a religious leader, and said, "We have to make people understand that he's not real." Obama's vast crowds, his wild-eyed devotees—it was a kind of mass hysteria.

She was like Cassandra, convinced she could see the future, filled with angst that no one believed her. She looked on in amazement as more and more superdelegates—so many old allies of hers and Bill's—flocked to Obama. Two days earlier, John Lewis had switched his endorsement from Hillary to her opponent. It was painful for Clinton, but she gave a free pass to black elected officials. She understood their position, the pressure they were under, the threats (which the Clintons kept hearing about) that they would be hit with primary-election challenges if they didn't toe the Obama line.

But people such as Senator Jay Rockefeller of West Virginia were another story. Hillary and Rockefeller were friends, she'd thought; they had fought side by side through the health care war of the early nineties. Now Rockefeller was telling Clinton he was backing Obama because his children were jazzed about him. Hillary had heard that explanation before. Was it simply an excuse? Or was it actually true? She couldn't decide which was more pathetic.

Even if Clinton won Ohio and Texas, her only route to the nomination was by way of the superdelegates.

She had to make them understand, had to make them see. She spent the final days before the primaries lashing out at Obama, trying to render him unacceptable. Her campaign drilled him over Rezko, whose corruption trial began that week. They thumped him over his economic adviser Austan Goolsbee, caught telling the Canadian government that Obama's anti-NAFTA stance was merely posturing. Hillary herself handed the likely Republican nominee a choice sound bite to use against her rival in the fall.

"I have a lifetime of experience I will bring to the White House," Clinton declared on March 3. "Senator McCain has a lifetime of experience he will bring to the White House. And Senator Obama has a speech he made in 2002."

The Obamans sloughed off Clinton as a terminal patient raging against the dying of the light. But if Clinton found her voice in New Hampshire, in Texas and Ohio she discovered a new persona: the fighter, the populist, the resilient underdog. She started speaking clearly, forcefully, and empathetically to hard-pressed voters who felt her pain. And she reaped the rewards: a ten-point win in Ohio and a three-point victory in the Lone Star State's primary. Onstage that night in Columbus, Clinton began her speech with a refrain that would thematically mark the rest of her campaign: "For everyone here in Ohio and across America who's ever been counted out but refused to be knocked out, and for everyone who has stumbled but stood right back up, and for everyone who works hard and never gives up, this one is for you."

Once again, Clinton had pulled a rabbit from her hat. Once again, she'd raised questions about Obama. Why couldn't he win the big states that would matter most in the fall? Why did he have trouble connecting with working-class voters? Why couldn't he close the deal?

Yet none of the doubts those questions raised was enough to alter the underlying dynamics or overriding mathematics of the race. For Obama to lose the nomination would require a magnum-force game changer. Something that might cause Democrats en masse to slam on the brakes and say whoa. Something that might lead the party to perceive Obama as Clinton saw him—as a "disaster in the making," as she put it.

Obama, with his epic self-confidence, couldn't imagine what that something could be. More than a year into the campaign, he had thwarted the efforts of his rivals to turn him into a parody. He was still Barack Obama. What he never guessed, though, was that the gravest threat he'd face—the threat now looming before him—wouldn't be posed by his enemies in the present. It would come instead from an old friend.

13

OBAMA AGONISTES

The Obamas ate breakfast in silence at their hotel in San Antonio the morning after Ohio and Texas. Their friends Jarrett and Whitaker tried to cheer them up, but it was no use. Bad vibes suffused the table.

Michelle was especially out of sorts—which is to say, pissed off. She'd been that way the night before, too, but her mood had worsened with the new dawn. She was tired, very tired, and she missed her girls. She was no campaign strategist, but she knew her husband's operation had poured $20 million into Texas and Ohio. And what had all that dinero yielded? Two big, fat losses. Michelle felt she was wasting her time on the road, spending countless days away from home, and yet failing to help her husband. She was unhappy with her schedule. Unhappy with her stump speech. Just unhappy. On the flight home to Chicago, she plugged her iPod headphones into her ears and spoke to no one.

Checking out was no option for Barack, but he was just as displeased as Michelle. He wanted the race against Hillary to be over. He still desperately needed some sleep.

But by failing to put Clinton out of her misery, Obama had all but guaranteed himself another three months of this hell. A seven-week chasm stretched out before him until the Pennsylvania primary on April 22, which, given its older and whiter demographics, he was virtually certain to lose. Many of the contests after that would be no picnic, either; the calendar, which had been his friend in February, was now his enemy. Meanwhile, the press was starting to treat him as what he was: the front-runner. Obama didn't much like it. At a press availability two days earlier, when reporters nagged him about Tony Rezko, he'd whined, "C'mon, guys, I just answered, like, eight questions"—and then stalked off, cutting them short. For more than a month since South Carolina, Obama had been in the catbird seat. Now he braced for his turn in the barrel.

No amount of girding, however, could have prepared Obama for what he saw on his TV screen eight days later. On March 13, ABC News aired a story about his pastor, Reverend Jeremiah Wright. Using excerpts from videotapes of Wright's sermons that were for sale at his parish, Trinity United Church of Christ, the story painted a picture of a preacher unhinged. In one clip, Wright railed about the treatment of African Americans: "The government gives them the drugs, builds bigger prisons, passes the three-strike law, and then wants us to sing 'God Bless America.' No, no, no! Not God bless America—God*damn* America!" In another, he referred to America as the "U.S. of KKK A." In still another, from a sermon delivered after 9/11, Wright bellowed, "We bombed Hiroshima! We bombed Nagasaki! And we nuked far more than the thousands in New York and the Pentagon, and we never batted an eye. We have supported state terrorism against the Palestinians and black South Africans and now we are *indignant* because the stuff we have done overseas is now brought right back into our own front yards!" Revolving on his heel, gazing heavenward, fluttering one hand in the air, Wright ominously concluded, "America's *chickens* . . . are coming *home* . . . to *roost*."

As the story went metastatic the next day, Obama was traveling from Washington to Chicago, where he had a pair of ed-board interviews scheduled with the Windy City's two daily papers. He had been pushing for some time to sit down with the press and try to clear the air about his relationship with Rezko. The suits had resisted, but with the crooked developer on trial and the media pressing on the subject, Obama felt it was imperative. But now, on top of prepping for the interviews, he had to deal with the Wright imbroglio.

"All right, let's get down to business," Obama said as he walked into his campaign HQ. "We've got about two hours and we have a lot to do."

He took a seat in a conference room amid sheer pandemonium among his aides. One of them had drafted a statement on Wright to release to the Huffington Post. But Obama rejected it and, in about twenty minutes, dictated one of his own, which called Wright's sermons "inflammatory and appalling." When the suits said the statement would be a sufficient response, Obama overruled them, saying he wanted to go on TV that night. "They're going to be looping Reverend Wright all weekend; the public needs to see me, too," Obama said. Then he prepared for the Rezko ed boards, and aced them. His performance that day—calm, methodical, precise, and strategic—impressed his team immensely. Anita Dunn, the strategist who'd run Hopefund, had joined the campaign after Nevada. *This is a guy I want in a foxhole with me*, she thought.

Beneath Obama's cool exterior, though, he was furious with his campaign for failing to unearth the Wright tapes before then. Obama had been a member of Trinity for twenty years. He knew Wright could be provocative, even incendiary. And so did much of the political community in Chicago. "This guy is going to be a big problem for Barack," Mayor Daley had warned his brother Bill, even before Obama launched his bid. The *Rolling Stone* story that prompted the downgrading of Wright's role at the announcement in Springfield tossed up another red flag. But the campaign's research department had inexplicably failed to follow up.

Michelle was even angrier than her husband, though the focus of her upset was elsewhere. From the moment she'd read the piece in *Rolling Stone*, she was through with Reverend Wright, ready to quit the church. "That's enough of that," she told Jarrett. Her husband's panicked advisers approached her to find out basic details about the Obamas' membership at Trinity; they knew hardly anything. How often did the family go to church? Had they been present for any of the controversial sermons? Michelle made it clear that she'd never much liked Wright. And that since the births of Malia and Sasha, in 1998 and 2001, the Obamas had rarely attended services.

Still, Obama had said that Wright "brought me to Jesus." He had declared himself a proud Christian. To admit that his religiosity was, in practice, limited, would have made Obama look craven at best, and like a liar at worst.

Obama's relationship to Wright and Trinity was, in fact, complicated. His initial attraction to the parson and his South Side ministry sprang from its commitment to the social gospel: the day care programs, the work with prisoners, the encouragement of HIV/AIDS testing—all the kinds of things that would have appealed to a young community organizer. Obama liked the admixture of working-class and buppie congregants at the church. He was impressed by Wright's reputation as a biblical scholar and had been inspired by his oratory; he had lifted the title of *The Audacity of Hope* from one of Wright's sermons. And although Obama considered the words that were causing the current controversy beyond the pale, he well understood the context—generational, cultural, and social—by which Wright had come to the views that animated them. His ties to his pastor were neither mainly religious nor political. They were quasi-familial. "He's like your uncle who says things you profoundly disagree with," Obama told *The Chicago Tribune* editorial board. "But he's still your uncle."

The evening that Obama released his initial statement about Wright, he conferred with Jarrett, Nesbitt, and Whitaker, then phoned Axelrod. Obama told his strategist that he wanted to give a major address on race—and wanted to do it on Tuesday, just four days later. Given how personal the speech would be, Jon Favreau waited to hear from Obama before he started working on a draft. Obama was busy campaigning the next day and didn't reach him until late that night.

"This is tough," Obama said, "but I'm running for president, and this is what you do when you run for president. I want this to be a teaching moment."

The idea of doing a big race speech had been on Obama's mind for months. Back in the fall, he'd brought it up, but the suits were wary, not wanting to mess with his post-racial brand. He'd raised it again the day after Texas and Ohio, when the exit polls showed that Clinton had won the white vote in the Buckeye State by thirty points. Convinced that he would be the nominee, Obama wanted to start dealing with issues he was destined to confront in the general election, of which race was plainly one. The Wright fiasco had simply sped up the timetable on the speech, filling Obama with—to swipe a phrase—the fierce urgency of now.

Yet even with the Wright snippets playing endlessly on cable, and conservatives baying for Obama's head—demanding to know if he was a closet black radical, as anti-American as the man *The New York Post* had dubbed the "minister of hate"—the suits were dubious. They feared the speech might make the problem worse, deepening instead of healing the gash that

Wright had opened up in the belly of Obama's candidacy. "Do you guys understand, this could be it?" Axelrod said. "This could be the whole campaign."

But when Obama emailed the speech text to his senior staff on March 18, the morning of the address, Axelrod was blown away. "This is why you should be president," he emailed Obama back.

Standing at the lectern at the National Constitution Center in Philadelphia, flanked by four American flags on either side of him, Obama delivered the remarks he'd titled "A More Perfect Union." The speech was candid, nuanced, and replete with context. It spoke to the resentments of both blacks and whites, tried to explain how they had arisen, what fueled them, why they were "grounded in legitimate concerns"—but then argued they had landed the country in a "racial stalemate" that had to be broken.

Obama denounced Wright's comments as "expressing a profoundly distorted view of our country," as "not only wrong but divisive—divisive at a time when we need unity." Yet Obama refused to cut his pastor loose. "I can no more disown him than I can disown the black community," he said. "I can no more disown him than I can my white grandmother . . . who once confessed her fear of black men who passed by her on the street, and who on more than one occasion has uttered racial or ethnic stereotypes that made me cringe.

"The profound mistake of Reverend Wright's sermons is not that he spoke about racism in our society. It's that he spoke as if our society was static; as if no progress has been made," Obama said. "But what we know, what we have seen, is that America can change. That is the true genius of this nation. What we have already achieved gives us hope—the audacity to hope—for what we can and must achieve tomorrow."

In the short term, politically, the speech was as effective as it was eloquent. It placed Obama on the elevated plane where he always thrived. It strummed the mystic chords of the media. It replaced the TV images of Wright fulminating with those of Obama soothing, synthesizing, and waxing hopeful.

Its longer-range effects were harder to gauge. Obama's refusal to disown Wright left him open to attacks from the right. Two days earlier, a video produced by conservative activists titled "Is Obama Wright?" had been posted to YouTube. It weaved together clips of Wright with other ephemera—shots of Obama at a campaign event without his hand over his heart during the national anthem, of him saying he wasn't inclined to wear an American flag lapel pin—to suggest that the senator was unpatriotic. It also featured footage of Michelle, speaking at a recent rally in Wisconsin, saying, "For the first time in my adult lifetime, I'm really proud of my country."

To many Republicans, Obama had long appeared to be a tougher general election opponent than Clinton. But with Wright's emergence, that assessment was being revisited. The question was whether many Democrats were thinking the same thing—and what, if anything, the Clintonites could do to spur the party's synapses to start firing in that fashion.

Harold Ickes proposed hiring a private investigator to look into the connection between Obama and Wright. Ickes was famously liberal; he'd worked for Jesse Jackson. But he was also famously tough and he was at least half-serious about the PI. He was meeting with the Clintons and the Hillaryland high command one day in late March, trying to figure out how to handle the Wright story. Everyone was pussyfooting around the thing, and Ickes had finally had enough. "This guy has been sitting in the church for twenty fucking years," he said. "If you really want to take him down, let's take him fucking down."

The Clintons wanted to take Obama down, but they weren't sure that going after Wright was the way to do it. Some Hillarylanders thought holding a candidate responsible for the words of his minister was unfair. Others thought pushing the story risked touching the third rail that race had become in the campaign. Even Penn was an advocate of Hillary personally keeping a safe distance. But like Ickes, with whom he shared nothing but fierce mutual enmity, Penn believed the campaign should be searching for evidence that Obama had been present for one of Wright's screeds. "The tape will speak for itself" was Penn's position.

Hillary reconciled herself to the wisdom of exercising restraint on Wright. But she saw a maddening double standard in play yet again. "Just imagine, just for fun, if my pastor from Arkansas said the kind of things his pastor said," she held forth one day to her aides. "I'm just saying. Just imagine. This race would be over."

Instead—in spite of Texas and Ohio, in spite of Wright—superdelegates were still swarming to Obama. Since Iowa, he had picked up fifty-three en- dorsements to Hillary's twelve. The flashiest of these was Bill Richardson, who signed on with Obama three days after his race speech. Richardson had been in bad odor with the Clintons since his deal with Obama in the Hawkeye State caucuses. Nevertheless, Bill Clinton had flown to Santa Fe to spend Super Bowl Sunday with Richardson and court him. Clinton swore up and down to his friends that Richardson had promised him five times he would at least refrain from endorsing Obama, even if he didn't back Hillary. Thus did Richardson, courtesy of James Carville, earn himself a new sobriquet in Clintonworld: Judas.

More disquieting to Hillary were the mounting calls for her to leave the race—the latest and loudest of which had emanated from Vermont Senator Patrick Leahy. But far from weakening her resolve, the suggestions that she quit only galvanized her commitment to stay in until the bitter end. They were trying to force her out, even though she still had a chance to win, and that struck her as mighty strange in light of Obama's weaknesses.

What Clinton failed to apprehend were the vulnerabilities that many Democrats continued to see in her, a number of which were on vivid display in the run-up to Pennsylvania. Cable was having a field day with a story that had become known as Snipergate. More than once on the trail, Hillary had described a trip she made to Bosnia as First Lady in 1996. In her telling, she arrived under sniper fire, racing across the tarmac with her head down. In late March, video surfaced of her being greeted at Tuzla airport by cheerful children, with Chelsea smiling beside her. The story reinforced every extant preconception about the Clintons' dodgy relationship with the truth.

Then, on April 4, Clinton was engulfed in yet another Hillaryland melodrama. *The Wall Street Journal* reported that Penn, in his continuing role as CEO of Burson-Marsteller, had just met with the Colombian ambassador in Washington to strategize about how to win passage of a free trade deal with the United States—a pact that Hillary and the labor unions opposed. The resulting furor forced Clinton to demote Penn, elevating Wolfson and the pollster Geoff Garin to jointly fill the role that her chief strategist had occupied.

To the outside world, the Penn fracas was another sign of a Clinton campaign in chaos, and a damning one for a candidate running on experience and competence. Inside Hillaryland, however, the situation was seen as even more disturbing. In the eyes of many, the chief strategist had shown his true stripes: that his paramount client was always himself, his preponderant aim his own enrichment. What Penn had done was a firing offense, his continued presence in the building a demonstration of Hillary's insecurity.

Clinton, it seemed, couldn't catch a break—and then, out of nowhere, she got one. On April 11, less than two weeks before the primary, the Huffington Post put online audio of Obama speaking at a private fund-raiser in San Francisco. "You go into some of these small towns in Pennsylvania, and like a lot of small towns in the Midwest, the jobs have been gone now for twenty-five years and nothing's replaced them," Obama told the group. "So it's not surprising then that [people there] get bitter, they cling to guns or religion or antipathy to people who aren't like them or anti-immigrant sentiment or anti-trade sentiment as a way to explain their frustrations."

Obama's "bitter/cling" comments seemed to be a heavenly gift to the Clintons. They billboarded a simple message about Obama that Hillary and Bill already believed was true: that he was, at bottom, a helpless and hopeless elitist. Unlike the Wright story, here was something the Clintons could push—and push it they did, immediately and furiously and with no fear of stumbling over racial trip wires. For the next ten days, Hillary would come at Obama guns blazing, armed with a line that, in the context of her new persona, was so well pitched and perfectly modulated that it almost sounded like poetry.

"Americans need a president that will stand up for them, not a president that looks down on them," she said.

The final Democratic debate of 2008 took place in Philadelphia on April 16. The event was being held in the same venue where Obama had given his race

speech a month earlier, the National Constitution
Center. So there was a certain grim coincidence when,
the day of the debate, Obama's BlackBerry buzzed
with the news that Reverend Wright was planning to
resurface. Obama was already in rotten spirits over everything that had happened in the past weeks. Now
his worst nightmare was planning a comeback tour,
complete with media interviews and public speeches.
Terrific.

The debate, sponsored by ABC News, did nothing
to elevate his mood. The first and second questions
to Obama, from Charlie Gibson, were about "bitter/
cling" and Wright. The third and fourth, from George
Stephanopoulos, were also about the reverend. Next,
by video, a voter from Latrobe, referencing the lapel
pin controversy, challenged Obama: "I want to know if
you believe in the American flag." Then Stephanopoulos asked about his association with William Ayers, a
former member of the Weather Underground (a group
that had bombed the Pentagon and the Capitol in the
early seventies), who lived in Obama's neighborhood in
Chicago and with whom he was said to be friendly.

Obama looked weary and defeated, as if he'd been
beaten with a stick. He soldiered through his answers,
calling the flag pin matter a "manufactured issue" and
saying that inferring anything from his acquaintance

with Ayers, "who engaged in detestable acts forty years ago, when I was eight years old . . . doesn't make much sense."

Hillary seemed to know a lot about Obama's ties to the erstwhile Weatherman; she noted in her rebuttal that the two men had served on a board together, citing dates and other details. Clinton's staff was surprised; Ayers hadn't been part of her prep. But Hillary had a number of friends—among them Sid Blumenthal, whose nickname was "Grassy Knoll"—regularly feeding her on the sly negative tidbits of dubious veracity about Obama. (In getting ready for that night, Hillary casually mentioned to her aides that she'd heard that Obama's mother was a communist.) Her advisers tried to prevent her from spouting such stuff in the debates. But every so often, she slipped something in.

After the face-off, Clinton was tickled pink over seeing Obama slammed so hard and on such earthy matters. Kibitzing in a hallway offstage, she told her aides, "I need you all to think about the best closing argument, what ads to go with, especially now with all this new material."

No brilliant closing argument would be required. Between "bitter/cling" and Hillary's resurgence on the trail, where her fighter's stance grew even more pronounced and effective, Clinton had Pennsylvania in her pocket. Six days later, she trotted to victory.

Obama took no comfort from the fact that the suits had told him all along he was foreordained to lose Pennsylvania. Hillary had killed him again among white voters, 63 to 37—and beaten him among every ideological cohort except the self-described "very liberal." More loudly than before, pundits were saying that Obama couldn't close the deal. Some were even starting to compare him to McGovern and Dukakis.

Obama flew out of Pennsylvania and scheduled a meeting with his team at his house for the next night. *Enough is enough*, he thought. The time for change had come.

Around four o'clock on April 23, a few hours before the rest of his brain trust would arrive, Barack and Michelle met with Jarrett and Rouse to get their read on the situation.

"I gotta tell you," Rouse said, "I'm a little uncomfortable having this conversation without Axe and Gibbs and Plouffe here."

"I don't know why," cracked Obama. "I talk to them all the time without you there."

It had been nine months since the Edley meeting spurred Obama to draw Rouse and Jarrett deeper into the campaign fold. Since then, he'd often expressed a desire to broaden the circle further, get more voices in the room, especially more female voices. But the suits would slow-walk him, and Obama wouldn't push it. As long as things were going fine, he was happy deferring to them, didn't mind the narrow pipeline. When things went badly, though, Obama would start making noise again—and things were certainly not tip-top now.

Rouse was all for more voices, but he saw a greater imperative. "You need to take more ownership of this campaign," he told Obama. You've got a great team here, you've got confidence in them, they've got your best interests at heart. But what it feels like to me is that they say, Here's our schedule for the week, here's our theme—and off you go. I think you're the best political mind we've got. You ought to be more engaged.

At seven, the rest of the brain trust arrived in Hyde Park. Attending by phone was Anita Dunn. Everyone could see from Obama's body language that he was tense. Instead of sitting back, relaxed, with his legs crossed as usual, he was hunched over his dining room table, his hands curled into fists, the trademark twinkle absent from his eyes.

Look, Obama said, I have not been my best the last two months. The "bitter" thing was a huge gaffe. I didn't perform well at the debate. My pastor was a big problem. But let's be honest, you guys haven't been your best, either. We're not going to lose the nomination. We've come too far. But we have a bunch of challenging states in front of us, and I don't want to limp across the finish line. I want to finish strong.

For the next five hours, Obama and his team chewed over what was wrong and how to fix it. Obama listened to everyone's ideas—and then told them how it was going to be. From then on, he said, the campaign would have a nightly conference call to run down what had happened that day and strategize about the next. The entire senior staff would be on the call. And Dunn, not Axelrod, would run it. Obama knew that many of his aides felt locked out of the loop by the suits, and were reluctant to disagree with them. He wanted that to end. He also wanted a nightly assessment of how they had fared in each twenty-four-hour news cycle. "We need to win every day," he said.

Before then, Obama had been fairly detached from the granular details of the daily back-and-forth—now he insisted on being up to his eyeballs in them. He wanted to know which surrogates were going to be on television. To see talking points and message plans. To be consulted on paid media decisions. To prescreen every ad before it aired.

Then there was the matter of Michelle. Since Ohio and Texas, her circumstances had only grown more trying. "Proud of my country" had turned her into something of a target; even John McCain's wife, Cindy, had taken a shot at her. ("I don't know about you, if you heard those words earlier," she said. "I am *very* proud of my country.") Michelle worried that she was hurting Barack's prospects, thought the campaign wasn't protecting her sufficiently, that it hadn't devised a real strategy for her.

That, too, was going to end, Obama said. He wanted to see a plan for Michelle. And not just some ideas vomited verbally; he wanted to see paper.

How long all these changes would remain in place was unclear. "I may not need this forever," Obama said. But it was how they would be doing business at least through the next two contests—the primaries in Indiana and North Carolina on May 6.

Obama believed that winning them both would force Clinton from the race. North Carolina, with its large black vote and high concentrations of college students and knowledge workers, promised to be relatively easy. But Indiana would be a bear. Obama decreed that they would go balls out to win the Hoosier State. Michelle would do whatever the campaign planned for her. Their daughters would even hit the trail with them for the final weekend.

We're all damn tired, Obama said. But we all need to get off our asses and end this thing, all right?

A fine plan, for sure—but there was a small wrinkle. The Jeremiah Wright comeback tour was about to begin.

Obama had tried to call Wright before his race speech, but failed to reach him; the reverend had just retired from the church and set off on a ten-day cruise. Obama was aware that Wright was angry about what had happened around the announcement in Springfield and disgruntled over the candidate's words in Philadelphia. Somehow Obama needed to break through all the acrimony and misunderstanding.

The two men arranged a secret meeting at the reverend's Chicago home. Obama explained that he hadn't intended to criticize Wright in his race speech—far from it. Disowning him would have been the expedient play, but Obama had resisted. He had tried to place Wright in historical context, tried to help others understand where he was coming from. Obama treated Wright as an old friend, a former mentor. He tried to raise his consciousness about the magnitude of what Wright was jeopardizing: Obama's run for the presidency represented something far greater than either of them individually. But Wright didn't seem either persuaded or placated.

He listened to me, heard me out, Obama told Jarrett afterward. I had a chance to express my concerns. We'll see.

That Friday night, in an interview with Bill Moyers on PBS, Wright spoke softly as he defended himself and argued that the clips of his sermons had been deployed to paint a caricature of him. "I felt it was unfair," he said. "I felt it was unjust. I felt it was untrue. I felt those who were doing that were doing it for some very devious reasons." Moyers asked Wright about his reaction to Obama's race speech. "I do what I do; he does what politicians do," Wright said. "So that what happened in Philadelphia where he had to respond to the sound bites, he responded as a politician."

Most of Obama's advisers heaved a sigh of relief at the PBS interview—but Jarrett did not. She knew immediately that Wright's impugning of Obama's motives would wound her friend. And she was right.

"How could he say that about me?" Obama asked Jarrett. "He knows that's not true. He knows I wasn't being a politician."

Personally painful as the Moyers interview may have been for Obama, it was Wright's appearance at the National Press Club on the morning of April 28, three days later, that was politically imperiling. Posing and preening, pontificating, apostrophizing, and mugging for the cameras, Wright declined to retract his "chickens coming home to roost" comments about America's complicity in 9/11. Asked about AIDS, he brought up the Tuskegee experiment and said, "Based on what has happened to Africans in this country, I believe our government is capable of doing anything." Asked about Louis Farrakhan, he said, "He is one of the most important voices in the twentieth and twenty-first century." Asked about Obama, he repeated and sharpened his attacks on his parishioner as a typical politician, and then added that he'd told Obama, "If you get elected, November the fifth, I'm coming after you, because you'll be representing a government whose policies grind under people."

Campaigning in North Carolina, Obama hadn't watched the performance live, but Jarrett, by phone, told him it was bad. Very bad. On the tarmac in Wilmington, Obama, under pressure from reporters to offer a reaction, could summon only a wan rebuke for an offense he had not seen. "He does not speak for me," Obama said. "He does not speak for the campaign."

Later, on the campaign's new nightly conference call, his advisers paraphrased for him what Wright had said. But Jarrett urged him, "You've got to watch this for yourself. You have to look at him."

When Obama did, late that evening in his hotel room, he was stunned. The first Wright eruption had filled him with sadness at the sight of his pastor self-destructing. But the sequel made him angry and indignant. With his race speech, Obama had declined to throw Wright under the bus. Now Wright appeared to be hell-bent on tossing Obama in front of a runaway train.

A press conference was arranged to follow a town hall meeting in Winston-Salem the next morning. A few minutes before Obama would walk out and face the waiting reporters, Gibbs found his boss in a men's room in a recess of the Joel Coliseum Annex, standing over the sink washing his hands, lost in thought.

Gibbs had traveled thousands of miles with Obama, seen him in almost every conceivable situation. Moments of stress. Moments of dolor. Moments of steely fury. But he had never encountered Obama in a moment of profound self-doubt. Even at the lowest moments of the campaign, nothing had shaken Obama's conviction that the country would see him in the way he wanted it to see him. See him as he saw himself. See him as he was. But Wright had stolen that certainty from Obama. His public image was up for grabs, along with the nomination.

"Do people really believe that I think that way?" Obama said softly. "Do people really believe that his views are my views? Why would people think that?"

Gibbs tried to reassure Obama, urged him to go out and say simply and forcefully that he found Wright offensive. Gibbs had no doubt what was at stake. The entire Obama enterprise had been based on the premise that Barack could transcend racial stereotypes, if not race itself. Now Wright—a stereotype of a stereotype—threatened to torpedo that underpinning. It was, both men agreed, the moment of maximum peril in the campaign. Obama touched Gibbs on the arm and said, "I know what I gotta do."

"The person that I saw yesterday was not the person that I met twenty years ago," he declared before the cameras. "His comments were not only divisive and destructive, but I believe that they end up giving comfort to those who prey on hate and I believe that they do not portray accurately the perspective of the black church. They certainly don't portray accurately my values and beliefs. And if Reverend Wright thinks that that's political posturing, as he put it, then he doesn't know me very well."

The next six days were brutal for Obama. His poll numbers took a hit in North Carolina and plummeted in Indiana, where the campaign now feared getting clobbered. He was campaigning harder than he ever had before. But Clinton was working just as hard, and was in a groove. At high school gyms, train depots, and fire stations, she turned in performances that were sharp, energetic, and laced through with antic, even madcap, populism—vowing to "go right at OPEC" over high gas prices, attacking Wall Street "money brokers" for their role in causing the recession. Her staff was bedraggled, shriveled; Hillary fairly glowed. "She's finally having fun," said one of her aides.

Obama was having no fun at all. He was consumed by visions of doom. First Texas and Ohio. Then Pennsylvania. Then Wright. Now the possibility of a drubbing in Indiana. Would the superdelegates start to think Obama was mortally wounded? That Clinton was correct that he was unelectable? *Maybe we're not going to survive,* he thought.

On the night before the May 6 primaries, Obama was in Indianapolis for a massive get-out-the-vote rally that included entertainment by Stevie Wonder. Twenty-one thousand people were there. Rain bucketed down from the skies all over them.

Jarrett, Nesbitt, and Whitaker had come from Chicago to lend Obama moral support. He needed it, Valerie thought. Her friend seemed despondent.

"I can't wait to call you Mr. President," Jarrett said, trying to buck him up after the rain-soaked rally.

"I don't know if I'm going to call you that, man," Nesbitt chimed in. "You're going to always just be Barack to me."

Obama laughed a little.

"Look, man," Nesbitt went on. "There's nothing you can do about Reverend Wright. He's a suicide politician. He had a plastic explosive strapped to his vest and he said, 'I'm blowing up everybody!'"

All of them started cracking up, mirthful tears streaming down their faces—until Axelrod walked in wearing an even more mournful expression than usual.

Bad news, he said. The polls don't look good. We're down twelve in Indiana, and it's tight in North Carolina.

"Get Axelrod out of here," Obama said, instantly deflating. "He's a downer."

A downer, and also wrong, it turned out—with enormous implications. The next day, Obama won North Carolina by a whopping fifteen points. And while Clinton carried Indiana, it was only by the barest of margins, a single percentage point.

From a stage in Indianapolis, Hillary made a half-hearted attempt to declare herself the victor of the night. "Not too long ago, my opponent made a prediction," Clinton intoned. "He said I would probably win Pennsylvania, he would win North Carolina, and Indiana would be the tie breaker. Well, tonight we've come from behind, we've broken the tie, and thanks to you, it's full speed on to the White House."

Not a soul believed her. Though Obama had failed to defeat Clinton in Indiana, he'd achieved several greater triumphs. He had beaten expectations. He had reassured the party that he wasn't irreparably damaged goods. And, not least, he had overcome his real nemesis—not Hillary Clinton, but Jeremiah Wright. Around midnight, Tim Russert appeared on MSNBC and summed up the meaning of Obama's trifecta unequivocally, with a single sentence that caused one set of hearts to flutter and another to stop beating: "We now know who the Democratic nominee is going to be and no one is going to dispute it."

14

THE BITTER END GAME

The voters of West Virginia didn't give a damn about Russert's certainty or Obama's hold on the nomination. A week later, in the state's primary on May 13, they delivered Clinton a victory by the kind of margin normally reserved for blowout football games: 67–26.

Obama had wanted to play hard in West Virginia, but his advisers told him no way. There were too many "bitter people" there, they said, employing what had become their rueful shorthand for white working-class voters. Obama bridled at the ever-growing perception that he couldn't win those voters, and wanted to dispel any impression that he wasn't competing for them. For three nights running, he kept asking, Are you sure we can't go? Are you sure we can't win? Are you sure we shouldn't even show the flag? Yes, we're sure, Plouffe said. It would be a waste of your time and our money.

But now, in the wake of a forty-one-point shellacking, the campaign faced the prospect of a welter of stories about Obama's weakness with a key general-election demographic. It needed something to quash that coverage, and to show the superdelegates that West Virginia had changed nothing, that the nomination was still in Obama's bag.

Barack had an idea. For the past week, his emissaries had been pushing hard to land (finally) the endorsement of Edwards, whose blue-collar cred might have given Obama a bump with the bitter people. They were close, so close, the go-betweens said, but apparently Edwards was still waffling.

"I'm going to call John one more time," Obama said on the campaign's conference call the night of West Virginia, "and tell him that if he wants to do this, tomorrow is the last day when it's gonna matter."

Obama had been chasing the endorsement since Edwards dropped out at the end of January. They talked by phone the day Edwards quit, and a few weeks later Obama trekked down to Chapel Hill to make his pitch. Obama and Elizabeth got into a squabble about health care, in which she criticized his reform plan as weak beer. Obama liked John well enough, but didn't exactly consider him a policy heavyweight. Being lectured to by his wife on substance—well, Obama found that pretty rich.

The trouble with Obama, from Edwards's point of view, was his refusal to get transactional. He wouldn't engage, wouldn't promise anything, wouldn't so much as deign to stroke Edwards's ego. When Edwards told Obama that he wanted him to make poverty a centerpiece of his agenda, Obama airily replied, Yeah, yeah, yeah, I care about all that stuff. Clinton, by contrast, proposed that she and Edwards do a poverty tour together, even hinted that Edwards would have "a role" in her administration. Edwards still had his eye on becoming attorney general, and thought the odds of getting that plum were better with Clinton than with Obama. But after South Carolina, the chances of Clinton claiming the nomination just kept falling—and Edwards didn't want to back a loser.

So, instead, Edwards sat there, perched on the fence, squandering his leverage. Making the situation all the more absurd was the birth in late February of Rielle Hunter's baby, a girl she named Frances Quinn. In a crib somewhere, secreted away, the out-of-wedlock child was peacefully gurgling. And yet here Edwards was, still believing, beyond all reason, that he could be nominated and confirmed down the road to run the U.S. Department of Justice.

Obama reached Edwards the night of West Virginia not long before midnight, and managed, however momentarily, to pierce his bubble of delusion. At 1:15 a.m., Obama sent an email to his staff: Edwards is a go.

The endorsement was unveiled seventeen hours later in Grand Rapids, Michigan. Edwards enjoyed the experience more than he thought he would. (His attitude on the flight up had been, let's get this over with.) And he didn't come away empty-handed. At a meeting with his donors in New York, Edwards bragged about securing a prime-time speaking slot at the Democratic convention, though for the Obamans, that was a small price to pay. Timed to coincide with the network evening news, the endorsement succeeded not only in stepping on Clinton's West Virginia headlines but in shifting the narrative about Obama's demographic dilemma.

There was another set of problems, not unrelated, that Obama was determined to fix, and they involved his wife. The criticism of Michelle over "proud of my country" had grown more vociferous and pointed; that week, the Tennessee Republican Party posted a four-minute Web video skewering her for the remark. Then there were the rumors buzzing in the political world about the "whitey tape": footage that supposedly existed of Michelle at Trinity United railing against the sins of Caucasian America, using the term "whitey." The chatter hit the blogosphere three days after West Virginia. A pro-Clinton site claimed the tape—"video dynamite"—was in the hands of the Republicans, who were planning to deploy it during the general election as an "October surprise."

The Obama campaign found the idea of the "whitey tape" preposterous. But after the Wright fracas, no one was taking any chances. Jarrett was dispatched to raise the topic with Michelle. "Did you ever say anything about 'whitey' at Trinity?" Jarrett asked.

What? Michelle said. I never spoke at Trinity and if I had, I would certainly not have used that word. Later, she joked to Jarrett, It's such a dated word. I'm much cooler than that!

Barack was in no mood for jest. He expected that the fall campaign would be ugly, and told himself he was ready for the freak-show attacks on him. *I'm a big boy,* Obama thought. *I can take it.* What he wasn't prepared for, what he wouldn't countenance, was seeing his wife in the crosshairs. "They're coming after Michelle," he told Jarrett. "I want to shut it down."

On May 18, while campaigning in Oregon, the Obamas taped a segment for the next day's broadcast of *Good Morning America.* When the interviewer brought up the Tennessee Republican Party Web video, Obama pounced. "If they think that they're gonna try to make Michelle an issue in this campaign, they should be careful," he said, fairly growling. "For them to try to distort or to play snippets of her remarks in ways that are unflattering to her, I think is just low class." Obama added, "These folks should lay off my wife."

In truth, Obama was talking as much about the whitey tape as the GOP video—and the folks he was addressing weren't just Republicans but Hillary and Bill. In case they were considering a last-ditch, scorched-earth campaign, he wanted to draw a bright line underscoring the limits of what he'd tolerate.

After the interview, Jarrett asked Michelle what she thought.

"Look at my husband," she said, beaming. "That's my husband."

Obama had reason to be concerned about where the Clintons' heads were at. Without a plausible road still open to carry Hillary to the nomination, they seemed to be left with only two options: giving up or going postal. Rahm Emanuel, one of the few people in the world talking to both sides, was counseling Obama to give Hillary space, even as he urged Bill Clinton not to turn the final days of the race into a shooting spree.

But Emanuel was blunt with Obama about one thing. Quitting, he said, simply wasn't in the Clintons' bloodstream.

Certainly there had never been any evidence of that particular form of plasma in the former president's veins. And his recent behavior gave no indication that he'd received a transfusion. Besides his small-town stumping, Bill Clinton's main assignment was continuing to make phone calls to superdelegates, in which he pressed the case for Hillary and against Obama aggressively—at times, too aggressively. Clinton's message, sometimes implicitly, sometimes explicitly, was that the country wasn't ready to elect an African American president. Some recipients of the calls found them discomfiting, others embarrassing; few found them effective. Complaints were registered with the campaign. Bill's call sheet was duly adjusted.

Hillary's avoidance of ringing up superdelegates had long driven Ickes and others in Ballston to distraction. From Texas and Ohio onward, with a loaded gun pressed against her temple, she finally got with the program. The calls she made were softer in tone, but not much different in substance, than her husband's. Citing her strength among white voters in rural Ohio and Indiana, she would refer elliptically to the racial attitudes that she believed would keep them from pulling the lever for Obama in the fall. "You know how people are," she'd say.

Yet after Indiana and North Carolina, the Clintons realized that highlighting Obama's existing vulner-abilities would do little to reverse the tide of superdel-egates flowing into his column. Desperately, feverishly, they clung to the hope that a bombshell of some kind would fall from the sky and explode on top of him. A corps of conspiracy theorists around them encour-aged such notions. Penn believed that a late-breaking story on Rezko might disqualify Obama. Blumenthal was obsessed with the "whitey tape," and so were the Clintons, who not only believed that it existed but felt that there was a chance it might emerge in time to save Hillary. "They've got a tape, they've got a tape," she told her aides excitedly. It just goes to show, Hillary added, "You never know what can happen."

Clinton had other, less fantastical reasons for re-maining in the race. After one of her rallies that May, she sat down with her friend Ted Strickland and asked what he thought she should do. "I'm under so much pressure to get out," she said.

"I think you should do what you perceive to be in your best interest," Strickland told her. "But let me tell you what a part of me wants you to do, and that's to fight this thing to the bitter end, because you deserve to do that. No one has a right to try to push you out of this race."

Hillary heard that kind of thing all the time, and not just from party bigwigs but from ordinary voters, the kinds of people who crowded ten deep along her rope lines now, the women and men screaming, crying, brandishing countless items for her to autograph: T-shirts, books (*Living History*), pink boxing gloves, crumpled cocktail napkins. (She always signed simply "Hillary.") As she'd located her groove on the campaign trail, she'd begun inspiring great passion and devotion in her fans, and it meant the world to her.

These people, her supporters, millions of them, wanted her to stay in. So did two of her most trusted advisers, Penn and Mills. And so, of course, did her husband.

The matter of Bill's approval and his example loomed large in Hillary's mind. "When he had his toughest test, impeachment, he never gave up, never quit," an old Clinton hand observed. "How could she ever lie down before the race was completely over? Losing is one thing, but throwing in the towel would mark her as a failure in his eyes."

But those were not the only voices in Clinton's ears. Quietly, discreetly, Garin and Wolfson were trying to escort her to a graceful exit. Their arguments didn't revolve solely around the fact that she could no longer prevail. They spoke to what came next. If Clinton stuck around and aimed to destroy Obama, which was what winning would require, the effort would not only miscarry (they were sure of that) but shred her reputation, hobbling her ability to have any kind of meaningful future in the party.

Clinton, however reluctantly, agreed. She resolved to strike a delicate balance, staying in the race until the end, but eschewing criticism of Obama.

That was easier said than done, as Clinton would learn to her regret. Barely twenty-four hours after Indiana and North Carolina, she was quoted in *USA Today* saying, "Senator Obama's support among working, hard-working Americans, white Americans, is weakening again."

When the inevitable ruckus ensued, Clinton wailed to her aides that she was merely trying to make a demographic point—that the press was yet again casting her words in the worst possible light. "I feel like I'm living in a fun house," she complained.

Two weeks later, it was more like a house of horrors. Campaigning in Sioux Falls, South Dakota, ahead of the state's June 3 primary, Hillary sat down for an ed-board interview with the Sioux Falls *Argus-Leader.* Clinton mentioned that she found the calls for her to leave the race strange. "Historically, that makes no sense," she said, "so I find it a bit of a mystery."

"You don't buy the party unity argument?" she was asked.

"I don't because, again, I've been around long enough," Clinton replied. "You know my husband did not wrap up the nomination in 1992 until he won the California primary somewhere in the middle of June, right? We all remember Bobby Kennedy was assassinated in June in California."

Clinton went on to her next event, at a supermarket in Brandon. As she spoke to a couple hundred voters in the produce section, she noticed a sudden commotion among the traveling press—reporters swarming around her aides, her aides waving their arms and yelling.

The cause of the uproar was a fresh story on the website of *The New York Post,* whose reporter had watched a video feed of the ed board and wrote of Clinton: "She is still in the presidential race, she said today, because historically, it makes no sense to quit, and added that, 'Bobby Kennedy was assassinated in June,' making an odd comparison between the dead candidate and Barack Obama."

Clinton, of course, had made no such comparison, but the horse had left the barn. Soon enough, the story was bannered on the Drudge Report and being jibbered about on cable news. Stoking the frenzy, the Obamans quickly put out a statement, saying her comment "was unfortunate and has no place in this campaign."

After Hillary finished in the produce area, her staff hustled her into the market's stock room and explained what was going on. Standing amid shelves of canned goods, they ran through the chain of events, explaining that her remarks had set off a firestorm—one in which much of the media was now reporting that she had said, in effect, that she was still in the race because Obama might get shot.

"Unfuckingbelievable!" Clinton said, and shook with fury. How could anyone report that? How could anyone think that I meant that? How could they think that *about me*?

Mo Elleithee, one of her aides, told her Wolfson was adamant that Hillary needed immediately to face the press and clean up the problem. We tried to explain, Elleithee went on, but the reporters are pushing back because Obama's safety has been such an issue.

"Don't talk to me about safety," Hillary snapped. "Don't talk to me about threats on your life. I've been living with threats for fifteen years. I've had threats on my daughter's life. I've had guns and knives confiscated from my campaign events this year. Don't give me a lecture on safety!"

A few minutes later, Clinton dutifully went out and made a statement. She mopped up the mess, or, at least, she tried to—but, really, she didn't care. All the frustration she'd felt with the press through the campaign was encapsulated in that moment. She flew back to New York late in the night, her anger draining away, replaced with dysphoria. Watching her recede into herself, deflated, dejected, one of Clinton's aides on the plane had a thought: *The campaign is over.*

On the night of Tuesday, June 3, Obama clinched the Democratic nomination. Having split the last two primaries that day with Clinton—him winning in Montana, her in South Dakota—and receiving a final-hours influx of support from superdelegates, he had made it to the magic 2,025. At the Xcel Energy Center in St. Paul, Minnesota, where the Republicans would hold their convention that summer, Obama strode onstage to the strains of U2's "Beautiful Day," clasping hands with Michelle, hugging her, then sharing with her the most famous fist bump in the history of humankind.

After the speech, Barack, Michelle, his team, and his friends retired to a bar inside the arena to watch Clinton's event in New York on television. The Obamans were expecting a concession speech—or, at least, remarks that were courteous and maybe even classy. So was the press. So were even some of her supporters.

But the address Clinton gave that night in the basement gym of Baruch College was instead seen by many as a churlish attempt to stomp on Obama's buzz. After being introduced by Terry McAuliffe as "the next president of the United States," Clinton didn't concede, didn't endorse, didn't so much as acknowledge her rival's historic triumph. "Now the question is," Hillary asked the crowd, "where do we go from here?"

Her audience chanted, "Denver! Denver! Denver!"

She seemed to revel in it.

Back in St. Paul, some brainiac in the Obama communications shop had decided it would be a good idea to let the media be in the bar while the Obama team viewed Clinton's speech. As Hillary spoke, all the air went out of the room. Obama walked over and punched Jarrett in the arm.

"*What?*" she said to him.

"The look on your face," Obama said, noting her sour expression. "The *press* is here."

The next morning in Washington, a conference call of the senior Hillarylanders was convened to discuss their boss's next steps. "We have three choices," Penn said. "She can just get out. She can negotiate. Or she can park." By parking, Penn meant suspend active campaigning but not concede—waiting around, hoping for a landmine to explode under Obama's feet.

The group quickly coalesced around option number one, but Penn's preferred option was that she park. "Let's kick the can down the road," he said, maybe all the way to Denver. Or at least let's negotiate. Hillary had won eighteen million votes; her support was a valuable commodity. She should extract concessions from Obama.

"We need to make him grovel," Penn said.

As the call was going on, Clinton and Obama were at the Washington Convention Center for the annual meeting of the Jewish lobbying group AIPAC. Obama spoke first, then Clinton. When Hillary finished, she hurried backstage for a photo shoot for an upcoming magazine cover story—and ran smack into Obama and his traveling party.

The unfolding scene was a semiotician's fantasia. For months, Clinton and Obama had battled (and battered) each other more or less as equals. But now there was no longer even a faint hint of parity. When they first spied each other in the cluttered hallway, Clinton hugged the wall deferentially to let Obama pass. Obama took her aside, put his hand on her shoulder, leaned in for a few words. When their chat was over and Obama marched toward the freight elevator to leave, his Secret

Service agents brusquely shooed away Clinton's aides: "Make way for Senator Obama! Make way for Senator Obama!"

The question was whether Hillary herself would heed that directive. A few minutes later, she would head off to Ballston to figure out her end game. She was somber, prideful, aggrieved, confused—and still high on the notion that she was leading an army, Napoleon in a navy pantsuit and gumball-size fake pearls. Clinton knew she was being pummeled for her speech the night before, but she'd convinced herself that she was, in fact, helping Obama. Her voters were angry, they felt insulted, they had to be coaxed along. If she'd simply endorsed her rival, her supporters might have washed their hands of both of them, either staying home in the fall or voting for McCain. The situation was volatile.

Clinton was hearing from countless allies about what she should do now, but much of their advice—as it had been all along through the marathon campaign—she considered useless. A war was raging inside her between rationality and denial. Maybe she should wait a week before doing anything. Or maybe two. Keep her options open. You never knew what could happen.

It didn't take long for Hillary's high command, huddled in a conference room in her headquarters, to disabuse her of those thoughts. Grunwald told Clinton that she had to avoid letting the past twelve hours become "the last snapshot" of her campaign. The perception that she'd behaved badly had taken hold in the media, and fairly or not, threatened to eclipse everything she had accomplished. She had to get out and get behind Obama, quickly and graciously, but do it in a way that served her interests and her image. "You should own the moment yourself," Grunwald said.

Tina Flournoy, a savvy labor politico who'd joined the campaign in its late stages, drew an analogy to the Civil War. A lot of people who weren't ready for the battle to end took to the hills, Flournoy said. You can go to the hills for a while, but you have to come down eventually. You can't stay in the hills.

Clinton polled the table as to whether Obama could win in November. "Yes," Flournoy said. "With your help, he can win." Everyone but Penn and Mills agreed.

Clinton was persuaded to exit and set in motion plans to concede and endorse Obama that weekend.

The former combatants arranged to meet secretly Thursday evening at the home of Senator Dianne Feinstein in northwest Washington. They had much to discuss—Hillary's role at the convention, what help Obama might offer in retiring her campaign debt, how they would campaign together in the fall—but only one thing really mattered at this moment: whether Clinton would be Obama's running mate.

Speculation on the topic had been raging in the media for the past few days. Many of Clinton's supporters considered the veep slot Hillary's due. BET's Bob Johnson had launched a public campaign on her behalf, telling the press that Clinton had informed him that "if asked to do this, she must accept because she believes that it is in the best interest of the party."

The truth was, Clinton's ambivalence at the prospect was deep. If Obama offered her the number-two spot, Hillary *did* feel she would have to take it—but mainly to avoid being blamed if she declined and then Obama lost in the fall. Though her husband was all for her being on the ticket, Hillary found it difficult to muster any enthusiasm for it. "I've already done that job," she told Penn.

Obama's view of the matter was complicated, too. For all the heartache and heartburn of the campaign, he respected and admired Hillary, but he wondered if she would ever be able to see herself as his subordinate. There was also the issue of the baggage she brought, especially that one steamer trunk permanently strapped to her bumper. You can't have three presidents in the White House, Obama told some friends at a dinner in New York.

The Feinstein meeting played out against this psychological backdrop. Seated in the California senator's living room, each with a glass of water, Obama and Clinton cut right to the chase. Hillary indicated she was willing to be considered, but unwilling to be vetted unless Obama was all but certain that he planned to pick her. Obama indicated he was willing to vet her, but that he was unlikely to pick her.

Then, as if to make Clinton feel better, but actually putting the sting in the tail, Obama added, "You didn't run to be vice president."

Clinton left the Feinstein meeting and focused on her official exit. The event was less than forty-eight hours off, a Saturday morning rally at the National Building Museum in downtown Washington. For many of those hours, Clinton's speechwriters labored over her speech, cranking out twenty drafts. Late on Friday night, the speech was locked—or so everyone thought. In fact, Hillary and Bill stayed up late revising and reworking, editing and reediting the thing. Early the next morning, their new text landed in the email in-boxes of the high command.

"Wow, they really, seriously, fucked this up," Garin wrote to his colleagues after reading it. "They have turned a gracious endorsement of Senator Obama into something that will (and should) be seen as stingy and small, and turned nice passages about the causes of the campaign into turgid and self-reverential prose. The problem isn't just what they took out, it's also what they put in. How many more uses of the word 'I' do they have here?"

A furious scramble ensued. The Clintons had removed the word "endorse"; it was put back in. The Clintons had deleted many of the references to Obama; they were reinserted. Hillary uttered not a peep of protest, insisting that her goal all along had been to give a speech that was generous and unimpeachable.

It wound up being an address the Obamans could have written themselves—though it would be best remembered for a stanza that spoke not to Clinton's praise for the winner but to what she'd accomplished even in losing. "Although we weren't able to shatter that hardest, highest glass ceiling this time," Hillary said before an adoring throng, "thanks to you, it's got about eighteen million cracks in it. And the light is shining through like never before, filling us all with the hope and the sure knowledge that the path will be a little easier next time."

The path to peace between the Obamans and the Clintonites would not be strewn with primrose. The battle between Barack and Hillary had been historic across every dimension, from the amount of money spent and the numbers of voters who had participated to its sheer closeness—roughly 150,000 votes out of nearly 36 million cast divided the candidates. The fighting had been too long, too messy, and too mean for cuddling to commence right away.

The candidates had agreed to have Plouffe and Mills work out the details of how the two campaigns would come to a practical détente. At the center of those negotiations was the matter of Clinton's $12 million debt. The Clintonites wanted the Obamans to help pay it off by asking his supporters to cough up contributions to her. The Obamans were reluctant, or, in Plouffe's case, downright recalcitrant.

Though the press was starting to hyperventilate about polls suggesting that Hillary's voters were up for grabs or even leaning toward McCain, Obama and the suits didn't buy it. Sure, there were a handful of PUMA—"party unity, my ass"—women who would vote for G. Gordon Liddy before they voted for Obama. But the suits were convinced that rank-and-file Clinton voters would be with Obama in November as long as the campaign handled Hillary with due respect.

On June 27, the public process of rapprochement began when Obama and Clinton traveled together on a joint campaign trip to the aptly named town of Unity,

New Hampshire, where each of them had received 107 votes in the state's primary.

The plane ride up from Washington was awkward, the press scrutinizing their every gesture as they sat next to each other in seats 2A and 2B. But the two-hour bus ride from Manchester was worse. Obama had a compartment to himself up front, Clinton one to herself in back, with a middle section in between. For most of the ride, they stood in their respective door-ways batting pieces of idle chitchat (about learning to sleep on planes, using BlackBerrys, eating strange food in strange lands) back and forth like a pair of nervous tennis players.

Axelrod approached Clinton and asked to have a word. They retreated to the rear cabin and huddled. Obama's strategist wanted to make sure there were no hard feelings between them. Afterward, Axelrod was elated with how the talk had gone. It was a really good conversation, he said. But Hillary had a slightly different view.

It was like a root canal, she told her friends. I wanted to throw up.

The event itself was a relief. Obama and Clinton, their outfits coordinated so that his tie matched her blue pantsuit, fell over themselves praising each other, as if the past eighteen months had never happened.

"For anyone who voted for me and is now considering not voting, or voting for Senator McCain, I strongly urge you to reconsider," Clinton said. When the crowd squealed for Hillary, Obama concurred, "She rocks, she rocks."

Three days later, from the road in Missouri, Obama called Bill Clinton. They spoke for twenty minutes and agreed to get together in the future, maybe over a dinner in New York, and for a public event, as early as July. Obama knew Bill was still upset about having been cast as a race-baiter in the campaign, and that what he wanted was a get-out-of-jail-free card from Obama. Obama didn't think Clinton was a racist, but he had no intention of exonerating him. *Let him get over it and then we'll see*, Obama thought.

A few weeks later, Michelle called Hillary to break the ice with her after a trip to Florida, where some of Clinton's supporters had held a fund-raiser for Barack. I feel bad because I hadn't called you, Michelle said. I was waiting for the right moment.

They talked about Hillary's experience raising a young daughter in the White House, about how Michelle should avoid getting caught up in the campaign attacks that were now coming her way. Don't let that get to you, Hillary advised. That's what they're going to do. It's the Republican playbook. Expect it.

. . .

The brave face she put on for Michelle notwithstand-
ing, Hillary was not a happy woman in the summer of
2008. The past haunted her, the future daunted her,
and the present was full of burdens. Still coping with
her loss and what it meant, she kept casting her mind
back, trying to grasp what had gone wrong with her
campaign, inviting members of her former high command to her Senate office to conduct extensive exami-
nations of their failure.

One day in July, Penn arrived at the Russell Building for his discussion with Clinton. For more than an
hour, Clinton held forth, while Penn mostly listened.

"Well, I thank you for everything you did for me,"
Clinton began. "I'm sorry you took so much incom-
ing fire. It kind of goes with the territory. I don't know
what else to say."

"Yeah, well," Penn replied with a shrug.

Clinton then launched into a lengthy overview of the
problems that beset her. "It was just dysfunctional, and
I take responsibility for that," she said of her campaign.
"I mean it just didn't work.

"Having said that, it would have been a very hard
campaign to run against Obama," she went on. "We
had the entire press corps against us, which usually

Bill and I could care less, but this was above and beyond anything that had ever happened. I mean, it was
just a relentless, total hit job, day in and day out. I don't
mind that, because people seem to do hit jobs on me,
but with a total free ride for [Obama]. It wasn't even a
one-to-ten parity, in terms of anything that we thought
would be put out there that might get traction. And
you know, it was really hard to run against an African
American when the entire Democratic Establishment
was scared to death. They could not deal with it."

Clinton then raised the subject of her campaign's
original sin: Iowa.

"If we had gone after Obama on the paid media, I
just am not sure," she said. "If we could have avoided
Iowa, which I think would have been very difficult—I
was the front-runner, blah blah blah, I had to prove
my bona fides. I don't see how we could have, frankly.
But I never felt good about Iowa, *ever* felt good about it."

Clinton shook her head in wonder at the Obama
phenomenon in the cornfields. "You know, the Oprah
thing," she said. "There was such a sort of a cultlike,
peer group pressure. . . . They had drunk the Kool-
Aid. And I am convinced they also imported people
into those caucuses, which we will never prove."

Clinton attributed her campaign's poor performance
in Iowa in part to its inside-the-Beltway myopia. "I

would never, ever run a campaign in Washington again," she said. "Ever, ever, ever. It's poison, it's toxic."

"I couldn't agree with you more," Penn said. "I'm told in Chicago he had a group of Obama partisans that, when they were losing, and they were almost out, they were willing to do whatever . . ."

"Whatever it takes," Clinton said, finishing Penn's thought. "And I would love to get all their internal documents about playing the race card, because I know it was their strategy."

If there was one Hillarylander whom Clinton blamed above all for the miscues, it was Solis Doyle. "I think she was a disaster, Mark, and I am so disappointed," Hillary said. "She turned out not to be able to manage. . . . She just was incapable. I put her in a position; she was unable to do it."

"I thought the deal was that she was going to make the trains run on time," Penn said.

"She didn't even know which trains she was supposed to schedule," Clinton said sarcastically. "And I feel terrible, because it wasn't a campaign worthy of me."

But Clinton had harsh words for Penn, too. "Whenever there was a problem, people begged me to fire you. That was the answer to everything: 'Fire Mark,'" she said. "Now why is that? Because you rub people the wrong way."

After telling Penn that she was "personally fond" of him, she said he was dismissive, insulting, irritating, and alienating to his colleagues. (At one point, she suggested he consider therapy.) "The Colombia thing, that really was beyond the pale," she went on. "I felt fucked. I mean I gotta tell you. I felt like we were on the upswing, and I just felt fucked."

"And I took responsibility," Penn said sheepishly.

Clinton, apparently all talked out about the past, turned to the here and now. "So what should I be doing?" she said. "I'm trying to stay low and out of the line of fire and not get in the way between [Obama] and the voters."

Penn focused on Denver and the importance of Hillary's speech. "He's got to really make sure that the night goes well," he said. "The truth is, him making you vice president is the best way to guarantee it."

"There's no way—no way," she said. "He can't tolerate that."

Nothing was weighing on Clinton's mind more than her campaign debt. "Bill and I never leave a debt unpaid," she said. "It's just that, I was shocked at how little [the Obama campaign] will help us. They aren't going to help us. I really, I thought when I started this I might be able to get about five million out of them. . . . You know how much we've got so far?"

"Five hundred thousand?"

"No, one hundred thousand. He's not going to help."

"That's why I wanted to negotiate first, withdraw second. Right?"

"The press—I couldn't. I am held to such a different standard. We're trying to get somebody to cover the fact that I've done more to promote unity than anybody in a comparable position—Bradley . . . you name it, Tsongas, Jackson, Kennedy. But you know it was like they just beat the hell out of me until I got out."

Penn ran through the latest poll numbers, expressing his view of Obama's chances against McCain as dicey.

"I want you to start thinking about how I avoid being blamed," Clinton said. "Because I shouldn't be blamed. But they are going to blame me. I somehow didn't do enough."

" 'She stayed in too long,' " Penn put in.

In a voice of mock horror, Clinton exclaimed, " 'Oh, she damaged him,' you know—screw you! I thought it was a competitive election. I can stay in as long as I want to stay in. Teddy Kennedy stayed in until the convention. Give me a break."

Penn, always on the lookout for business, said he wanted to try "to reconcile with the Obama campaign."

"They're never going to reconcile," Clinton said dismissively. "Ain't gonna happen. Ain't gonna happen. Ain't gonna happen. They are vindictive and small. They don't think they need me. They had that conversation with Bill, they never called and asked him to do anything. They don't care about a former president."

Clinton returned to Obama's prospects in the general election. "I think it's fifty-fifty whether he wins, right?" she said, noting that Obama's VP choice was critical, giving odds on whom he would pick: "Biden, one-in-two chance. Bayh, one-in-four chance. Kaine and Sebelius, both which I think are terrible choices, one-in-eight chance."

For a year and a half, Hillary had spent every waking moment not just trying to defeat Obama, but convincing herself that he was a lightweight, a nose-in-the-air elitist totally unfit to be the leader of the free world. A little more than a month after he ended her dream, she hadn't become unconvinced. But now she would be forced to sit back and watch him run against McCain—a man whom Clinton considered a friend, but one whose election would be tantamount to re-electing Bush to a third term.

"The campaign was a terrible disappointment," she said. "I hate the choice that the country's faced with. I think it is a terrible choice for our nation."

PART TWO

15

THE MAVERICK AND
HIS MELTDOWN

The morning after the midterm elections of 2006, John McCain was in the community room of his condominium complex in Phoenix, Arizona, surveying the damage that had been inflicted on the Republican Party—and listening to his lieutenants talk about how he was primed to benefit. The night before, McCain and his wife, Cindy, had hosted a viewing shindig in the same room, which Cindy had catered extravagantly, laying out an opulent spread. The remains of that feast were gone now, replaced by a modest breakfast buffet: fruit, juice, coffee, and those pastries that her husband liked so much.

McCain had been up until the wee hours. He needed that coffee. Arrayed around him were his chief political advisers: longtime stalwarts John Weaver, Rick

Davis, Mark Salter, and Carla Eudy, along with a new presence, Terry Nelson. This was the first time they'd all been together to talk about 2008.

On a large-screen TV, the yakkers were yakking about the horrific results from the previous day. Republicans had lost everything: the House, the Senate, a majority of governorships and state legislative chambers. (Nearly a hundred seats in McCain's beloved New Hampshire—that hurt!)

McCain had seen it coming. Like Obama, he had been his party's top draw in the run-up to the midterms. With Bush holed up in the White House, toxically unpopular even in many red states, McCain had tirelessly traversed the country, offering aid to candidates in tough races, pushing to save seats. But it was no use. "This is as bad as it's ever been" for the GOP, he told anyone who would listen.

McCain's advisers viewed the devastation as a bad news/good news story. On one hand, a poisonous environment would greet whomever the party chose as its nominee. On the other, those circumstances made it all the more likely that the nominee would be their boss.

Since 2000, when McCain waged a spirited but doomed challenge to Bush to become the Republican standard-bearer, the Arizona senator had been an icon.

With his war heroism, famously independent streak, and reformist stances on matters such as campaign finance, McCain's maverick image was sterling. He was, as Weaver liked to put it, "the *Good Housekeeping* seal of approval in American politics." A familiar presence on the late-night talk show circuit, he was wry and funny; his winking irony and accessibility made him a favorite of the press. And though he'd spent years collecting Republican enemies by defying party orthodoxy—even flirting with the notion of becoming John Kerry's running mate—he had more recently embarked on a determined, and not unsuccessful, effort to redeem himself with the GOP Establishment. He had put aside his feud with Bush, supported the Iraq War, and built ties to conservative activists and donors. In a party governed by primogeniture, he was now the presumptive front-runner.

A front-runner's operation was very much what his advisers had in mind. McCain's bid in 2000 had been a ragtag affair, more cause than campaign. In 2008 his team proposed the polar opposite. They would build a battleship that was sturdy, well funded, disciplined, imposing. Outsider romance would be sacrificed for insider clout. The model they were mimicking was the one that beat them. They were aiming to create a McCainiac emulation of the Bush machine.

The architect of that approach was Weaver, the forty-seven-year-old Texan strategist who'd been McCain's political guru for a decade. Lanky and laconic but intense, Weaver had temporarily left the Republican Party in a huff, disillusioned by the Bush campaign's dismantling of McCain. But Weaver was convinced that McCain belonged in the White House, and he had come to see the Bush model as the best means of making it happen. To that end, Weaver had imported Nelson, who in 2004 had served as the Bush team's political director, to be campaign manager. He and Weaver were all about going big: big endorsements, big donors, big spending.

Bigness didn't sound too bad to Davis, either. A Washington lobbyist by trade, Davis, also forty-seven, had managed McCain's last run. He was loyal, fleet, droll, and aimed to please. Despite McCain's expressed disdain for the culture of Beltway banditry, he always wanted Davis on his team. The guy got things done, and Cindy loved him. He would be McCain's campaign chief executive.

The planning for McCain's run had been slowly building for months; this meeting, in a way, was both a culmination and a launch. Davis talked about operations, everything from budgets to office space to a proposed logo. Weaver presented a strategic overview, discussing the calendar, organization, and McCain's competitors. The field hadn't fully taken shape, but it was looking weak. There was Rudy Giuliani, the former mayor of New York City, whose universal name recognition put him at the top of the national polls, but whose social liberalism would make him a hard sell in an ever-more-conservative Republican Party. There was Mitt Romney, the former governor of Massachusetts, who was handsome, rich, and successful—but unknown across the country and a Mormon, a faith regarded by many Evangelicals and Catholics with suspicion and distrust. The rest were a collection of the anonymous, the toothless, and the marginal. Certainly there was no one on the horizon who possessed the attribute that was making McCain look so good to so many Republicans, even those whose instinctive reaction to him was to balk: he was the only GOP candidate who appeared capable of beating Hillary Clinton, the odds-on favorite for the Democratic nomination.

Through the whole presentation, McCain sat there looking vaguely bored, saying almost nothing. His detachment was striking, but not entirely unusual. If all candidates fall along a range from micromanagers to hands-off delegators, McCain deserved a category all his own: ultra-laissez-faire. In his rational brain, he knew that a serious presidential effort required scores of staffers, high-priced consultants, polling, advertising, policy development, and more. But he really just didn't give a shit. The details made his head hurt. A fighter pilot through and through, McCain liked to follow his instincts. He envisioned himself getting in his jet and taking off; whatever he left behind on the carrier deck ceased to exist in his consciousness. All that mattered was him, the plane, and the mission. His approach to political combat was the same. Wherever he was, whatever he was saying, whoever was listening—*that* was the campaign. The rest was noise. As far as McCain was concerned, he could win the election with a roster of events, a few *Meet the Press* appearances, and a sheaf of airplane tickets.

Even so, this was a pretty important meeting, his advisers thought. Yet McCain seemed absent, as if he didn't want to be there. When Weaver finished laying out plans for the months ahead, McCain finally opened his mouth and said, Do we really have to start this early?

Nelson gazed on in disbelief. He'd been on board only a couple of weeks, after McCain, wearing a dress shirt and his boxer shorts (a favorite outfit of his), offered him the job in a hotel room somewhere.

Now, for neither the first time nor the last, Nelson looked at his new boss and wondered, *Do you really want to be president?*

. . .

The truth was, McCain had a lot of reasons to dread the start of the race. For all his progress in making himself more acceptable to the Establishment, he knew that winning his party's nomination would be no cakewalk. Conservative activists still distrusted him for his apostasies on taxes, campaign reform, interrogation techniques, and judges. The religious right would never warm to him. And there were plenty of Establishmentarians who saw his legendary temper as a problem of no small consequence. Some worried his hotheadedness made him unsuited for the Oval Office; others, that he might blow his stack in public and blow up his candidacy. Though he'd been better in recent years at keeping his petulance at bay (or under wraps), McCain was still prone to outbursts of profanity—sometimes in front of campaign volunteers—that made his advisers wince.

Iraq, too, had become a problem for McCain, politically and emotionally. He was a military man, from a family of officers. He worried about the safety of the troops, including his own sons, two of whom were in the service. Long before the campaign began, McCain burned over what he saw as the Bush administration's mismanagement of the conflict, and he was carrying that anger into the race. "Just incompetent," he'd say. "Just terrible."

McCain had been outspoken in pressing Bush to commit more U.S. forces to Iraq, even as Americans had turned decisively against the war and favored a timetable for withdrawal. His advisers warned him that his stance was damaging him politically, hurting him with voters as well as donors. He didn't care. "You're not gonna get me to change my opinion on Iraq," McCain would say. "I'd rather lose the campaign than lose a war."

By late 2006, McCain had another vulnerability, and an unexpected one. Suddenly, out of nowhere, his status as a media darling was fading. He was losing the constituency he had proudly, and only half-jokingly, called "my base."

Once, McCain could do no wrong in the eyes of the press. Now, when he engaged in a rapprochement with the Reverend Jerry Falwell or favored tax cuts, the media scalded him for what it deemed transparent efforts to curry favor with the right. When he embraced the Iraq War more fervently than Bush, columnists didn't praise his adherence to principle, they scorched him for being out of step with the country. His treatment in the blogosphere was even worse.

The new media reality depressed McCain, and the time-honored backroom chores of politics didn't thrill him much, either. Like his friend Hillary Clinton, he found pleading for money and endorsements about as pleasant as a hot poker in the eye. Also like Hillary, McCain took his work in the Senate seriously, especially now on Iraq.

Through the fall of 2006, Weaver and Salter fretted over McCain's gut. Salter, at fifty-one, was McCain's speechwriter and the co-author of all his books, as well as his supremely patriotic and fatalistic alter ego. Don't just drift into a presidential, he warned McCain. You've got to decide you really want to do this.

Salter and Weaver were well aware that two other concerns were weighing heavily on McCain. The first was Cindy's opposition to his running. The Bush campaign's demolition of her husband had taken place in South Carolina, amid shadowy attacks that had wounded her lastingly and deeply. Most despicable was the smear campaign alleging that the McCains' younger daughter, Bridget, adopted from Bangladesh, was John's illegitimate child from a liaison with a black prostitute. But there were also rumors spread that Cindy was a drug addict and that John's long captivity in Vietnam had left him mentally unstable.

South Carolina was never far from Cindy's mind. The thought of it being repeated made her sick. She wasn't merely press shy, she was just plain shy, and she was worried about her servicemen sons, Jack and Jimmy—and especially about Jimmy, a Marine headed for a tour of duty in Iraq. Her fear was that he might be targeted for harm if his father were a candidate.

As the end of 2006 approached, McCain continually told his team, Cindy isn't ready. His advisers tried to reassure her: things would be different this time; she would be protected. But Cindy wanted guarantees, some of them impossible to offer—that the children would be able to maintain their privacy, for instance. Gradually, eventually, her stance softened. The McCains were a military family, and if John wanted to serve, Cindy wasn't going to stand in his way. Four words defined her ethic: "I support my husband." Yet even then she made no bones about being unhappy that John was making the race or about her refusal to play a large or public role. Smiling, nodding, shaking the occasional proffered hand? Fine. Daily events, multistate trips, full-on surrogacy? Not gonna happen.

What gave the McCainiacs even greater pause were John's frequent references to his age and physical condition. McCain was sixty-nine and a cancer survivor. I'm not the man I was when I ran in 2000, he said. Presented with schedules packed with events from early morning until late at night, McCain would say, "Are you guys trying to kill me?"

There was nothing lighthearted about his tone—he was cranky, peevish. When his staff sang hosannas to his stamina, he would wave them off.

One day, McCain asked Weaver if he was simply too old to run.

"Only you can tell us that," said Weaver.

"Let's do it . . . I guess," McCain replied.

The front-runner's campaign got under way in December 2006. And just as McCain's advisers wanted it to be, it was Bush-scale big—at least on paper.

The initial budget devised by Davis was a monster. The fund-raising plan called for the campaign to haul in a record $48 million in the first quarter of 2007. That figure was derived largely by looking at the numbers that Bush had racked up in his 2004 campaign—as an incumbent president with the best-oiled cash-accumulating apparatus ever assembled (in the pre-Obama era, that is). Yet nobody seemed to question whether that was an appropriate yardstick.

At the same time, Weaver and Nelson—who were responsible for spending, while Davis and Eudy handled the collecting of cash—began hiring dozens of high-end consultants and staffers, many of them veterans of the Bush team in 2004. They opened offices around the country and rented space for an enormous headquarters not far from Clinton's, in suburban northern Virginia.

The split structure of McCainworld was no accident. From the moment the November meeting in Phoenix ended, there were two McCain campaigns, one led by Weaver and one by Davis, two men with a long-standing history of personal enmity. No one could really explain where it had begun, but it was so profound they could barely stand to be in the same room together. Weaver had brought in Nelson partly to keep Davis from being campaign manager. By January, John and Terry were lobbying to have Rick canned.

McCain had known all along that Weaver and Davis detested each other. His attitude toward it was studied indifference. Like Hillary, McCain valued loyalty above all else and avoided confrontation at all costs. He instructed Weaver, Davis, Nelson, and Salter (who didn't much care for Davis, either), "I don't want any more decisions being made unless all four of you agree." But that was only a recipe for gridlock and feuding, which quickly became the hallmarks of McCainworld, just as they were in Hillaryland.

There was no ignoring the ramifications when it came to money, though. While Weaver and Nelson were spending like whiskey-addled sailors, the campaign's early efforts to raise cash through direct mail

and on the Web were falling flat. Many would-be contributors were turned off by McCain's ardent support
for Bush's just-announced troop surge in Iraq. Making
matters worse, McCain spent December engaging in a
passive-resistance boycott against calling donors or attending fund-raisers.

By the start of 2007, the campaign was already more
than $1 million in the red. And McCain had virtu-
ally no finance events on his schedule for the first two
months of the year. The candidate was livid, but he
blamed the problem not on the fund-raising, but on the
campaign's spending.

The first sign of trouble was when McCain made his
maiden visit to his campaign fortress in Alexandria,
Virginia, in the middle of January. Carrying a Star-
bucks cup, he walked into the war room and found
sixty-odd people (some of whom were unpaid interns,
though he didn't know that) gathered there to greet
him. He stopped in his tracks, his mandible dropping
to his sternum. He turned in a slow circle, took it all in,
mumbled a few words of greeting and thanks, and then
stormed off in the direction of Nelson's office.

"What the fuck are all these people doing here?" he
yelled at his campaign manager. "Where are we getting the money to pay for all of this? What is it they do?
Get rid of half of them."

Not long after, McCain examined the personnel lists, looking for cuts, and grew incensed. "I am not fucking authorizing these fucking hires," he insisted to Nelson. "Why do we need all these people? Who are these fucking Bush people? Where is the fucking money?"

McCain's reaction to the spending was even worse on the road. When he hit the trail in the winter months of 2007, he saw evidence of excess all around him, and would call Nelson and Weaver in a fury. Why did there have to be a live band at one of his events? Why were there *two* boxes of donuts on his campaign bus?

Then there was the bus itself, an upgraded version of McCain's fabled Straight Talk Express from 2000. The sleek new rig had deluxe furnishings, satellite television, a fancy bathroom, a full kitchen, and a big private office that doubled as a bedroom. Cindy mocked it as a "rolling Ritz-Carlton."

As the cash crunch mounted into March and McCain's fits became more frequent, Weaver reached a breaking point. Everyone is at fault for not vetting the fund-raising plan—including you, he told McCain.

"We started too fucking early," McCain replied. "We should have waited. I shouldn't be running right now."

"We didn't choose to be the front-runner," Weaver said. "We *are* the front-runner. We have to conduct ourselves as the front-runner."

Weaver warned McCain that the first-quarter fund-raising numbers were due out soon and they were going to be bad. He wasn't kidding. Released in early April, the figures revealed that McCain had raised a meager $12.5 million—$35.5 million shy of the campaign's original projections. Worse, he had finished third among his rivals; Romney led the pack with $21 million, while Giuliani had raised $15 million. The press coverage was brutal.

Weaver, Nelson, and Salter met McCain in his Senate office to talk about how to improve the balance sheet. Salter and Weaver bellowed back and forth with McCain, but they all agreed on the bottom line: if they didn't fix their financial situation, they didn't need to worry about laying people off. McCain's campaign would be over before the race had even started.

"**Fuck you!** Fuck, fuck, fuck, fuck, fuck, fuck, fuck, fuck, fuck, fuck!!!"

McCain let out the stream of sharp epithets, both middle fingers raised and extended, barking in his wife's face. He was angry; she had interrupted him. Cindy burst into tears, but, really, she should have been used to it by now.

Cindy Lou Hensley had always looked like a beauty queen (or a senator's wife) with her ice-blue eyes and flaxen waves and delicate mien. She first met John McCain in Hawaii, where he was a war hero still recovering from his injuries, still married to his first wife, Carol. Phoenix-born Cindy was just twenty-four, and wildly smitten with the dashing older man in his dress whites. Within a few months, she was a misty military wife, saluting and serving.

A quarter of a century and four children later, the dazzle had faded, even as the duty and the bond remained. But for all her taut Stepford smiles, Cindy was no typical political spouse. She was the sole heir to her family's multimillion-dollar beer distribution business and chair of the company. She loved her home in Arizona, her job, her charities, and, above all, her children. While John spent months and months in D.C., she maintained her base and raised the kids. The setup worked for both of them.

When she was dragged back into campaign service in 2007, Cindy wanted to be an asset to her husband. But they were so fixed in their ways, so unused to compromise or relinquishing control, they could barely remain polite. John was impatient and indifferent, Cindy intent on asserting her needs. After an argument over a Secret Service detail—Cindy wanted the protection; John hated the intrusion—she flounced back to Phoenix. When you get it, call me, Cindy said, and I'll come back on the trail, but otherwise I'm going home.

She summoned her husband out of campaign discussions to talk about Jimmy, over in Iraq. If their
daughter Meghan, out on the stump, complained to her
mother about blogosphere attacks on the family or annoying staffers assigned to her, Cindy would throw a
fit. She'd agree to attend events and rallies, and then
cancel abruptly.

The McCains fought in front of others, during
small meetings and before large events, to the amazement and discomfort of the staff. Things could escalate
quickly. She cursed him; he cursed her. She cried; he
apologized. Cindy fought back, too. I never wanted
you to run for this, she said. You ruined my life. It's all
about you. When it came time to film campaign videos
of the couple, the camera crews had to roll for hours to
capture a few minutes of warmth.

There were moments of tenderness, to be sure.
When Cindy was depressed or overwhelmed, John was
able to cheer her up or calm her down. He implored his
staff to accommodate his wife, and refused to make any
major decisions without her input. They were aware of
each other's quirks and needs, crazy about their children, and they talked to each other by phone all day
long. They looked after each other's health, and often
served as staunch mutual protectors.

But there were also rumors. In the spring of 2007,
whispers from Arizona reached Salter and Weaver that

Cindy had been spotted at a Phoenix Suns basketball game with another man. The man was said to be her long-term boyfriend; the pair had been sighted all over town in the last few years.

Members of the McCain senior staff discussed the un-settling news, amid their growing concerns that Cindy's behavior had been increasingly erratic of late. Weaver and others suspected that the Cindy rumor was rooted in truth. It was upsetting, Weaver believed, but not a threat. The legitimate press would never write about a spouse's personal life—unless that spouse was Bill Clinton.

Then the campaign heard that a supermarket tab-loid was working on the story. It could blow up at any time. At a meeting in mid-April, Team McCain pre-pared a full-bore media plan to deal with the fallout if the story broke. Soon after, Weaver delicately ap-proached McCain. Did he know about this? Could he talk to Cindy?

McCain appeared distraught, but not surprised. He seemed aware of the situation, and, incredibly, sug-gested it was a matter he preferred be dealt with by the staff.

This is something a husband needs to do, Weaver told him.

McCain called his wife. She denied an affair. You'll have to come out on the road with me, he told her.

You'll have to travel more now. People will need to see us together.

So she did. Davis, who'd always gelled with Cindy, was assigned to spend more time with her, and for a while she was by her husband's side at rallies and town halls, just in case the story bubbled up—or bubbled over.

There was silence on the small charter flight from New York to New Hampshire on April 24. McCain was on his way, finally, *finally*, to officially kick off his candidacy the next day. Weaver, Salter, and Nelson were steaming mad. With no money, a feuding staff, and the stench of loserdom setting in, they'd been working for weeks on an idea for the announcement that would jolt McCain's campaign back to life. The candidate had signed off on it—but now, just hours beforehand, he had changed his mind.

"I don't want to do it," McCain said to Weaver. "And I don't want to argue about it."

"This far down the road, you owe us a chance to discuss it," Weaver angrily replied. But no discussion was forthcoming.

The idea was as simple as it was radical: a one-term pledge. McCain would promise that if he won the White House, he would spend four years in residence and then step down. The pledge would embody the theme that McCain cared only about solving the country's problems and not about indulging his ambition. It would say that he was going to tackle the hardest issues—Iraq, immigration, ethics, entitlements, runaway spending—with no regard for reelection. It would mitigate what the campaign's polling showed was his most significant liability: his age. It would be a bold statement about political sacrifice, a larger-than-life, maverick move.

Salter and Weaver had come up with the pledge and pushed it hard. McCain had reservations, but knew his campaign needed electroshock. His advisers plotted the rollout, taking extraordinary steps to keep the idea quiet, fearing that the loose-lipped McCain would spill the beans himself. The announcement speech was written. The press release was drafted. All systems were go.

But not everyone thought the pledge was a good idea. Some considered it crazy, in fact. One of them was Lindsey Graham, the South Carolina Republican senator who was one of McCain's closest friends; another was Rick Davis. They told McCain that the pledge would marginalize him and the office of the presidency. That it would make him a lame duck from day one.

A few hours before the flight to New Hampshire, McCain was with Cindy in New York at the Mandarin Oriental hotel, looking over his remarks. When Salter and Brett O'Donnell, McCain's speech coach, arrived, McCain startled them by saying he was having doubts about the pledge. Meghan McCain entered the suite and trashed the idea, saying it was lame. Her dad now apparently agreed.

The next day, it was damp and chilly in Portsmouth for the kickoff. Dressed casually in a sweater, looking grim and awkward, McCain stood next to Cindy. His speech, having been hurriedly purged of all references to the pledge, was a disjointed mess. Later, in Manchester, McCain gave it again at Veterans Memorial Park downtown. Weaver looked around at the vast space and said, "You could have a fucking Rolling Stones concert here." But the park was nearly empty.

McCain's campaign was formally off the ground, but it remained a hugely troubled enterprise. The candidate was depressed and fatigued, feeling helpless, picked to pieces by something he couldn't control. He contemplated how much better his life would be if he just pulled the plug on his campaign. *If I'd known this before, I never would have run*, McCain thought. "This wasn't the campaign I wanted," he told his advisers.

Long gone was the tough, spry McCain of the 2000 race, the cocky, joyous McCain of the Senate. This McCain was angry, angry every single day, as angry as Weaver had ever seen him. McCain knew what was being said about his implosion; he obsessively read the papers and the tip sheets, collected political gossip, and watched cable news. A mocking Maureen Dowd column could ruin his entire day.

"The press is out to get me" became McCain's new catchphrase. No more was he accompanied by a merry band of accomplices filing stories about his charm. Now, trailing behind him, eager to catch every snort and frown, were stern scribes, overcaffeinated bloggers, and curious civilians with camera phones.

McCain was erupting over everything. At a scheduling meeting to discuss Meghan's college graduation, McCain learned that the commencement was a multiday affair that would require him to make several round trips to New York. "How many fucking times do I have to go to fucking New York this week?" he yelled. "How many fucking times can you fucking graduate from fucking Columbia?"

Agitating him further was a policy debate about which he cared greatly, and for which he was catching major flak. The issue was immigration reform. With Bush's support, Congress was taking up a proposal that would allow a path to citizenship for some illegal immigrants. In late May, McCain stood alongside Ted Kennedy and announced his support for the bill.

Weaver and Salter begged McCain to ease up. He was already the face of the Iraq surge. Now he was becoming the face of what opponents called "amnesty." Just tone down the rhetoric, his advisers pleaded.

McCain refused. He was disgusted by Republicans in Congress and talk radio gasbags such as Rush Limbaugh who bashed immigrants. "They're going to destroy the fucking party," he would say.

As McCain's town hall meetings devolved into shouting matches over immigration, the candidate let his frustration show through. He called Lindsey Graham in despair. Listen to these people, McCain said. Why would I want to be the leader of a party of such assholes?

By the time the immigration bill collapsed in the Senate on June 28, 2007, the damage was done. The issue had more than injured McCain politically. It had thoroughly crippled his already lame and halting fund-raising. The second quarter had the same unhappy result as the first. He raised only $11 million, which left him just $2 million in the bank, and the political world switched from describing him as a "troubled front-runner" to predicting, and then assuming, he would be forced to quit the race.

McCain returned from a Fourth of July trip to Iraq with Graham more riled up than ever, but still capable of some gallows humor. "I'm the only one I know who would go to Iraq to get away from it all," he said.

In that spirit, he had resolved to finally make some changes in the campaign. With his polling numbers receding both nationally and in key states, he blamed Nelson and Weaver for running things into the ground, and he wanted Davis to take over.

After one last climactic shouting match in the Senate office, Nelson announced that he was quitting, jumping before he was pushed. Weaver, out of frustration, disdain for Davis, and solidarity with Nelson, decided to say sayonara, too.

McCain wanted Weaver to stay. They were brothers-in-arms from 2000, and no one, including McCain himself, had spent anything like the amount of time that Weaver had thinking about how to get him elected president. But too much poison had flowed between them.

With Weaver's conspicuous departure, McCain lost his wingman, and was visibly uncomfortable answering reporters' questions about the situation. "I'm very happy with the campaign," he repeated stiltedly, making himself seem deluded in addition to desperate.

McCain was on the verge of losing Salter, too. Close to Weaver, disillusioned by the spiteful family feud, he told McCain that he'd continue to write his speeches, but little more. But McCain pleaded with Salter to stay—"Forget about this shit; we're friends, we've been friends for twenty years"—and Salter relented.

McCain's highest priority was fixing the money situation. Davis took over the shriveled operation, its staff shrunk by Nelson at McCain's insistence from nearly three hundred to around forty, and zeroed out every other possible expense. Publicly, the moves were seen as the slow winding down of the operation. McCain had gone from a campaign bleeding internally to spilling its entrails all over the carpet.

The candidate gave pep talks to his remaining staff, his donors, his backers. In every case, he tried to be upbeat about his chances without sounding ridiculous. He showed more emotion than usual in thanking people for sticking by him.

With his closest friends, he was more torn. "I guess I never should have fucking run," he said. "I'm gonna do what I need to do, everything I need to do, and then we'll probably lose." He knew he risked further embarrassment, but he was willing to take the hit: I know they're gonna make fun of me. I know what they're gonna say. I watch cable. I get it.

McCain went to New Hampshire on July 13, trailed by national reporters who hadn't covered him for months but who wanted to be present at the cremation.

Jimmy McCain, who almost never campaigned with his father, came along. The senator was quietly defiant, vowing to stay in the race, with the Granite State the key to his comeback.

Cindy and Salter weren't dreaming of a resurrection. They were worried about John, about his entire career being defined by a botched mission of a few months. Their goal was to wrap up the campaign without further damage to his reputation or a plunge deeper into debt. "He's not gonna be the nominee," Salter told one of his colleagues. "I just want the campaign to last long enough so we can tell people one last time, 'Go fuck off. We made it this far.'"

McCain had a series of conversations with Charlie Black, a longtime friend and Republican strategist—and another Washington lobbyist. Despite all the speculation, McCain wasn't inclined to leave the race right away, but he wanted to know if he still had a chance to win. He was irritated and sad, burdened with a sense of responsibility for letting everyone down.

There was a narrow path back, Black told McCain, mostly because the other candidates seemed so weak. Giuliani? He would never roll up his sleeves and do the hard work. Romney? Conservatives would never fall in behind him; he was the moderate former governor of Massachusetts, for heaven's sake. The others? Please.

McCain stood head and shoulders above them all. It was like what happened with Ronald Reagan in 1980, Black reminded McCain. The Gipper had been the front-runner, but his campaign ran out of money at the end of 1979 and his staff was in turmoil. Reagan had come back, and so could McCain.

Black advised McCain that he needed to adopt a distinctly un-McCain-like approach: he needed to lower his profile. He had to do whatever he could to get as little national media attention as possible. "Every time you get covered it's going to be, 'That idiot McCain was the front-runner and screwed up his campaign,'" Black said. "So our goal is to be off the radar screen.

"Look," Black added, "for the next three months, all the stories are just gonna say, 'McCain's dead and buried.' Your only job is to keep your head down, go to those early states, and keep right on campaigning. We'll see where we are after Labor Day. If we aren't dead and buried, we're in this."

16

RUNNING UNOPPOSED

Rudy Giuliani took little personal pleasure in the prospect of McCain's demise. The two men were friends, and not just faux political friends. They actually liked each other. They'd first met at New York's City Hall in the late nineties, when Giuliani was mayor. They bonded over sports, baseball in particular, with Giuliani touting his beloved Yankees and McCain his Arizona Diamondbacks. In that awful autumn after the Twin Towers fell, when their teams met in the 2001 World Series, they'd made a show of attending several of the games together. More than once in the course of the 2008 presidential, Giuliani had said publicly that if he weren't running, he would probably be supporting McCain.

Not that Giuliani didn't see the political upside for him in the unraveling of his pal's campaign. He would've had to be blind to miss that—and Giuliani had an eagle eye when it came to his own advancement. Since he entered the race in February, he had led the field in virtually every national poll, riding his celebrity as "America's Mayor" and his brassy reputation as a hero of 9/11. With his hawkish profile on national security and moderation on social issues, Giuliani was chasing many of the same voters as McCain. In the wake of the maverick's meltdown, he seemed positioned to scoop them up, along with a chunk of McCain's donors. He looked like the new front-runner.

Yet to the members of the politico-industrial complex, Giuliani's candidacy was a chimera. The idea that the Republican Party would select a man of his background and views as its nominee struck them as implausible when they were being polite, risible when they were being honest. They contended that Romney was the runner to watch in the aftermath of McCain's implosion. Or maybe Fred Thompson would be the one to seize the moment; the former Tennessee senator and Hollywood actor, familiar from his regular role on *Law & Order*, had been making noises for months about a late entry into the race. But Hizzoner? No way.

McCain himself agreed. Even at his lowest depths, he never felt threatened by Giuliani. Asked why by his advisers, McCain would shrug and say, "Rudy's Rudy."

Giuliani's defects, from a conservative point of view, were readily apparent. He was pro-choice, pro–gay rights, pro–gun control. He was thrice married, and had carried on a public affair with wife number three while going through a messy divorce from wife number two. When the latter, Donna Hanover, kicked him out of Gracie Mansion, he cohabited with two gay men. There were pictures all over the Internet of him in drag—face painted in rouge, head adorned with a blond wig, shoulders draped in a feather boa—from a New York variety show.

And those were just the liabilities that Giuliani brought into the campaign with him. The past six months had exposed more. He had fallen far short of his fund-raising goals. He had failed to master the retail politics rituals of Iowa and New Hampshire, never shedding his swollen entourage or his preference for photo ops over town hall meetings and intimate voter coddling.

Most puzzling was his timidity. Giuliani was supposed to be a tough guy, but in the face of attacks by his opponents, his performance had been as limp as an overcooked Chinatown noodle. Challenged in debates, he would bare his cartoonishly big teeth and respond with lame jokes. When his advisers, trying to fire him up, showed him vicious direct-mail attacks on him by the Romney forces, Giuliani would just chortle. He never discouraged his aides from producing negative TV ads against his foes, but whenever they showed him a new spot or proposed script, he invariably rejected it.

Giuliani's aides were at a loss to explain his softness. Some attributed it to his bout with prostate cancer in 2000. Others thought he feared that getting tough would provoke retaliation. Still others believed Giuliani didn't want to be president badly enough to assail his fellow Republicans. But mostly, when his advisers were trying to make sense of the bizarreness of Giuliani's behavior, they talked about his wife—and the operatic piece of psychotropic theater that was the Rudy and Judi Show.

Judith Nathan had been in the spotlight since 1998, after she and Giuliani collided one night at a cigar bar. The tabloid coverage of her had never been flattering, but once her husband entered the presidential race in early 2007, it turned into a horror show.

First came the story that Judith had actually been married twice—not once, as she had previously suggested—before wedding Rudy in 2003. ("JUDI GIULIANI'S SECRET HUSBAND REVEALED.") Two weeks later, she suffered a far worse headline: "JUDI'S JOB WITH PUP-KILLER FIRM." Years earlier, it seemed, she had worked for a medical supply firm that, yes, exterminated puppies as part of its sales demonstrations.

Rudy's famously thin skin was a suit of armor compared to the gossamer sheath that enveloped Judith; after every negative story, she became hysterical. The press hates us, she howled to her husband's advisers. They hate Rudy. They love Donna. And, "They're fucking me!"

Judith had the same view, also loudly expressed, of the press staffers assigned to her. They're all out to get me, she'd say. Nobody gives a shit about me.

Three successive communications teams tried to assist her, but found it hard sledding. She refused to provide the background information that would enable them to defend her and which only Judith had at her disposal. When they asked about the details of the puppy story, she professed selective amnesia. "I don't remember exactly what happened back then," she said. "It was a long time ago."

She was equally evasive about her whereabouts, insisting that aides never call or email her directly, but instead stay in touch through her assistant. So mysterious was she that Rudy would joke, I'm going to make her the head of the CIA if I win.

One cool night that summer, in the private room of a New York restaurant, the Giulianis convened a group of about a dozen campaign advisers and friends of Judith's to discuss rehabilitating her image; she called them Team J. As they sat down to dinner, each attendee was handed a sheet of paper by Judith's assistant: a nondisclosure agreement that swore them to silence about the evening's talk.

With wine flowing, Judith observed that her press coverage had not been to her liking. She wasn't being handled well, wanted to get back to basics. "What role should I play?" she asked the group.

Rudy's pollster, Ed Goeas, tried to be helpful. "First of all, you're his third wife. What you should be is humble," he said.

Judith scrunched up her face and pouted.

Humility wasn't Judith's strong suit. Nor was leaving Rudy to his business. She called him constantly when he was traveling without her, no matter where he was or what he was doing. On several occasions the calls arrived when Giuliani was meeting with donors or making speeches. He invariably picked up the phone. "Hello, dear," he said when she interrupted him while he was onstage addressing the annual meeting of the National Rifle Association. "I'm talking to the members of the NRA right now. Would you like to say hello?"

His staff concluded that Giuliani had no choice but to answer Judith's calls, because ignoring her risked dire consequences—more dire than wrecking some speech. To the NRA members, Rudy apologized, but added, "It's a lot better that way."

Team Giuliani faced a problem more imperiling, if less sensational, than Judith. Of the early-voting states, Iowa and South Carolina had proved inhospitable to the mayor's liberal leanings, and New Hampshire voters, who should have been a natural fit, were not taking to him, either. The campaign had always been premised on the notion that Giuliani was a national candidate—that his strength in places such as New York and California would carry him through. The question was how he could survive until those states started voting on Super Tuesday. The answer was Florida.

The Florida primary on January 29 was the fifth contest in the Republican race. The Giuliani strategy was to do well enough in New Hampshire to allow him to stay alive until the vote in the Sunshine State, then win there and be off and running.

Taking Florida was a credible objective. Replete with transplants from New York and elsewhere in the Northeast, and with large urban and suburban pockets of centrist Republicans, the state seemed fertile ground for Giuliani's pitch. It was one place where McCain's expected immolation would boost Giuliani on primary day. But the mayor had his eye on a more concrete asset that he wanted to swipe from John: Florida governor Charlie Crist.

Crist had been elected the year before to the top job in the ultimate battleground state. With his lean frame, snow-white hair, and perpetual tan, he was the most popular elected official in Florida, a prodigious fund-raiser, and a topic of endless fascination. Though Crist's political skills were respected, many insiders saw him as something of a cipher. In becoming governor, he had won a bitterly contested GOP primary after facing down dual allegations of having fathered a child out of wedlock and being gay.

McCain had endorsed Crist in his primary fight; Giuliani had remained neutral. Crist expressed gratitude to McCain on a regular basis, including several reaffirmations of a promise to endorse McCain's presidential bid. "Don't worry, I'll be there at the right time," Crist assured him.

But now that McCain was tanking, Crist seemed to be reconsidering his options. "I campaigned my ass off for him," McCain groused to his lieutenants. "And now that fucker is not going to keep his end of the bargain."

McCain was right to be worried, for even Crist's closest allies often said of him, "Charlie is all about Charlie." Crist's political team was aggressive and demanding. Jim Greer, his handpicked Florida state party chairman, started actively exploring what the governor could receive in return for his endorsement, suggesting to Giuliani directly that a "right of first refusal" on the VP slot might do the trick. The Charlie Bazaar was open for business.

One fine July weekend, Giuliani made his play, inviting Crist to fly up and spend the weekend in the Hamptons. Giuliani and Crist played a round of golf. They smoked cigars at the Giulianis' home in Bridgehampton. And they shared an epic meal. Sitting outside under a stand of trees with Judith and a handful of their respective advisers, they talked long into the night about the paths that had carried them to prominence. The evening went splendidly, the Giulianis thought. Crist was reveling in the courtship. The endorsement seemed within Rudy's grasp. He invited Crist back to his house the next morning for a private conversation.

When Crist arrived, Giuliani made his appeal—and was thrilled with the reply.

"I'd like to support you," Crist said.

The next day, Giuliani shared the news with his aide Tony Carbonetti. "I think we got him; it went very well," Giuliani said.

Carbonetti was familiar enough with Giuliani's lexicon to know what that meant: Rudy thought it was a done deal. Seeing Giuliani's strong poll numbers in

Florida, Crist had apparently concluded that Rudy was the horse to ride. Carbonetti, a no-nonsense fixer who'd been Rudy's chief of staff at City Hall, followed up with Crist's main political guy, George LeMieux, flying to Tallahassee to meet with him and plan the endorsement.

Giuliani's team so valued their new prize that they proceeded to build their entire fall strategy around it. Their secret plan was to start running TV ads in New Hampshire in November, followed shortly thereafter by a surprise trip to Florida to claim the Crist endorsement. Then a classic fly-around to all the state's major cities, for a series of press conferences and fund-raisers. After that, Crist and Giuliani would travel together to New Hampshire for some joint campaigning. The publicity, money, and show of force that Crist would confer in Florida would so impress the national media and the voters of New Hampshire that the endorsement would have a gigantic spillover effect.

Over the next few months, Giuliani was buoyed by the confidence of having a prepackaged bombshell tucked in his breast pocket. Crist's close friend and top fund-raiser, Harry Sargeant, was helping Giuliani raise money, a heartening sign that the political families were engaged. Even as he began to slip in the polls, Rudy remained serene.

Until, that is, his campaign began hearing the same message over and over from their allies in Florida.

No one could quite pin down what it meant, but the message filled Giuliani with unease: There's a problem with Crist.

The candidates lined up at the urinals, Giuliani next to McCain next to Huckabee, the rest all in a row. The debate was soon to start, so they were taking care of business—and laughing merrily at the one guy who wasn't there. Poking fun at him, mocking him, agreeing about how much they disliked him. Then Willard Mitt Romney walked into the bathroom and overheard them, bringing on a crashing silence.

Romney was the guy on whom much of the smart Beltway money had been betting from the start. His résumé was impressive: former CEO of Bain and Company and founder of Bain Capital; savior of the blighted 2002 Salt Lake City Olympics; one-term governor of Massachusetts. His pedigree was glittering: his father, George, had been a governor of Michigan and a presidential candidate, too. His personal life was impeccable: he had married his high school sweetheart, Ann, with whom he had had five strapping sons. He was well spoken and terrific looking, with blindingly white choppers, a chiseled jaw, and a helmet of glossy dark hair.

Romney was running a textbook Republican campaign. He had hired a squad of A-list consultants, pollsters, and media wizards. He'd raised more money than anyone in the field and had millions of his own to draw on. He'd courted the GOP Establishment; worked to neutralize the most vocal potential sources of opposition; racked up oodles of endorsements; and carefully tailored his policy positions to appeal to social, economic, and national security conservatives, the three legs of the Republican stool.

But Romney's efforts to get right with the right landed him in trouble. For most of his life, he had been a middle-of-the-road, pro-business pragmatist, unequivocally pro-choice, moderate on tax cuts and immigration. Running against Ted Kennedy for the Senate in 1994, he pledged that he'd do more for gay rights than his opponent, and declared, "I don't line up with the NRA" on gun control. By 2008, Romney had reversed himself on all of this, which quickly gave rise to charges of hypocrisy and opportunism. Even before he announced his candidacy, a YouTube video began making the rounds that captured him firmly stating his liberalish social views, comically juxtaposing them with his newly adopted arch-conservative stances. From then on, the flip-flopper label was firmly affixed to Mitt's forehead.

Unlike Giuliani, Romney had no reticence about slashing at his rivals. But the perception of him as a man without convictions made him a less-than-effective delivery system for policy contrasts. The combination of the vitriol of his attacks and his apparent coreless-ness explained the antipathy the other candidates had toward him. McCain routinely called Romney an "as-shole" and a "fucking phony." Giuliani opined, "That guy will say anything." Huckabee complained, "I don't think Romney has a soul."

His own team's view was more generous, but no less damning. For all Romney's business acumen and affectations—he sometimes gave PowerPoint presen-tations instead of stump speeches—his advisers found him indecisive, an incorrigible vacillator. He would wait and wait, asking more and more questions, con-sulting with more and more people, ordering up more and more data. The internal debates over his message and even his slogan went on for months, without end or resolution.

By the summer, Romney was stuck in single digits almost everywhere except New Hampshire, where his status as a former Bay State governor and the owner of a vacation home on Lake Winnipesaukee made him a quasi-hometown boy. In trying to explain his failure to catch on, his advisers pointed to another issue, which they shorthanded as TMT—The Mormon Thing. For the Evangelical portion of the Republican base, with its suspicions about Mormonism, Romney's religion was a significant roadblock. (Friends of President Bush would call him from Texas and say of Romney's chances, You've got to be kidding; he's in a cult.) Compounding the problem was the candidate's unwillingness to talk openly about his faith, until it was too late.

Worse, Romney had a propensity for stumbling into the wrong kind of headlines. There was the story about how his gardeners were illegal aliens. There was the one about the time that he and his family went on vacation and put their dog in a crate strapped to the roof of their car for the twelve-hour drive. Oh, and also the one about his "lifelong" devotion to hunting, which turned out to mean he'd done it twice. "I'm not a big-game hunter," Romney said, then explained that his preferred prey were rodents, rabbits, and such—"small varmints, if you will."

Romney found his failure to break through frustrating. "It's not fair," he said to his aides. He was being defined as a flip-flopping Mormon—or a Mormon flip-flopper. He couldn't fathom why the caricature of him was sticking, had no ability to see himself as others might. When Romney's staff showed him the devastating YouTube video, his first reaction was, "Boy, look how young I was back then."

That two candidates as flawed as Giuliani and Romney were the best poised to step in and capitalize on

McCain's implosion was stark testament to the weakness of the rest of the Republican field.

There was Mike Huckabee, the former governor of Arkansas. He was looking good in Iowa, with his cheeky quips and syrupy drawl. But he was raising no money and had limited appeal outside his rural, religious conservative base.

There was Fred Thompson, around whom buzz continued to build all summer as he dithered over taking the plunge. But once he finally hit the trail in September, his candidacy was one long snoozefest, both for the voters and apparently for him; Thompson behaved as though he would rather have been anywhere but on the hustings, ideally in his La-Z-Boy.

And then there were the other entrants: Sam Brownback, Tom Tancredo, Ron Paul, Tommy Thompson, Duncan Hunter, and Jim Gilmore, all of whom were such long shots that they were better described as no shots.

Of course, that described McCain, too. Or so everyone in politics thought.

"Hey, boy, it's John. How ya doing?"

By the summer of 2007, McCain had added a new number to the speed-dial list on his phone. The cell phone was the one piece of modern technology he understood, and it was indispensable to him. McCain lived by the speed dial, was forever calling up and checking in with a wide and sundry orbit of confidants and confrères. The circle of calls was a perfect reflection of McCain's character and of his approach to politics and campaigns. He wanted to hear from a lot of people. He wanted to talk about what he wanted to talk about, not what he was supposed to talk about. He wanted to do it spontaneously, randomly, on his schedule. McCain would listen to everyone, take in their advice, then bounce that advice off the next person in the loop, and so on, ad infinitum. The circle of calls was not designed for the making of firm decisions. More often, it abetted avoiding them. It fed McCain's solipsism; he was the only fixed point. But although the circle was an infinite loop, it wasn't a closed circuit. Every so often, a brand-new voice would be jacked in.

Steve Schmidt lived in Sacramento, California, and barely knew McCain, though in their handful of encounters they'd hit it off. At thirty-six, with a Kojak-bald head, a linebacker's frame, and a Bluetooth headset invariably plugged into his ear, Schmidt was a strategist who had run the rapid-response unit for the 2004 Bush campaign, headed up Dick Cheney's press shop, and orchestrated the confirmation hearings of John Roberts and Samuel Alito to the Supreme

Court. Wanting out of national politics, he'd moved to California to manage the reelection campaign of Governor Arnold Schwarzenegger. He was put on retainer by the McCain campaign when it was still operating under the Bush model, but he had given up his fee in March when the roof started to cave in.

With his campaign in free fall, McCain called and asked Schmidt, "Will you help me?"

"I will help you, but it's your campaign now," Schmidt said. "Everyone assumes it's over. You have nothing left to lose. You should do what you want to do." Schmidt's assessment of McCain's prospects matched those of Davis and Black: McCain probably wasn't going to be the Republican nominee. But it wasn't impossible, and at least now he had a clean slate on which to redraw his approach.

Schmidt's conversations with McCain quickly grew in frequency. He was talking to the candidate at least three times a day now, trying to help guide him toward a path to revival—but occasionally thinking, *Holy shit, how the fuck did I get in the middle of this monstrosity?*

The first call would come like clockwork around eight in the morning, as Schmidt took his dog on a six-mile walk past the manicured lawns of the gated communities that surrounded the one where he lived. One August morning when Schmidt and McCain were gabbing, the talk turned to Iraq. The two men had a bond on the subject of the war. As a White House staffer, Schmidt had been sent to Baghdad to help figure out how to sell the conflict to a skeptical American public. He'd come back from his assignment so disillusioned that he declined to prepare a written report on his findings. He told the White House chief of staff that it wasn't in the administration's interest to have him commit his pessimistic views to paper. Like McCain, Schmidt believed that the war had to be won and that the Bush administration had bollixed the job. Both men had devoured the recent spate of books that chronicled just how bad things were; both had close relatives serving in Iraq.

When McCain talked to Schmidt on the phone, the candidate was always resolute: under the leadership of Army general David Petraeus, the troop surge was working. But on TV, McCain was hedging, saying it might work, it could work, it was working in some ways. Rather than run away from his own position, Schmidt insisted, McCain should embrace it. The Senate was about to debate the surge policy, with the Democratic candidates pushing their party to the left and forcing a vote that would mandate a troop withdrawal ahead of what the White House planned. This is a big, defining issue, Schmidt told McCain.

Your strategic imperative is completely different from every other candidate's, Schmidt said. Romney's strategic imperative is to win the Iowa caucuses. Giuliani's is to win in New Hampshire, then take Florida. Yours is to create a comeback narrative. You are a reader of literature. You understand what a narrative arc is. You were on top and then you fell, and now we're at the part of the story where, before you can have any hope of winning, we have to create the comeback. And the way you create the comeback is by making this race about something other than your political fortunes. It's gotta be about a cause greater than self, which is what your campaign is supposed to be about. The thing this campaign ought to be about now is stopping the Democrats from surrendering in Iraq at the moment when we're winning.

Schmidt proposed a low-budget campaign tour of the key states, with McCain accompanied by some of his POW buddies and other veterans. Put together a caravan, the strategist said. Stay in cheap hotels. Do American Legion halls and VFW posts. Down some beers at night. Have some fun.

McCain loved the idea. The campaign, once so big and bloated, now was reduced to a simple mission, just as it should be. "That's right. I'm gonna do it," he told Schmidt. "I'm gonna do it."

On September 5, Schmidt's galvanizing advice about his message on Iraq still ringing in his ears, McCain appeared with the other candidates at the University of New Hampshire for a debate. With Petraeus scheduled to testify before Congress the following week on the progress of the surge, Romney was asked a question about his attitude toward troop withdrawals. "I don't have a time frame that I've announced," Romney said. "The surge is apparently working. We're going to get a full report on that from General Petraeus . . . very soon."

McCain spoke next—and let Romney have it. "Governor, the surge *is* working. The surge is working, sir. It is working."

"That's just what I said," Romney replied.

"No, not *apparently*," McCain said sharply, cutting him off. "It's working!"

A week later, the No Surrender Tour commenced in Waterloo, Iowa, and from there continued to New Hampshire and South Carolina. The crowds were small, the staging often ragged, the events in cramped, dark, smoky rooms. But the impact was apparent—and not just on the press narrative, but on McCain himself. He was now at the center of a high-profile fight where he had moral certainty that his cause was just and his fear of the opposition was nil. He was distancing himself from the White House's mushy rhetoric and slamming the totems of the left. Surrounded by friends, he started joking again, enjoying himself, some of his confidence returning. Fatalistic as ever, he tried to keep his excitement in check. But his political nerve endings began to tingle.

My God, I might be pulling this thing back in, he thought.

McCain flew down to Florida to raise some money. A fund-raising event had been set up for him on October 2 at the Governors Club in Tallahassee. As long as he was in the neighborhood, he arranged to pay a call on the governor himself. If he couldn't get Crist to endorse him, at least he might be able to hold him neutral.

One of McCain's top Florida supporters, Kathleen Shanahan, was with him when he finished up the donor event. On the way to the statehouse, she verbally took McCain by the lapels and shook him. She was worried that if she didn't say something, McCain, being McCain, would almost certainly sit down with Crist, make small talk, tell some jokes, and waste the moment.

"Don't go over there and bullshit your way through this meeting," Shanahan said. Crist was under all sorts of pressure from Giuliani, Romney, and Thompson, and there was no telling which way he might jump. "You have to be serious; you've got to tell him why you need Florida, why you need Charlie, why you can win."

"I hear you," McCain assured her.

McCain marched into Crist's office and got down to business. He followed Shanahan's script to the letter. No one likes Rudy Giuliani more than me, McCain said, but he's not going to be the nominee of this party, and you'd be wasting your support if you endorsed him. There's no way he's going to win. You should support me. I'm going to win this nomination. My campaign is revived.

Afterward, Crist told his advisers that he cared about McCain, was grateful for his backing in the governor's race. He might not endorse John in the end, Crist said, but otherwise, the senator's speech had convinced him. He intended to remain neutral—for now.

A few weeks later, in early November, the Giuliani people got the word from Florida that Crist's endorsement was being suspended until further notice. Giuliani tried to reach Crist, but he was out of the country, on a Latin American trade mission—having taken Giuliani's nomination strategy with him.

Giuliani's campaign was in a precarious place. Bernard Kerik, the mayor's former driver and then police commissioner and business partner, whom Giuliani had lobbied Bush to nominate as federal director of homeland security, had just been indicted on corruption and tax evasion charges. Worse, on November 27, Politico reported that Giuliani's mayoral office had allegedly used murky accounting practices to cover up government funding of his security during secret visits to Judith's Southampton condo when she was his mistress. Together, the stories created the kind of political-personal reek around Giuliani that many had predicted would be as likely to derail his presidential bid as would his liberal positions on social issues.

Without Crist's endorsement, Florida was almost certainly gone for Giuliani, though he would gamely continue to stump there. Where else did he have to go? Among the first four states, Giuliani's people believed New Hampshire was their only shot. But his poll numbers there were falling fast, which led him to throw in the towel on the Granite State. In doing so, Giuliani was making the single significant change—in strategy, personnel, or message—he ever attempted in reaction to his campaign's decline. He was also helping pry the door open for the resurgence of McCain.

New Hampshire was the only state that mattered to McCain. He knew he was in a binary situation: If he lost the primary, he was through; if he won it, he'd be the front-runner again, and this time, when it counted.

Had it been any other state, McCain's emerging sense of optimism would have been even more guarded than it was. But being all-in on New Hampshire? That wasn't too bad. Man, he loved that place.

And why not? New Hampshire had given McCain his nineteen-point win over Bush in 2000, the greatest political victory of his life. More important, it was the perfect place for the kind of campaign that he had to run now. It was small, intimate, pure retail, and everybody already knew him. McCain was flat broke, after all. He had no staff. He had no pollsters. All of it was gone. Instead of the Cadillac campaign that his advisers once had in mind, he was driving around in the political equivalent of a Ford Pinto—with a hamster wheel for an engine, and Rick Davis sprinting furiously on the thing to keep it spinning. And weird as it might sound, McCain preferred it this way. Living off the land, guerilla-style, hand to mouth. In a way, the collapse of his campaign had been the best thing for McCain, because when the campaign disintegrated, so did the crippling campaign dysfunction.

McCain was at his best in the town hall meetings that were a staple of New Hampshire's quirky political culture. They were how he won the state in 2000, and ever since the No Surrender Tour, town halls in New Hampshire were the oxygen that sustained him.

Week by week, day by day, he could feel himself picking up steam. For one thing, the crowds were getting bigger; he always took a mental count. For another, they were getting friendlier. At a town hall up in North Haverhill in late November, the audience was practically hanging from the rafters. And when it was over, a stream of people came up and said, unprompted, "I'm voting for you."

Equally heartening for McCain was this: no longer was he getting blistered by the anti-immigration forces. Oh, sure, he still had to defend his position on the issue. The hot-eyed ranting had ceased, however, and that was a good sign.

McCain's advisers were glad to hear his rosy reports from the road. But contrary to what he might have believed, they knew he couldn't win the state on town halls alone. Back in September, the campaign had scraped together just enough money to get him on the air in New Hampshire. McCain's advisers wanted to use the famous footage of him in Hanoi filmed after his capture, the pictures of him prone and in excruciating pain, his broken bones encased in slipshod dressing. McCain resisted, as he had throughout his career, the exploitation of his suffering for political gain. But Salter and Schmidt brought him around. "You don't have an option of not talking about who you are and what made you who you are," Schmidt said. "That decision got made the day you decided to run for president of the United States. Whether you like it or not, that's reality, and if you don't do it, we don't have a prayer."

McCain reluctantly agreed, and the ad stirred up a lot of press attention. Several weeks later at a debate, McCain snapped out a sound bite for the ages. "A few days ago, Senator Clinton tried to spend one million dollars on the Woodstock concert museum," he said. "Now, my friends, I wasn't there. I'm sure it was a cultural and pharmaceutical event." Pause. "I was tied up at the time."

The audience roared, and the campaign took the cue. The quip became part of another TV ad for New Hampshire.

McCain had taken New Hampshire a bit for granted at the start, as he ran around trying to raise money to pay for that Bush machine his lieutenants were building. He'd made it easy for Romney to seize the top slot in the polls. The funny thing was, as events unfolded, this worked to McCain's advantage, with Romney writing him off for months. Now the former governor found himself under siege in Iowa, where Huckabee was coming on strong. More good news for McCain; it let him continue to fly under the radar.

One day in late October, out of the blue, McCain told Charlie Black, "We gotta get to twenty percent by December first" in New Hampshire. Black had no idea where the number or target date had come from. Davis didn't know, either. The goal struck them as arbitrary, but what the hell? If it helped McCain to have a tangible marker, fine.

McCain talked about the goal incessantly from then on. Twenty percent, twenty percent, twenty percent. Then, in late November, they all looked up, and there he was: Fox News put him at 21 percent, just eight points behind Romney.

Over Thanksgiving, McCain made another trip back to Iraq, accompanied again by Graham and also by Democratic senator Joe Lieberman, of Connecticut. While they were there they met with General Petraeus and visited Jimmy McCain in Anbar Province.

McCain and Lieberman had developed a close friendship through the years, and the war was a big part of it. Lieberman was inarguably the most hawkish Democrat in the Senate. He and McCain saw eye to eye on almost everything when it came to Iraq, but the bond was deeper than that. It was forged around the antipathy they both had for the bases of their parties, which was reciprocated in spades. Though Lieberman had been Al Gore's running mate in 2000 and was a fairly standard issue Democrat on most social and economic issues, his foreign policy stances had made him an enemy of the left and especially of the netroots, which had successfully targeted him for defeat in the 2006 Connecticut Democratic primary. Lieberman now called himself an Independent Democrat. McCain could relate to that.

The day after returning from Iraq, McCain phoned Lieberman. New Hampshire is going to be everything for me, he said. And there's a lot of independents who are going to vote in the primary. I want to ask if you'd think about giving me your support. If you can't, I'll understand. You're in enough trouble with your party already, but I know it would help me out a lot.

Give me a couple of days to think it over, Lieberman replied. It's a big step, but you know how I feel about you. We've been through a lot together and particularly on the war.

A former Democratic vice-presidential nominee endorsing a Republican? It sure was a big step. Lieberman talked it over with his wife, a couple of staffers, a few friends back home. One of them said, I think you're crazy—but McCain's campaign won't last long, so this will be a brief interlude. For Lieberman, deciding to support McCain would mean crossing another

Rubicon. The calumny that would be hurled at him from the left, he knew, would be intense.

On the other hand, not a single Democratic candidate had asked for Lieberman's endorsement, not even his fellow Connecticut senator, Chris Dodd. For all the distance between him and his party, Lieberman still found that level of ostracism surprising—and painful, very painful. He believed that McCain had shown guts by putting his campaign on the line to stick with the surge. Also that he'd be the best president in a dangerous world. *I don't agree with him on everything, but I agree with him on a lot of big things, and war and peace is one,* Lieberman thought. *Besides, the guy's my friend.*

Lieberman's endorsement came on December 15 in New Hampshire. For McCain, it capped a three-month run of favorable press, rising poll numbers, and the new story line that he had created through the sheer force of his personality. Between Christmas and New Year's, a series of polls showed him ahead in New Hampshire for the first time since the early spring.

McCain had gone from front-runner to corpse to contender in less than a year. Everyone assumed he was flying high: the Mac was back. But the truth was, dangling over his head was a sword of Damocles invisible to almost everyone, if no less menacing for that. The blade was in the form of a newspaper article that was threatening to drop any day. McCain thought it might kill more than his shot at the nomination. He thought it might destroy his career and his reputation—even though the woman at the heart of the story insisted that she'd never even been alone with him.

17

SLIPPING NOOSES, SLAYING DEMONS

Vicki Iseman was a small-town girl in Gucci Gulch. She came from rural Pennsylvania, born in the same burg as Jimmy Stewart, where she was a high-school cheerleader. She arrived in Washington in 1990 with a degree in elementary education and everything she owned stuffed inside two plastic garbage bags. She landed a job as a receptionist at a lobbying shop called Alcalde and Fay. Eight years later, she became the youngest partner in the firm's history. On paper, she gave every appearance of being a familiar Washington archetype: ambitious, workaholic, politically connected, thin and blond and pretty. But she was more a striver than a climber, more earnest than gimlet-eyed. Her clients were mid-level corporations, mostly telecommunications companies that no one had ever heard of. She didn't work the social circuit or want to be a public figure; she had no interest in appearing on *Hardball*. She seemed slightly wonderstruck by how far she'd come. When her college newspaper interviewed her in 2002, she talked about the great view of the nation's capital she had through her office windows, and proudly listed the celebrities she had been lucky enough to meet: Melanie Griffith, Bo Derek, Britney Spears, and Rudy Giuliani.

McCain was another boldface name with whom Iseman was acquainted by then. As the chairman of the Senate Commerce Committee in the late nineties, he held sway over regulations that affected companies she represented. Iseman supported McCain in his 2000 race and helped him raise money for it. In February 1999, she and the senator flew down to Miami and back together on the corporate jet of one of her clients to attend a fund-raiser. The shared transport may have seemed like little more than a convenience to the lobbyist and the senator—but to McCain's advisers, it looked like trouble.

With his wife three thousand miles away, McCain was on his own for months at a time when he was in Washington. As a rule, his aides saw no need to police him and had no desire to play chaperone. The level of scrutiny accorded the private life of an ordinary senator was minimal, anyway. But with McCain preparing for his first presidential bid, the glare of the spotlight was about to increase a thousandfold. Appearances mattered now more than ever. So when a rumor that

McCain was having an affair with Iseman started flitting through Washington, his advisers blanched. Some thought it was true, some thought it was false, but they all feared that it could pry open a can of worms.

The Iseman problem never reared its head publicly in 2000, and the qualms of McCain's team receded for years thereafter. But in the first half of 2007, just as McCain's new campaign was launching and faltering in the same breath, a reporter from *U.S. News & World Report* began pursuing a story that McCain and Iseman had been sexually involved. Iseman denied it. The McCainiacs pushed back hard. *U.S. News* ran an article on McCain and lobbyists, but mentioned neither the allegation nor Iseman.

Now, in November 2007, the Iseman problem had returned with a vengeance. *The New York Times* was on the case, with four staffers assigned to the story.

Iseman's colleagues at Alcalde told her that reporters had been calling and asking questions about her relationship with McCain. When one of them left a message for her, she refused to return the call. But she started to panic as she discovered the scope of the *Times*'s investigation. She called Rick Davis and told him about the unsettling intrusion into her life. "What is going on? Where is this coming from?" Iseman asked. "Is it Weaver?"

Iseman had known Davis, a fellow lobbyist, longer than she had known McCain. She trusted Rick— unlike Weaver, whom she loathed. Back in 1999, after the Miami trip, Iseman and Weaver had clashed, with Weaver instructing her to steer clear of McCain, and they hadn't spoken since.

Davis tried to soothe Iseman, who sounded desperate and a little unhinged. But he shared her surmise that his former rival was the culprit. Ever since his departure, Weaver had been carping to reporters about the McCain campaign; Davis blamed him for some nasty leaks in the wake of the implosion. Within Team McCain there was a strong suspicion that all roads in the *Times* inquiry led back to Weaver.

But the sourcing behind the Iseman story was the least of the campaign's worries about it. The perception that McCain, the great reformer, was too close to the capital's influence peddlers had hurt him badly before; in 2000, the Bush campaign had skewered him mercilessly over that contradiction. Allegations of infidelity aside, the *Times* could do McCain damage on the hypocrisy front. The publication of the story might also incite more unwelcome snooping around in McCain's bedroom—which would be bad enough by itself, but potentially devastating in a party dominated by religious conservatives who didn't trust McCain to begin with. Already, as word had spread in media circles about what the *Times* was chasing, at least a half-dozen new delvings into McCain's personal life had been undertaken by news organizations. At the same time, the campaign was coping with an incipient revival of the story about Cindy's alleged extramarital wanderings; McCainworld heard that there might be an incriminating surveillance videotape of her and another man.

As November turned to December, the public picture of McCain's campaign was all about revival. But privately, his advisers were living in terror. Behind the scenes, no single issue was consuming more of the staff's time or psychic energy than the Iseman problem—and nothing was weighing more heavily on the candidate's mind. Outwardly, McCain was coming on strong in New Hampshire, but inside, he was coming undone.

From early in the morning until late at night, he was distracted, tense, and gruff. Like Iseman, McCain was hearing that a wide range of his past and present associates was being contacted by the *Times* for the story. He dispatched friends with connections at the Gray Lady to try to penetrate its veil of mystery. "Where do you think we are on this?" McCain would ask. Umpteen times a day, he'd phone Davis, Salter, Black, or Schmidt, all of whom were dealing with the story in one way or another. What's happening with the *Times*? Have we heard from them? What do they want? What do we have to do?

McCain's attitude about the likely outcome was dark. "They're out to get me, boy," he'd say. Or, "They're coming after us." Or, "They're going to fuck us."

Finally, in early December, McCain decided he could take it no more. He thought the way the paper was handling the story was shoddy, its tactics bordering on harassment. He believed he had a solid relationship with Bill Keller, the executive editor of the *Times*. On a conference call with Davis and the rest of the campaign's top brass, McCain said, "Fuck it, I'll talk to Keller."

McCain was astonished when, after reaching Keller, almost the first thing out of the editor's mouth was: Is it true? "I have never betrayed the public trust by doing anything like that," McCain replied, and then got off the phone in a hurry.

The next two weeks were a frenzy within the McCain camp as the *Times* appeared to be moving toward publishing the story—which, apart from whatever seamy stuff it might contain, was apparently going to take a substantial look at McCain's efforts on behalf of corporate interests and their water-carriers. Salter was spending three quarters of each day doing nothing but diving into cardboard boxes, excavating ancient records, and pulling up documents in response to the *Times* reporters' detailed questions.

On a parallel track, the campaign was preparing its defense strategy. Schmidt's well-honed and long-held view was that you couldn't go wrong in Republican politics by attacking the *Times*. To help with handling the media circus that was bound to ensue, McCain hired the Washington power lawyer Bob Bennett, who had served as Bill Clinton's personal attorney during the Paula Jones sexual harassment case.

Meanwhile, Iseman hired a lawyer of her own— actually, her second—and was in a bad way. She felt sick, wasn't eating, had lost a parlous amount of weight; her paranoia was stratospheric. She was talking with Davis constantly, sharing with him her answers to the written list of questions the *Times* had provided at her request—a degree of coordination about which few were aware. At the top of her reply, Iseman wrote, I am a private citizen. You are destroying my life. She again insisted that she never had a romantic relation-ship with the senator.

The McCain campaign braced for the story to run the week before Christmas, and sent Bennett to meet with the *Times* reporters. Then, on December 20, the Drudge Report blared an item with the headline

"MEDIA FIREWORKS: McCAIN PLEADS WITH NY TIMES TO SPIKE STORY." The banner was a reference to the Keller call, but the tantalizing part of the post was elsewhere. The reporters "hoped to break the story before the Christmas holiday," it said, "but editor Keller expressed serious reservations about journalism ethics and issuing a damaging story so close to an election."

The revelation that the *Times* was pursuing such an explosive line of inquiry caused the political world to gasp. The Romney campaign saw the item and worried that the piece would never be considered fit to print. For Romney, the publication of the story before New Hampshire would all but guarantee that he won the state. For McCain, the calculation was the converse: if the story ran, he was dead.

The whole thing was excruciating for McCain; fending off such personal attacks, true or false, felt like South Carolina all over again. "I do find the timing of this whole issue very interesting," McCain told the Associated Press on the day the Drudge item appeared. "And we're not going to stand for what happened to us in 2000."

But Schmidt was certain that no act of defiance would be necessary at that point. They don't have the story, he told McCain. If we get to Christmas and they don't publish, we'll be fine. They're not going to put something out a few days before Iowa. It's just not going to happen.

"I hope you're right," McCain replied, using one of his favorite expressions. What it meant was: Don't bet on it.

In the days before the New Hampshire primary on January 8, the McCain campaign was suffused in an aura of nostalgia: the Straight Talk Express crisscrossing the snowbanked byways, with McCain in the back of the bus cracking wise, the hack pack huddled around him. McCain's town hall meetings were jammed, his wit and spontaneity on display. The Sunday before the vote, at an event in Salem, he was questioned by an audience member who objected to his support for Bush's tax cuts as fiscally irresponsible. "You're still in purgatory," the man said.

"Thank you," replied McCain. "That's a step up from where I was last summer."

McCain was openly, fanatically superstitious. In New Hampshire, he carried with him his lucky penny and lucky compass, and not only stayed in the same room in the same hotel as he did in 2000, but slept on the same side of the bed. And though such behavior might have struck some as obsessive-compulsive, it reflected his awareness of the role that blind luck had played in his revival.

Mark McKinnon, the former media adviser to President Bush who was now filling that role for McCain, observed that his current boss's winning required that he draw a political inside straight. In the last months of 2007, McCain had been dealt the first two cards in that hand: the apparent success of the Iraq surge, and the reduction in the heat surrounding immigration. The results of the Iowa caucuses on January 3 delivered him a third. Huckabee trounced Romney by nine points, leaving McCain's only serious competition in New Hampshire reeling. The fourth card came courtesy of the *Times*, which made good on Schmidt's optimism and continued to hold back the Iseman story. And the fifth was slapped down in front of him by New Hampshire, where he won the primary by five points over Romney. Accepting his hard-earned victory, he told the crowd, "We are the makers of history, not its victims."

McCain's luck at the table continued in the Michigan primary on January 15, though it was less than evident at the time. In a state with the nation's highest unemployment rate and a manufacturing base hollowed out to the point of collapse, McCain had chosen candor over pander—"Those jobs aren't coming back," he declared—and paid the price at the polls, losing to Romney by nine points.

Yet McCain's long-run prospects were bolstered by the curious strategy pursued by Huckabee. With his energetic base of Evangelical support, Huckabee stood as McCain's greatest threat in the next primary, in South Carolina, which came four days after Michigan. But seduced by the notion that his appeals to economic populism would play well in Michigan, Huckabee and his team decided to devote several days and a pile of cash—precious resources, of which he had little—to the state. Not only did Huckabee finish a distant third, but he also missed the chance to get a jump on McCain in South Carolina.

With all eyes transfixed on the Democrats, the Republican primary in the Palmetto State might as well have been occurring in Bora-Bora for all the attention it received. Yet in the contemporary history of the GOP, no contest had been a more reliable bellwether in determining who would eventually claim the Republican nomination. Since 1980, when Lee Atwater pushed his native state to the front of the presidential calendar, every winner of South Carolina had gone on to become the party's standard-bearer.

The McCains were nervous as they entered the sprint to primary day. The polls showed a tighter race than John had hoped it would be after his victory in

New Hampshire, his lead over Huckabee in the low single digits. Cindy, still scarred by the memories of 2000, was uncomfortable every moment she spent on the ground. And her husband was only minimally less haunted. The possibility of another crushing loss in South Carolina—one that, in light of McCain's still-threadbare financial circumstances, might effectively end his campaign—filled him with dread.

In one crucial respect, however, the McCain of 2008 was a very different animal in South Carolina than the McCain of 2000. No longer the insurgent, no longer the rabble-rouser, he was the candidate of the Establishment. His most loyal supporter, Lindsey Graham, was the state's senior senator, and had done yeoman's work in corralling the endorsements of local elected officials early on—and holding them in place during the dark days of 2007. At events across South Carolina in the days leading up to the balloting, McCain stood arm in arm with those officials. He also basked in the glow of the support of the state's war veterans, some of whom had turned viciously against him in 2000. In almost no other way had McCain's campaign wound up resembling the Bush model, but he was grateful for these two exceptions.

By primary night, no one had a clue as to what might happen. Romney had pulled most of his advertising to focus on Florida—that was good. Giuliani had failed to make the smart move and campaign along the affluent

South Carolina coast, where there were scads of pro-choice voters—another boon to McCain. But when the polls closed, neither the networks nor the AP were prepared to project a winner. The early returns were screwy, the forecasting models were messed up. It was going to take a while.

In the McCains' hotel suite, the tension was nearly unbearable. Always optimistic, Graham began doing his own analysis as the results from certain counties came in, predicting victory. But McCain didn't want to hear happy talk, even from Lindsey. Don't say that, he snarled through gritted teeth. You don't know that. Just shut up.

Watching her husband pace around the room only made Cindy more anxious. "Is everything going to be okay?" she whispered to Davis, on the brink of tears.

When word arrived after eight o'clock that McCain had narrowly won, joy washed over Cindy, excitement over her husband—which was unusual. Normally for McCain, the relief of not losing was a more powerful emotion than the thrill of winning. But South Carolina was different. It was about vindication, about slaying demons, about putting paid to the past. McCain wasn't a drinker, but that night, there was champagne.

Yet the sweetness of South Carolina lasted only a few hours. McCain now faced what everyone expected would be the decisive primary of the season: Florida, on January 29. With Huckabee and Giuliani effectively finished, McCain was finally going one-on-one against the rival he most disdained, Romney. If McCain prevailed in Florida, the nomination would be his. But if he lost, he would be heading into Super Tuesday mortally wounded, facing a candidate with tens of millions of dollars in personal wealth and little apparent reluctance to spend it.

For the next ten days, Romney campaigned like a conservative incarnation of Bill Clinton circa 1992. "The economy, stupid" was his leitmotif. McCain talked of little besides Iraq, slamming Romney—in a dishonest way—for wanting to prematurely withdraw American troops. (Earlier in the year, Romney had said he favored "a private timetable" for drawing down U.S. forces.) But by the weekend before the vote, the polls remained razor-edge close. McCain and Romney were in a dead heat.

Both men had long hoped that Charlie Crist would be their ticket to ride in the Sunshine State. But after all the hide-and-seek of 2007, Crist seemed to have decided to sit out the primary. "I'm not going to endorse anybody; whoever's going to win is going to win," he told his adviser LeMieux on the Friday night before the Tuesday primary. The assurance quickly went out from Cristworld to the Republican candidates: Charlie wasn't going to put his finger on the scale.

The next day, however, Crist, out sailing with his fiancée, felt a pang of conscience. The governor's internal polling showed McCain slipping as Romney poured money into the state. Crist harkened back to the endorsement McCain had given him in 2006. *The guy's been really good to me,* he thought. *I can't leave my friend behind.*

The following night, McCain was in St. Petersburg for the Pinellas County Lincoln Day Dinner. Crist was slated to introduce him. Upstairs in McCain's suite at the Hilton where the event was being held, he asked John for a word alone—and told him he would be endorsing him at the dinner downstairs in a few minutes.

Crist's intervention propelled McCain to a five-point win in Florida. The other Republican candidates and their advisers may have seen Charlie as a liar, a manipulator, and a no-account betrayer, but he was all right with John. To Crist's betrothed on primary night, McCain said, "God bless him."

The next three weeks may have been the most glorious of McCain's political career. After Florida, much of his party fell into formation and smartly saluted him. Giuliani dropped out the next day and threw his backing to McCain. Arnold Schwarzenegger and Texas governor Rick Perry climbed on board the day after that. McCain's face graced the cover of *Time*, above the tagline "The Phoenix." And on February 5, Super Tuesday, he racked up a clutch of big-state wins—California, Illinois, New Jersey, New York— that put him within shouting distance of clinching the nomination.

And yet there was still one enemy lurking that potentially had the power to hang McCain: *The New York Times*. The only questions were whether the Iseman story was in fact a noose around his neck, and whether the paper would ever try to cinch it tight.

All along, Schmidt had assumed that the piece would eventually run. The *Times* had invested too much time and effort in pursuing the matter just to let it drop. He was even more certain when, over the weekend of February 16 and 17, the campaign heard that *The New Republic* was working on its own story about the internal deliberations at the *Times* over whether to publish the opus. There was no way the *Times* would let itself be scooped or embarrassed, Schmidt believed. The Iseman story was coming and coming soon, Schmidt told McCain.

On February 20, it came. Just hours before the piece went live on the Web, Schmidt and Salter learned from the *Times* that it was being posted and was set to run in the paper the next day. McCain and his wife were campaigning in Toledo, Ohio. Schmidt and Salter had to get there fast. They raced to Reagan airport in Washington, but their flight was delayed, so they grabbed a plane to Detroit instead, rented a car, and drove the sixty miles south. Along the way, they studied the story on their BlackBerrys.

It ran to more than three thousand words, the majority devoted to McCain's dealings with lobbyists. But the story also contended that, in 1999, some of McCain's aides and advisers had confronted him over an alleged affair with Iseman, and that McCain had "acknowledged behaving inappropriately and pledged to keep his distance" from her. It also recounted the Weaver-Iseman dustup, with Weaver confirming by email and on the record that he had told Vicki to stay away from John. Weaver's chief concern, he said, was that Iseman had been bragging to others that she had professional sway over McCain, which threatened the senator's image as a reformer.

It was nearly midnight when Schmidt and Salter finally reached Toledo. They found the McCains in their hotel suite. Cindy was distraught, had clearly been weeping. John was hardly in better shape. He said he was sure the campaign was over. That the story wasn't politically survivable. That he wouldn't be the nominee.

"I don't know how we get through this," McCain said.

Schmidt was having none of it.

"This is going to be fine," he said. "The story is outrageous. Someone's going to get crushed on this, and it's going to be *The New York Times*."

Emphatically, Schmidt laid out his plan for a counterattack. First thing the next morning, McCain would hold a press conference for the reporters traveling with him, Cindy by his side. We're not going to put a clock on this, Schmidt said. You're going to take every question. You'll deny the story, you'll express your unhappiness with the *Times*, and you'll do it in the proper tone. "You can't get up there looking pissed off," Schmidt said. "You have to be measured in the response."

Although both McCains were furious at Weaver for having gone on the record in the story, Salter told McCain that he had to speak positively about his former wingman at the press conference; they needed to avoid giving Weaver an excuse to peddle anything further to the press. As for Iseman, they all agreed that McCain should call her a friend, which was what he said she was.

The next morning, John and Cindy met the press. In a dark suit, blue shirt, and blue tie, McCain performed to his advisers' precise specifications. He was calm. He was collected. He showed not the slightest flash of even the mildest annoyance. He answered many questions with a simple yes or no. He said that Weaver was a friend. And that the same was true of Iseman.

Asked about the *Times*, he said, "This whole story is based on anonymous sources . . . I'm very disappointed in that."

The press conference not only achieved its intended effect but had some ancillary benefits. McCain never believed he would see the day when the raving right rallied around him in unison, yet that was what was happening now. Sean Hannity, Rush Limbaugh, Laura Ingraham—every one of them scorned McCain. Yet within hours, they'd all hastened to his defense, because they hated the *Times* even more. ("For the first time in history, John McCain won talk radio," Charlie Black drolly observed.)

The McCainiacs had feared that the *Times* story would open up the Pandora's box that was the senator's personal life. Although *The Washington Post* and *Newsweek* promptly ran their own similar anonymously sourced versions of the Iseman tale, the stories disappeared without a trace. The unequivocal denials of McCain and Iseman, and the criticism of the *Times* for venturing into tabloid territory, produced the same dynamic as had the paper's 2006 piece on the Clintons' marriage: the Gray Lady was forced to play defense, and McCain assumed the self-righteous pose of the aggrieved. Never again would the campaign face another serious press inquiry about the candidate's personal life.

In defusing the Iseman story, McCain cleared the final remaining obstacle to his nomination. But the victory came at a cost. For two years, McCain's relationship with the media had been souring, but this turned things from sour to rancid—at least in his mind, where it counted. The campaign's dealings with the *Times* in particular would never be the same again, either. There was no turning back, no way to restore even a modicum of trust with the most important print outlet in the country.

Having dodged bullet after bullet, McCain clinched his party's nomination on March 4 by winning the primaries in Texas, Ohio, Rhode Island, and Vermont, and concluding one of the greatest political comebacks in modern American history. The next morning, he flew from Dallas to Washington to have lunch at the White House and claim his first reward: the endorsement of one of the least popular Republicans in the country. The task of simultaneously embracing and maintaining sufficient distance from George W. Bush presented McCain with his initial political challenge as the presumptive nominee. He handled it awkwardly, garbling his words as he told reporters in the Rose Garden, "I intend to have as much possible campaigning events together as is in keeping with the president's heavy schedule."

The weeks between March and June, when the general election would unofficially begin, should have been a period of enormous opportunity for McCain. His approval rating, according to Gallup, was 67 percent, as high as it had ever been. In head-to-head polling matchups, he was running even with both Obama, by then the likely Democratic nominee, and Clinton. The two Democrats were pummeling each other, spending many tens of millions of dollars to do it, and the rancor in their party was growing every day. McCain, on the other hand, had an extended period to regroup after more than a year of chaos. He had won the nomination with no money, no organization, no well-defined message, and no sophisticated strategy. Now he had a chance to acquire all those things. The question was whether he would even try.

On April 2, McCain arrived in Annapolis, Maryland, for one of the stops along his weeklong "Service to America" biography tour. The idea was for him to travel to places of significance in his life story, reintroducing himself to voters and redefining his image. He would visit his high school in Alexandria, Virginia;

military installations in Mississippi and Florida where he'd been based; his political HQ in Arizona; and Annapolis, which he entered as a plebe in 1954. After leading the pledge of allegiance at a local diner, where scrapple-scarfing patrons huddled in booths beneath a sign that read "DELICIOUS PANCAKES, MAPLE SYRUP, MARGARINE," he arrived at a grander setting: the Navy football stadium. But no throng of midshipmen-cum-McCainiacs surrounded the candidate on the podium. In front of him instead were sixty folding chairs occupied by wizened dignitaries; behind him were thirty-five thousand seats, occupied by no one.

McCain was cranky about the setting. "What is going on with this?" he asked his aides. But the speech was hardly better than the TV pictures. He sought to explain how a callow, shallow hellion had become a man of honor. At the academy, McCain said, he was "childish" and prone to "petty acts of insubordination." But then came the horrors he suffered in Vietnam, and the lessons Annapolis had sought to teach him took hold.

"It changed my life forever," McCain said. "I had found my cause: citizenship in the greatest nation on earth." But his next sentence—"What is lost, in a word, is citizenship"—sounded like a non sequitur, and that's because it was. The prompter was at fault: it had devoured a page of his script.

Nevertheless, McCain's consiglieri professed themselves pleased with the tour. "It was open-field running for us," McKinnon told a reporter. "While the Democrats continued to attack each other and claw their way to the bottom, McCain was able to communicate a positive message and create a compelling narrative about the values he learned growing up that make him best qualified to be president."

But for many Republicans, the biography tour began to instill pessimism about the party's nominee. McCain had failed to drive a message. He had failed to bore in on the weaknesses of Obama. He had failed to make news of any kind. The press coverage of the tour was perfunctory when not derisory. On *The Daily Show*, Jon Stewart dubbed it the "Monsters of Nostalgia Tour," cracking that it had "all the allure of an Atlantic City senior citizens' outing without all the awkward sexual tension."

Republicans worried, too, that McCain's organization was ramping up far too sluggishly. Although its leadership—Black, Davis, McKinnon, Salter, and Schmidt—was well regarded, it seemed stretched too thin. The campaign had just four full-time finance staffers and no significant online fund-raising presence. In March, it brought in a mere $4 million over the Web and through direct mail.

But the greatest Republican concern was about McCain himself: that in selecting a septuagenarian senator more comfortable in Washington than anywhere else, a dark-humored war hero with a distinctly premodern sensibility, a man who thought that being on *Meet the Press* was more important than going to church—actually, that being on the show *was* going to church—the party had chosen Bob Dole all over again.

The comparison seemed all too vivid, and its implications all too dire, on the night of June 3. As Obama celebrated having locked up his party's nomination, McCain delivered a televised speech that made Republican hearts sink across the land. In front of an unsightly green backdrop, he stammered through an uninspiring and uninspired text. His people knew it was a disaster from the moment he took the podium; they prayed the cable networks would cut away.

The general election was now upon McCain. In his three unmolested months, he had accomplished next to nothing. His organization was still too small. He was still in the poorhouse. He still had no real message and no clear strategy.

McCain wasn't happy about any of this. But panicked he was not. The guerilla approach had won him the nomination. Why couldn't it work against Obama?

PART THREE

18

PARIS AND BERLIN

John McCain and Barack Obama entered the general election jointly holding out the hope of a different kind of fall campaign. For all of their intellectual, generational, and stylistic differences, McCain and Obama had much in common. Both candidates argued that Washington was broken, in need of root-and-branch reform, and ascribed its dysfunction to hyperpartisanship and the pernicious power of special interests. Both cast themselves as anti-politicians and post-ideological avatars. To gain their respective nominations, both relied on the support of centrist independents and even a handful of members of the other party. Neither had any inclination to turn the election into another bitterly polarized knife fight. Both boasted of being ready and able to lead a more civil and constructive conversation.

There was one minor hitch with this rosy scenario, however. McCain and Obama didn't like each other. Not even a little bit.

Their very first entanglement had ended in a fit of unusually public acrimony. It was in February 2006, when McCain asked Obama to collaborate with him on ethics reform. McCain always kept an eye peeled for young turks who shared his propensity for bucking the system, and he didn't care if they happened to be Democrats. As a freshman congressman in the early eighties, McCain had been taken under the wing of Democrat Mo Udall, the legendary Arizona representative who was the liberal conscience of the House and a ringing voice for reform. The Udall precedent was on McCain's mind when he reached out to Russ Feingold, the novice Wisconsin Democratic senator who became his partner on campaign-finance reform. And it was what drove McCain to approach Obama, the designated Democratic captain on ethics.

Obama indicated an interest in working with McCain on a bipartisan initiative. But after attending a meeting of a McCain-led splinter group, Obama backed away, neglecting to call the Arizonan to let him know, instead sending a formal letter on February 2 announcing that he intended to push the Democratic version of ethics legislation—a letter that was released to the press before it reached McCain.

McCain felt that he had extended his hand and Obama had slapped his face, and he directed Mark Salter to brush the whippersnapper back. Over his boss's signature, Salter fired off a letter to Obama (that wound up in the hands of reporters posthaste) bristling with scorn and oozing sarcasm. "I'm embarrassed to admit that after all these years in politics I failed to interpret your previous assurances as typical rhetorical gloss routinely used in politics to make self-interested partisan posturing appear more noble," it said. "I understand how important the opportunity to lead your party's effort to exploit this issue must seem to a freshman Senator, and I hold no hard feelings over your earlier disingenuousness."

Salter's chin music was the first time anyone in either party had tossed a high hard one at Obama—and it echoed through the Senate, where decorum made that kind of personal affront about as common as cut-off shorts at a confirmation hearing. The same day, Obama wrote back to McCain, expressing cool puzzlement and ostensible solicitude. But when he was asked about the exchange by the press, Obama didn't hesitate to throw a brushback of his own.

"The tone of [McCain's] letter, I think, was a little over the top," he said. "But John McCain's been an American hero and has served here in Washington for twenty years, so if he wants to get cranky once in a while, that's his prerogative."

Did you just call McCain "cranky"? a reporter asked.

"You got my quote the first time," Obama said tartly.

Back in his office, Obama was blunter with his aides about his sentiments. "I'm not interested in being bitch-slapped by John McCain," he said.

As far as McCain was concerned, the ethics ker-fuffle was just the first in a series of incidents that revealed Obama's true colors. In 2007, when McCain was paying a brutal price politically for his work alongside Kennedy on immigration reform, Obama joined a bipartisan group of senators who'd agreed to band together and oppose amendments from the right and left that would scuttle the legislation. But then Obama promptly turned around and voted for several liberal provisions. A year later, he criticized McCain for coming out against a new GI Bill that would have guaranteed money for college to anyone who served three years in the military. "I can't believe [that] he believes it is too generous to our veterans," Obama tut-tutted.

McCain didn't believe any such thing; he worried that the bill would create retention problems in the armed forces. Having his commitment to veterans questioned set off McCain's first flare of genuine ire toward Obama. "I will not accept from Senator Obama, who did not feel it was his responsibility to serve our country in uniform, any lectures on my regard for those who did," McCain snapped.

McCain never thought any of this would be of consequence in the presidential race. All along, he believed that he would be running against Clinton—and relished the prospect. He liked Hillary, respected her, had become friendly with her in the Senate. They had traveled to the far reaches of the globe together and enjoyed each other's company. (The vodka shots they'd shared once in Estonia had become the stuff of lore.) His disappointment when she lost was palpable.

By the start of the general election, McCain's view of Obama was firmly fixed and strikingly similar to the one that Hillary held: Obama was a lightweight, a line-cutter, a go-along-to-get-alonger who pretended to be a man of independence, and who bore none of the scars of political sacrifice that McCain wore as medals of honor. Honor was the core concept here, the soldier's highest virtue. McCain believed Obama lacked it, along with guts.

McCain was fortified in his dim opinion by the people closest to him. Graham and Salter were always

trashing Obama, and Cindy had been genuinely offended by Michelle's "proud of my country" remark.
In the past, she rarely said a word about John's opponents, let alone an opponent's spouse. But as a mother
of two sons in the service, she couldn't restrain herself;
after she took her shot at Michelle on the stump, her
husband gave her an approving thumbs-up.

The Obamas were a good deal less emotionally
wound up in their opinions of the McCains. For all of
Michelle's angst about the fallout from "proud of my
country" and becoming a target of the right, she was
taken aback when Cindy joined the fray. Michelle absorbed her counterpart's slam with private defiance.
*Oh, so it's gonna be like this? So this is how you want
to play?* she thought. Barack, meanwhile, regarded his
past run-ins with McCain as faintly ridiculous. McCain
had behaved like an arrogant jackass, happy if he could
pat Obama on the head and have him follow his lead,
but then all self-righteous and indignant if Barack took
a different path. *Whatever.*

Nothing Obama had seen had altered his conviction
that the political environment was fertile for a Democratic victory. "If I lose the nomination to Hillary, I can
hold my head up," he told his team on a conference call
that spring. "But if I lose the general election to John
McCain, I'll be run out of town on a rail."

. . .

On June 4, not long after the news broke that Clinton intended to concede, Obama received a congratulatory call from McCain. The two men pledged comity in the coming campaign and joked about how the pundits had written them both off a year earlier. But McCain also took the opportunity to press a proposal that he and Obama conduct ten joint town hall meetings, one each week between June 12 and the Democratic convention. For McCain, the upside was obvious: a chance to go toe-to-toe with Obama in a format he loved (and generate tons of free publicity to boot). For Obama, the payoff was less evident. In May, he'd declared that he would welcome debating McCain "anywhere, anytime." Now Obama said he was open to the idea but made no commitments.

The truth was Obama had an array of more pressing concerns to deal with. After waging a nomination fight of unprecedented length and strain, he and his exhausted team had no time to rest their heads. In the span of a few weeks, they had to plan two vast and vastly complicated events: an ambitious trip abroad in July, to help Obama buff up his foreign-affairs bona fides, and the convention in August. At the same time, the Obamans had to devise a state-by-state electoral strategy for the fall, and take the measure of their new adversary.

Obama's lead pollster, Joel Benenson, quickly slammed together a presentation on the state of play. The good news, he reported, was that Obama was leading McCain by 49 to 44 percent among likely voters. The unexpected news was that the economy was now by far the most important issue, especially to undecideds. The neutral news was that neither Obama nor McCain was strong on that issue. The most surprising (and most heartening) news was that the perception of McCain as a maverick change agent was confined to the Beltway; in the rest of America, voters viewed him as Bush redux. The implications for Team Obama's message were plain. Every effort they expended for the next four months should be devoted to shackling McCain to Bush on the economy.

The Obamans had grand aspirations for remaking the electoral map. Plouffe's plan was to target seventeen battleground states, including some—Indiana, North Carolina, North Dakota—that hadn't voted Democratic in decades.

That Plouffe was thinking so boldly owed much to the breadth of Obama's appeal. But it had as much to do with the resources at his disposal. On June 19 the campaign announced its decision to opt out of accepting public financing for the general election, making Obama the first candidate to do so since that system was implemented in the aftermath of Watergate. The decision was a reversal for Obama on two levels: he was a longtime champion of the public system, and had signed a commitment (on an interest group question-naire) in November 2007 to stay in it. The U-turn un-dercut the reformist image that Benenson's data showed was a vital advantage for Obama against McCain. But the unholy amount of money being sucked in by the campaign's Web fund-raising machine represented an even greater edge.

McCainworld learned about the decision around the same time it was becoming clear that Obama had no intention of doing the joint town halls. McCain wasn't surprised by either outcome, but they bolstered his sense of Obama as a phony. What bothered him more was the failure of the press to challenge Obama on his hypocrisy. *If I'd done that, they'd kill me*, he thought. McCain and his advisers had been astonished by how far in the tank the media had been for Obama during his race against Clinton. Now McCain, his relations with the press already strained, braced for a similar double standard.

Steve Schmidt agreed with all of that, but thought it was slightly beside the point. The McCain campaign would be limited to the $84 million provided by the public financing system (although the Republican National Committee would supplement that with spending of its own); the Obamans were likely to raise four or five times as much. Making matters worse, the lengthy Democratic nomination fight meant that the Obama forces had operations in nearly every state, firing on all cylinders—whereas McCainworld was sputtering along, forever on the verge of needing roadside assistance.

In mid-June, after the green backdrop debacle, Schmidt had a candid conversation with McCain about the state of the campaign.

"How do you think things are going?" he asked his boss.

"Not well," said McCain.

"I think that's about right," Schmidt said. The structure of the campaign was still a mess. There was no political operation. Basic things weren't getting done. We either need to fix this now, Schmidt said, or not only will we lose, but we're in danger of going down as the worst-run presidential campaign in the history of American politics.

For the first time in months, McCain seemed galvanized. He called a meeting of his senior advisers at his condo in Washington and elevated Schmidt to run the show alongside Davis.

Almost instantly, McCainworld was imbued with a new degree of discipline and order. Nicknamed Bullet by Bush uber-strategist Karl Rove and Sergeant Schmidt by McCain, the shaven-headed operative brought to his task two signal strengths: a relentless focus and zero tolerance for bullshit. He hired a top-flight political director. He instituted a regular message call at eight o'clock every morning. He sought to limit McCain's cell phone use to keep him from terminal drift. He even took up the matter of housekeeping at the campaign's disheveled HQ. "This place looks like a fucking gypsy camp," Schmidt told the office manager over the July 4 weekend. "I want it painted and cleaned up by Monday."

Schmidt also took the draconian step of curtailing his boss's access to the media. The old days of reporters indulging McCain's freewheeling disquisitions—on everything from the caprices of his Senate colleagues to the temptations of Brazilian table dancers—and not writing about them were long gone. Now the coverage was constant, glaring, and driven by the quest to trip him up.

And so, in July, a barrier between McCain and the reporters covering him was installed on his jet. Press availabilities were cut back. Literally, figuratively, and symbolically, a curtain came down on the Straight Talk

Express—just as one was rising on the Obamapalooza World Tour.

It was, by every measure, an extraordinary spectacle, with a sprawling itinerary that would have posed real challenges to a sitting president and his team. Eight countries in ten days, including two war zones: Kuwait, Afghanistan, and Iraq on the first leg; Jordan, Israel, Germany, France, and England on the second. And yet the Obamans miraculously pulled it off without a hitch. The pictures beamed around the world were priceless: Obama visiting an army base and effortlessly sinking a three-point shot in front of hundreds of cheering soldiers; Obama in a helicopter with General Petraeus, both in sunglasses and grinning like mad; the soaring speech in front of two hundred thousand at the Victory Column in Berlin; the interviews with each of the broadcast network anchors, who had tagged along for the trip.

The reaction of the McCain campaign was unambiguous. It went on the attack. It released an ad unveiling the campaign's slogan, "Country First," with its insinuation that Obama put something else (i.e., his ambition) above the nation. It aired another claiming that Obama, while he was in Germany, "made time to go to the gym, but canceled a visit with wounded troops—seems the Pentagon wouldn't allow him to bring cameras." On the trail, McCain spat venom over an interview from abroad in which Obama said that, although the surge appeared to have been effective, he still opposed it. "It seems to me that Obama would rather lose a war in order to win a political campaign," McCain said.

Schmidt doubted that any of it was working. We're almost out of time, he said to Davis. Obama is up by double digits now. He could be up twelve or fifteen points heading into their convention. Bill Clinton's going to give a great speech. Hillary's going to give a great speech. Obama's *definitely* going to give a great speech, and even if he doesn't, the press will say he did. So now we're down twenty heading into our convention. On the first night, we have Cheney and Bush; after that, we could be down twenty-five. If we don't figure out something immediately to arrest Obama's lead, we're done.

On July 27, the day after Obama returned stateside, Schmidt and a small group of McCain advisers met in a conference room at the Phoenix Ritz-Carlton to take up that task. "We're running against the biggest celebrity in the world," Schmidt said. Obama was flying at an altitude no politician had ever before attained. He was flying so high that there was no way to shoot him out of the sky or pull him down to earth. Their only hope,

Schmidt went on, was to push Obama higher. Push him from twenty thousand to forty thousand feet, above the so-called death line on Mount Everest, where there's not enough oxygen to breathe.

You said he's a celebrity, noted Fred Davis, McCain's lead adman. "Well, let's turn that against him. Big celebrity? So's Britney Spears! So's Paris Hilton!"

The room exulted. Linking Obama with such famously insubstantial household names might shove him straight into the asphyxiation zone. Davis rushed off to produce some ads based on the concept. A version featuring Oprah was scuttled by Schmidt. ("Don't politicize Oprah. She's more powerful than you can comprehend, like Obi-Wan Kenobi.") A version including Ellen DeGeneres was nixed as well. But the incarnation with Britney and Paris was good to go.

The ad, called "Celeb," hit the air on July 30. "He's the biggest celebrity in the world," a female voice intoned over soft-focus images of Spears, Hilton, and Obama in Berlin. "But is he ready to lead?" The ad's unveiling was accompanied by an email from Davis: "Only celebrities like Barack Obama go to the gym three times a day, demand 'MET-Rx chocolate roasted-peanut protein bars and bottles of a hard-to-find organic brew—Black Forest Berry Honest Tea' and worry about the price of arugula."

The message wasn't difficult to decode. Not only was Obama a celebrity, but he was precious, self-infatuated, effete, hoity-toity—a celebrelitist.

"Celeb" quickly became ubiquitous on cable. It went viral on the Web. Trivial and trivializing, the talking heads snorted. Pathetic. And some liberals discerned a subtext in the ad that was more insidious. They saw the juxtaposition of Obama with the comely white women as an attempt to stir up fears of miscegenation. They pointed to a shot of the Victory Column and called it phallic. They cited an earlier McCain negative spot that showed Obama draining his three-pointer and found a racial angle there as well: that McCainworld was trying to portray Obama as a blinged-up, camera-hogging NBA point guard, Allen Iverson with a Harvard Law degree.

Obama seemed to see something, too. On the day that "Celeb" went up, he was campaigning in Missouri. At his first stop, in Springfield, Obama said, "Nobody really thinks that Bush or McCain have a real answer for the challenges we face, so what they're going to try to do is make you scared of me. 'You know, he's not patriotic enough. He's got a funny name. You know, he doesn't look like all those other presidents on those dollar bills, you know. He's too risky.'"

McCain was on a hair trigger over accusations or imputations of racism. He had warned his team to steer clear of anything that might open him up to that charge. He was emphatic that Reverend Wright was off-limits. McCainworld, however, feared that innocence wasn't a sufficient defense when it came to racial matters. John and Cindy had talked at length about the charges that had been leveled against the Clintons during the Democratic nomination fight. They believed that those accusations had been unfair, saw the Obama campaign's hand in the besmirching of Hillary's and Bill's reputations, and had vowed not to let the same thing happen to them. So when Obama let loose with his "other presidents" comment, McCain and his lieutenants were gripped with a sickening sense of déjà vu.

"We gotta call bullshit on this," Schmidt said.

"Do whatever you have to do," McCain told Davis. "This is not right."

The next morning, Davis put out a press release that minced no words. "Barack Obama has played the race card, and he played it from the bottom of the deck," Davis's statement said. "It's divisive, negative, shameful, and wrong."

The Obamans had never been so directly challenged on playing the race card—except by Bill Clinton in South Carolina, when his head was in the process of exploding. The campaign's reaction was furious backpedaling. "What Barack Obama was talking about was that he didn't get here after spending decades in Washington," Gibbs tepidly told the AP. "He was referring to the fact that he didn't come into the race with the history of others. It is not about race."

But, of course, it was. Obama himself had made the same point more explicitly six weeks earlier, when he said at a rally in Jacksonville, Florida, "We know what kind of campaign they're going to run. They're going to try and make you afraid of me. 'He's young and inexperienced and he's got a funny name. And did I mention he's black?'" But outside the context of the McCain negative-ad assault, that remark had gone unnoticed.

On his nightly call after the Davis broadside and the Gibbs retreat, Obama wasn't happy. The campaign had failed to defend him as well, as vigorously, or as forthrightly as he thought it should have. Obama understood the strategic imperative of maintaining a postracial métier. And he grasped the tactical wisdom of sometimes playing possum, of not letting race swallow the campaign. But he also believed that his campaign tended to be too gun shy when the issue was forced upon them.

"You guys are trying to pretend I'm not black," Obama said urgently. "I'm black!"

534 · GAME CHANGE

You can't pretend this isn't an issue, he went on. Of course it's an issue. You know McCain is playing the race card by accusing me of playing the race card. They're making sure that race is injected into this campaign. They're going to keep doing it in a lot of ways, and when they do it we have to fight back.

Axelrod's head wasn't buried in the sand with respect to Obama's pigmentation or its political implications. He had no doubt that the McCain campaign would employ an assortment of race-freighted messages against Obama. In "Celeb," Axelrod saw a bid to paint Obama as a figure undeserving of his success—the affirmative-action nominee. From his experience with other African American candidates, he suspected that coming next would be volleys on a pair of issues that pushed racial hot buttons: crime and taxes.

But the Obamans were preparing for far more nefarious assailments than that, if not directly from McCainworld, then from shadowy independent groups on the right. The degree of Chicago's readiness was a well-kept secret; there was no sense in admitting publicly how concerned they were about Obama's vulnerabilities surrounding his race and background. But their worries were considerable, especially about the consistent thread they picked up from voters that wove together the false rumors about Obama being a Muslim with the charge that he was insufficiently patriotic.

While the cash-poor McCain campaign was coming up with negative ads on the fly, scribbling scripts, in effect, on the backs of napkins, airing the spots without ever testing them, the well-heeled Obamans were running a stealthy high-tech lab to discover which attacks were most dangerous and to develop responses. Dozens of Obama-funded faux negative ads against Obama were produced and tested: about Wright, Ayers, Muslimism, the flag pin—the works. And some were devastatingly effective.

Obama had begun inoculating himself against the charges that his brain trust presumed were on the horizon. But some efforts he resisted as too ham-handed. At one point, he and his ad team were preparing to shoot a spot designed to deal with Muslimism and patriotism in one throw. "If I have the privilege of taking the oath of office, I would do so with my hand on the Bible and pride in my heart," the script read. Obama began to recite it, then stopped and grimaced. "Guys, I can't do this," he said. "There are limits."

Despite all the study and safeguarding, however, Obama and his campaign were caught off guard and knocked off balance by "Celeb" and its aftermath. Through the entire nomination fight, Clinton had never found a consistent negative frame in which to put her opponent. But McCainworld had conjured one almost by happenstance—and the whole of the rightward realm, from the Republican National Committee to the flying monkeys of conservative talk radio, was pounding away at Obama in a concerted fashion, just as it had done to Dukakis, Gore, and Kerry. The frame was dead simple: McCain equals country first; Obama equals Obama first.

After weeks of bombardment over the airwaves, Obama's negative ratings were inching upward, just as Hillary and Bill had predicted. Now he faced a trio of challenges in rapid succession: selecting his running mate, making peace with the Clintons, and delivering a dynamite convention speech. The last of these might have been a gimme (this was Obama, after all), but the first two would require the savvy of a Metternich and the patience of a saint. And there was no room for error. On August 1, the Gallup tracking poll made Obama versus McCain a dead heat.

19

THE MILE-HIGH CLUB

The senator arrived in Minneapolis in disguise, having shed his uniform of suit and tie, wearing a baseball cap pulled down low on his forehead and a pair of aviator shades. The Obama people told him they were worried he'd be recognized, so he was traveling incognito. When he climbed off the private jet from Washington on August 6, a young woman hustled him into a waiting car with tinted windows. As they set off for the Graves 601 Hotel, the site of the secret meeting, the senator couldn't stop talking. This is the first time in decades, he said to his escort, that I've been on a job interview.

Joseph Robinette Biden, Jr., didn't want to be vice president—at least not at the start. He liked to trot out an old chestnut for his aides: A woman has two sons; one goes off to sea, the other becomes vice president; neither is heard from again. No, what Biden wanted was to be secretary of state. That was a real job. But then Obama began pushing the VP thing, and Biden's competitive juices started flowing, especially when he thought about the other names supposedly on the short list. Tim Kaine? Evan Bayh? Kathleen Sebelius? *Nothing against them,* Biden thought, *but if that's the group, I'm the guy.*

It was that kind of cogitating that had gotten Biden into the 2008 race in the first place—that and a hunger for redemption. Twenty years had passed since his first White House bid ended in ignominy, when he was caught lifting lines from a British politician's speech. He'd survived two brain aneurisms and turned himself from a gabby showboat into the (still-gabby, still-showboaty) chairman of the Senate Foreign Relations Committee, and one of the party's leading voices on judicial matters, too. He'd abstained from running in 2004, although the political circumstances would have been better for him. This time, he was ready. His wife, Jill, was ready. At sixty-four, he saw it as his last chance.

Biden knew he was a long shot, but he was also convinced he was more qualified than his opponents. In 1988, he had believed he could do the job of getting elected. Looking at 2008, he believed he was up to the task of being president.

His campaign ended, in effect, on the day it started, cut down in its tracks by his mortal enemy: his own mouth. It was that first morning, January 31, 2007, when Biden was quoted in *The New York Observer* calling Obama "the first mainstream African-American who is articulate and bright and clean and a nice-looking guy." Biden spent the day of his announcement apologizing, to Obama among others, for having tiptoed into a racial minefield in concrete shoes. The gaffe resurrected every caricature of Biden as a victim of terminal logorrhea and instantly crippled his fund-raising. A year later, he snared 1 percent of the vote in Iowa, finished fifth, and dropped out that same night.

A week later, Biden's inner circle assembled around the kitchen table at his home in Greenville, Delaware, just outside Wilmington. They spent five hours having lunch, gazing out the big kitchen windows at the frigid lake beside the house, speculating and scheming about what might come next for Joe.

Biden had acquitted himself with honor after his disastrous opening salvo. His debate performances were top-notch—funny, smart, and even disciplined. Somehow, despite his drubbing, Biden came out of the campaign standing taller than when he entered. "People agree," said his adviser John Marttila, "that your stature has been enhanced."

The question was whether to cash in that currency by supporting either Clinton or Obama. Joe was close to Hillary, extremely close, treating her with the warmth and protectiveness of an older brother. (He kept a picture in his Senate office of Hillary laughing as Biden whispered in one ear and her husband whispered in the other.) But while he'd started out, like all the veterans in the field, thinking Obama was too big for his britches, not ready to be president, Biden had revised his opinion. "He's the real deal," he told the table.

Biden was inclined not to endorse anyone. His inner circle agreed, arguing that it made no sense to foreclose any possibilities, of which they saw two. Secretary of state was the obvious one; they all assumed he'd be in the running, especially if Hillary won. But Biden might even have a chance at being on the ticket. With the Democrats headed toward choosing the first female or the first black nominee in history, a white male with gravitas could be tempting for either Clinton or Obama.

Although Biden made a show of scoffing at the running-mate talk, he was willing to proceed with the strategy his staff devised for a kind of soft campaign. There would be no lobbying. No phone calls. No talking up his name. Biden would go back to the Senate, try to build on the best aspects of his performance in 2007. He would hammer the GOP on foreign policy, offer advice to Clinton or Obama if they sought him out—and keep his yap shut about everything else.

Biden informed Barack and Hillary that he wouldn't be endorsing them, but also pledged to each that he wouldn't endorse the other. "My word as a Biden" was one of his pet phrases. (The family name meant a lot to Joe.) And he was giving them his word now.

For the next five months, Biden talked incessantly to Clinton and Obama. They just kept calling him. At first it was mostly about policy, but later, as the race dragged on and Hillary's chances faded, Biden began to play honest broker, trying to engineer a peaceful end to the brawl. He counseled Clinton that she should ignore the pressure to drop out, make up her own mind, but delicately added that it made sense for her to stay in only if she believed she had a realistic shot of winning (say, one in three). To Obama, Biden said, Don't push her over the cliff; you've got to respect her; let her take her time; a graceful exit is in everyone's interest. After Obama's race speech in March, Biden had become an avid fan, telling aides it was the best oration he had heard since Dr. King. But his respect for Clinton was undiminished. In fact, he told Obama point blank that he should pick her as his running mate.

Biden's advisers were beside themselves when they heard that. What the hell was Joe doing, they asked each other, boosting Hillary for *his* job? But Biden didn't care. He thought Hillary had earned it, and doubted he'd be in the veepstakes running anyway.

Anyone who knew the history between Obama and Biden would have shared that skepticism. In their first two years together in the Senate, Biden's behavior toward Obama was similar to McCain's, condescending and patronizing to the point where it rankled. "Can you believe this guy?" Obama said to his Senate staff. "Can you believe what Biden did today?"

In the course of 2007 and 2008, however, Obama had changed his mind about Biden just as Biden had flipped on Obama. He liked the way Joe had handled himself on the trail. Appreciated his working-class appeal. (The unions loved Joe, and so did the cops, after his championing of the crime bill in the nineties.) That clean-mainstream-articulate thing? In public, Obama took a little potshot at Biden when it happened, to appease the African American groups. But in private, the comment rolled right off his back. When Biden called him to atone, Obama told him, Joe, you don't have to explain anything to me.

Not long after he clinched the nomination, Obama started hinting to his brain trust that he was leaning in Biden's direction. He mentioned it to Axelrod and Jarrett, and gave the same impression to Rahm

Emanuel, whom Obama had asked to throw some ideas in the hopper about potential veeps.

One night on the phone, Barack complained to Emanuel, You haven't given me a single name. Emanuel flatly said that he wasn't going to. Why? asked Obama.

It's just like 1992, Emanuel replied, when he'd been involved with Bill Clinton's VP-selection process. They examined some forty names that year, but all along, Clinton kept bringing up Gore, singing the praises of his book *Earth in the Balance*.

This is over, Emanuel told Obama. You've decided on Biden. We're just going through the process to make sure your gut's right.

Process mattered to Obama. Head overruled gut, as always. The screening system he implemented was rigorous and methodical. On June 4, not even twenty-four hours after the nomination fight ended, Obama announced that his selection committee would be run by Caroline Kennedy and former deputy attorney general Eric Holder. Two weeks later, the Obama campaign said that Patti Solis Doyle was joining Team Obama as the eventual VP nominee's chief of staff. (The move enraged Hillary's supporters, since it seemed to signal that Clinton was off the table for the number-two spot.) By July, Obama's pollsters were focus-group-testing potential running mates with voters in Cleveland and Milwaukee.

The first list the committee handed Obama had a dozen names. Many of those that appealed to him were problematic. He liked Tom Daschle, but Daschle had become a Washington influence peddler. Sebelius, the Kansas governor, had no national experience or foreign policy chops, and as Solis Doyle argued, her selection might offend Clinton's supporters on the grounds that if Obama was going to choose a woman, it should be Hillary. Virginia senator Jim Webb refused to be vetted. Obama's pollsters reported that voters strongly preferred that the nominee choose a gray-headed Washington insider, and that Chris Dodd tested well. But Dodd's connection, as chairman of the Senate Banking Committee, to the subprime mortgage debacle made him a nonstarter.

Obama was less than thrilled with the slimness of the pickings, and, despite his reverence for process, kept raising a name that wasn't on any ledger: Clinton.

Let's just run through the Hillary option again, he would say to his brain trust. She's tough, she's smart, she's prepared to be president, she has a constituency—she got eighteen million votes. You can't just dismiss all that.

The brain trust shook its collective head, reminding Obama of all the hassles that Clinton would bring, not least of them Bill. They told Barack their research showed that swing voters had a hard time accepting him and Hillary suddenly holding hands and crooning "Kumbaya." Jarrett and Plouffe were dead set against putting Clinton on the ticket. And so was Michelle, who had yet to forgive or forget Hillary's comment about RFK.

By the end of July, the Clinton option was finally buried and the list was whittled down to three: Virginia governor Tim Kaine, Indiana senator Evan Bayh, and Biden. Of the group, Kaine was the person with whom Obama felt the closest personal bond. Both were Harvard Law grads; both had spent time overseas as children; and, bizarrely, both their mothers and maternal grandparents hailed from the same tiny town of Eldorado, Kansas. Obama knew Bayh less well, but his political appeal was manifest. He was the young, handsome, former two-term governor of the Hoosier State, one of the red states that the Obamans hoped to capture, and the centrist scion of the state's most famous political family.

Kaine and Bayh submitted eagerly to the investigative cavity search that being short-listed entailed. After the first round of interviews, Kaine's wife said to him over dinner, "Tim, if there's anything you haven't told me, I think you should, because it's probably going to come out." They both cracked up. (Their teenage son was less mirthful when the vetters grilled him about his Facebook profile.) Bayh, self-conscious about a recent weight loss, explained in detail to the vetters about his apparent digestive trouble with dairy and gluten, then arranged for a $5,000 consultation with a specialist recommended to him by Hillary.

The phones rang for all three finalists in the first week of August, summoning them for interviews with Obama. Bayh was smuggled into St. Louis; Kaine, into small-town Indiana.

The Biden interview in Minneapolis came last. For ninety minutes they sat in the suite at Graves 601, feeling each other out. Obama ribbed Biden about the financial details his vetters had turned up. "All these years, and you still have no money," Obama teased.

The salient question for Obama was, did Biden really want the gig? He'd seemed hesitant throughout the vetting process. Did Biden think the job was too small? Did Biden think Biden was too big? Would he rather be secretary of state?

Biden replied that it all depended on how Obama envisioned the job of VP. The role he could embrace was that of counselor in chief; weighing in on every important decision, foreign and domestic; contributing his expertise on congressional relations, legislative strategy, judicial appointments, all of it. The key, Biden said, was building a relationship based on candor—at which point, Obama laughed.

"I *know* you'll be candid," Obama said. "Are you prepared for me to be?"

"Absolutely," Biden answered.

The next day, Russia invaded Georgia, markedly enhancing Biden's prospects as the short-lister with the most bombs-and-bullets cred. He talked the idea over with Jill and his family, who said they were all for it. After months of living with the concept, Biden had come around; he wanted the job, and bad.

A week or so later, Biden received a call: the Davids wanted to see him. Axelrod and Plouffe arranged to meet him in Wilmington, at the home of his sister, Valerie. Once again, the senator showed up in disguise. You could never be too careful, apparently, even in your hometown.

The Davids had their worries about Biden, and one above the rest. Could he manage to keep his gyrating gums under control for the duration of the fall campaign?

Sitting outside by the pool, Biden reassured them that he could keep his mouth in check, cited examples of how he'd done it before, promised he could do it again. In talking about how he could control his talking, Biden kept talking and talking—offering a soliloquy that, had it been a one-man play, might have been titled *QED*.

The Davids silently noted the irony, then pressed Biden for a commitment: not a vow of silence, but a pledge to stick to the script he was handed, to keep a firm grip on his tongue. Biden told them that, if he got the nod, he would be a good, and tight-lipped, soldier. He gave them his word. As a Biden.

On August 22, three days before the start of the Democratic convention, Obama phoned Kaine and Bayh, delivering his verdict with the identical phrase: "I've decided to go in a different direction." He knew Biden was the right call. The working-class thing. The gray-hair thing. The foreign-policy thing. Oh, and the attack-dog thing. Obama was convinced that he could count on Biden to maul McCain.

Still, right up until the moment he rendered his decision as final, Obama kept chuckling, shaking his head, and thinking, *I can't believe I'm picking Biden.*

And neither, really, could McCain, who heaved a sigh of relief when he learned the news with the rest of the world the next morning. McCain and his team had feared that Obama would tap Hillary, creating a megawatt media explosion that would block out the sun, consigning McCainworld to icy darkness.

"Well, good for Joe," McCain told one of his advisers. "But, boy, Obama will never get a word in edgewise now."

. . .

As the new Democratic vice-presidential pick was elevated and celebrated, the previous one sat in North Carolina wondering how it had all gone so wrong.

The past month had been sheer hell for Edwards; his life was falling apart. On July 22, the *National Enquirer*, which had become his own personal tormentor and truth squad, ran a story about him paying a secret visit to Rielle Hunter and her baby. Two weeks later, it published a grainy "spy photo" of Edwards holding the little girl.

Edwards, panicked, assembled a handful of his former staffers—Ginsberg, Prince, Jennifer Palmieri— to strategize about how to handle the latest installment of his rolling crisis. The group was at a loss, but Edwards settled on the idea of performing a mea culpa on ABC News's *Nightline*. Don't do this interview unless you plan to tell the whole truth, Palmieri told Edwards, because if you lie, you're going to make things infinitely worse. Edwards replied that he was going to confess to the affair, but deny paternity of the child. He didn't want to jeopardize his chances of being Obama's attorney general.

Palmieri couldn't believe her ears. "That, John?" she said. "That was gone a long time ago." Palmieri had been on the phone with the Obama campaign, which was sending the clear, if gentle, signal that there was no longer even a slot available for Edwards to speak at the convention, that it was time for him to stand down with dignity. "You have to call Obama right now" and back out, Palmieri said.

"I don't want to give up on that yet," Edwards insisted.

Elizabeth hadn't given up yet, either. Confronted with the picture in the *Enquirer* of her husband cuddling the baby, she told Palmieri she still believed that John was not the father. "I have to believe it," Elizabeth said. "Because if I don't, it means I'm married to a monster."

As Palmieri predicted, the *Nightline* interview, on August 8, only brought more misery for Edwards, as the world gained a vivid picture of his pathology. When reality began to sink in, he started calling his old staffers and apologizing. Edwards finally accepted that he wasn't going to be attorney general. Not only wasn't he speaking at the convention, he wasn't even welcome in Denver. Edwards felt like an outcast. His weight plummeted. His countenance turned sickly. Some of his former aides began to fear that he might kill himself. And though the extent of his ruin didn't reach that depth, the months ahead held something horrible enough for Edwards: a final and all-too-public reckoning with the truth.

Some days before the convention got under way in Denver, Obama found himself on a campaign swing through Boston, the city where his meteoric and historic ascent began. Riding with Gibbs, Obama noted wryly, "We were here about four years ago, weren't we?"

"Yeah," Gibbs replied, "and our lives have been fucking complicated ever since."

Obama stared out the window and said, "Very complicated."

With his running mate chosen, the next challenge for Obama was to make his convention a success. And the central wrinkle was the former First Couple. The Clintons of Chappaqua rarely made an inconspicuous appearance at any social occasion. They were almost always, naturally and unavoidably, the center of attention. The question was whether, or how well, the Clintons would behave—and judging by two recent incidents, Obama had reason to be nervous.

In early August, on a trip to Africa, Bill Clinton had given an interview to Kate Snow of ABC News. After observing mulishly that "everybody's got a right to run for president who qualifies under the Constitution,"

Clinton pointedly refused to affirm Obama's readiness to occupy the Oval Office. (He also renounced his friendship with Congressman Jim Clyburn and declared, with a Nixonian echo, "I am not a racist.") Two days later, a video surfaced of Hillary at a reception in California, speaking to a crowd of female supporters about the need for "catharsis" in Denver, seeming to suggest that her name be placed in nomination and a roll call vote conducted. The press seized on Clinton's comments and speculated about trouble brewing.

Two months after the Obama-Clinton trip to New Hampshire, Unity was still just a place on the map. Neither Hillary nor Bill had a shred of personal affection for, or connection with, Obama—whereas they continued to share a rapport with McCain. The Arizonan regularly phoned Bill and chatted with him about foreign policy. Boy, McCain gets it, the Clintons would tell people. John McCain is tough. The country might have been facing a "horrible choice," as Hillary had said to Penn, but some of the Clintons' friends got the impression that the couple was more than copacetic with the Republican prevailing.

Still smarting over the hits to his reputation on matters racial, and still blaming the Obamans, Bill was also now grumpy over what he perceived as being given the high hat. After the perfunctory Barack-Bill phone call in June, there had been no follow-up. No meal. No event. No requests for Clinton's counsel. And certainly no absolution. The first communication the former president's office received about the convention was a form letter that went to all of the delegates—letting Bill know he was eligible for a discounted hotel room in Denver.

As was typically the case with the Clintons, Hillary was looking forward while her husband was looking back. Despite her ongoing frustration over the Obamans' failure to assist in paring down her debt—they refused even to send out email solicitations to their Web donors, for crying out loud—she had started campaigning for Obama, saying all the right things on the stump, trying to inoculate herself from being blamed if he lost. For the first time, Hillary was willing to admit that Obama had what it took to win. After what I went through with this guy, she said to a friend, I can tell you, he's plenty tough.

But Hillary also believed that Obama was capable of screwing it up. And that his minions were severely underestimating the difficulty of inducing her supporters to shift their loyalties to him. An NBC News/*Wall Street Journal* poll that month found that only half of her voters were behind Obama—and 21 percent were for McCain. Hillary's talk of catharsis wasn't either idle chatter or malevolent cauldron-stirring. She was simply pointing out that her people needed to have their voices heard before they would rally around the Democratic nominee.

Although he had little direct contact with the Clintons, Obama had a lucid sense of where they stood. "She's okay," he told one of his advisers. "He's taking a lot longer to get over this."

Obama's attitude toward the couple was sharply differentiated. From the moment he clinched the nomination, any rancor he felt toward Hillary evaporated. He needed her support, wanted her on his team, and was willing to work for it. But Bill was another story. Obama saw no benefit in kissing the ring, let alone the ass, of 42. *I'd be happy to call if it would make a difference,* Obama thought. *But why waste my time if the guy's just going to keep crapping all over me?*

When it came to the convention, the Obamans assumed both Clintons would play nice, if only because it was in the couple's self-interest not to be perceived as the skunks at the garden soirée. The endless Clinton negotiations were annoying, to be sure. ("How did you deal with these people?" Plouffe asked Solis Doyle.) The unpredictability of the couple was a chafing distraction. But it was clear the Clintonites had no intention of setting off a bomb in Denver. They didn't want a floor fight. Their demands weren't crazy. They weren't even certain they wanted the roll call vote. Team Obama had hoped to confine both Clinton speeches to one evening. But word came back from Hillaryland that she expected a night to herself, and the Obamans were fine with that. A certain amount of Clinton drama, whipped up by an adrenalized media, was inevitable, they knew. Their aim was simply to keep it from consuming the convention.

The convocation opened on the hot, dry Monday afternoon of August 25—and even before it was gaveled into session, Team Obama was receiving the first of many kicks in the teeth. On the streets of Denver, there were pro-Clinton, anti-Obama marchers. The papers were full of stories quoting Clinton delegates promising defiance. Cable news was riveted by the ravings of the PUMA faction. That night on CNN, James Carville, whom the Obamans (not unreasonably) saw as a conduit for the Clintons, trashed the first day's proceedings. "If this party has a message, it has done a hell of a job of hiding it tonight," Carville moaned. "I look at this and I am about to jump out of my chair."

The collective reaction of the Obamans was: What the fuck? Hillary's speech was the following night,

Bill's would be on Wednesday. If the Clintons were lackluster or subversive, the Obamans would have only one night to salvage the convention.

The Clintons themselves were lying low, sulking and stewing in their suite at the Brown Palace Hotel. They thought the convention was a mess, that their supporters were being treated like second-class citizens, forced to bow and scrape for passes and other goodies. Beyond that, however, both Clintons were obsessed with their speeches. They realized the stakes involved.

Hillary felt the pressure more than her husband. The eyes of the world would be on her Tuesday night as never before in the campaign. But by that morning, her speech was in good shape, she thought. She went over to the Pepsi Center, the sports arena where the first three days of the convention were taking place, to practice it on a prompter with the convention's dedicated speech coach, Michael Sheehan. When she was done, she returned to her room to rest. In the afternoon, she wandered down the hall to the small meeting room where her speechwriting team had been laboring over her text, to rehearse it one last time. She picked up the speech, began to look it over—and was stunned to discover that the thing had been rewritten. It was unrecognizable.

"*This* is my speech?" Clinton said. What the hell happened to it?

Your husband happened, her speechwriting team informed her. Bill had shown up with a pile of hand-written notes, ideas about how to restructure the speech to make it better. New lines, language, themes. The speechwriters had dutifully incorporated his edits.

Hillary was furious, apoplectic.

"This is *my* speech!" she said, and then stalked out of the room and back to her suite.

A few minutes later, Bill walked into the conference room looking sheepish and chastised. The speechwriters were frantically trying to reconstruct the address. There was paper strewn all over the long table, hard copies of various versions of the text. Standing over the addled aides as they cut and pasted on a laptop, Clinton attempted to pitch in. This was here, I added this, I like this, I like that, the former president said.

It was late in the afternoon by then; Hillary had only a couple of hours before she had to be onstage. Report-ers were calling, asking why the Clintonites had yet to provide an advance text, accusing them of holding out. Earlier, the edgy Obamans had checked in with Sheehan about the speech and dispatched strategist Larry Grisolano to the Brown Palace lobby to take the one sneak peek that the Clinton people would allow.

Sheehan and Grisolano reported back. It's great, they said. They had no idea that the speech had been rewritten and now was being rewritten again in an effort to restore it.

Hillary arrived at the Pepsi Center in a frenzy, still making edits in the back of the car. Then she walked onstage and knocked the ball clear into the upper deck. "Barack Obama is my candidate, and he must be our president," Hillary proclaimed. "Nothing less than the fate of our nation and the future of our children hang in the balance."

The next afternoon, the roll call began. The negotiations between the two sides over this had been protracted, but not as tense as the media claimed. The Obama forces had come to realize that Clinton wasn't wrong; that the depth and passion of her support were greater than they'd imagined; that some degree of catharsis was indeed required. The Clintonites, meanwhile, had come to fear that a full roll call vote might wind up embarrassing Hillary, as large numbers of her delegates defected out of a desire to come together behind the nominee. A compromise solution was engineered, with some states casting their votes for each candidate, but then a call for acclamation—by none other than Hillary herself, making a surprise appearance on the convention floor. "In the spirit of unity," she said, "with the goal of victory, let's declare together in one voice, right here, right now, that Barack Obama is our candidate and he will be our president!"

With Hillary having done her duty, that left Bill. There had been some tsuris between the Clintonites and Obamans over his speech, but again, less than the hyperventilators in the press made out. When the Clintonites learned their boss would be appearing on a night dedicated to foreign policy, they objected, insisting that Clinton wanted to talk about the economy. (Barack, who had relented and called the former president a few days before the convention, told his people, "He can talk about whatever he wants to talk about.") And as with Hillary, there was no advance text submitted for approval, which unsettled some of the Obamans.

Bill knew they were anxious, but he refused to rush. I'm going to take my time, and when I'm done, I'm done, he told Terry McAuliffe. If it's not done until a minute before, so be it.

It was done a little earlier than that, but not much. Once again, Grisolano legged it over to the Brown Palace to take a gander. When he finished perusing the speech, Grisolano looked up at the Clintonite who'd delivered it and smiled.

"Hey, you gotta do me one favor," Grisolano said.

"What's that?"

"Tell him not to change a thing."

. . .

Obama shared that assessment as he watched Bill Clinton up on stage. Clinton did more than a dazzling job with his oratory. He did more than blow the room away with his charm. He said, with clear premeditation, precisely the words that Democrats in the hall and around the country wanted, needed, to hear from him: "Everything I learned in my eight years as president, and in the work I have done since in America and across the globe, has convinced me that Barack Obama is the man for this job . . . Barack Obama is ready to be president of the United States." Whether or not Clinton believed those words was, in a way, immaterial—as Obama understood. When it was over, Obama remarked to one of his aides, He went out there and did something that was really hard for him.

With all the Clinton-related commotion in the first three days of the convention, there were few other moments that broke through. Ted Kennedy's speech on Monday night was an exception. The senator, who had been diagnosed with a lethal brain tumor three months before, hauled himself to Denver and delivered what would be (and what everyone in the hall knew would be) his last convention speech—on behalf of the young senator to whom his endorsement had meant so much.

The other exception, on the same night, was Michelle Obama's speech. Ever since "proud of my country," Michelle's public image had been in a bad way. In the campaign's focus groups, voters volunteered their misgivings: that she was unpatriotic, seemed entitled or angry. (*The New Yorker* had captured the caricature on its cover that summer with a sketch portraying her as a gun-toting radical with an Angela Davis afro.) The Obamans knew this was their last best chance to rescue her from becoming a toxic spouse in the vein of Teresa Heinz Kerry.

Stealing a page from the Clinton playbook of 1992, they set out to use the convention stage to humanize her; to portray Michelle as the loving mother, sister, and daughter that she was, and one reared not in privilege but in a blue-collar home. Working with Hillary's former speechwriter, Sarah Hurwitz, and the speech coach, Sheehan, Michelle revised and rehearsed for more than a month. The payoff was worth it. Her performance, slightly nervous but winningly sincere and at times bracingly direct ("I love this country"), wowed the crowd and sent her approval ratings soaring, never to return to earth.

Obama's speech on Thursday night was, of course, the convention's culmination, and another of those big-game moments that the candidate seemed to live for. Obama had amped up expectations by deciding to mimic John Kennedy's 1960 acceptance at the Los Angeles Coliseum, delivering his before nearly one hundred thousand people at Invesco Field, home of the Denver Broncos. That Obama would be stirring and poised was not in question. Of course he would. The question was whether he would be effective—making the case for himself and against McCain in terms more concrete and compelling than he had so far.

After taking the outdoor stage amid the starbursty sparkle of thousands of camera flashes, Obama worked his way through an oration less thrilling than some of his best, but more strategic. He did biography, invoking his mother, his grandfather, and his grandmother, citing the last's rise from the secretarial pool to middle management "despite years of being passed over for promotions because she was a woman" as a nod to Clinton's voters. He strafed McCain as a Bush clone who was clueless about the economy: "I don't believe Senator McCain doesn't care what's going on in the lives of Americans; I just think he doesn't know." He hinted at McCain's hot-headedness, questioning whether he had the "temperament" to be commander in chief. And he deconstructed the negative campaign his rival had been running against him. "I've got news for you, John McCain," he bellowed. "We all put our country first."

Obama happened to be speaking on the forty-fifth anniversary of Martin Luther King, Jr.'s "I Have Dream" address on the Washington Mall, and he closed with a graceful reference to the "young preacher from Georgia" who said, "We cannot walk alone. . . . We cannot turn back." Axelrod and Gibbs, watching from the wings, were in tears. For them, the speech was one of the rare moments, in the midst of the campaign's bustle and insanity, when the magnitude of what they had accomplished sank in.

As the convention closed, Axelrod was well pleased. After the lost weeks of July and August, in which McCainworld had stolen a march on the Obamans, the Democrats had recaptured the flag.

The chattering classes agreed with Axelrod. The convention had been a triumph. The Democrats had found their way to peace and unity. Barack and Michelle had killed. And the Clintons had piled aboard the bandwagon—at least publicly. Hillary and Bill were still bruised and still mopey. But as they flew back east from Denver, one thing had changed. They both were starting to believe that Obama was probably going to win.

Obama believed it, too. The next morning, he rode out to the airport and boarded his campaign jet. He was headed to Pennsylvania with Biden to begin the fall campaign in earnest. The Republican convention was scheduled to start the following Monday. McCain was due to announce his running mate any minute now. The Democratic ticketmates wondered who it would be—and then, like that, Axelrod appeared in the forward cabin and broke the news.

"Wow," said Obama, picking his jaw up off the floor. "Well, I guess she's change."

But Biden looked confused. Swiveling his head, speaking for millions, he blurted out, "Who's Sarah Palin?"

20

SARAHCUDA

The plan was always for McCain to shock the world with his vice-presidential pick. For weeks his top advisers had been dreaming and scheming, touching bases and laying groundwork, secretly readying an announcement at once unconventional, unexpected, and unprecedented, which would throw the press and both parties for a loop and redraw the political map. The surprise that McCainworld intended to spring was a running mate named Joe Lieberman. But then something happened on the way to the Republican convention in St. Paul—and, presto chango, there was Palin.

McCainworld's core conviction was that McCain's VP choice had to be a game changer. The campaign assumed the progress it had made with "Celeb" was a temporary blip. That Obama's financial advantages would continue to create a crushing imbalance. That the three quarters of the electorate who were telling pollsters the country was on the wrong track and blaming the GOP would punish McCain at the polls. If McCain's running mate selection didn't fundamentally alter the dynamics of the race, it would be lights out.

From thirty thousand feet, the process by which McCain sought his number two looked altogether normal for many months. He'd begun back in April, with about as much time at his disposal to make his choice as any nominee in history. A tight circle of his aides, with his input, produced a long list of possibilities. A prominent Washington attorney with a reputation for probity and discretion—A. B. Culvahouse of O'Melveny and Myers—was retained to head the vetting team. As the list was winnowed, Culvahouse and Co. conducted extensive research on the surviving finalists, preparing a lengthy and intrusive questionnaire and arranging face-to-face interviews with A.B. The customary premium was placed on keeping the pick a surprise, and a plan was developed to maximize its impact: announcing the selection soon after the Democratic convention, ideally the very next day, to stop Obama's momentum cold.

Yet three of the five short-listers produced by this seemingly rigorous process failed to meet its chief goal. Mitt Romney, Charlie Crist, and Minnesota governor Tim Pawlenty all had their virtues, but game changers they were not. The fourth, New York mayor Mike Bloomberg, qualified for the label—but he also was a divorced, pro-choice, pro-gay, anti-gun, Jewish plutocrat who had switched his party affiliation from Democrat to Republican to independent as nonchalantly if as he'd been changing his loafers. Not one of them generated much enthusiasm in McCainworld, or, more important, in McCain. But, for reasons both personal and political, the fifth man did.

McCain's affection for Lieberman had only grown since the Democratic senator from Connecticut endorsed him in December. Joe became a fixture on the Straight Talk Express, traveling all over during the nomination fight, even to locales where his presence made McCain's advisers skittish. When McCain suggested that Lieberman campaign with him in South Carolina, Davis thought, *God, what are we doing? A liberal, Jewish Democrat—who was Gore's running mate—in South Carolina for the Republican primary?* But McCain wasn't remotely fazed. "Don't worry about it," he told Davis. "It won't be a problem."

Lieberman was chummy, too, with McCain's other regular sidekick on the road, Lindsey Graham; the trio was dubbed the Three Amigos. Between Lieberman's

Shecky Greene humor and Graham's tall tales about falling asleep during meetings with foreign leaders, McCain was in stitches much of the time when his pals were around. A favorite pastime of the amigos was watching that funny YouTube video of John Edwards fixing his hair. "Let's look at it again!" McCain would command, and soon they'd all be clutching their sides, emitting peals.

The political case for picking Lieberman as VP was straightforward, if audacious. McCain's lieutenants maintained that it was essential that their candidate distance himself from Bush and reclaim the reformer's mantle. Nothing would do that better, went the argument, than presenting the country with a kind of national unity ticket, a pairing that literally embodied bipartisanship. Lieberman's support for the Iraq War made him reasonably popular among Republicans. His long tenure in Washington would reinforce the campaign's message of experience and drive the perception that McCain had made his choice with governing, not politics, in mind. The pick would fairly shout McCain's slogan, "Country First."

Many of McCain's most influential advisers— Schmidt, Graham, the former Bush White House communications director Nicolle Wallace—were strongly in favor of the Lieberman option. The worst-case scenario, Wallace contended, was that Lieberman's pro-choice stance would cause a walk-out of social conservatives from the convention, and even that would have its benefits, sending a message of independence. Astonishingly, no one among the senior staff objected to Lieberman on ideological grounds. Most of them, in fact, saw his selection as the campaign's best chance to win, assuming they could get Lieberman approved at the convention.

In mid-July, Davis called Lieberman and asked if he'd be willing to be put on the short list and vetted. "Gee, this really surprises me," Lieberman said. "John doesn't have to do this to thank me for supporting him."

"No, no. He's not doing it to thank you. He's very serious about this."

"Honestly, Rick, I don't intuitively see how this could happen," Lieberman said. "Well, if he's serious, it's an honor. I'm happy to go forward."

For Lieberman, endorsing McCain had moved him further away than ever from the Democratic Party. And he had already taken another step in that direction by agreeing to speak at the GOP convention. His decision to be considered for the VP slot was driven in part by one thought: *Am I ever going to have another opportunity at this?* Yet, given the political climate,

Lieberman couldn't also help but wonder, *Am I going to have the unique honor to be the only person in history to lose twice as vice president on two different tickets?*

As July turned to August, Lieberman received from Graham encouraging reports about his prospects. "Schmidt gets this," Lindsey said. "He did Schwarzenegger's campaign. He knows we have to get independents." Graham added, "Cindy is for you."

Lieberman still couldn't quite see how the McCain forces could get him through the convention, given his liberal views on almost every issue save national security. "If he chooses me, do you think I'd get nominated?" he asked Graham.

"Of course, you'd be nominated," Lindsey said. "Some minority of the convention would walk out. But I think that's not so bad for John."

McCainworld had a two-pronged plan for minimizing the negative convention fallout. First, the pick had to be a complete surprise, sprung at the last minute, before the opposition had time to coalesce, so Lieberman could be defined on the campaign's terms. And second, McCain would agree to take the one-term pledge he'd abandoned in the final hours before his announcement in the spring of 2007, thus eliminating the risk that he would die in office during his second term and leave a

Democrat in charge. McCain, once again, balked at the pledge, but his advisers assured him it would be necessary if he went with Joe. Grudgingly, McCain seemed to assent, while Lieberman readily agreed.

For much of August, McCainworld pursued the Lieberman option with singular focus. Davis and his deputies began calling delegates, state chairmen, and other party leaders around the country, feeling out their level of resistance to a pro-choice pick (without mentioning any names). Davis crafted a convention strategy to see Lieberman through—everything from a whip operation, to a sophisticated communications roll-out, to a lunch with conservative grandees that Charlie Black would attend the Friday beforehand to explain the rationale and rally them to the cause.

No one was more gung ho about all this than Graham. He couldn't stop talking about it with McCain, hectoring him about why Lieberman was his only hope. With the Mormon thing, you can't pick Romney; you'll lose by eight, Graham contended. You can't pick Pawlenty—he's a nice guy, but nobody's ever heard of him; you'll lose by six.

McCain played his cards close to his chest. I hear you, he said. I gotcha.

But Graham's eager advocacy, and his Biden-like loose lips, wound up sinking the Lieberman option.

On August 13, while Graham was traveling with McCain on a campaign swing, he floated the idea of a pro-choice running mate to a group of wary social conservatives in Michigan, asking which they would prefer: a running mate who opposed abortion but caused the GOP to lose or one who supported abortion rights and carried the party to victory?

Within days, the indiscretion had leaked, flooding the mainstream press and the Web with speculation about Lieberman and Republican pro-choice former Pennsylvania governor Tom Ridge, sparking a flaming tizzy in the rightmost precincts of GOP Nation. "If the McCain camp does that," bellowed Rush Limbaugh, "they will have effectively destroyed the Republican Party and put the conservative movement in the bleachers."

Anticipating this kind of reaction from the right, McCain's advisers had been quietly trying to recruit a conservative counter-chorus to sing Lieberman's praises. When they approached Karl Rove, he not only declined but told them that picking Lieberman was a terrible idea. If you nominate him, he'll probably get through the convention, Rove argued, but the battle will be bloody. The vote will be close, the story line will be bad, McCain will leave St. Paul with a split party—and no time to put it back together.

That Sunday, August 24, Rove took his concerns to Lieberman directly, pleading with the senator by phone to turn down the VP slot if McCain extended his hand.

"You know him," Rove said. "He's so stubborn he may simply get this in his mind and carry it to you. And you may be the only person who can save McCain from himself."

Lieberman listened politely and said, "I hear you. I'll think about it," and then hung up, turned to his wife, and marveled at the fantastic strangeness of the situation.

Lieberman had no intention of taking Rove's advice. But, as it happened, McCainworld was in the process of rendering the question moot. That same day, out in Arizona, McCain's senior advisers were meeting again at the Phoenix Ritz-Carlton and reluctantly coming to the conclusion that Rove was right. In a pair of meetings, one with McCain present, pollster Bill McInturff informed the group that research data he'd been studying indicated that a pro-choice pick would cost McCain votes among Republicans and gain him few, if any, among independents. With a lot of work and elbow grease, we can get Joe through the convention, Black added. But then we're going to have to spend September healing the party instead of concentrating on swing voters and Obama.

The depth and severity of the problems raised by picking Lieberman finally hit home with McCain. "I understand," he said in a tone of resignation—and from that point on, Joe's name was never seriously raised again.

That night, Schmidt and Davis drove over to McCain's Phoenix condo for dinner. The Republican convention was a week away, and they were nowhere. In the meetings earlier that day, there was no support for Romney, Crist, or Bloomberg. That left Pawlenty.

"Here's my view of the politics of it," Schmidt told McCain as they feasted on deep-fried burritos. "In any normal year, Tim Pawlenty's a great pick, a nobrainer. But this isn't a normal year. We need to have a transformative, electrifying moment in this campaign."

Schmidt and Davis then placed a new option on the table: Sarah Palin.

Palin's name had been on the longest of the long lists, but that was it. Davis told McCain that if he wanted to consider the governor of Alaska, he needed to phone her that night and ask her if she'd be willing to be vetted—and arrange to meet with her, pronto.

McCain was impassive, but agreeable.

"I'll call her," he said. "Let's call her."

A few minutes later, McCain reached Palin on her cell phone at the Alaska State Fair. Fifteen minutes after that, McCain hung up. And Palin was on her way.

She was forty-four years old, had occupied the Alaska statehouse for twenty months, and had an 80 percent approval rating, making her, as Schmidt pointed out, "the most popular governor in America." She'd attended five colleges and been a beauty queen, a sportscaster, and the two-term mayor of Wasilla, the tiny town where she lived with her snowmobiling husband, Todd, and five children. She was pro-life, anti–stem cell research, pro-gun, and pro–states rights. She had captured the governorship by running as a reformer, pledging to clean up the corrupt clubhouse politics of Juneau, and she was often at odds with Alaska's regnant Republican kingpin, Senator Ted Stevens. Her nickname from her high school basketball days was "Sarah Barracuda." She was intensely competitive, apparently fearless, and endlessly watchable.

McCain had met Palin in February, at the annual winter meeting of the National Governors Association in Washington. She was part of a small group of western-state governors whom McCain had convened to talk about energy policy. Later that day, he and Palin spoke again, for ten minutes or so, at a reception; two nights later, they shared a table at a fund-raising dinner and chatted a bit more. Afterward, McCain told Black that he liked the cut of Palin's jib. She's damn impressive, he said.

It was six months later when Schmidt and Davis came to the same conclusion, almost by accident. In July, Davis, who was in charge of McCain's VP process, was casting about for unconventional possibilities and sat down one day in front of his computer with a list of names of female Republican officeholders. When he stumbled upon a video of Palin appearing on *Charlie Rose*, Davis was bowled over. And so was Schmidt, who screened the clip and proclaimed, She's a star!

As the Lieberman option became more and more imperiled at the end of August, Schmidt and Davis—afraid that this new VP idea would leak, too—kept talking furtively between themselves about Palin. She seemed to be the answer to their prayers. In a way, she was the anti-Lieberman, hard right and totally fresh. Davis considered her a triple threat: a governor, a conservative, and a would-be historic pick. Schmidt upped the ante, saying that Palin was the only candidate who might achieve all four objectives he saw as critical for McCain: excite the GOP base, rouse women voters, create space between him and Bush, and help him recapture the maverick label.

On the evening of Wednesday, August 27, three days after McCain phoned Palin, she arrived at the airport in Flagstaff, Arizona, in a private Learjet from Anchorage. Palin was ferried to the home of a wealthy McCain supporter, Bob Delgado, to meet with Schmidt and Salter.

It was now thirty-six hours from the campaign's Friday target for unveiling its veepstakes winner. But McCain was leaving the next morning, so the count-down clock was actually set closer to T minus twelve hours. At that point, Culvahouse and his team had de-voted just five days to vetting Palin, digging into public records, her hastily completed seventy-four-part ques-tionnaire, and her tax returns—less investigation than a potential assistant secretary of agriculture would re-ceive. Palin had spent just a few hours filling out the questionnaire, which had consumed weeks for other short-listers. She had never met Schmidt. She had never met Salter. Now, in a rush, against a deadline, with little background information, the two McCain advis-ers had to determine if she was ready for the big stage.

After offering Palin some pizza, Schmidt com-menced his grilling. Governor, he said, in Alaska you're the boss. You have a staff, advisers, and your husband, all valuable in having helped you get where you are. None of them will have a seat at the table here. Senator

McCain is the boss in this effort, and your job, if you're chosen, is going to be to do what's asked of you and get comfortable real fast with the people we put around you. What's your reaction to that?

I understand completely, Palin said.

Should this go forward, Schmidt went on, by dinnertime Friday you'll be one of the most famous and recognizable people on the planet. Your life will never be the same. Have you thought about the impact on your family? Would you and they be a hundred percent committed to this project going forward?

Yes, a hundred percent, Palin said.

Do you have confidence in your lieutenant governor and your staff to fulfill your constitutional duties as the governor of Alaska in your absence? Schmidt asked. Because unless there's an earthquake or a natural disaster of some magnitude, you won't likely be back home again until after Election Day. You can't be distracted by your day job. You need to be focused on *this* job.

Yes, absolutely, I understand, Palin said.

You and Senator McCain have differences on some issues, Schmidt continued. He is pro-life, but he's in favor of exceptions in the cases of rape, incest, and the life of the mother being at risk; you are not. Senator McCain is in favor of stem cell research; you are not. We'll never ask you to make a statement that contradicts your beliefs, but we expect you to support his positions as the policies of the administration you'd be part of. And we may ask you to appear in ads advocating those positions. Do you have a problem with that?

No, I don't, not at all, Palin said.

Schmidt and Salter both warned Palin that her private life would be subjected to harsh, at times unfair, attacks. Nothing you've experienced has prepared you for this, how ugly it can be, Salter said. Nothing, nothing, nothing.

I understand, Palin said.

Salter had read about Palin on his flight to Arizona, and was concerned about hints that she might be a creationist. "Governor," he said flatly, "do you reject the theory of evolution?"

No, Palin said. My father is a science teacher. He showed me fossils. I know how things evolved. I just don't think that evolution excludes a role for God.

Schmidt and Salter were approaching Palin from different perspectives. Schmidt, the discipline fiend, wanted to be sure Palin was ready for what she'd face and would toe the line. Salter, the ur-loyalist, wanted to safeguard McCain's brand, to make sure he wouldn't be teaming up with a female Pat Robertson. But neither one was poking or prodding to find every possible weakness in Palin. They asked her nothing to plumb the depths of her knowledge about foreign or domestic policy. They didn't explore her preparedness to be vice president. They assumed she knew as much as the average governor, and that what she didn't know, she would pick up on the fly. They weren't searching for problems. They were looking for a last-second solution.

What reassured them was Palin's preternatural calm and self-possession. Never once did she betray any jitters or lack of confidence.

Later that night, Palin spoke for three hours by phone with Culvahouse. Over the previous weekend, he had assigned a Washington lawyer named Ted Frank, who'd worked on the screening of Lieberman, to prepare a written vetting report on Palin. Thrown together from scratch in less than forty hours, the document highlighted her vulnerabilities: "Democrats upset at McCain's anti-Obama 'celebrity' advertisements will mock Palin as an inexperienced beauty queen whose main national exposure was a photo-spread in *Vogue* in February 2008. Even in campaigning for governor, she made a number of gaffes, and the *Anchorage Daily News* expressed concern that she often seemed 'unprepared or over her head' in a campaign run by a friend."

The longest section of the vetting report dealt with an ongoing ethics investigation in Alaska known as

Troopergate, in which Palin stood accused of improperly pressuring and firing the state public safety commissioner after a messy dispute with members of her family.

The report contained a disclaimer: Given the haste in which it was prepared, the vetters might have missed something.

But Culvahouse seemed to sense that the momentum in McCainworld behind picking Palin was gathering such force that the vet might be irrelevant. "We may be slowing a freight train with boxes of feathers," he said to his colleagues.

The first thing Palin told Culvahouse on the phone that Wednesday night concerned a matter that she'd left off her questionnaire (and neglected to tell Schmidt and Salter). Her teenage daughter, Bristol, was pregnant out of wedlock.

"Is she getting married?" Culvahouse asked, then added, jokingly, "Is she getting married *tomorrow*?"

The lawyer pressed Palin about her critics in Alaska who charged that she was too inexperienced when she ran for governor. Palin replied disarmingly, People are still attacking me back home, but you'll notice they no longer say I'm in over my head.

The next morning, Culvahouse spoke to McCain by phone. Overall, the lawyer was impressed with how

Palin handled herself, but he advised McCain that, compared to the alternatives, there were more potential land mines with Palin.

"What's your bottom line?" McCain asked.

"John, high risk, high reward," Culvahouse said.

"You shouldn't have told me that. I've been a risk taker all of my life."

Shortly afterward, Palin rolled up to the senator's ranch in Sedona with Schmidt and Salter. McCain and Palin walked down to a creek that ran through the property. For about an hour, they spoke privately beneath a sycamore tree.

After they finished talking, McCain introduced Palin to Cindy, took a short stroll alone with his wife, and then approached his advisers for a final powwow about the pick. Salter contended that Pawlenty was young and energetic, a party modernizer but a solid conservative, and an able communicator who could connect with blue-collar voters. Palin, he said, was untested, would undermine the experience argument against Obama, and might damage McCain's stature. "This is your reputation," Salter stressed.

Schmidt conceded that picking Palin could go bad, but he maintained that Pawlenty would gain McCain nothing. "If I was running," Schmidt said, "I'd rather lose by ten points trying to go for the win than lose by one point and look back and say, 'Goddamn it, I should have gone for the win.'"

The most important decision of McCain's campaign was squarely in his hands, and the circumstances could hardly have been odder or more telling. Unlike Obama and his methodical process, McCain was flying by the seat of his pants. He had left himself no time and no other options; if he went with Pawlenty or any conventional pick, he believed that he would lose. Yet, in judging Palin, he was relying on a vetting so hasty and haphazard it barely merited the name. No one had interviewed her husband. No one had spoken to her political enemies. No vetters had descended upon Alaska. There had been almost no follow-up on any issues that the investigation had raised. Palin's life still was a mystery to McCainworld. And she was still a stranger to McCain.

But although McCain didn't know much about Palin, what he knew, he liked. She reminded him a lot of himself: the outsider's courage, the willingness to piss all over her party. (He loved that she'd taken on that pork-barreler Ted Stevens, whom he despised.) He saw in Palin a way of seizing back and amplifying his own message of change—real change, not the bogus Obama version. "Trust your gut, John," Cindy told him, and McCain knew that she was right.

McCain walked up to the deck outside his cabin, where Palin was waiting, and offered her the job. They shook hands, embraced, went back down to the creek to pose for some pictures—and then McCain was off.

Palin collected herself and her things and left for the airport in Flagstaff with Salter and Schmidt. They boarded an afternoon charter flight to Dayton, Ohio, where she would rejoin McCain the next morning for the announcement of her selection.

In the air, Palin, in a black fleece and black skirt, her hair pinned up with a clip, appeared perfectly serene— which again struck Schmidt. Five days earlier, this woman, for all her success in Alaska, had been living in relative obscurity, without even the faintest inkling that she was being seriously considered to be McCain's running mate. And yet here she was, totally unruffled, utterly unflustered, not even terribly excited.

"You seem very calm, not nervous," Schmidt said to her quizzically.

Palin nodded and replied, "It's God's plan."

The lord's stratagem certainly appeared to be working the next morning in Ohio. The campaign had pulled off a hell of a coup, secrecy-wise. When Palin took the stage with McCain, jaws dropped and eyes popped across the country and around the world. Before a throng of more than ten thousand, the biggest crowd the campaign had yet seen, Palin delivered a knockout speech, filling her partner with delight, a gratifying gift on what was his birthday. After name-checking Geraldine Ferraro, the Democratic VP nominee in 1984, she gave a shout-out to Clinton and made a bid for her disaffected supporters. "Hillary left eighteen million cracks in the highest, hardest glass ceiling," Palin said. "But it turns out the women of America aren't finished yet, and we can shatter that glass ceiling once and for all."

In Ohio, Schmidt, drawing on his experiences managing the Alito and Roberts nominations, told Palin that the introduction of a veep was a lot like a space launch. The period of time from the ignition of the rocket until the capsule was in orbit was ten or twelve minutes of violent kinetic energy, Schmidt said. That's the dangerous part. But once the vehicle escaped Earth's atmosphere, it was safe.

Schmidt's analogy was all too apt—and that was the problem. A successful space launch requires years of meticulous planning by scientists and engineers, stress-testing the components of the rocket, running through countless simulations, discovering every potential pitfall, implementing fail-safe systems. McCainworld had done precisely none of that with Palin. Her record and background, like those of any nominee, presented political challenges, but none was insurmountable with sufficient preparation. But the swiftness of the vetting, the obsession with covertness, and the suddenness of the pick meant that the campaign was ill equipped to present and defend McCain's choice.

From the moment Palin stepped onstage in Ohio, McCain headquarters was in turmoil. The phone lines were jammed with calls from reporters trying to figure out who she was. The McCain press shop was just as clueless as the journalists. There were no basic talking points in circulation or any of the materials from the Culvahouse vet, let alone some secret, comprehensive Palin briefing book. Frantic staffers were reduced to Googling Palin's name or hitting the State of Alaska website, which was constantly crashing due to overload.

Meanwhile, Palin's team was being assembled almost entirely on the fly. Her designated sherpa, the Republican operative Tucker Eskew, was hired on the spot that Friday after he sent an unprompted email to Nicolle Wallace with some ideas about how to put forward Palin. (Great! Yes! Have you got sixty-three days? Wallace wrote Eskew back.) Palin's traveling chief of staff, Andrew Smith, was first approached that Sunday; a friend of Schmidt's, he had almost no political experience. Before the announcement, most of the members of Team Palin couldn't have picked their new boss out of a lineup or properly pronounced her name. They had no answers to even the most routine questions about her.

By the time Palin arrived in St. Paul on Sunday night, August 31, there were plenty of queries. What foreign countries had she visited? Had she ever been to Iraq? Had she really killed the infamous Bridge to Nowhere in Alaska, as she claimed? Did she worship at a Pentecostal church where people spoke in tongues? Had Todd been arrested for driving drunk? Had her son, Track, been busted for drugs? And, most incendiary of all, was her infant son, Trig, who had Down syndrome, really her baby—or was he Bristol's?

As the media typhoon whipped through St. Paul on Sunday, the McCain operation was also dealing with a genuine meteorological event. Hurricane Gustav was about to hit the Gulf Coast, raising the specter of the Republican failure to handle Katrina. Davis decided to cancel the first day of the convention, relinquishing one night of precious airtime. But there happened to be a silver lining to that cloud. For months McCain and his aides had been dreading the prospect of Bush and Cheney onstage. Charlie Black had floated the idea of having Bush spend convention week in Africa, speaking to the delegates via satellite and restricting himself to the administration's programs to combat AIDS and malaria. At the same time, Black tried to convince Cheney to decline his convention invitation; Black thought the VP had agreed, but then signals got crossed and Cheney accepted. Now, with Monday night scotched, Cheney's appearance had been, too. And Bush would be relegated to delivering a short talk by video hookup from the White House.

On Monday, the embattlement of the McCain press shop reached code red. To stamp out the Trig rumors—whipped up by photos on the Internet showing a supposedly very pregnant Palin looking remarkably svelte—Sarah and Todd acknowledged that Bristol was expecting, and therefore couldn't be the five-month-old baby's mother. But now *The National Enquirer* was reporting that Palin had had an affair. Another story popped up claiming that she had once been a member of the secessionist Alaskan Independence Party (AIP). And even more threatening politically, reporters were starting to turn their attention to Palin's vetting. The press shop insisted the vet had been thorough, but journalists were skeptical, especially since McCainworld was having such difficulty nailing down simple facts about Palin.

Schmidt and Davis had a lot on the line here. The questions about the vet went to their performance and credibility, and to the core of McCain's sense of responsibility about governance. McCain was seventy-two and had a history of cancer scares. How seriously had they really examined the woman who would be in line to replace him?

The next morning, Schmidt and the senior staff gathered in the communications bunker in the Minneapolis Hilton. When Schmidt asked if the campaign had figured out if Palin was ever a member of the AIP, he was told they still weren't sure.

Schmidt exploded, pounding the table, hollering, ranting, and cursing. Goddamn it, he shouted, we are under attack! This is a fight for survival! We have to get our shit together!

A few days earlier the campaign had dispatched a SWAT team to Alaska to help deal with the Palin inquiries. Schmidt wanted to get them on the horn and have the history of her AIP registration checked immediately.

"But it's two in the morning in Alaska," someone said.

"The phones don't work at fucking night there?" Schmidt bellowed. "Call them! And keep calling them until they pick up!"

Schmidt had been involved in two presidential campaigns, two Supreme Court fights, and any number of corporate crisis-management brouhahas, but never had he experienced anything so intense, so savage, or so crazy. Under fire, he shifted to a tactic he had turned into an art form: blaming the liberal media. From *The New York Times* to the lefty blogosphere, the press was trotting out "smear after smear after smear," on a "mission to destroy" Palin, Schmidt charged.

Yet the truth was that Palin's critics weren't only on the left. The reaction to her selection in much of the GOP Establishment ranged from stupefaction to scorn. When Bush first caught the news of the pick on a basement television set in the West Wing, he thought at first he heard "Pawlenty." (*Interesting*, he mused.) But then he realized that the name was Palin, and he was completely baffled. (*Where did that come from?*)

The current occupant of the VP's chair had a harsher reaction. Palin was woefully unprepared, and McCain had made a "reckless choice," Cheney told his friends.

Similar criticisms were pouring into the ears of reporters from GOP consultants and operatives galore. The former Reagan speechwriter Peggy Noonan was caught on a live microphone on MSNBC saying of McCain's decision, "I think they went for this, excuse me, political bullshit about narratives. Every time the Republicans do that—because that's not where they live and it's not what they're good at—they blow it."

Mike Murphy, one of McCain's key strategists in 2000, chimed in, "The greatness of McCain is no cynicism, and this is cynical."

McCain was upset about Murphy's remark. "Why would he say that? Why would he say that?" he asked his aides lamentingly.

But McCain himself did Palin no favors in an interview with ABC News's Charlie Gibson in St. Paul. "Can you look the country straight in the eye and say Sarah Palin has the qualities and has enough experience to be commander in chief?" Gibson asked.

"Oh, absolutely," McCain said—and then cited Palin's largely ceremonial role as commander of the Alaska National Guard, an argument his own campaign had rejected as ludicrous.

On the eve of Palin's Wednesday night convention speech, her nomination was struggling to achieve liftoff. "This is the worst mishandling of a VP choice since McGovern tapped Eagleton," a prominent GOP strategist said darkly to a reporter. "I'll bet she is off the ticket inside of ten days."

Cloistered in a suite on the twenty-third floor of the Hilton, Sarah Palin barely noticed the storm raging outside. Not that the atmosphere of anarchy didn't penetrate her quarters. Quite the contrary. The place was a freaking madhouse, a Grand Central rush hour of aides, kids, and minions. But Palin had to concentrate. There was so little time and so much to do, so much to learn, so much to change. She was having an Eliza Doolittle moment, and it was keeping her mighty busy.

Take that Tuesday afternoon. Palin was sitting there in her suite, getting ready to go shoot some footage that the admen could use in the new spots and videos they were cooking up now that she was on the ticket. Boxes of Manolo Blahniks were piled up four feet high and stretching twenty feet along one wall of the living room. Neiman Marcus bags were everywhere, along with several rolling garment racks loaded with suits and dresses—maybe sixty outfits, beautiful threads, purchased by a New York personal shopper whom Nicolle Wallace had found for her. A fleet of Hollywoodish stylists in tight black jeans and high heels were hovering and strutting. In the corner, an elderly African American seamstress was hunched over a sewing machine.

Palin was in her robe, seated at a desk. Wallace was there coaching her on the pronunciation of the proper names in the text of her address, repeating them over and over like a speech therapist. Every so often, they would pause so that Palin could model a new outfit. If they liked it, fine; if not, they would often suggest an alteration. Lose the lapel! It would be better sleeveless! And the seamstress would go to work.

When Fred Davis, McCain's media guy, walked into the suite, a couple of the stylists were applying some kind of hot-iron contraption to Palin's hair. There was steam coming off the top of her head that looked to Davis like smoke. For a moment he thought, *Oh my God, her hair's on fire!*

Palin greeted Davis, whom she knew slightly from some work he had done on her gubernatorial race. She wanted his opinion on a matter of no small importance.

"My brand is hair up, isn't it?" she asked.

Yes, it is, Davis said.

In the first forty-eight hours in St. Paul, Palin's existence was a political version of *Extreme Makeover*—and the clothes were only part of it. To Schmidt's way of thinking, Palin faced three big hurdles. The first was her convention speech on Wednesday night. The second was her inaugural national interview, which would take place ten days hence with Charlie Gibson. And the third was Palin's debate in early October with Joe Biden. In Schmidt's view, they had no time to waste. For Gibson (and other future interviews), and especially for Biden, Palin needed to get on top of international affairs.

The trouble was, the outside world kept intruding. The McCain people knew so little about Palin that every time a press controversy erupted, someone had to race to the suite and find out directly from her what was true and what was false. Palin had barely settled in on Sunday night before she had to deal with drafting the statement concerning Bristol's pregnancy. Palin called her daughter in Alaska to tell her the revelation was coming—I love you, she reassured Bristol, you're a good person—then turned to her fledgling team and said, all business, "Where were we?"

By and large, Palin's reaction to the parade of controversies traipsing through her suite was a blend of equanimity, steely focus, and naïveté. Watching cable, she would point to some famous personality spouting one of the stories about her and say, "Who is this person?" (Palin meant it both sarcastically and literally; she was green enough to the national scene that she couldn't tell the players without a scorecard.) Of all the tales she rebutted that week, only one shattered her aplomb. After Schmidt told her about the *Enquirer*'s accusations of infidelity, she briefly lost her composure while rehearsing her speech.

It was amid this bedlam that Schmidt's desired policy tutoring took place. Schooling Palin were Steve Biegun, a longtime Republican foreign-policy hand,

and Randy Scheunemann, a McCain national security adviser. In the days since the pick, Schmidt had spent enough time with Palin to get a sense of how much instruction she would need. "You guys have a lot of work to do," he warned Scheunemann. "She doesn't know anything."

Scheunemann and Biegun took Schmidt at his word. They sat Palin down at a table in the suite, spread out a map of the world, and proceeded to give her a potted history of foreign policy. They started with the Spanish Civil War, then moved on to World War I, World War II, the cold war, and what Scheunemann liked to call the "the three wars" of today—Iraq, Afghanistan, and the global war on terror. The tutorial took up most of Monday, starting early and going late. When the teachers suggested breaking for lunch or dinner, the student resisted. "No, no, no, no, let's keep going," Palin said. "This is awesome."

Palin was particular about her study aids. Early on, she told her team that she absorbed information best from five-by-seven index cards. With Scheunemann and Biegun, she became obsessive, wanting to put every pertinent piece of information, including the names of world leaders, on separate cards. Soon enough, she had multiple towering stacks of cards, which she referred to constantly, sitting quietly and poring over them, lugging them back to her room to memorize late at night. It quickly became a running joke on Team Palin: Don't get between Sarah and her cards!

Tuesday night and all of Wednesday were given over to Palin's speech, which was written by Matthew Scully, a former Bush White House wordsmith. A speech coach was imported from New York to help Palin convey her personality through the text. Wallace taught her to say "NEW-clear," not "NUKE-u-lar," writing out the letters for good measure: *N-E-W-C-L-E-A-R*. Palin worked tirelessly on her address, pounding out more than a dozen run-throughs.

Tucker Eskew watched the rehearsals carefully. She was good, he could see, and she would be even better from the stage. *She's a red-light-on performer,* he thought—kind of like Obama. But McCain aides were still nervous as the moment of truth arrived. Palin hadn't spoken that often from TelePrompTers in her career, and she certainly had never experienced anything like this kind of pressure, a situation in which the stakes were so high, where everyone was watching. As Palin strode out onstage, the heebie-jeebies even overcame Eskew. *What if it's a bomb?* he thought.

The roar of approval inside the hall was deafening. The faithful were resentful of a media they believed had treated the VP nominee unfairly, turning at one point toward the press seats and chanting, "Shame on you!" They wanted to be wowed by Palin. And they were.

In a shantung Valentino jacket and black skirt, Sarah was glamorous, homespun, spunky, and snarky. She bragged that when she became governor, she shed the office of its luxury jet: "I put it on eBay." She said she "told the Congress 'thanks, but no thanks,' for that Bridge to Nowhere." She described herself as "just your average hockey mom," and threw in an ad lib that she'd used before but wasn't in her text. "You know, they say the difference between a hockey mom and a pit bull?" she said. "Lipstick!"

What was less expected was the delight that Palin took in baring her fangs, and sinking them into Obama. "I guess a small-town mayor is sort of like a community organizer, except that you have actual responsibilities," she quipped. She said, "We tend to prefer candidates who don't talk about us one way in Scranton and another way in San Francisco." She called Obama an elitist, an egotist, a taxer, a spender, an appeaser, and an accomplishment-free zone. By the end, it was clear why that barracuda moniker had stuck.

Watching on a television in a room backstage, McCain went from pacing fretfully, to murmuring, "She's really good," to enthusing, "She's incredible," to grabbing Wallace and exulting, "Oh, my God, great job, she did a great job!"

Then Wallace told McCain that Palin's achievement was even greater than he knew: her prompter had been malfunctioning throughout the speech; the text hadn't paused during periods of applause, so a couple of lines were always missing from the screen when she resumed.

"If that happens to me tomorrow night," McCain replied, "we're fucked."

No one, besides maybe Salter, had high expectations for McCain's speech. But for all its shortcomings, it reflected clearly the consensus in McCainworld that reviving the candidate's independent, cross-partisan image was essential. The only time that McCain uttered the surname Bush was when he was referring to Laura. Only thrice did he use the word "Republican," once in relation to Palin and twice in the context of decrying corruption.

But McCain's speech didn't matter; the only story line out of St. Paul was Palinmania. Some armchair GOP psychologists had surmised initially that the reason McCain picked Palin was that he didn't want to be overshadowed by his running mate. But for the next week, as the two of them campaigned together across the country, they were greeted by massive,

beaming crowds who were there mainly to see her—
and McCain loved it. Everywhere they went, Palin
described McCain as "the one great man in the race,"
as he grinned from ear to ear. "Change is coming, my
friends!" McCain crowed over and over.

Donations and volunteers spiked up. Cable and
radio could talk of little else but Sarah. The Palin pick
deprived Obama of his post-convention bump; the
weekend after the GOP convention, McCain was trailing him by a trifling two points. And according to an
ABC News/*Washington Post* poll, McCain's standing
among white women had improved by a net twenty
points (from 50–42 behind Obama to 53–41 ahead) in
the blink of an eye.

On September 10, McCain and Palin appeared together in Fairfax, Virginia, a few miles from the campaign's headquarters. Fifteen thousand people swarmed
into Van Dyke Park—little girls wearing "STRONG
WOMEN VOTE MCCAIN-PALIN" T-shirts, their
mothers chanting, "Sarah! Sarah! Sarah!" Later that
afternoon, Palin would board a flight to Alaska for her
interview with Gibson. At the moment, though, she
stood there on stage, perched atop a pair of ruby-red
heels, looking less like Eliza Doolittle than Dorothy:
the girl swept up in the cyclone, lifted out of her black-
and-white world and deposited in a Technicolor Oz.

. . .

Obama and his people certainly felt as though a house had been dropped on their heads. Since the moment Palin's selection was announced, they had been struggling to calibrate a response to her and the variables she injected into the campaign. In Palin, the Obamans were confronting something with which they had no experience, a phenomenon so new and fascinating to the press and public that it eclipsed even their boss. For the first time, they understood how the Hillarylanders felt during much of the Democratic nomination fight—helpless, flummoxed, unable to break through.

In the hours after the announcement, Team Obama turned to Hillary herself for help, asking her to put out a tough statement criticizing the pick as a transparent ploy that female voters would see right through. Clinton not only declined to do that, but she did the opposite, calling Palin's nomination "historic" and saying that Palin would "add an important new voice to the debate."

Hillary had no intention of assisting in the trashing of Palin; she thought it would annoy her supporters. She also believed the pick might prove to be smart politics, and in this, she was seconded by her husband. When Democratic elites initially scoffed at Palin, ridiculing her outré tastes—the passion for weaponry, the hankering for mooseburgers—Bill Clinton went into Bubba mode, cautioning them not to underestimate her appeal. Don't be so sure of yourselves, he said. Good old boys, they can relate to her.

The reaction of the Democratic Establishment to Palin was wildly schizophrenic. In the days just after she burst on the scene, she was discounted as just a pretty face, and McCain was mocked for having squandered his only argument against Obama—experience—and for disqualifying himself with a nakedly political pick. But as Palinmania built over the week following the Republican convention, panic spread through the Democratic ranks. The Obamans were swamped with phone calls and email from donors, operatives, and members of Congress demanding that Palin be taken down, slamming the campaign for being too soft and passive, urging them to do . . . something!

Team Obama was split over how to handle the Palin perplex. On one side were advisers convinced she would inevitably self-destruct. On the other were those who shared what Plouffe described as the "bedwetting" tendencies of much of the Establishment. (One member of the campaign's media team, Steve Murphy, referred to Palin as a Republican female Barack Obama.) In focus groups, voters were split roughly into thirds: those who dismissed her out of hand, those who weren't sure what to think, and those who found her a breath of fresh air. "She is the change that Barack Obama talks about," said one voter in the latter camp.

Obama attempted to retain his balance through the outbreak of Palinmania. When his team's first instinct was to criticize Palin's selection, he dialed them back. He counseled them repeatedly to keep their eyes (and train their fire) on the top of the ticket. When Jarrett informed him of a series of meetings she'd had in New York with frantic Democrats in that first week after the conventions, Obama said, "Just tell them to calm down."

A couple of days later, Jarrett received a viral email that pictured Obama staring forward sternly and pointing in the direction of the camera. Above his head were the words "EVERYONE CHILL THE FUCK OUT," and below that, the message "I GOT THIS!" She forwarded it to Obama.

"That's what I was trying to tell you!" Obama replied.

Yet Palinmania and the media dynamics it unleashed were a quantum force that even the Democratic nominee could not resist entirely. The day before Palin set off back to Alaska, Obama was in Virginia, too, and he offered an observation about McCain's new message of change. "I guess his whole angle is, 'Watch out, George Bush—except for economic policy, health care policy, tax policy, education policy, foreign policy, and Karl Rove–style politics—we're really going to shake things up in Washington,'" he said at a rally. "That's not change. That's just calling something [that's] the same thing something different. You know, you can put lipstick on a pig, but it's still a pig."

The McCain campaign was perfectly aware that Obama was making no allusion to Palin's lipstick-on-a-pit-bull convention line; the lipstick-on-a-pig phrase was common parlance, particularly in politics. But the team saw a "Celeb"-like chance to clog up the cable airwaves, harness the right-wing freak show to its advantage, and keep Obama and his people on defense. Within hours, McCainworld accused Obama of referring to Palin as a pig and demanded an apology, and the story exploded as planned.

Obama's frustration with the media was intense, but the next day, he felt he had no choice but to respond—by calling for an end to the absurdity, even as he fueled both it and the dominance of Palin in the campaign discourse for another day.

All through the campaign, in moments of annoyance at its triviality, Obama would tell Axelrod that when it was over he planned to write a book entitled *This Is Ridiculous*. And the lipstick-on-a-pig imbroglio was definitely that. But there was no denying one brute reality: a week after the conventions, McCain had pulled even in the polls again. Some even had him a little bit ahead. Obama smirked and reprised for Axelrod another of his favorite sayings: "This shit would be really interesting if we weren't in the middle of it."

21

SEPTEMBER SURPRISE

Obama showed up at Axelrod's office wearing jeans, a leather jacket, and his White Sox cap. It was September 14, a rainy Sunday afternoon in Chicago, and Axelrod had called a small circle-the-wagons meeting to talk about how to turn things around after ten solid days of pounding. The candidate wasn't supposed to be there, but when he heard about the meeting, Obama decided to hijack it. He had just gotten word that the apocalypse was nigh.

He began by letting his people know that he wasn't entirely happy. Since the Republican convention, his campaign had been too much on its back foot, was playing subpar ball. The ads, the messaging, the strategy, the tactics—all of it needed to be stronger. The first of his three debates with McCain was less than two weeks away, in Oxford, Mississippi. "I've got to perform," he said. "But we've all got to sharpen our message."

Obama thought the campaign needed to be more forceful and pointed in offering a contrast with McCain on the economy, and shift the focus away from Palin. Larry Grisolano had come to the meeting pushing a proposal: two-minute TV ads with Obama addressing the camera directly, laying out his economic agenda. Obama immediately approved it.

The American economy had been in recession since the end of 2007, driven there by the collapse of the mid-decade housing bubble and the subprime mortgage market. By September, the financial system had spiraled into an ever-deepening crisis, as one venerable institution after another buckled under crushing losses. The investment bank Bear Stearns had gone belly up in March. Merrill Lynch and the insurance titan AIG were imploding. The federal government had just seized control of the foundering mortgage giants Fannie Mae and Freddie Mac. And now Lehman Brothers, one of Wall Street's most storied firms, was on the brink of bankruptcy.

Financial economics was hardly an area of expertise for Obama, nor had he said much about the unfolding crisis during the campaign. But behind the scenes, he was building relationships with a handful of influential financial figures: former Federal Reserve chairman Paul Volcker, former SEC chairman William Donaldson, and UBS Americas chairman Robert Wolf, who was one of Obama's most prodigious fund-raisers and had become his go-to guy on questions involving the money markets.

Over the weekend of September 13 and 14, Wolf was among a clique of bankers and policy makers, including Treasury Secretary Hank Paulson, locked in a marathon meeting at the New York Fed, wrestling with the fate of Lehman. Every so often, Wolf would step out and phone Obama with status reports. Obama was also in touch with Paulson, to whom he'd started to reach out as the crisis worsened. By Sunday, the picture that Wolf and Paulson were painting wasn't pretty. Lehman was likely to go under the next morning, with potentially calamitous fallout on Wall Street and stock markets around the world.

At the meeting in Axelrod's office, Obama revealed nothing specific about what he was hearing. But he told the room that an event might be coming overnight that would change the political landscape dramatically, turning the final two months of the campaign into an all-economics-all-the-time affair.

If this event happens, the country may be in for a bad stretch, he said. We're going to have to deal with it in some way, because the impact could be devastating. I told Paulson that we'd be cooperative and try to help out the administration. We're not going to mess around playing politics. In any case, the right politics here, I think, is to behave responsibly.

Obama knew that economic issues favored the Democratic side in the campaign. But these external forces were too unpredictable for comfort—especially with the race so close and the Palin surge still in effect. Obama's confidence wasn't shaken, but his voice betrayed concern. "It's a very volatile situation," he said. "We could still lose this thing."

The next morning, Lehman announced it was seeking Chapter 11 protection, after the government declined to intercede to save the firm. The filing set in motion the largest bankruptcy in American history. It triggered a financial panic that would provide Obama and McCain with a real-time test of political temperament, skill, and leadership. And it marked the start of an extraordinary ten-day period that would more or less decide the election.

McCain greeted the day of Lehman's demise at a rally in Jacksonville, Florida. The Dow was already plunging its way toward a five-hundred-point decline between the opening and closing bells. "There's been tremendous turmoil in our financial markets and Wall Street, and it is—people are frightened by these events," McCain said. "The fundamentals of our economy are strong, but these are very, very difficult times."

In his maladroit way, McCain was trying to heed the advice of his chief economic adviser, Douglas Holtz-Eakin, who had counseled him not to talk down the economy and assured him that its underlying strength—its workers, its factories—was intact. McCain, indeed, had uttered the same line before and it had gone unnoticed. But in the context of Lehman, "fundamentals" was a gaffe of historic proportions.

Matters fiscal and monetary were always the weakest policy link for McCain, which he had admitted publicly more than once. Holtz-Eakin begged him to please stop saying that aloud, particularly in light of its truth, but there was no hiding McCain's rudderlessness over the next three days, as he lurched from blunder to blunder.

On Tuesday, McCain declared the financial situation "a total crisis"—an effort to clean up the "fundamentals" mess that instead looked like an abrupt about-face. That same day, he stated his adamant opposition to a proposed federal bailout of AIG; the next morning, after the bailout had been announced, he flipped to reluctantly supporting it. The day after that, he attacked

SEC chairman Chris Cox, saying, "If I were president today, I would fire him," only to have it pointed out that no president, real or hypothetical, has that power. Making an awful week worse, one of McCain's main economic surrogates, former Hewlett-Packard CEO Carly Fiorina, went on MSNBC and observed, "I don't think John McCain could run a major corporation." (With that, Fiorina provoked an unnamed McCain adviser to give to CNN.com one of the priceless blind quotes of 2008: "Carly will now disappear.")

The Obamans could barely contain their glee. Their boss's reaction shifted quickly from incredulity to disdain. When he first heard about "fundamentals," Obama said to Axelrod, "Why did he say *that*?" Three days later, after the Chris Cox episode, a friend emailed Obama asking what he thought explained McCain's wild swings and oscillations.

"No fucking discipline," Obama replied.

As McCain bumbled publicly, Obama was privately conducting for himself what amounted to an on-the-fly series of postgraduate seminars, holding lengthy conference calls night and day with his party's brainiest economic savants. Many of the people to whom Obama turned were Clinton veterans: former treasury secretaries Bob Rubin and Larry Summers, former Council of Economic Advisers chief Laura Tyson. Obama also turned to Clinton himself, calling the former president several times, soliciting his advice, impressing him (for the first time, really) with his approach to the crisis.

Obama was talking regularly with Fed chair Ben Bernanke and daily, sometimes more often, with Paulson. The treasury secretary was astonished by the candidate's level of engagement. On one occasion, Obama kept his plane on the tarmac for a half hour after the final event of his day, with a long flight ahead of him, so he could finish a conversation with Paulson. On another, Obama called Paulson late at night at home and spent two hours discussing the intricate details of regulatory reform. As much as the substantiveness of the discussions struck Paulson, so did their sobriety and maturity. I'll be there publicly for you at any time, Obama told him. I'm going to be president, and I don't want to inherit a financial system that's collapsed.

McCain was in communication with Bernanke and Paulson, too, but to less useful effect. In one exchange with the Fed chairman, McCain compared the causes of the crisis to some recent management troubles at Home Depot. It's kind of like that, isn't it? he asked Bernanke. No, it's not, a flabbergasted Bernanke replied.

When Paulson tried to get McCain on the phone urgently, it would often take a day for his messages to be returned, and even then, it might be Lindsey Graham on the other end of the line instead of the candidate. At one point, McCain insisted on putting Palin on a call with Paulson—whereupon she proceeded to spout an assortment of populist, anti–Wall Street bromides that the secretary, a former CEO of Goldman Sachs, found weirdly off-key and completely pointless.

In the wake of Lehman and AIG, the credit markets were frozen shut and the capital markets in disarray. Paulson and Bernanke convinced Bush that a gargantuan bailout fund was necessary to stave off disaster. The administration, in turn, gave Paulson the lead in devising and selling the idea to Congress. It had little choice. The White House had no credibility on the economy, no competence to fashion complex financial transactions, and no ability to deal with the Democrats who controlled Capitol Hill. Paulson, who had spent much of his time in office reaching out across the partisan aisle, had each of those virtues. Bush and his people viewed Paulson, said one, as "our Petraeus on the economy."

On September 19, Paulson and Bernanke held an emergency meeting in Speaker Nancy Pelosi's office with a bipartisan clutch of congressional leaders. Paulson argued that, without quick and momentous action, economic Armageddon would ensue; Bernanke was visibly shaking, his voice trembling when he spoke.

The leadership agreed to move rapidly on a bailout bill. Two days later, Paulson presented his proposal to Congress: a three-page request for $700 billion with essentially no strings attached.

Both parties recoiled from the plan, but their respective leaders began trying to build a workable bill around it. Pelosi made it clear that House Democrats wouldn't support the bill without a substantial number of Republican votes, to protect the Democrats if public opinion turned against it. John Boehner, the House minority leader, was on board, but after a meeting of the House Republicans on Tuesday, September 23, it was evident to Boehner that there was no support among his people for anything that resembled the Paulson plan. The next day, the point was reinforced when, in a private meeting, House Republicans hooted down Dick Cheney, who had come to the Hill to sell the bill.

As the nature and dimensions of the dilemma became stark, all eyes in the capital shifted to McCain. The new conventional wisdom was that if the Republican nominee supported the bill, his party would rally around him and it would pass. If he didn't, the bill was doomed. Democrats said so. Republicans said so. The media said so. The question was what McCain was thinking. And for the moment, he wasn't saying.

McCain was twitchy that Wednesday morning as he and his senior lieutenants filed into his suite at the Hilton in Midtown Manhattan. McCain had a jampacked schedule in New York for the next twenty-four hours: debate prep, an appearance on the *Late Show with David Letterman*, a speech at the annual meeting of the Clinton Global Initiative. But McCain was fixated on other things. Obama had phoned him an hour earlier; he'd missed the call, had no idea what it was about, and that unsettled him. And then there was the financial crisis, which he was sure would be the death of his campaign.

Earlier that morning, McCain had met with thirteen Republican CEOs and Wall Street tycoons—including Steve Schwarzman of the Blackstone Group, Henry Kravis of KKR, John Thain of Merrill Lynch, and Jimmy Lee of JPMorgan Chase—who were, at least nominally, economic advisers to his campaign. Almost to a person, their view of the severity of the crisis was identical to Paulson's. And despite their free-market pedigrees, so was their conviction that a massive government intervention was required, and pronto, to keep the world from self-immolating.

Up in the suite, the fog of pessimism, both economic and political, was thick as porridge. For the next several hours, McCain and his advisers grappled with how to respond to the Paulson plan and to the crisis more broadly. In other circumstances, a massive federal bailout bill would be the kind of thing McCain would oppose on instinct and on principle; and he knew that many grassroots Republicans were against it.

Yet from the rambling, chaotic conversation, agreement emerged on three interlocking points that suggested a different course. First, if what they'd just heard from the financial hot shots was to be believed, the risk of an imminent global meltdown unless the government acted was high. Second, the Paulson plan didn't have the votes to pass. And third, if the bill went down and the economy cratered, Republicans—and McCain in particular—would be blamed and the election over. "Checkmate," said Schmidt.

Presidential campaigns are routinely consumed with faux existential crises, but this was a real one. Casting about for salvation, McCain briefly latched on to the idea of joining forces with Senator Clinton on a piece of legislation she'd introduced to ameliorate the epidemic of foreclosures that were plaguing the housing market. Impulsively, McCain grabbed his cell phone and called her; two minutes later he hung up and told the group, "She doesn't want to do it."

To Schmidt, Davis, and Salter, there seemed only one plausible route to survival: McCain had to fly to Washington and stitch together a passable bill. Schmidt pointed out that Harry Reid had been quoted the previous day saying, "We need the Republican nominee for president to let us know where he stands and what we should do." The ball was being handed to McCain, Schmidt said. He should take it and run for daylight—not only steaming into the capital to save capitalism, but suspending his campaign, pulling his ads from the air, and calling for the first debate to be postponed until an agreement on the bailout had been brokered.

"It's a big risk," McCain mused. "It's a big gamble." But gradually he warmed to the notion. McCain's instinct when he saw a problem was to charge straight at it and try to solve it. He started thinking, *I can do this. I can cut this deal.*

In the early afternoon, with no final decision made, Team McCain headed to the Morgan Library and Museum on Madison Avenue for McCain's debate prep session. His maiden face-off with Obama was set to take place two days later, but this was to be McCain's first full dress rehearsal. The campaign had built a mock-up stage and had camera crews in place to document the proceedings. Former Ohio congressman Rob Portman was on hand to play Obama.

McCain was grouchy about the prep session from the get-go. When his aides tried to do a formal introduction of the candidates, McCain snapped, "We don't need to worry about that crap. It's just bullshit. I'm here at the podium, let's just do the debate."

But they didn't get too far—the interruptions were ceaseless, as McCain's aides scrambled to figure out the details of how the campaign suspension might work. Finally, Schmidt interrupted and told McCain that they needed to decide. Are we doing this? he asked.

Charlie Black and Brett O'Donnell, McCain's debate coach, had doubts about pulling out of the showdown in Oxford. If you say you're not going to do the debate and then end up doing it, they argued, you're going to look like a fool. But McCain brushed them off. Convinced that the gamble was worth it, he was all in.

McCain set off back to the Hilton. In the car he called Bush and informed him of his decision, and asked if the president would host a meeting at the White House for him, Obama, and congressional leaders to discuss the bailout bill. Bush feared such a meeting would inject a destabilizing dose of politics into a fragile situation. He told McCain that his intercession would undercut Paulson and wasn't likely to help solve the problem.

After hanging up, Bush instructed his aides, Find out what's going on here. But before they had a chance, McCain was on TV, standing at a lectern at the Hilton, announcing the suspension and calling on Bush to convene a conclave.

McCain also phoned Obama before making his announcement, finally returning his rival's call from six hours earlier. Obama, in Florida doing his own debate prep, told McCain he thought that, in the spirit of bipartisanship, the two of them should release a joint statement of principles concerning the bailout. McCain replied that they should go further: get off the campaign trail and head to Washington to mediate. Obama was noncommittal, but believed that McCain had agreed to the joint statement. A few minutes later, he learned otherwise when McCain popped up on TV. "Man, that was quick," Obama said to Axelrod in disbelief.

McCain had one more crucial call to place, to David Letterman. McCain had been on the *Late Show* a dozen times. He considered Dave a pal. But, though McCain was staying overnight in New York to keep his commitment to Bill Clinton's CGI, he decided it would be in poor taste to be yukking it up in the midst of a crisis. Letterman did not take the news of the last-minute cancellation well. "He's pissed," McCain told his aides. "We'll make up."

By the late afternoon, McCain finally got some good news. Bush had agreed to host the meeting. The president called Obama to extend an invitation for the following day. Obama sensed reluctance in Bush's voice, but, like the president, he felt he had no real choice but to accede to McCain's wishes.

The news of McCain's suspension drew gales of derision from the press. No one was willing to give him the slightest benefit of the doubt—as McCain and his people felt the media surely would have lent Obama— that his motivations were anything less than craven. Pundits said he was using the economic meltdown as an excuse to delay debating Obama. Democrats were instantaneous in criticizing McCain for disrupting the negotiations over the bill. Reid, who a day earlier had called for McCain to make his voice heard on the financial rescue, issued a statement (which he read by phone to McCain) that said, "We need leadership; not a campaign photo op."

McCainworld had assumed that the suspension would be viewed as an authentic, characteristic act of putting country first. But after "Celeb," the selection of Palin, and lipstick-on-a-pig, combined with the pratfalls of the week of the fifteenth, McCain was now seen as a typical, and faintly desperate, politician— and his campaign a campaign of stunts. The return to

Washington might have escaped ridicule. The combination of the suspension and the move to postpone the debate was a gimmick too far.

The weasely image of McCain was reinforced that night, when Letterman exacted his revenge. In the midst of acidly mocking McCain, the host discovered that he was still in New York—not racing to a plane, but preparing for an interview with CBS News's Katie Couric. Tapping into a live feed of McCain having his makeup applied on set, Letterman said, "Hey, John, I got a question. You need a ride to the airport?"

As any good stuntman will attest, it's all in the execution—and in staging his return to Washington on September 25, McCain left a great deal to be desired. There was no careful coordination with House Republicans or the White House. There was no media strategy, no plan for a press conference. Nothing. McCain just showed up in his Senate office that morning and said, Okay, let's see what I can do to get something moving here.

The optics of the day were especially poorly managed. A series of meetings was hastily arranged, but they were private; so rather than images of McCain conferring with conservatives, there were shots of him wandering the halls of Congress, as he moved from room to room, looking like a gypsy. He showed up in Boehner's office, where a gathering was already under way with a handful of Republican House leaders. After listening to two and a half minutes of discussion about their concerns regarding the bill, McCain said he was on their side if it would get a deal done. Boehner and his colleagues were happy to have an ally, but they were also bemused. If House Republicans had been asked to vote for their least favorite senator (in either party), McCain would likely have won in a landslide; and he in turn had always considered them a bunch of yahoos. McCain had only just shown up and knew next to nothing about the issues in play around the bailout. And he said not a word about how he planned to approach the meeting with the president later that day.

Davis asked Boehner's chief of staff if there was anyone in his office who could staff McCain at the White House; his campaign aides were legally prohibited from doing so. A young aide named Mike Sommers, who had been in the thick of the fight over the Paulson plan, was assigned the task.

Sommers rode with the nominee to the meeting, prepared to provide McCain with more detail on what House Republicans were looking for. McCain, after all, was now their de facto champion—and he was headed for the high-stakes gathering he'd requested. But McCain spent the trip down Pennsylvania Avenue talking on the phone to Cindy. I'm on my way to the White House, he said. What are we doing for dinner tonight?

When they arrived at their destination, McCain and Sommers hopped out of the car beside the West Portico. As they walked toward the door, McCain suddenly stopped and looked at Sommers blankly.

"What do I need to know about this meeting?" he asked.

Obama, meanwhile, had strategized extensively with Reid and Pelosi, who agreed to defer to him. Obama had no agenda to push; he was annoyed at having to be there rather than preparing for the debate. (He'd resolved to show up in Oxford whether McCain did or not.) *They're driving this, so let's hear what they have to say,* Obama thought.

Just before the meeting, Bush was briefed by his adviser Ed Gillespie.

"What's McCain going to say?" Bush asked.

"We have no idea," Gillespie said.

The meeting took place in the Cabinet Room. When the Democrats showed up en masse, Obama worked the room as if he were mayor of the White House, introducing himself and shaking hands with all the staff. McCain stood off to the side and said little.

The nominees and congressional leaders took their places around the oblong mahogany table. After asking Paulson for a rundown of the situation, Bush talked about how the credit market couldn't be fixed until the political market was appeased. The president didn't care what the rescue plan looked like. If Hank says it will work, I'm for it, he said.

"Madame Speaker?" Bush said, turning the floor over by protocol to Pelosi.

"Mr. President, Senator Obama is going to speak for us today," Pelosi replied.

"Harry," Bush said to Reid, "is Senator Obama speaking for the Senate Democrats as well?"

"Yes, Mr. President, he speaks for all of us here today."

Obama took the floor and held forth for five or six minutes. I appreciate the urgency here, he said, and mentioned his regular conversations with Paulson. Obama ticked off four items central to the bill: executive compensation, golden parachutes, oversight, and flexibility. "I think just about everyone has agreed on these," he said, then added a sly dig at the House Republicans. "I understand there are some who may not be as far along as the rest of us.

"We can argue about how we got here, but that's not the issue," Obama went on. "The issue is how to solve the problem."

Boehner spoke next, airing his caucus's complaints with the Paulson plan and putting forward a smaller, less intrusive alternative.

"This is interesting," Reid said, "because John Boehner seemed like he was a socialist last week, and suddenly he's finding free-market principles."

Pelosi and House Financial Services Committee chairman Barney Frank piled on Boehner. "I can't invent votes," Boehner said, defending himself. "I have a problem on my own hands." Others chimed in. The pace was rapid-fire, though the volume was low.

At that point, Obama more or less took over. House and Senate Democrats and Senate Republicans are ready to make this deal, Obama said. We can't be going forward and creating a new one. (One Republican in the room mused silently, *If you closed your eyes and changed everyone's voices, you would have thought Obama was the president of the United States.*)

The meeting was now more than forty minutes old. McCain had yet to contribute.

"Can I hear from Senator McCain?" Obama asked, as if he really were running the session, although he first went back to Paulson with a question. When Paulson finished, the treasury secretary told McCain that he'd like to hear from him, too.

McCain thanked the president for hosting the gathering, then thanked Paulson. He said the situation was dire. He noted that progress had been made, but that House Republicans had concerns, which he listed. His comments sounded like introductory talking points, presented as if the first forty-five minutes of the meeting hadn't happened.

All hell broke loose. Frank, Pelosi, and Republican senators Richard Shelby and Mitch McConnell started loudly squabbling. Frank, agitated, turned on McCain.

"John, what do you think?" Frank asked sharply.

"I think the House Republicans have a right to their position," replied McCain.

"Fine. You agree with that position?"

"No, I just think they have a right to their position."

Bush had heard enough. "You ready to end this?" he said to Reid, who signaled his assent.

"All right, I think we understand where we are," said Bush. "We have work to do, and all I'm asking you is to make sure we go forward." Placing his hands on the table for emphasis, he stressed how important it was that some kind of deal happen quickly.

"We can't let this sucker fail," Bush said, and, with that, the meeting was over.

Bush was dumbfounded by McCain's behavior. He'd forced Bush to hold a meeting that the president saw as pointless—and then sat there like a bump on a log. *Unconstructive*, thought Bush. *Unclear. Ineffectual.*

McCain told his aides the reason he was silent was that, from the moment the Democrats deferred to Obama, he knew that the meeting would accomplish nothing. Their disruptive behavior at the end had only confirmed his opinion.

To whatever extent McCain's chagrin was sincere, it reflected another bedrock miscalculation in his decision to suspend his campaign. The premise of the strategy was that McCain could return to the capital and play the above-the-fray bipartisan dealmaker. But in any election year, the fray is boundless. The idea that the opposition party would let McCain waltz back into Washington and stage-manage a triumph with November 4 only forty days away was folly. Yet in the face of a determined Democratic resistance, McCain had failed even to wire the outcome on the Republican side. By the night of the White House meeting, the costs of those mistakes were apparent on every TV screen in the land, as Democrats lustily tore McCain limb from limb and Republicans were mute.

"If you're going to come riding into Washington on a white horse to slay a dragon, you better have the dragon tied up and tranquilized and ready to die," a longtime friend of McCain's concluded. "You don't come in and not slay the dragon and walk out with a whimper."

A bevy of Obamans were waiting in Mississippi, wondering when they might next see their man—and if he was going to end up on stage tangling with McCain or talking to himself. The next morning, less than twelve hours before the debate was scheduled to begin, the answer remained a mystery. And then, just like that, McCain's campaign issued a statement that the candidate was suddenly "optimistic that there has been significant progress towards a bipartisan agreement" and was therefore suspending his suspension. The jousting match was on.

The topic of the first debate was supposed to have been domestic policy, per the decree of the nonpartisan Commission on Presidential Debates. But over the summer, when the two campaigns met to negotiate details, Obama's team, led by Emanuel, had proposed a switcheroo to foreign policy. For press consumption, Axelrod explained that the change reflected Obama's confidence on the topic—and that was half true. The other half, however, was that Obama believed that McCain's foreign-policy strength was vastly overstated. *He doesn't know as much as everyone thinks he does,*

Obama told his advisers. The surge? Check. Wasteful weapons systems? Check. Everything else? Whiff.

Obama's preparation for the debates had been extensive. He was aware that his performances against Clinton had not been among his most shining moments, and he was still smarting from his one onstage encounter with McCain, in August. Invited to a joint forum on social and religious issues at Rick Warren's Saddleback Church, Obama had prepared little— *Prepare? For Pastor Rick? I know this stuff*—and been creamed. (His answer that deciding when a fetus was entitled to human rights was "above my pay grade" was widely ridiculed.) In the past, Axelrod had run Obama's debate prep, and it had been, like the strategist himself, disorganized and loose-limbed. For his debates with McCain, Obama had given authority to veteran Democratic strategists Tom Donilon and Ron Klain and forensics specialist Michael Sheehan, who put him through his paces with repeated dress rehearsals, DVDs of himself to study, and meticulous briefing books.

For McCain, the chaotic session at the Morgan Library was not an aberration. He detested debate prep, resisted it with every fiber of his being. "Not today" was his reflexive response to the suggestion that he practice. He thought he didn't need it, thought he knew the issues, and hated being quizzed. During a rehearsal for the first GOP debate in 2007, O'Donnell pressed him on a question to the point where McCain finally snapped. "John, what is the difference between a gay marriage and a civil union?" O'Donnell asked. McCain replied, "I don't give a fuck."

When he arrived that morning in Oxford, indeed, McCain had yet to complete a single formal run-through. One hold-up revolved around who would play Obama in mock debates. The campaign had settled on someone it thought would be the ideal stand-in: Michael Steele, the African American former lieutenant governor of Maryland. Not only would Steele be a feisty sparring partner, he could also help McCain become aware of potential racial rhetorical traps. Steele said yes when O'Donnell approached him, and spent all summer gearing up for the task, studying Obama briefing books and watching Obama videos. But McCain stalled, worried that the press would find out he had picked a black Obama placeholder and accuse him of tokenism. After more than a month of paralysis, the idea was scrapped and Rob Portman was brought in with just two weeks' notice.

On the afternoon of the debate, McCain was nervous. His advisers took it in stride. Charlie Black believed that if a presidential candidate said he wasn't skittish before his first general election debate, he was lying, was insane, or didn't comprehend the stakes.

Perhaps Black should have added a fourth option— freak of nature—to describe Obama, who was as calm as ever. An hour before the debate, Valerie Jarrett went to his hotel room and knocked on the door; she was a nervous wreck. When Obama appeared, he took a look at her face, put his hand on her shoulder, and said, "Valerie, I got this."

Jarrett headed out to the auditorium, where she met up with Michelle, who was a basket case herself. Jarrett told her about her exchange with Barack a few minutes earlier.

"Well, then, I guess he's probably got it," Michelle said, smiling.

An audience of more than fifty-three million watched the debate that night. They saw Obama present himself as composed and reassuring. They saw him project an aura of confidence and competence on foreign policy. And they saw him pierce McCain with one poison-tipped sound bite regarding the Republican's record on Iraq: "You said we knew where the weapons of mass destruction were. You were wrong. You said that we were going to be greeted as liberators. You were wrong. You said that there was no history of violence between Shiite and Sunni. And you were wrong."

McCain's advisers, worried that his disdain for Obama might show through, had advised their man to look at the audience and not at his opponent. He followed that directive all too well, not making eye contact with Obama all night. He seemed dismissive and cranky and ill at ease. The debate was McCain's chance to redeem himself; instead, he spent ninety minutes reinforcing his weaknesses and doing Obama no damage. He lost every post-debate insta-poll and was pummeled mercilessly by the cable talking heads. "Do you think he was too troll-like tonight?" Chris Matthews asked one of his guests afterward. "Seriously. Do people really want to put up with four years of that? Of [him] sitting there, angrily, grumpily, like a codger?"

The following Monday, September 29, the Paulson bailout plan was voted down in the House of Representatives, 228 to 205; not a single Republican pulled the lever in its favor. The stock market immediately plunged nearly 800 points. Five days later, Congress finally passed a slightly modified, but still $700 billion, version of the bill. But by now, all confidence was gone. The following week, the Dow fell by almost 2,000 points, losing more than 18 percent of its value—the biggest weekly percentage drop in the 112-year history of the Exchange.

McCain and his advisers were right: the collapse of the economy hurt the GOP. But it was the performances of both candidates during those ten September days after the fall of Lehman that mattered most. In a time of turmoil, Obama demonstrated a capacity to withstand pressure and keep his balance. The crisis atmosphere created a setting in which his intellect, self-possession, and unflappability were seen as leaderly qualities, and not as aloofness, arrogance, or bloodlessness, as they had sometimes been regarded in the past. In the Obama campaign's focus groups, doubts about his readiness began to fall away—while at the same time, voters described McCain as unsteady, impulsive, and reckless.

This view was shared by Democrats and Republicans alike, by those watching the crisis unfold from afar and those with a front-row seat. Jim Wilkinson, a longtime Republican operative, served as Paulson's chief of staff during the crisis, and his impression of the candidates could hardly have been clearer. "I'm a pro-life, pro-gun, Texas Republican," said Wilkinson. "I worked all eight years for Bush. I helped sell the Iraq War. I was in the Florida recount. And I wrote a letter to John McCain asking for my five-hundred-dollar contribution back, when he pulled that stunt and came back to D.C. Because it just wasn't what a serious person does." To his amazement, Wilkinson determined that he would be voting for Obama.

Even one of Obama's harshest critics was now writing off McCain. None other than Hillary Clinton was finally convinced that there was no stopping Barack. In the midst of the financial crisis, she said to a friend, "God wants him to win."

Clinton wasn't alone in the conviction that the outcome of the race was basically settled. But October turned out to hold its own abundance of surprises—shaking the campaigns and appalling or delighting voters, depending on their inclinations. The shocks to come weren't discharged by McCain or Obama, though. Instead, the game changers of the final month were on the undercard.

22

SECONDS IN COMMAND

Sarah Palin was alone in her room at the Millennium Broadway Hotel in New York staring at her index cards. It was September 23, the night before McCain suspended his campaign, and Palin was scheduled to begin a series of interviews the next morning with Katie Couric. Around nine o'clock, Nicolle Wallace arrived to spend some time doing prep. Couric was sure to ask her about the financial crisis, Wallace said, showing Palin a statement that McCain had just released on the subject. "If you internalize this," Wallace explained, "you should be able to field basic questions about the bailout."

Wallace knew Couric well, having worked as a political analyst at CBS between her stints at the White House and the McCain campaign. She shared her insights with Palin on other areas the anchor would almost certainly pursue, such as abortion rights. But Palin, who had spent the day meeting foreign leaders who were in Manhattan for the U.N. General Assembly, was exhausted and distracted. She had a hard time processing the statement on the bailout, and when Wallace tried to raise other topics, Palin would not engage. For three hours, the prep session went nowhere, as Palin kept downshifting into small talk. "What's Katie like?" she asked.

By the eve of the Couric interviews, McCainworld was nursing an array of worries about Palin, from her character to her knowledge level to her focus. With her meteoric rise had come fantastic scrutiny, and although Palin had survived so far, the chinks in her armor were becoming apparent—especially to those observing her at close range.

The first signs of trouble appeared immediately after the convention, when the campaign staff began digging in a systematic way into Palin's background, and noticed that she had a tendency to shade the truth. Had she really said "thanks, but no thanks" to the Bridge to Nowhere? Well, no. Had she really sold the state jet on eBay? Not exactly. Had she and Todd really been without health insurance until he got his union card? Actually, the story was more complicated. At McCain

HQ, a white board was set up with a list of controversies the press was exploring, from Troopergate (which the Palins unvaryingly called "Tasergate," a reference to one of the more lurid details of the case) to the charge that, as mayor of Wasilla, Palin had sanctioned requiring women to pay for their own rape-exam kits. The campaign quickly discovered that consulting her about any issue on the board invariably yielded a sanitized version of reality.

Another source of concern was Palin's lack of fealty to the commitments she'd made to Schmidt and Salter the night before her selection. Palin had promised to support McCain's positions, even those she disagreed with. But one day in September, when the campaign arranged an elaborate and expensive setup for her to shoot a pro-stem-cell-research television ad, she showed up and refused to read her lines. You should have sent me the script before, Palin declared. I'm not saying this.

Palin had also pledged to banish Alaska temporarily from her thoughts and concentrate on the task at hand. But she and Todd were fixated on her reputation in the state, concerned that her image was taking a beating in Alaska because of the wave of attacks on her. They wanted the campaign to run television ads there, though Alaska was solidly Republican and money was tight in McCainworld. Todd griped about how few McCain-Palin yard signs he saw when he drove around back home. Sarah voiced so much anxiety over her gubernatorial approval ratings that Schmidt promised to commission a poll in Alaska to prove that her fears were groundless.

Then there was the matter of Palin's substantive deficiencies. On September 10, she was preparing to fly back to Alaska to see her son Track ship off to Iraq and to tape her first network interview with ABC News's Charlie Gibson. Before the flight to Anchorage, Schmidt, Wallace, and other members of her traveling party met Palin at the Ritz-Carlton near Reagan airport, in Pentagon City, Virginia—and found that, although she'd made some progress with her memorization and studies, her grasp of rudimentary facts and concepts was minimal. Palin couldn't explain why North and South Korea were separate nations. She didn't know what the Fed did. Asked who attacked America on 9/11, she suggested several times that it was Saddam Hussein. Asked to identify the enemy that her son would be fighting in Iraq, she drew a blank. (Palin's horrified advisers provided her with scripted replies, which she memorized.) Later, on the plane, Palin said to her team, "I wish I'd paid more attention to this stuff."

But after cramming furiously, Palin managed to emerge intact from the Gibson interview—stumbling only over whether she agreed with the "Bush doctrine" ("In what respect, Charlie?") and in discussing why the proximity of Alaska to Russia afforded her insight into its behavior on the world stage ("They're our next door neighbors, and you can actually see Russia from land here in Alaska").

Now, with the convention and a network interview behind her, Palin had just the last of her three major hurdles left to surmount: the vice-presidential debate on October 2 at Washington University in St. Louis. It was obvious that she would need to spend much of her time on Biden prep, but McCainworld believed it couldn't simply bunker Palin and have her disappear from public view. She was a star, a sensation, and the press was howling that, Gibson or no, she was being sheltered from cross-examination.

Hence the decision to grant Couric a multi-part interview. As CBS promoted and unspooled the segments over the following week, Palin could go dark to study while keeping her visibility high.

What no one realized was how severely Palin's bandwidth was constricted; her road show was becoming a traveling circus–cum–soap opera. Her children—a pregnant, hormonal young woman; a lively teenage girl;

a rambunctious child; a special-needs infant; and a son just decamped for Iraq—consumed a vast amount of her psychic energy. Her focus on Alaska (and especially the Alaskan media, with which she had been friendly but which she was now certain was turning against her) and her attempts to prepare for her meetings with world leaders devoured even more. One of Palin's private email accounts was hacked, and the gossip website Gawker posted messages that she'd sent, as well as Bristol's cell phone number. And on the season premiere of *Saturday Night Live*, on September 13, Tina Fey debuted her withering, hilarious, uncanny caricature of Palin, mocking her interview with Gibson: "I can see Russia from my house!"

All of this had taken a toll on Palin by the time Wallace sat down with her at the Broadway Millennium. Wallace's husband, Mark, a former Bush campaign official who was also part of Palin's team, had warned his wife about a phenomenon that he and others thought of as "the two Sarahs." One minute, Palin would be her perky self; the next, she would fall into a strange, blue funk. With prep going nowhere, Nicolle decided it was best to put Palin in a positive state of mind. She cooed over the governor's wardrobe for the next day and said they'd get down to business again in the morning at six o'clock.

When Wallace returned bright and early, she found Palin in a pink bathrobe, her eyes glassy and dead. The candidate was furious and embarrassed about a report in *The New York Times* detailing how the press had been blocked from the first few minutes of her meeting the day before with Afghan president Hamid Karzai. As hair and makeup stylists worked on Palin, Wallace ran through potential interview questions. The candidate was unresponsive. Wallace read Palin the newspaper. The candidate sat in silence. After two futile hours, as they were about to set off to meet Couric, Palin announced, "I hate this makeup"—smearing it off her face, messing up her hair, complaining that she looked fat. Wallace, in a panic, summoned a makeup artist to ride in the motorcade and repair the damage.

On the drive across town to meet Couric at the U.N., Palin could speak of little else besides the Alaska poll that Schmidt had promised but she suspected had never been conducted. I'm trying to trust you people, Palin said to Wallace, but how *can* I trust you?

Palin and Couric greeted each other cordially and then taped the first two segments of the series: a sit-down interview and a walk-and-talk outside the U.N. Everyone in earshot understood immediately the scale of the disaster.

Palin's answers about the bailout were halting and incoherent. When Couric asked her to name examples of McCain's efforts to regulate the economy, Palin said, "I'll try to find some and bring them to you." Asked again about the relevance of Russia's closeness to Alaska, she replied, "As Putin rears his head and comes into the airspace of the United States of America, where do they go? It's Alaska." Asked to name a Supreme Court case, besides *Roe v. Wade*, that she disagreed with, Palin awkwardly hedged—"Of course in the great history of America there have been rulings that there's never going to be absolute consensus by every American"— and then came up empty.

A snippet from the interviews aired on CBS that night, but in the clamor over McCain's campaign suspension, nobody noticed. The next morning, Couric went on the network's *Early Show* to promote her exclusive, commenting mildly that Palin wasn't always responsive in replying to certain questions.

At that moment, Wallace was in the middle of an appearance on *Today* and felt her cell phone vibrate madly. As she left NBC, she checked and saw that Palin had been calling nonstop. Soon enough, the governor called again.

Katie said I struggled to answer questions! Palin shouted.

Wallace held her tongue.

Palin shouted again, Are you *listening*?

I'm listening, said Wallace. You did struggle to answer a lot of questions.

I don't know what you guys are trying to do to me, Palin fumed. Why did you make me do Katie?

For the next twenty minutes, as Wallace walked the thirteen blocks back to her apartment, Palin screamed and Wallace yelled back. The reason the interview sucked was because you didn't try, Wallace said. You didn't show up and you didn't fight. The reason Gibson worked out is because even if you didn't know every answer, you clawed your way through the whole thing.

Wallace could barely fathom Palin's hissy fit and her attempt to blame others for her failure to prepare. Wallace had been Palin's closest confidante in McCainworld, but now Nicolle was through with her—and the feeling was mutual.

Palin thought Wallace and McCainworld had tossed her into the lioness's mouth, that Couric had been bound and determined to devour her. She wanted nothing more to do with network anchors, especially since they got in the way of her talking to Alaska reporters. "I want to do what I want to do," Palin said stubbornly to Wallace. "Now I know what Hillary meant when she said she had to find her voice."

. . .

That afternoon, Palin left New York and flew to Philadelphia to spend the next week concentrating on debate prep. She and her team—led by Mark Wallace and including Tucker Eskew and Steve Biegun—checked into the Westin downtown, took over a conference room, and got to work.

The next two days, by all accounts, were a total train wreck. Never before had Palin's team seen her so profoundly out of sorts for such a sustained period. She wasn't eating (a few small bites of steak a day, no more). She wasn't drinking (maybe half a can of Diet Dr Pepper; no water, ever). She wasn't sleeping (not much more than a couple of hours a night, max). The index cards were piling up by the hundreds, but Palin wasn't absorbing the material written on them. When her aides tried to quiz her, she would routinely shut down—chin on her chest, arms folded, eyes cast to the floor, speechless and motionless, lost in what those around her described as a kind of catatonic stupor.

Some on her staff believed that Palin was suffering from postpartum depression or thwarted maternal need. (Again and again, she talked about Trig, who most of the time was back in Alaska with Todd. I miss my baby, Sarah would say, I miss sleeping with my baby.) Others pointed to the Couric interview, the second excruciating slice of which aired the Thursday night they arrived in Philly, subjecting Palin to more ridicule. Still others cited the sheer magnitude of the pressure she was under, given her oft-expressed sense of obligation not to let McCain down, an apparent fear of humiliation, and the searing scrutiny she was receiving.

Wallace, with a sense of desperation setting in, tried to buck Palin up. Sure, they were in a rough patch, he said, but it was worth it, right?

"No," Palin answered darkly. "If I'd known everything I know now, I would not have done this."

On Saturday, September 27, Wallace sent an urgent SOS to McCain headquarters. On a call with Schmidt, Davis, and Salter, he described how Palin was performing, how dire the circumstances were, especially with the debate just five days away. They began discussing a new and threatening possibility: that Palin was mentally unstable.

Schmidt had heard that Palin was accusing him of lying about the Alaska poll—in fact, it had been conducted; her approval rating was in the seventies—which led him to believe that she was becoming irrational. He and Davis planned to take the train to Philadelphia the next day to assess the situation themselves.

Given the acuteness of Wallace's concern, McCain's advisers felt they had to bring the candidate into the loop that Saturday. Bluntly, they described to him their unease about Palin's mental state. McCain suggested that they move the debate prep to his spread in Sedona. Give her room to breathe. Let her bring her family. A change of scenery might do her good. Cindy would be there to support Palin, and a doctor friend of the McCains would be on hand to observe her.

Schmidt and Davis weren't the only McCainiacs who trekked to the Westin on Sunday. Wallace had also summoned Joe Lieberman, to help Palin grasp elements of foreign policy, and also to get an outside perspective on whether she was doing as badly as he thought. A month earlier, when McCain informed Lieberman that he'd lost out to Palin in the veepstakes, Lieberman had been disappointed, if unsurprised, but more confused than anything. He was so unfamiliar with Palin that he mixed her up momentarily with Linda Lingle, the Jewish Republican governor of Hawaii; after all, "Sarah" *was* a Hebrew name.

Lieberman had met Palin at the convention in St. Paul and established a bit of a rapport with her— another reason for him to be at the Westin. But the Palin he saw now scarcely resembled the confident, brassy woman he'd watched bring audiences close to rapture on the trail. She was sitting there being fed questions, saying virtually nothing, to the point where her coaches asked Lieberman to take the lectern and start answering instead.

Schmidt and Davis arrived and were appalled by the scene they found. The room was hot and claustrophobic; the shades were drawn. The place was full of half-eaten hotel food and stank of moldering french fries. Palin, looking dazed, was surrounded, as usual, by stacks and stacks of index cards.

Schmidt cleared the room and said to Palin, Governor, the debate's on Thursday and this isn't working. We're going to move the show to Sedona and we're going to fix it. The Katie Couric interview did not go well, and it didn't go well because you didn't prepare; and there can never be another instance of something not going well because of that. You're not the first politician to have a bad interview. Ronald Reagan said that trees cause pollution and went on to be a great president. No one will remember this stuff if we have a good debate.

Schmidt thought Palin looked thin and drawn. Your road crew tells me that you're not sleeping, he said. No one running for the office of vice president should be getting less than eight hours of sleep a night. If you need to take sleeping pills, you should.

Schmidt then brusquely brought up Palin's weight. It's my understanding that you might be on the Atkins diet, he said. That goofy diet is bad for you. I want you off it today. I'm alarmed by your weight loss and it's noticeable even in just a couple weeks. In order to perform at your highest level, you have to have a balanced diet.

Palin offered not a word of protest.

When Schmidt finished, he walked out in the hall and buttonholed Lieberman. "She's down," Schmidt said. "This whole process is affecting her confidence."

Lieberman couldn't have agreed more, although he wasn't sure that having a former VP nominee show off his debating chops was the best way to build Palin up. The situation was wildly unconventional already: a Democratic senator being imported into a top-secret lockdown to assist a Republican vice-presidential candidate whose mental stability was in question. Now Schmidt asked Lieberman to perform another unorthodox intervention.

"You're both very religious," Schmidt said. "Go in there and pray with her."

As it happened, Palin had already been prayed for that day. A group of Republican congresswomen had offered their blessings via conference call with her. But Lieberman went back and took a less direct tack, providing Palin with Talmudic wisdom. Invoking the influential Orthodox rabbi Joseph Soloveitchik, he spoke about the covenant of faith, which is the relationship between God and man, and the covenant of destiny, which is what men make of themselves.

"Look," Lieberman said kindly, "you gotta be saying to yourself, 'What am I doing here? How did this happen?' This is your moment to make it really count for something."

Palin seemed touched. "Joe," she said. "I can't figure any other reason I'm here except that I was meant to be here."

Palin's immediate rendezvous with destiny was in Ohio the next day, where she stopped on the way to Sedona to join McCain for a rally and to tape the final parts of her interview with Couric. Palin wanted to blow off Katie, but the campaign felt that doing so would be a PR nightmare. Palin acquiesced, but not entirely. Rather than prepping for Couric, she allowed herself to become consumed by a different media opportunity: a questionnaire from the *Mat-Su Valley Frontiersman*, the local Wasilla newspaper, which she insisted on filling out herself. Hours before she was scheduled to meet Couric, Palin emailed several members of her team, "How 'bout I do the Katie interview after I get the Frontiersman interview questions and reply to them? It's been my priority."

The irony was rich, therefore, when the question of Couric's that tripped up Palin that day was one about her reading habits: What newspapers and magazines did she read to stay abreast of the world? "Most of them," Palin said. Specifically? "All of them, any of them that have been in front of me all these years." Can you name a few? "I have a vast variety of sources where we get our news, too," Palin said. "Alaska isn't a foreign country."

Debate camp commenced that night in Sedona with an outdoor buffet hosted by Cindy. Palin was thrilled to see her family and spent much of the time cradling Trig, but beyond that, she was subdued. To prevent leaks about the ongoing crisis, Schmidt had drastically narrowed the circle around Palin, cutting out much of her staff and foregoing the idea of a professional politician to stand in for Biden. (Randy Scheunemann, one of her foreign policy tutors from St. Paul, was assigned the job.) Davis had pleaded with Mark McKinnon, who had decided to sit out the general election because he wanted no part of flaying Obama, to ride to their rescue; he agreed, but just for that one night.

After dinner, they all retreated to a small room tightly packed with two lecterns and a camera, in one of the McCain compound's guest buildings. A run-through was attempted, in which Palin kept getting lost fifteen seconds into her answers, stopping suddenly and saying, No, no, wait, let me start over, or, Shoot, I don't know this.

The session ended after an hour. Schmidt, Mark Wallace, and McKinnon stepped outside into the cool desert air, the night pitch black around them.

"What do you think?" Wallace asked McKinnon.

"Oh. My. God."

The next day, Schmidt decreed the banishment of Palin's hundreds of index cards. Instead, she was given twenty-five or thirty containing full-blown questions and answers, based on her team's best guesses at what the debate queries would be, along with scripted pivots out of dangerous territory and onto safer ground. There was no time for Palin to learn enough to be turned into Jeane Kirkpatrick in the next forty-eight hours. But after seeing her handle the prompter malfunction at the convention, Team McCain knew that she had an impressive capacity for learning by rote.

They moved the lecterns outside and set them up by the creek for daytime rehearsals. Between sessions, Palin, dressed in a hockey jersey and soccer shorts, would go off by herself, sit on the porch or on a swing under a tree, and study up on her preset questions, committing the answers to memory.

The change of venue and routine seemed to have an effect. That night, Palin made it all the way through her formal run-through. When she finished, the room broke into applause. Priscilla Shanks, the speech coach who had worked with Palin at the convention, shouted out, "She's back! She's back!"

Schmidt and Wallace took a dimmer, more angst-ridden view. Outside Sedona, the stakes around the debate had continued to rise. On October 1, the night before the showdown, CBS ran the last, and arguably the worst, of the Couric clips: the one featuring Palin's muffed Supreme Court answer. The previous Saturday, Tina Fey had unleashed her second stab at Palin on *SNL,* in a sketch spoofing the initial Couric sit-down, using nearly identical language to what the nominee had said about the bailout bill; a devastating mash-up juxtaposing the reality with the parody was zooming around the Web. And while Palin's performance in prep had improved markedly, she was still committing howlers that, if let loose during the debate, would be cataclysmic events.

She also continued to stumble over an unavoidable element: her rival's name. Over and over, Palin referred to Obama's running mate as "Senator Obiden"—or was it "O'Biden"?—and the corrections from her team weren't sticking. Finally, three staffers, practically in unison, suggested, Why don't you just call him Joe?

Palin stared at them quizzically and said, "But I've never met him."

In far-off Delaware, things were running more smoothly, at least on the surface. At the Sheraton Suites Hotel in Wilmington, the opposing side had taken over the second floor and transformed it into a down-to-the-millimeter replica of the debate stage in St. Louis. The height of the lecterns. The distance between them. The lighting. The color scheme. All of it was identical to the real thing. And then the Obamans and Bidenettes saw the press pictures of Palin rehearsing in her gym shorts by a tree. They had to laugh.

But only for a second. Then they went back to being tied up in knots with fear that Joe would botch his big moment.

It wasn't hard to imagine how it could happen. The expectations for Palin were subterranean, while the bar for Biden was set around Jupiter. There wasn't much to win here, in other words, but there was plenty to lose—and there were at least two obvious ways that Biden could do it. He might be condescending to Palin because he thought she was an ignoramus. Or he might be patronizing to her as a woman, which, given Joe's old-school Sinatraesque tendencies, was just as likely.

The Obamans were pushing a simple strategy: Ignore Palin. Don't engage her. Whatever happens, don't let her lure you down any rabbit holes with her crazy syntax and run-on sentences.

But Joe couldn't resist—not at first. A week or two before the three days of formal debate camp started on September 29, the campaign put him through his paces in a mock run-through against Anita Dunn. She played the part by reading from a script assembled almost entirely out of verbatim Palin quotes. That's too incoherent, Biden exclaimed. Is that really what she says? No, that can't be her answer. But, I mean, she's not saying anything. How am I supposed to respond to that, folks?

And into the rabbit hole he went.

It only got worse once they brought in the actual stand-in for Palin, the governor of Michigan, Jennifer Granholm. Lithe and alluring like Palin, Granholm came with talking points and a strategy, having glutted herself on YouTube videos of Palin's Alaska debates. Pushing the readiness regimen past the point of absurdity, the Obamans ran Granholm through her own pre-prep prep against a fake Biden. The result was a perfect Palin: charming, folksy, disciplined, flirty—and mean.

Biden's first sessions with Granholm were bad enough to put a scare into Axelrod and Plouffe.

Biden was in *Meet the Press* mode, ponderous and long-winded. Granholm, aware that family was Biden's soft spot, made cracks about his son Hunter's lobbying history, and Joe turned defensive. When Granholm dangled bait by playing dumb, he turned scornful and chauvinistic.

But Biden worked diligently with Michael Sheehan, who trained him using what Sheehan—with due generational aptness—dubbed an "Arthur Murray pattern." Describe the situation; explain how it will be worse under McCain; describe how it'll be better under us. One-two-three, one-two-three, one-two-three. Biden quickly got the hang of it.

He also figured out other means of avoiding rabbit holes. In one session, Granholm was tossing in non sequiturs—explanations that started nowhere and ended up even farther off the map—when she tried to entice Joe into hole-diving with an answer on race that concluded with a wayward reference to *Guess Who's Coming to Dinner*.

Biden paused. "I really have nothing to add to that."

By the night of the debate, the Obamans were expressing confidence, but their doubts weren't far beneath the surface.

"You feel like he's ready?" Obama asked Dunn an hour before the debate.

"He's totally ready," Dunn assured him (and herself).

"You know," Obama said, "I think I'm just going to watch this by myself."

The debate began with its best-known moment: Palin striding onstage in a fitted black suit, extending a hand to Biden, and saying, "Hey, can I call you Joe?" From there, the next ninety minutes unfolded as almost no one expected they would. Neither Palin nor Biden gaffed. Neither said anything egregiously stupid. Neither went for the other's throat, as both aimed their shots at the top of the opposite ticket.

When it was over, the Obamans exhaled and Biden was triumphal. Coming off the stage, he said to his aides, "You guys owe me. You don't know how much restraint that took."

McCainworld was ecstatic. Five days earlier, many of them had feared that Palin's psychological fragility might lead to a fiasco. Palin had not only survived, but fought Biden to something like a draw. In their suite at the Four Seasons, the Palins stayed up past midnight celebrating, drinking champagne, talking about what came next. More rallies. More rope lines. And more attacks on Obama.

Let's go, let's go, let's go, Palin said. Let's get out there and win this election!

. . .

The debate propelled her back onto the trail with a fresh head of steam, a renewed sense of confidence, and an appetite for Obama's jugular. On October 4, *The New York Times* provided Palin an opportunity to capitalize on all three when it published a front-page article about the topic that Hillary Clinton always believed would come back to bite Obama: former Weather Underground subversive William Ayers.

Though the story concluded that Obama and Ayers "do not appear to have been close," the next day McCainworld instructed Palin by email to lay into the Democratic nominee as "someone who sees America as imperfect enough to pal around with terrorists who targeted their own country." Palin eagerly agreed, and, with a few syntactical tweaks, delivered the message as written.

For McCainworld, it would be one of the precious few times in the election's final month that Palin stuck to the script. With the debate-related tumult behind them and any possibility gone that Palin would be a game changer, McCain's strategists hoped that she would continue to be useful in firing up the base and not create too many disruptions or distractions. But it wasn't long before the signs appeared that Palin was going rogue.

The most widely publicized example was an interview she gave to the *Times*'s in-house conservative columnist, William Kristol, on October 5, the same day she thrashed Obama for "palling around with terrorists." When Kristol asked why, if Ayers was on the table, Reverend Wright was not, Palin said that Obama's pastor should be fair game and implicitly criticized McCain for not leading the charge. McCain was rarely bothered when Palin scampered off message, mainly because he did the same so often himself. But this was an exception. He'd drawn a hard line around Wright and couldn't understand why his running mate would have crossed it.

At the same time, Palin was waging a persistent internal crusade to reverse one of the campaign's major strategic decisions. On the day of the VP debate, McCainworld let it be known that it was pulling its resources out of Michigan, a key battleground state that it had determined was out of reach in the wake of the financial crisis. Palin had visited there more than once, thought she connected with its blue-collar voters and could put the state back in play, and lobbied to be allowed to return. When her traveling chief of staff, Andrew Smith, pointed out to her that McCain,

Schmidt, and Davis had reached their conclusion on the basis of complex calculations involving the polls and the budget, Palin simply shrugged and uttered one of her signature phrases: "I know what I know what I know."

Regardless of what Palin thought she knew, Schmidt and Davis turned her down flat about venturing back into Michigan. But Palin refused to give in, sending email after email suggesting ways that she could squeeze a visit to the Wolverine State into her schedule. "It's a cheap four hour drive from [Wisconsin], I'll pay for the gas," Palin wrote to the senior staff on October 8. "I'd just be sleeping at that midnight drivetime anyway."

She was emerging as a big-time control freak. With her family now accompanying her most everywhere, making air-travel logistics a pain, she directed the campaign to "schedule bus transportation instead of flights wherever possible, even if that means late night drives in the bus." She became maniacal about monitoring her media coverage; she was constantly channel-surfing and blogosphere mining, and when she came across any mention that was less than flattering, she insisted that her staff try to have it corrected. Palin also showed an unusual wariness about the politicians and donors brought aboard her campaign plane and bus, insisting that she prescreen them before their seats were confirmed. "I want to google them myself so I can know my comfort level," she emailed her team on October 9. "Photos, etc with them may come back to haunt me if I can't vet these folks myself."

Palin's concern with such appearances was seen by some as an indication that she already had her sights set on 2012. But in truth, she and Todd continued to be far more preoccupied by her status in Alaska than just about anything else. Any issue related to the state put them on high alert, and incited some of their worst propensities toward parsimoniousness with the truth. On October 10, when the Alaska legislature issued a report on Troopergate stating that Palin had abused her powers but not broken the law, Palin proclaimed to reporters that she'd been cleared of all wrongdoing. When her staff told her she would have to walk back her statement because it wasn't true, she said, "Well, why was I told otherwise?"—neglecting the fact that her talking points had made the results of the report quite plain.

A few days later, Palin got into a fight with Schmidt when she insisted that the campaign put out a statement denying Todd's involvement in the Alaskan Independence Party. Palin contended that Todd had mistakenly registered with the party and rectified the error; she also claimed the party had nothing to do with secession. Schmidt curtly informed her that secession was the party's reason for existence and that, according to the campaign's records, Todd had been a member for seven years.

For Schmidt and Davis, Palin was a time sink the size of the Lake Eyre Basin. She pestered them with complaints that her schedules were so tight that she didn't have time to get in a daily run. She never took no for answer; she just kept asking different senior staffers until she found someone who told her what she wanted to hear. Every media opportunity put before her produced a conniption.

In mid-October, Palin was considering an offer to do a guest spot on *Saturday Night Live*. Schmidt was in favor, saying it would show the country that she could laugh at herself. After watching some clips, Palin was chary. "I had no idea how gross 'celebrities' could get," she wrote in an email to HQ. "These folks are whack."

Palin eventually came around and did the program on October 18. The moment that everyone was waiting for was fleeting. She and Tina Fey crossed paths briefly on-screen but spoke not a word to each other. Even so, the charge from it was electric, and rightly so.

For all the emphasis McCainworld had placed on Palin's big three image-making challenges, none of them had done as much to shape public perception of her as Fey—and Couric. Pop culture has always been a part of presidential contests, but never before had there been anything quite like the Fey-Couric double act: two uptown New York ladies working independently but in tandem, one engaged in eviscerating satire, the other in even-handed journalism. The composite portrait they drew of Palin was viral and omnipresent. The sparkle of celebrity made it irresistible, and devastating. Faced with the footage of Reverend Wright, Obama was able to slay the dragon with his words. Faced with Fey-Couric, Palin was powerless. Everything she did or said only fed the beast. By the time she went on *SNL*, the definitional war over her had ended. She retained the ardor and loyalty of her fans, who continued to turn out for her, root for her, and defend her. But in the eyes of the broader public—and even more so those of the national media and political Establishments—any traces of her image as a maverick reformer had been erased. For them, Palin had been reduced to nothing more than a hick on a high wire.

Rogue as Sarah Palin may have gone that October, she didn't have a monopoly on the practice, even among running mates. The debate aside, Biden had basically been coloring outside the lines since the Democratic convention. With the Palin tornado making so much noise and kicking up so much debris, it just wasn't nearly as noticeable—until, one day, it was.

In an effort to demonstrate his commitment to being a team player, Biden told Obama when he accepted the VP slot, "I'll do anything you want me to do, but there are two things I won't do: I won't wear a funny hat and I won't mess with my brand."

The Biden brand meant a great deal to Joe, almost as much as the Biden name. To him, the brand was about substance, about truth-telling, about making hard choices even if they were politically awkward or painful. Biden thought of it as a Democratic version of the McCain brand—the old McCain brand, that is.

But what Biden quickly discovered was that Obama's policies were awfully thin, not terribly specific, more rhetoric than substance. Right after the convention, at a prep session at his house in Wilmington for an appearance on *Meet the Press*, Biden listened to a bunch of the Obamans talk him through the Democratic ticket's position on taxes. "That's our policy? *That's* our policy?" he said incredulously. "Well, it's your campaign. I'll say what you want me to say. But after Election Day, all bets are off."

Then one day in the middle of September, a disturbing bulletin reached O-Town. Apparently, Biden had been hanging around with the reporters in the back of his new plane, running his mouth about how he was more qualified to be president than Obama. On paper, of course, it was arguably true. But that didn't make it go down any easier with the suits; actually, it struck a nerve. Axelrod was a fan of Joe's, but this made him angry. He and Plouffe had warned Biden about precisely this kind of scenario that August day in Wilmington. Right out of the chute, Joe was breaking the deal they'd made.

A chill set in between Chicago and the Biden plane. Joe and Obama barely spoke by phone, rarely campaigned together. Not only was Biden kept off Obama's nightly campaign conference call, he wasn't even told it existed. (When the idea of having Biden join was put to Plouffe, his response was "Nah.") A different daily call was set up for Joe, with the Davids, so they could keep a tight rein on him.

The frostiness soon began to run in both directions. Biden had an endless stream of complaints about Chicago. He was frustrated with the staff, didn't like the advertising, didn't love how he was being deployed. After his comments about being more qualified than Obama, his access to the press was severely limited, and he didn't like that, either. Are you part of the Chicago team or are you on my team? Biden would ask new staffers dispatched to join his road show. Are you with me or are you with them?

Then the cold war turned icy, when Biden started making public gaffes, some politically maladroit and some just plain goofy. In the span of a few days in late September, he equated paying higher taxes with patriotism; made a comment at odds with Obama's position on clean coal; and offered a historical reference to the 1929 stock market crash in which he said that FDR was then the president (it was Hoover) and went on television (which hadn't yet been invented) to soothe the nation. In an interview with Couric, Biden was asked about an Obama TV ad that knocked McCain for being computer illiterate. "I thought that was terrible," Biden said. "I didn't know we did it and if I had anything to do with it, we would have never done it."

In Chicago, irritation mounted over Biden's indiscipline—not least inside Obama, whose unflappability burst into flames when it came to his running mate. One night during a debate prep session, Obama approached one of his advisers and said grumpily, When are you going to fix this problem with Biden?

Joe's insertion of both feet into his mouth on October 20 took the tensions into a new and nasty place. At a fund-raiser in Seattle, Biden seemed to be showing off for the wealthy donors, trying to impress them with his farseeing vision, his exclusive knowledge. (Also, he wasn't at his sharpest; he was dog-tired and had a cold.) "Mark my words," he told the muckety-mucks. "It will not be six months before the world tests Barack Obama like they did John Kennedy. . . . Watch, we're gonna have an international crisis, a generated crisis, to test the mettle of this guy."

On Obama's nightly call, the candidate hit the ceiling. (Axelrod was already up there, needing to be peeled off, having let fly a string of F-bombs when he first found out what Biden had said.) "Golly, man!" Obama said, with more anger in his voice than "gollys" normally carry. He was, in fact, as pissed off as most people on the call had ever heard him, more so than he'd been at even the wickedest jabs from Hillary Clinton. "How many times is Biden gonna say something stupid?"

Obama asked if Solis Doyle, Biden's chief of staff, was on the call. "Yes, I'm here," she said abashedly.

"Listen," said Obama. "Tell Joe I love him. I love him. But he can't be doing this."

A couple of days later, Obama phoned Biden and laid into him. You're supposed to have my back, he said, not be out there creating problems.

With two weeks to go before Election Day, Biden's remark was gift-wrapped booty for the McCain campaign, a ready-made TV spot. And, indeed, soon after the comment, just such an ad hit the air, complete with

Biden's voice and pictures of terrorists and a frightened child. Its message spoke directly to the stubbornest doubts that some voters still had about Obama, and to their fears about the risks entailed in electing him.

More than that, though, what rankled Obama was that Biden hadn't bothered to pick up the phone and apologize. Worse, Biden didn't say that he was sorry when Obama called; he showed no remorse for his Seattle comments or understanding that they posed a real political problem.

Biden knew he'd screwed up, of course, but he went into a defensive crouch. He told his aides it wasn't really a gaffe, that he was just speaking the truth—as the Biden brand demanded. He got a little chippy.

Well, gosh, Biden said. I guess it's a good thing I didn't say anything about bitter people who cling to their guns and religion.

On October 22, Palin ticked the box next to the only remaining network to which she had yet to grant a sit-down, NBC. After finishing her talk with anchor Brian Williams, she tapped out an email to the campaign's senior staff that had an air of resignation and a certain poignancy. "Was not a good interview," Palin wrote. "So hang on to your hat w[ith] the criticism and mocking that will ensue. Just a head's up—doubt anything can be done about it—the gotcha questions started right out of the shoot and as usual I was perplexed at the whole line of questioning and I'm sure that showed through."

Palin was still as rogue as ever, but the thrill was gone. The only pleasure she seemed to take was in her crowds; she worked her rope lines hungrily, for two hours at a time, lingering over every hand she touched. Otherwise, Palin was demoralized, isolated, and confused. On her plane, when confronted with an uncomfortable topic by her advisers, she was still dropping her head and refusing to respond, even as they stood there awkwardly waiting for a reply. She had no idea whom to trust anymore or really where to turn. On the day of the NBC interview, Politico broke a story that the RNC had spent $150,000 for clothing for her and her family. It was the first shoe to drop in what over the next week would become a hailstorm of expensive footwear. CNN reported that someone close to the campaign called her a "diva." Politico reported that "a top McCain adviser" called her a "whack job." The maelstrom not only eclipsed Biden's mega-gaffe but signaled the death of whatever was left of Palinmania.

The invective was the visible outcropping of a deeper fault line. McCainworld had split into internecine factions surrounding Palin and her candidacy, roughly divided between those who still had faith in Palin and those who did not. The tensions were bursting forth in the form of proxy warfare in the media, infuriating McCain. Schmidt and Davis ordered the campaign's email system searched to determine who was behind the snipes in the press. Palin's loyalists on her plane pointed at Nicolle and Mark Wallace for the "diva" comment. In fact, the source was veteran Republican fund-raiser and strategist Wayne Berman, a close friend of McCain's.

Palin had long since lost faith in McCainworld. She felt belittled and lectured to by the senior staff; whenever an aide told her Schmidt was waiting to talk to her on the phone, Palin's reflexive reaction was, "Do I have to?" She was raising so much money for the campaign and drawing such mammoth crowds, yet she received no respect in return. If I'm doing all this, she would ask, why can't I have input? Increasingly, she was a picture of isolation, either listening to her iPod or surfing cable channels on her seatback TV on her plane. When politicians or donors traveled with her, she rarely spoke more than a few words of greeting to them; she stared at her speech text and avoided engagement.

The truth was, the McCain people did fail Palin. They had, as promised, made her one of the most famous people in the world overnight. But they allowed her no time to plant her feet to absorb such a seismic shift. They were unprepared when they picked her, which made her look even more unready than she was. They banked on the force of her magnetism to compensate for their disarray. They amassed polling points and dollars off of her fiery charisma, and then left her to burn up in the inferno of public opinion.

The face-to-face exposure of the campaign's senior advisers to Palin was minimal in the last month before Election Day. She was on the road; they were at headquarters or with McCain, their paths rarely intersecting. But after witnessing her near-breakdown during debate prep and monitoring her subsequently by phone and email, some in the upper echelons of McCainworld began to believe that Palin was unfit for high office.

McCain was aware that his senior team considered Palin troubled and troubling, but he was shielded from the fullness of their distress. Several of his lieutenants agreed that should McCain's electoral prospects miraculously improve and winning in November become likely, they would have to confront the nominee as he started to plan how his administration would function. It would be essential, they believed, that Palin be relegated to the largely ceremonial role that premodern vice presidents inhabited. It was inconceivable that Palin undertake the duties of a Gore or a Cheney—or that, if McCain fell ill or died, the country be left in the hands of a President Palin. Some in McCainworld were ridden with guilt over elevating Palin to within striking distance of the White House.

They were hardly alone in such harsh judgments. Obama, who had cautioned his advisers not to jump to conclusions about Palin's potential when she was first selected, ultimately came to believe that the process used to pick her, the man who did the picking, and the woman who was picked were all suspect. He took to mimicking Palin's stylized "You betcha!" in front of his campaign team.

In late October, Obama's focus group maestro, David Binder, was conducting a session with a group of swing voters in a Cleveland suburb. A middle-aged woman let loose with a string of not-unfamiliar broadsides against Obama. He's a Muslim. He's soft on terrorism—because he's a Muslim. He doesn't put his hand on his heart during patriotic rituals. We're not even sure he was born in this country.

Binder was confused. This was supposed to be a group of undecided voters. If you think all these terrible things about Obama, he asked the woman, how can you possibly be undecided?

Because if McCain dies, Palin would be president, she said.

23

THE FINISH LINE

Thirty-five thousand souls filled the sprawling field in Kissimmee, Florida, just outside Orlando. It was nearly midnight on October 29 and the air was shockingly cold, but people didn't seem to mind. They were there to get a glimpse of history, to feel the magic, to witness the commingling of the Democratic future and the Democratic past. They were there for the one and only joint campaign appearance of Barack Obama and Bill Clinton.

Obama and Clinton came out onstage, clasped hands in the air, and then 42 began to speak. His thirteen-minute talk was amped up to the point of being hyperactive. He flapped his arms, clenched his fists, pointed toward the sky. "Folks, we can't fool with this," Clinton said. "Our country is hanging in the balance. This man should be our president!" Obama returned the compliments, singing a song in the key of Clinton, praising his economic record, calling him "a great president, a great statesman, a great supporter," a "political genius," and a "beloved" figure "around the world."

Yet beyond the histrionics and the headline—Barack and Bill, finally side by side—the chemistry between the two still seemed less than stable, the body language awkward. Clinton's speech was formulaic, lacking a single warm personal anecdote or insight (both trademarks of his). Obama's expression conveyed no greater satisfaction than if he were being endorsed by the mayor of Kissimmee.

The subject of Clinton campaigning on Obama's behalf had come up seven weeks earlier, when the two men finally had their much-anticipated tête-à-tête. Obama, who was in New York on September 11 for various memorial events, ventured to Clinton's Harlem office for lunch. Though he showed deference to Clinton by walking in alone—no staff, no security, no posse—and respect for his stature by asking questions about governance instead of politics, the meeting had a stilted feel. Clinton's staff and the Obamans had engaged in a tug-of-war over whether to include a Harlem stroll and photo op as part of the visit (with each side ascribing ulterior race-related motives to the other).

Obama, who had a vicious stomach bug, spent much of the lunch trying not to puke on Clinton's shoes.

Clinton offered to hit the trail for or with Obama. But neither party was thrilled by the prospect. Clinton told CNN's Larry King that he planned to start "after the Jewish holidays," which he'd never been known to observe. The Obamans, meanwhile, had determined through their polling that Clinton's presence would help only in a handful of states, mainly with Latinos. (Not only would the Florida event be held in Hispanic-heavy suburban Orlando, but it would also feature actor Jimmy Smits.) Their primary interest in holding a joint event—*one* joint event—was to keep the press from badgering them about doing none.

That Clinton could be of service to Obama in so few places was as much a testament to the latter's strength as to the former's weakness. By the start of the last full week of the campaign, an NBC News/*Wall Street Journal* survey had Obama up by ten points; the ABC News/*Washington Post* tracking poll put the number at eleven. He was leading in every state won by Kerry in 2004, and either ahead or within the margin of error in ten states carried by Bush in the previous election: Colorado, Florida, Indiana, Iowa, Missouri, Nevada, New Mexico, North Carolina, Ohio, and Virginia.

The significance of Obama's financial advantage over McCain was impossible to overstate. Armed with the tens of millions that kept pouring into O-Town over the Web, the campaign was moving cash around the country as if it were Monopoly money. Just before the Kissimmee rally, Obama and Biden had taken part in an unprecedented thirty-minute prime-time infomercial that cost $7 million and ran on CBS, NBC, MSNBC, Fox, BET, TV One, and Univision—attracting thirty-three million viewers, nearly twice the number of the top-rated network show, *Dancing with the Stars*.

By the end of October, Obama and his team were beginning to face the fact: victory was within their grasp. With Wall Street in flames and the economy falling further into recession, Obama knew that the challenges that awaited him in the White House would be daunting. On the stump, he seized the mantle of FDR, repeating the famous line, "The only thing we have to fear is fear itself." His aides began reading books about Roosevelt's first hundred days in office—and also, yes, *Team of Rivals*.

With such burdens looming, Obama put aside the petty and personal, reconciling with his running mate. The repair of the breach was initiated by Biden, whose close aide Tony Blinken figured out from his sources in the campaign that Obama was still angry over Joe's failure to apologize for his Seattle remarks. When Blinken explained why it might have gotten under Obama's skin, Biden said, "Oh, I get that."

Biden called Obama and came quickly to the point. You know what, I've gotta tell you, I was totally remiss, he said. I want you to know I understand that what I did was not only bad for me—it was bad for you and it endangered our common prospects. I never said I was sorry and I want to apologize.

Obama was grateful. Biden felt magnanimous. A warm and lengthy conversation ensued, with more to come. After weeks of distance, a partnership was taking root. Joe was a proud guy. Acts of contrition didn't come naturally to him. But this one, he admitted, was worth it. And no funny hat was required.

McCain never needed a rapprochement with his running mate. On the upswing and the down, through the nastiest and gnarliest moments, not an ill word escaped his lips regarding Palin. If McCain was disappointed in her or in his own judgment, he hid it from even his closest intimates. He treated Palin chivalrously, inquiring regularly about her well-being and that of her family. We asked a lot of her, McCain said, and he meant it.

McCain blamed Palin's problems on the press, and on members of his team for feeding the hounds. The leak-fueled stories about her drove him so nuts that he stopped watching cable news. (His staff convinced him that leaving the TV tuned to ESPN would be a boon to his spirits.) Indeed, both John and Cindy held the media responsible for much of what had gone wrong in the homestretch of the campaign—and that was a long list. October had been a month of misery for the McCains.

The second and third debates with Obama had gone no better than the first. In Nashville, Tennessee, on October 7, they'd met in a town hall–style format that should by all rights have worked to McCain's advantage. Instead, he rattled around the stage looking slightly lost (*Like a crazy uncle in search of a bathroom*, one of his top advisers thought), making hokey jokes that fell flat, flinging edgy barbs, and telling stories that referenced Ronald Reagan, Teddy Roosevelt, Tip O'Neill, and Herbert Hoover, making him seem every bit his age and then some. Eight days later, at Hofstra University, in New York, McCain started strong and got off his best line of all three confrontations: "Senator Obama, I am not President Bush. If you wanted to run against President Bush, you should have run four years ago." But the split-screen format used for the final debate enhanced the focus on McCain's facial expressions. He smirked, glowered, scowled, rolled his eyes; he looked angry. The insta-polls after each debate told the same story. Viewers judged Obama the winner of both by somewhere between twenty and thirty points.

McCain was frustrated and resentful. The campaign had planned to carpet-bomb Obama with negative ads in October, including some that would have used his own voice from the audio versions of his books. With the economy unraveling, however, McCainworld realized such tactics would seem cheap and hollow—and would be ineffective, to boot.

But now McCain lashed out at his opponent on his own in ways remarkable for their tone and subtext, suggesting that Obama was a dangerous, possibly corrupt, possibly Manchurian unknown. "Who is the real Barack Obama?" McCain said at a New Mexico event two days after the *Times* published its piece on Ayers. "What does he plan for America?" Forty-eight hours later, he referred directly to the former Weatherman. "He wasn't a guy in the neighborhood. [Obama] launched his political career in his living room."

Cindy McCain was equally vitriolic, a startling turnabout from a woman who for so long shunned the spotlight. Obama has "waged the dirtiest campaign in American history," she said one day. The next, she averred about the Democratic nominee's position on a war-funding measure, "The day that Senator Obama cast a vote not to fund my son when he was serving sent a cold chill through my body." A week later, she reprised her attack on Michelle Obama before a pom-pom-waving crowd in Florida. "Yes," Cindy said, "I have always been proud of my country."

As the election barreled toward its conclusion, something dark and frightening was unleashed, freed in part by the words of the McCains and Palin. At rallies across the country, there were jagged outbursts of rage and accusations of sedition hurled at Obama. In Pennsylvania and New Mexico, McCain audience members were captured on video and audio calling the Democrat a "terrorist." In Wisconsin, Obama was reviled as a "hooligan" and a "socialist."

With the brutish dynamic apparently on the verge of hurtling out of control, a chagrined McCain attempted to rein it in. In Minnesota, when a man in the crowd said he would be afraid to raise a child in America if Obama were elected, McCain responded, "He is a decent person and not a person you have to be scared of as president." A few minutes later, he refuted a woman who called Obama "an Arab."

McCain's efforts to tamp down the furies were valorous, though they did nothing to erase his role in triggering the reaction in the first place. The civil rights hero John Lewis, whom McCain admired enormously, compared the Republican nominee and his running mate to George Wallace and said they were "playing with fire."

Another prominent African American was watching with alarm. Colin Powell had been friends with McCain for twenty-five years. The senator had been actively seeking his endorsement (as had Obama) for nearly two years. Powell warned McCain that his greatest reservation was the intolerant tone that seemed to be overtaking the Republican Party. McCain's selection of Palin bothered Powell because he saw her as polarizing. He was dismayed by McCain's deployment of Ayers as an issue, perceived it as pandering to the right. And then there were the hate-soaked rallies, which he considered anti-American. *This isn't what we're supposed to be,* he thought.

Powell had leaned toward staying neutral, but these outbursts were all too much—and McCain had moved only belatedly to stop them. Obama, by contrast, had displayed terrific judgment during the financial crisis, Powell thought. And his campaign had been run with military precision; the show of overwhelming force struck the general as a political realization of the Powell Doctrine. On October 19, he endorsed Obama on *Meet the Press.*

The general's repudiation was a stinging blow for McCain. Beyond their longtime friendship, Powell represented the same brand of Republicanism as McCain's. Tough on defense. Fiscally prudent. Pragmatic and nondoctrinaire. McCain had to wonder what had become of him if his current incarnation was repelling someone like Powell. He was startled by the crazies at his rallies. Who were they? Why were they there? And what did they see in him?

In the final two weeks of the race, McCain began to try to salvage something of his reputation. He put away the harshest of the personal invective against Obama and went back to talking about the economy, rash spending, and Iraq.

He seemed ever more resigned in his public comments to a graceful exit. "I've had a wonderful life," McCain told Fox News. "I have to go back and live in Arizona and be in the United States Senate representing them, and with a wonderful family and daughters and sons that I'm so proud of, and a life that's been blessed."

He wanted to go out on a high note, to recapture some of the old McCain spark, but it was hard to do. On November 1, he and Cindy appeared on *Saturday Night Live*. In a skit that cast him as a TV huckster, he fell flat. On the same day, he received the most unwanted endorsement in the universe: that of Dick Cheney.

There was no love lost between Cheney and McCain, who'd clashed bitterly over the conduct of the war in

Iraq, the performance of Donald Rumsfeld, and inter-rogation techniques. When Cheney's friends learned about the endorsement, they laughed. That wasn't Cheney saluting McCain, they thought. It was him flip-ping the senator the bird.

The next day, McCain traveled to New Hampshire for one last town hall meeting in the state where his presidential aspirations first took wing. The trip made absolutely no sense politically. The polls had Obama ahead there by double digits. But McCain had been agitating for the Granite State curtain call since a visit there in mid-October. To Mike Dennehy, his top New Hampshire strategist, he said, "I want to go to Peter-borough." Dennehy knew that McCainworld HQ would resist. "Just call them and make it happen," McCain said.

Peterborough, population 6,100, was the place where McCain first tasted the flavor of a New Hampshire town hall, in 1999. Just nineteen people attended. Months later, the Peterborough Town House was packed on the eve of his galvanizing 2000 primary win, and the scene had repeated itself in January 2008, as he pulled off another—albeit very different—New Hampshire surprise.

And so, in the early evening of November 2, McCain made the hour-long bus trip west from Manchester airport—a lunatic expenditure of time in the final hours of a national campaign, but his superstitions were in full flower. On the bus, he swapped memories with some of his old New Hampshire hands. Dennehy recalled that the first time in Peterborough they had to bribe people with free ice cream to get anyone to come. I'm glad we're going back, McCain said wistfully. We've come full circle.

Standing with Cindy onstage in the Peterborough Town House, dressed in a black jacket with its collar upturned and an open-necked shirt, McCain took questions from the packed hall for half an hour and ended with a flourish:

"My friends, it's time for all of us to stand up and fight for America. America is in difficulty. We've got to fight for America, we've got to fight for our children, we've got to fight for freedom and justice, we've got to fight for the men and women who are serving in the military. We've got to fight for America, the things we stand for and believe in. Our best days are ahead of us. America never quits. America never gives up. We will succeed. We will win. Let's win this election and get our economy and our country going again."

McCain was no fool. He could—and did—read the polls as closely as anyone. But in every candidate, fatalism, realism, and hope live in delicate equipoise.

McCain's pollster, Bill McInturff, was seeing some tightening in the numbers around the country. Obama wasn't over 50 percent. The electoral math was difficult, but not impossible. Some of the key battleground states seemed to be in reach; New Hampshire had closed to four, McCain had heard.

Maybe the smart set had it all wrong.

Maybe an upset was still somehow possible.

Maybe, maybe, maybe.

As McCain was getting off his campaign bus at the airport, about to bid adieu to the state he loved so much and that loved him so much back, he turned to Dennehy, a flash of optimism in his eyes, and asked, "How many we down by?"

Dennehy knew the truth, but couldn't bear putting it into words.

"Let's not talk about that tonight," he said.

As McCain was departing New Hampshire, Obama was arriving in Cleveland, Ohio, rolling up to find eighty thousand people on the city's downtown outdoor mall listening to Bruce Springsteen belt out "Thunder Road." At the end of Springsteen's set, Obama took the stage with Michelle and the girls and shared a warm moment with Bruce, his wife, Patti, and their kids. Springsteen, who hit the trail in 2004 for Kerry, had joked earlier about being glad to be invited back, not being seen as some kind of jinx. Now Obama added to the levity. When he got to the part in his speech where he asked the crowd how many of them made more than $250,000 a year—the floor for his proposed tax increases—The One made a point of telling The Boss that he needn't bother to answer.

Obama brought up McCain's endorsement by Cheney, noting that the VP had said he was "delighted" to support the GOP nominee. "You've never seen Dick Cheney delighted, but he is! It's kinda hard to picture, but it's true!" As Obama giggled, the skies grew dark and it began to drizzle. "Did you notice that it started when I started talking about Dick Cheney?" Obama joked. "That's all right. We've been through an eight-year storm, but a new day is dawning. Sunshine is on the way!"

The next morning, November 3, Obama woke up in Jacksonville, Florida, to the heaviest of all weather: on the last day of his presidential campaign, his grandmother Madelyn Dunham had died at eighty-six.

The news came as no surprise to Obama. Dunham had fought a long battle with cancer, and had been at death's door for months. Ten days earlier, Obama had briefly absented himself from the trail to fly to Hawaii to see her, knowing all too well that it could be for the last time. Dunham had been Obama's guardian for much of his youth, while his mother lived in Indonesia. He called her Toot; she called him Bear. He wanted desperately for her to make it to Election Day, to live to see him achieve his dream.

Obama betrayed no emotion in Jacksonville. His speech at Veterans Memorial Arena that morning was rousing. He recalled that, on September 15, McCain had appeared in the same venue and declared that "the fundamentals of our economy are strong."

"Well, Florida, you and I know that's not only fundamentally wrong, it also sums up his out-of-touch, on-your-own economic philosophy," Obama said, "a philosophy that will end when I am president of the United States of America."

Obama's next stop was in Charlotte, North Carolina, late that afternoon, where twenty-five thousand people gathered to see him in a field opposite Duke Centennial Hall at the University of North Carolina. The weather had been fine all day long, but as soon as Obama's jet touched down, the skies began to threaten. As the crowd waited for him, the heavens opened up and a vicious downpour began.

On the way to the event, Obama stopped by his Charlotte HQ to shake hands with volunteers and call a few voters. When one of the voters raised the subject of health care, Obama turned away from the pool reporters and said into the phone, "Obviously this is happening in my own family . . . my grandmother stayed at home until recently." When he turned back, Obama was visibly deflated, looking drawn and tired.

When he finally arrived in the field at UNC, the rain had stopped, the crowd was drenched, and they were ready for him. He stepped to the lectern and began his speech with a remembrance of his grandmother. He said, "She died peacefully in her sleep with my sister at her side, and so there's great joy as well as tears." He said, "She has gone home." Haltingly, he said, "I'm not going to talk about it too long because it's hard to talk about."

Even so, Obama wanted everyone to know a little about Toot. He called her a "quiet hero," like a lot of quiet heroes in the crowd and in the country. "They're not famous," Obama continued. "Their names aren't in the newspaper. But each and every day, they work hard. They watch out for their families. They sacrifice for their families. . . . That's what America's about. That's what we're fighting for."

As Obama said all this, his voice was mostly steady, but tears were streaming down his cheeks—the first time he had wept publicly since taking the national stage. Obama reached inside his pocket, pulled out a white handkerchief, wiped his eyes, and carried on, returning several times to the woman who had shaped his character as much as anyone in the world.

A few hours later, Obama and his traveling crew pulled into the Prince William County Fairground in Manassas, Virginia, for his final campaign rally. The scene was surreal, mind-boggling, like something out of a movie. The buses rolled up into a muddy parking lot behind the stage. The floodlights illuminated a swirling mist rising into the dark night sky. Beyond the camera risers surrounding the stage were a pair of trucks with uniformed, heavily armed, Secret Service tactical teams standing on top, scanning the horizon through their binoculars. And beyond the trucks were some ninety thousand Obama fans on a gently sloping hillside, stretching literally as far as the eye could see.

How fully Obama understood the alchemy or the tides of history, the collision of man and moment, that brought him to that place, putting him on the verge of winning the White House, was impossible to know. But he seemed to grasp the need for closure. At the end of his speech, he returned to the story of Edith Childs, the city councilwoman in Greenwood, South Carolina, who early in his campaign bequeathed to him the rallying cry that marked his breakthrough in the Iowa caucuses: "Fired up! Ready to go!"

Obama hadn't uncorked this riff in months, but he turned on the turbochargers in Manassas and delivered it with gusto, coiling his body, bouncing up and down, sweeping his arms, tracing with his fingers in the air. By the time he got to the end—"One voice can change a room, and if it can change a room, it can change a city, and if it can change a city, it can change a state, and if it can change a state, then it can change a nation, and if it can change a nation, it can change a world; come on, Virginia, let's go change the world!"—the crowd let loose a roar that shook the ground beneath their feet.

Returning to the airport, Obama boarded his jet and prepared to head back to Chicago. He made his way down the aisle and into the rear cabin, where the press corps mingled. He thanked the reporters for having accompanied him on his astonishing ride. He gave a photographer a birthday kiss. He shook every hand on the plane.

"Okay, guys, let's go home," Obama said. "It will be fun to see how the story ends."

Epilogue

TOGETHER AT LAST

On the morning of November 5, Barack Obama had breakfast with his family, saw his kids off to school, donned sunglasses, and went to the gym. The previous night, the nation's first African American president-elect had secured a victory that was as dazzling as it was historic. His 53 percent of the popular vote was the largest majority secured by a Democrat since Lyndon Johnson. He swept the blue states, captured the battlegrounds of Pennsylvania, Ohio, and Florida, and picked up red states across the country: Colorado, Indiana, North Carolina, Virginia. He dominated among black voters (95–4), Hispanic voters (66–32), and young voters (66–32). His share of the white vote, 43 percent, was higher than what Gore or Kerry had attained—and among whites age eighteen to twenty-nine, he trounced McCain, 68–31.

Obama made his way to his transition headquarters on the thirty-eighth floor of the Kluczynski Federal Building in Chicago's Loop. Sitting down with Biden; his soon-to-be chief of staff, Rahm Emanuel; his three transition co-chairs—Jarrett, Rouse, John Podesta—and a handful of others, he began examining the possibilities for his Cabinet. Most of the names on the lists were predictable, but one was not. Obama was leaning heavily toward Hillary Clinton for secretary of state.

Among those most intimate with Obama, it came as no surprise. Since the summer, he had been telling Jarrett and Nesbitt that he wanted to find a role for Clinton in his administration. Obama's inclination was abetted by Podesta, whom he'd appointed to run a kind of pre-transition planning effort after securing the nomination (and whom Clinton had tapped, albeit prematurely, to handle the same task). At the first Podesta-led meeting to discuss potential Cabinet picks, in Reno, Nevada, in late September, Hillary's name was on the lists for State and Defense. The next morning, Jarrett asked Obama, "Are you serious about Senator Clinton?"

Obama replied simply but emphatically, "Yes, I am."

Obama shared his thinking with few people before Election Day, but when he did, his praise for Clinton was effusive. She's smart, she's capable, she's tough, she's disciplined, Obama said again and again. She wouldn't have to be taught or have her hand held. She wouldn't have to earn her place on the world stage; she already had global stature. She pays attention to nuance, Obama told Jarrett, and that's what I want in a secretary of state, because the stakes are so high. I can't have somebody who would put us in peril with one errant sentence.

Three other names were raised in the meeting at the Kluczynski Building: Daschle, Kerry, and Richardson. Daschle and Richardson were on the short list only as courtesies; Obama had other things in mind for both of them. Kerry was eminently qualified and desperately wanted the job. But he would have been a predictable pick—there was no wow factor with Kerry. Choosing Clinton would send a powerful message about Obama's bigness.

Much of Obama's campaign brain trust was resistant to the idea. The suits were skeptical that Hillary would be, could be, a loyal team player. The arguments against her varied among them, but all were forcefully and fully aired. She would pursue her own agenda. She would undermine Obama's. She would be a constant headache. She came attached to her globe-trotting, buckraking, headline-making husband, whose antics were the very antithesis of the no-drama-Obama way of doing business.

Jarrett was wary, too, though her worries revolved around the question of the chemistry (or lack thereof) between Barack and Hillary. "You'd better really make sure that you two can work together," Jarrett advised the new president-elect, "because you can't just fire her."

Obama listened to the objections and more or less dismissed them. Sure, he needed to sit with Clinton and get comfortable. Sure, the Bill problem needed to be dealt with. But Obama shared none of his brain trust's lingering animus over the campaign. It was time to saddle up and get down to governing—and he saw Clinton as an invaluable asset. He told his quailing advisers to keep their eyes on the prize. More than once he calmly reassured Jarrett, "She's going to be really good at this job."

The following week, on November 13, Hillary met with Obama in his transition office in Chicago. She had some theories about why she was there, but being offered secretary of state was not among them. Two nights earlier, over dinner in New York with her and

Bill, Terry McAuliffe had asked about the rumors swirling in Democratic circles that the gig might be tossed her way. It's the craziest thing I've ever heard, Hillary replied.

Not that she thought a job offer was out of the question. But she expected it to be a token unity gesture, something both sides knew she would almost certainly turn down—maybe Health and Human Services. When the chatter about State picked up, she assumed that the Obamans were floating it and was suspicious about their motives. Why are they putting my name out? she asked her friends. How does it help them? What game are they playing?

But now here she was, sitting alone with her former nemesis, and Obama was talking about the job in earnest. You're head and shoulders above anyone else I'm considering, he said. Obama made it clear that they would have to come to terms regarding Bill's foundation and library-funding, as well as his money-making ventures. He explained how he envisioned their relationship if she took the post: one president, one secretary of state, no overlap. He didn't formally offer her the job, but he left no doubt that she was his choice.

Obama knew that Clinton would be reluctant, that he'd have to do some wooing. But at the same time he was selling, he was also evaluating. *Do we click?*

Will she respect the fact that I'm the president? Can she work for me? By the time the meeting was over, all those questions had been answered to his satisfaction. The conversation confirmed his instincts. He was surer than ever that he wanted Clinton, and he would do what it took to get her.

Hillary's head when she flew out of Chicago was in a different place. *I'm not taking this job,* she thought, *And I'm not going to let anyone talk me into it— anyone.* But she also remembered a formulation that James Carville was fond of: "Once you're asked, you're fucked."

That was precisely how Hillary felt for the next few days. She had less than zero interest in working for Obama—for doing anything other than going back to the Senate, licking her wounds, and putting her energies into paying down her multimillion-dollar debt. She was looking forward to reclaiming some semblance of the life she'd had before the campaign. Going to the theater. Dining out. Spending time with Chelsea. She was sixty-one years old and staring down the likelihood that she would never be president. And she was tired—oh, so tired.

The pressure on her to take the job was enormous, though, and all the more so because the whole drama was playing out in public. Hillary had flown commercial from New York to Chicago and been spotted on the plane. Then the press pool saw her three-SUV motorcade pulling out from the garage of the Kluczynski Building. Everyone Hillary encountered had an opinion—or, rather, they all had the same opinion, which was that she should accept. Being America's ambassador to the world at a hinge-of-history moment was a job commensurate with Clinton's skills, they argued. Biden was on the phone with her making that case persistently; so was Podesta.

Emanuel took a more aggressive tack. He told her she'd be making a big mistake if she turned it down. That a refusal would wound Obama before he even took office. That she had to play ball for her own sake as well as the party's. The conversations occasionally got heated. Voices were raised. Phones were slammed.

There were other reasons for Clinton to say yes. The Senate wasn't proving as welcoming as she'd hoped, not by a long shot. She had come back thinking that her campaign had enhanced her status, that she could snag for herself some kind of plum position—a subcommittee chairmanship, a specially created health care panel, something. But Kennedy shot her down on health care, and Reid sidestepped her other requests. (Behind the scenes, he and Schumer were beseeching the Obamans to take Hillary off their hands.) The conspiratorial whisperers in the Senate were no longer whispering. They were telling her not to get ahead of herself, to take a seat, take a number.

There was the Bill Factor, that unremitting source of speculation far and wide. The conventional wisdom held that the former president would be the death knell of the Madame Secretary scenario. Would he open the books and reveal the donors to the William J. Clinton Foundation and the Clinton Global Initiative? He'd always fought that tooth and nail. Would he accept restrictions on his travel, his speaking, his business activities? Please.

But the conventional wisdom couldn't have been more wrong. Faced with tough, unequivocal demands from the Obamans—demands that many of his people considered beyond the pale—Bill said, fine. Publicly and privately, he vowed to do "whatever they want." There was no way he was going to let himself be cast as a stumbling block. Back-channeling regularly with Podesta, Emanuel, and Biden, he became the loudest and most ardent voice urging his wife to take to the job.

Hillary felt the pull of patriotism and the call of duty. She believed that when the president asked a person to serve, there was an imperative to say yes. And yet, after five days of tumultuous to-ing and fro-ing, she decided to decline Obama's offer. Her reasons were many and, to her, dispositive. Secretary of state, of all jobs, seemed designed to turn her life upside down in myriad ways—in particular, the constant travel and omnivorous jet lag. She felt protective of her husband, too, especially after the torching of his reputation in the campaign. No matter how willing Bill claimed to be, she didn't want to see his philanthropic efforts crimped, his important work helping the sick and underprivileged curtailed. And she kept coming back to the question of her debt. For some politicians, lumbering around millions of dollars in the red was no big thing. She considered it immoral; she wanted to be shed of the burden, and quickly. But how was she supposed to accomplish that as secretary of state? Her people asked the Obamans (again) for help, but the transition team refused. And then there was something that she told one of her friends: she had spent a lot of years working for one guy and had no desire to do it again.

On the morning of November 19, the top officials of Hillary's and Bill's staffs held a conference call to coordinate the rejection. To fend off charges that Bill's activities had thwarted the deal, they planned to send the full list of his contributors to Obama's transition office in Washington. Thousands of pages had to be printed out and rushed there that afternoon.

Hillary informed Emanuel and Podesta of her decision. She wanted to talk to Obama to put the thing to rest.

Emanuel and Podesta had a lot on the line. They'd been among Hillary's most forceful advocates internally—and now she was about to drop a heaping pile of public embarrassment in Obama's lap. The advisers decided that they had no choice but to stall. The president-elect is unavailable for a call, they told Clinton. He's indisposed.

Hillary's staff tried to plan a time for the conversation. Again and again, it was pushed back. A 2:30 call was scheduled. At 2:17 p.m. Abedin sent around an email to Mills and others: "We hear that President-elect Obama will not do the call at 2:30. Instead, he wants her to talk to Podesta—talk to him in an hour, so 3:30." Hours later, Clinton had still not reached Obama. At 7:37, Abedin wrote: "The call has been scheduled for 10 P.M. Eastern." At 9:42: "God knows what's going to happen." At 10:27: "Call will not happen tonight."

Clinton was in New York for a reception at Chelsea Piers commemorating the renaming of the Triborough Bridge in RFK's honor. She flew back to Washington late on a charter flight, arriving at Whitehaven around midnight—and there, miraculously, she managed finally to reach the elusive Obama.

It's not going to work, an anguished Hillary told him. I can't do it. It was a long, hard campaign, and I'm exhausted. I have this debt to pay down, and I can't do that as secretary of state. I'm tired of being punched around; I feel like a piñata. I want to go home. I've had enough of this. You don't want me, you don't want all these stories about you and me. You don't want the whole circus. It's not good for you, and it's not good for me. I just can't do this.

Hillary, look, you're exactly right, Obama said. Those are all real concerns, they're all real problems, and it's fair and legitimate for you to raise them. And the truth is, there's really nothing I can do about them. But the thing is, the economy is a much bigger mess than we'd ever imagined it would be, and I'm gonna be focused on that for the next two years. So I need someone as big as you to do this job. I need someone I don't need to worry about. I need someone I can trust implicitly, and you're that person.

Hillary raised a matter far more intimate than her personal reluctance. You know my husband, she said. You've seen what happens. We're going to be explaining something that he said every other day. You know I can't control him, and at some point he'll be a problem.

I know, Obama replied. But I'm prepared to take that risk. You're worth it. Your country needs you. I need you. I need you to do this.

For both Obama and Clinton, it was a strange and rare moment—one of almost incomprehensible candor and vulnerability. For nearly two years, Clinton's posture regarding her husband had been fierce and unyielding. Never once had she wavered in Bill's defense. Never once had she been anything but defiant in the face of his screwups. Only rarely had she ever acknowledged, even to her closest friends, the damage that he had inflicted on her candidacy. And yet now, here she was, laying down her guard with her former rival, admitting not only that her husband could be a thorn in her side, but, in effect, that she'd known it all along.

Obama's tacit admission was equally revealing. As a public figure and a private man, his signal characteristics were supreme self-possession and self-reliance. He needed no one, was better and smarter, cooler and more composed, than anyone around him. But here he was conceding to Clinton that her help was crucial to the success of his presidency. For the first time, after all the bitterness and resentment that had passed between them as combatants, they had suddenly metamorphosed into different creatures with each other—human beings.

It was nearly one o'clock in the morning on the East Coast. I don't want this to be your final answer, Obama said quietly and in conclusion. I want you not to say no to me. I want you to keep thinking. I want you to sleep on it.

The next morning, Hillaryland prepared to announce Clinton's decision to the world. The previous day, she had signed off on a statement she would deliver before the cameras at a press stakeout site on the Senate side of Capitol Hill. It said:

"I spoke this morning with President-Elect Obama to convey my deepest appreciation for having been considered for a post in his administration. It is not something I sought or expected. In fact, it took me by surprise when he first mentioned the possibility a week ago. . . . [I]n the end, this was a decision for me about where I can best serve President-Elect Obama, my constituents, and our country, and as I told President-Elect Obama, my place is in the Senate, which is where I believe I can make the biggest difference right now as we confront so many unprecedented challenges at home and around the world."

In Chicago, at the Kluczynski Building, Obama walked into Jarrett's office and told her where he was with Clinton. She said no last night, Obama reported— but she'd called him back that morning. "She's going to do it," he said.

Jarrett studied Obama. In the course of the campaign, their conversations had numbered in the thousands. She couldn't remember a time when he seemed prouder, more satisfied.

It was November 20. The election was sixteen days in the past. But today, Obama had pulled off the grandest game changer of them all. On the brink of great power and awesome responsibility, he and Clinton were on the same team.

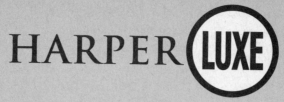

THE NEW LUXURY IN READING

We hope you enjoyed reading
our new, comfortable print size and found it
an experience you would like to repeat.

Well – you're in luck!

HarperLuxe offers the finest in fiction and
nonfiction books in this same larger print size and
paperback format. Light and easy to read, HarperLuxe
paperbacks are for book lovers who want to see
what they are reading without the strain.

For a full listing of titles and
new releases to come, please visit our website:

www.HarperLuxe.com